ICSA Study Text

Interpreting Financial and Accounting Information

ICSA Study Text

Interpreting Financial and Accounting Information

2ND EDITION

Numa Fudong and Chris Lang

icsa
The Chartered **Governance** Institute

First published 2019
Published by ICSA Publishing Ltd
Saffron House
6–10 Kirby Street
London EC1N 8TS

© ICSA Publishing Ltd, 2021

All rights reserved. No part of this publication may be reproduced, stored in a retrieval system, or transmitted, in any form, or by any means, electronic, mechanical, photocopying, recording or otherwise, without prior permission, in writing, from the publisher.

Typeset by Paul Barrett Book Production, Cambridge
Edited by Benedict O'Hagan

British Cataloguing in Publication Data
A catalogue record for this book is available from the British Library.

ISBN 9781860728150

Contents

How to use this study text — xii
About the authors — xiv
Acronyms and abbreviations — xv

Part one
The need to regulate financial reporting — 1

1 The regulatory framework and the role of International Financial Reporting Standards — 4

1 Introduction — 4
2 The need for a regulatory framework — 5
3 Agency theory and the role of corporate governance — 7
4 The role of financial reporting and accounting standards — 9
5 Arguments against accounting regulation — 10
6 National and company law — 10
7 International Financial Reporting Standards — 12
8 Barriers to global harmonisation — 16
9 Principal differences between IFRS and UK GAAP — 17
10 Environmental reporting — 19
11 Social accounting — 22

2 The Conceptual Framework for Financial Reporting — 27

1 Introduction — 27
2 The need for a conceptual framework — 29
3 The objective of general purpose financial reporting — 31
4 Qualitative characteristics of useful financial information — 33
5 Financial statements and the reporting entity — 35
6 The elements of financial statements — 36
7 Recognition and derecognition of the elements of financial statements — 38
8 Measuring the elements of financial statements — 41

9	Presentation and disclosure	42
10	Concepts of capital and capital maintenance	43

Part two
Understanding and interpreting financial statements and reports   49

3 Presentation of single entity published financial statements   53
1	Introduction	53
2	The objective of financial statements	55
3	Presentation of financial statements	56
4	Fair presentation and compliance with IFRS	57
5	Overriding concepts of financial statements	57
6	Structure and content of financial statements	60
7	Statement of financial position	61
8	Statement of profit or loss and other comprehensive income	67
9	Statement of changes in equity	72
10	Statement of cash flows	74

4 Other contents and features of published financial statements   86
1	Introduction	86
2	Content of the annual report and financial statements (or accounts)	87
3	The strategic report	88
4	The directors' report	91
5	Notes to the financial statements	93
6	Segment reporting	95
7	Reporting the substance of transactions	98
8	Limitations of published financial statements	100

5 Accounting policies based on IFRS   105
1	Introduction	105
2	Accounting policies	107
3	Accounting for inventories	114
4	Accounting for plant, property and equipment	117
5	Accounting for events after the reporting period	121
6	Revenue from contracts with customers	124
7	Provisions, contingent liabilities and contingent assets	128
8	Accounting for leases	131

6 Financial reporting by groups of companies — 134
1. Introduction — 134
2. Requirement to prepare consolidated financial statements — 135
3. Principles for the consolidation of financial statements — 136
4. Business combinations, fair value measurement and goodwill — 140
5. Consolidated statement of financial position — 147
6. Consolidated statement of profit or loss and OCI — 150
7. Investments in associates and joint ventures — 151
8. The IAS 28 equity method — 152
9. A parent company's separate financial statements — 153
10. Exemptions from preparing consolidated financial statements — 154

7 Analysis of published financial statements — 157
1. Introduction — 157
2. The need for financial analysis — 158
3. Fundamental analysis — 160
4. Economic analysis — 161
5. Industry analysis — 163
6. Company analysis — 165
7. Trend analysis — 165
8. Ratio analysis — 171
9. Profitability ratios — 172
10. Limitations of ratio analysis — 180
11. Accounting irregularities and creative accounting — 180

Part three
Sources of finance, their associated risks and returns — 187

8 Working capital management — 190
1. Introduction — 190
2. The nature and purpose of working capital — 192
3. The working capital cycle — 192
4. Working capital management: profitability versus liquidity — 195
5. Working capital ratios — 196
6. The management of inventories — 202
7. The management of trade receivables — 208
8. The management of trade payables — 210

9	**Sources of short-term finance**	**214**
1	Introduction	214
2	External sources of short-term finance	215
3	Bank and institutional loans	215
4	Overdrafts	217
5	Debt factoring	218
6	Invoice discounting	219
7	Alternative finance and online innovations	220
8	Internal sources of short-term finance	224
9	Controlling working capital	224
10	Reducing inventory levels	225
11	Tighter credit control	228
12	Delaying payments to trade payables	229
13	Sale of redundant assets	230
14	Retained earnings	231

10	**Financial markets and the identification of financing needs**	**232**
1	Introduction	232
2	Identification of financing needs: budgeting and forecasting	233
3	The need for cash and cash management	239
4	Financial markets	240
5	Private versus public markets	242
6	The role of the stock exchange	244
7	Efficient market hypothesis	245
8	AIM	247
9	Other sources of finance from the private market	247

11	**Sources of long-term finance**	**252**
1	Introduction	252
2	Equity or ordinary shares	253
3	Retained earnings	256
4	Preference shares	257
5	Bonds and debentures	258
6	Bank and institutional loans	263
7	Leasing	263
8	Securitisation of assets	266
9	Private finance initiatives	267
10	Government grants and assistance	269

Part four
The cost of capital and capital structure   273

12 The cost of capital and capital structure   276
1 Introduction   276
2 The importance of the cost of capital   277
3 Cost of equity using the capital asset pricing model   278
4 Cost of equity using the dividend valuation model   283
5 Cost of debt   284
6 Weighted average cost of capital   286
7 Capital structure   288
8 Factors affecting capital structure   289
9 Financial gearing   292
10 Operating gearing   295
11 The traditional approach to capital structure   297
12 The Modigliani and Miller theory of capital structure   299
13 Real world approaches   302

13 Project appraisal techniques   306
1 Introduction   306
2 Identification and analysis of projects   307
3 Factors affecting project appraisal   308
4 Project appraisal techniques   309
5 Non-discounting methods:
   payback period   310
6 Non-discounted methods: accounting rate of return   313
7 Discounted cash flow techniques based on the time value of money   316
8 Discounted cash flow methods: net present value (NPV)   320
9 Discounting annuities   323
10 Discounted cash flow methods: internal rate of return   324
11 Discounted cash flow methods: discounted payback   328
12 Impact of inflation and tax on project appraisal   329
13 Capital rationing and use of the profitability index   331

14 Risk assessment in investment appraisal techniques — 334
1. Introduction — 334
2. Risk and investment decisions — 335
3. Risk assessment models — 336
4. Sensitivity analysis — 336
5. Scenario analysis — 340
6. Simulation modelling — 341
7. Expected net present value — 342
8. Event tree diagrams — 347
9. The role of portfolio management — 348

15 Company analysis and company valuation methods — 355
1. Introduction — 355
2. Investment valuation ratios — 356
3. Earnings per share — 357
4. Price/earnings ratio — 359
5. Relative value measures — 363
6. Valuation using the dividend valuation model — 364
7. Valuation using discounted cash flows — 365
8. Valuation using the capital asset pricing model — 365
9. The application of efficient market hypothesis in company valuation — 367
10. Shareholder value analysis — 368
11. Economic value added — 372
12. Measuring value creation — 374

Part five
Interpretation and evaluation of accounting and financial information — 379

16 Interpretation and evaluation of accounting and financial information — 380
1. Introduction — 380
2. Accounting and financial ratios — 381
3. Interpretation and evaluation — 384
4. Limitations of ratios — 384
5. Introduction to the case studies — 385

6	Company A: a FTSE 100 manufacturing company	386
7	Company B: a retail baking company	393
8	Company C: an early stage IT company	401

Appendix	411
Test yourself answers	413
Glossary	466
Index	476

How to use this study text

This study text has been developed to support the Interpreting Financial and Accounting Information module of The Chartered Governance Institute's qualifying programme and includes a range of navigational, self-testing and illustrative features to help you get the most out of the support materials.

The text is divided into three main sections:

- introductory material
- the text itself
- reference material.

The sections below show you how to find your way around the text and make the most of its features.

Introductory material

The introductory section includes a full contents list and the aims and learning outcomes of the qualification, as well as a list of acronyms and abbreviations.

The text itself

Each part opens with a list of the chapters to follow, an overview of what will be covered and learning outcomes for the part.

Every chapter opens with a list of the topics covered and an introduction specific to that chapter.

Chapters are structured to allow students to break the content down into manageable sections for study. Each chapter ends with a summary of key content to reinforce understanding.

Features

The text is enhanced by a range of illustrative and self-testing features to assist understanding and to help you prepare for the examination. You will find answers to the 'Test yourself' questions towards the end of this text. Each feature is presented in a standard format, so that you will become familiar with how to use them in your study.

These features are identified by a series of icons.

The text also includes tables, figures and other illustrations as relevant.

Reference material

The text contains a range of additional guidance and reference material, including a glossary of key terms and a comprehensive index.

Stop and think

Test yourself

Making it work

Case study

How to use this study text xiii

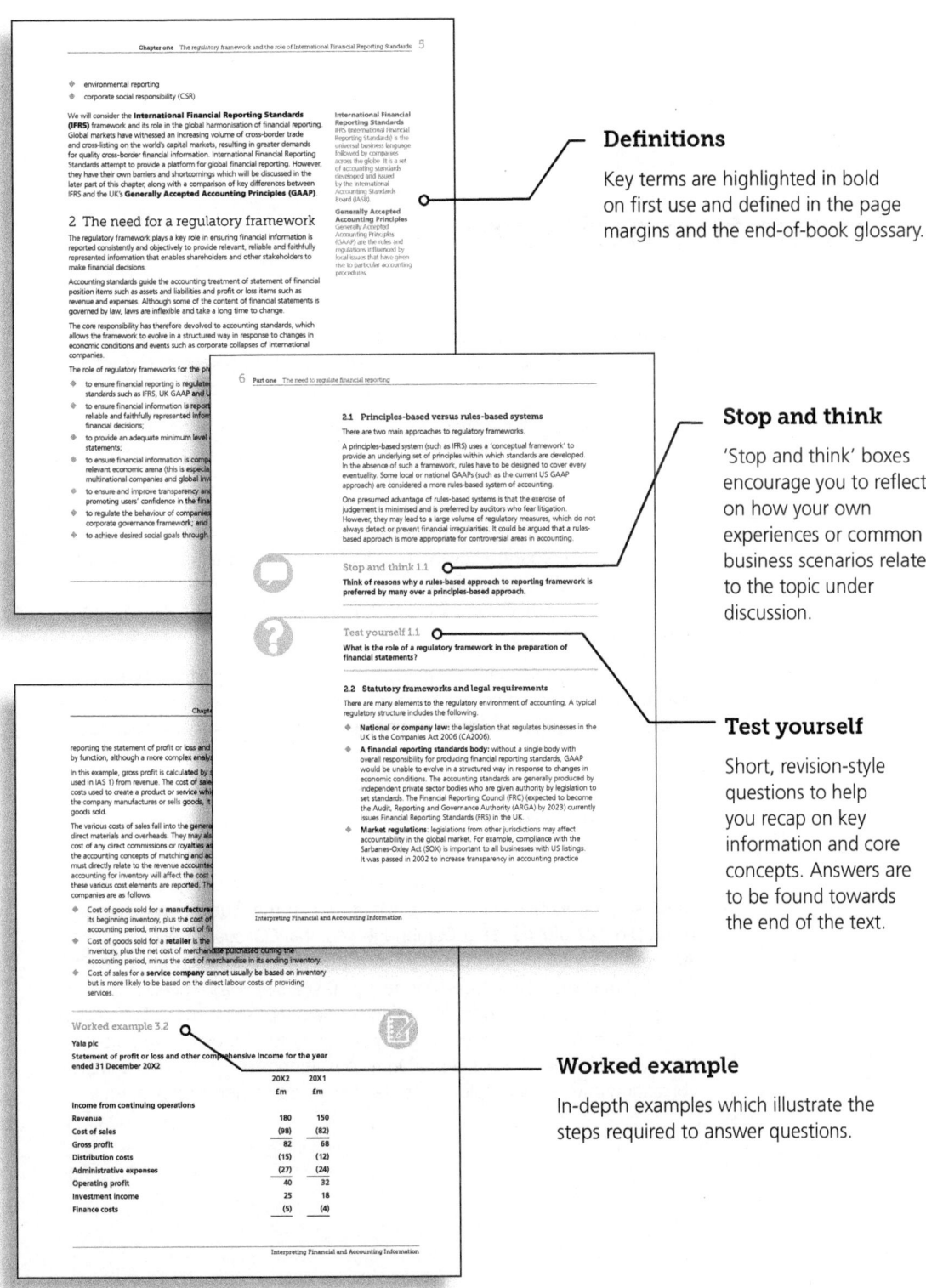

Definitions

Key terms are highlighted in bold on first use and defined in the page margins and the end-of-book glossary.

Stop and think

'Stop and think' boxes encourage you to reflect on how your own experiences or common business scenarios relate to the topic under discussion.

Test yourself

Short, revision-style questions to help you recap on key information and core concepts. Answers are to be found towards the end of the text.

Worked example

In-depth examples which illustrate the steps required to answer questions.

Interpreting Financial and Accounting Information

About the authors

Numa Fudong is a fellow member of the Association of Chartered Certified Accountants (UK) with a BSc (Hons) in applied accounting from Oxford Brookes University and a B.Com. (Hons) from SRCC, Delhi University.

Numa has a wealth of experience as a senior finance professional, having worked in both the private and public sectors including the audit commission, a big four accounting firm and a number of large multinational corporations across various industries. She is also the director of a company through which she provides consulting services within strategic finance, financial controllership, risk, audit and corporate governance. She has provided technical accounting guidance, including the drafting of complex sets of financial statements under IFRS, UK and US GAAPs and the support of clients through complex transactions and business changes.

As a consultant, she combines her functional finance expertise and project management capabilities with other broad skills and experiences in financial reporting, audit, tax, process reengineering, compliance and risk management.

Chris Lang graduated in 1989 from the University of Nottingham, with a BA Hons in History, specialising in modern economic history. Chris qualified as a Chartered Management Accountant in 1994.

Chris held senior financial roles at the University of Cambridge and Middlesex University, before becoming a Director at two Further Education Colleges, being Director of Finance at Cambridge Regional College for over 11 years. All these roles led to Chris gaining experience in corporate governance and financial management; indeed for nearly 20 years he was a director and/or the company secretary of a host of trading subsidiaries. Since 2015, Chris has been Chief Operating Officer and Company Secretary for Professional Services Firms International Limited (PSFI), a premium consulting firm. PSFI deliver practical consulting and learning solutions to leaders of professional service firms.

Acronyms and abbreviations

ABS	asset-backed securities
AF	annuity factor
AIM	Alternative Investment Market
ARGA	Audit, Reporting and Governance Authority
ARR	accounting rate of return
C/S ratio	contribution to sales ratio
CA2006	Companies Act 2006
CAPM	capital asset pricing model
CDO	collateralised debt obligations
CGU	cash-generating unit
CODM	chief operating decision maker
CSR	corporate social responsibility
CSV	creating shared value
DCF	discounted cash flow
DDM	dividend discount model
DPR	dividend payout ratio
DVM	dividend valuation model
EFG	Enterprise Finance Guarantee
EIS	Enterprise Investment Scheme
EMAS	Eco-Management and Audit Scheme
EMH	efficient market hypothesis
EMS	environmental management system
ENPV	expected net present value
EOQ	economic order quantity
EPS	earnings per share
EU	European Union
EVA	economic value added
FASB	Financial Accounting Standards Board
FCA	Financial Conduct Authority
FCF	free cash flow
FG	finished goods
FIFO	first in, first out
FRC	Financial Reporting Council
FRS	Financial Reporting Standards
FV	future value
GAAP	Generally Accepted Accounting Principles

GDP	gross domestic product
GHG	greenhouse gas
IASB	International Accounting Standards Board
IASC	International Accounting Standard Committee
IAS	International Accounting Standard
IFRS	International Financial Reporting Standard(s)
IPO	initial public offering
IRR	internal rate of return
ISA	International Standard in Auditing
ISO	International Organization for Standardization
JIT	just in time
LSE	London Stock Exchange
MBS	mortgage-backed securities
MM	Modigliani and Miller
MVA	market value added
MV	market value
NBER	National Bureau of Economic Research
NCI	non-controlling interests
NHS	National Health Service
NOI	net operating income
NOPAT	net operating profit after tax
NPV	net present value
NRV	net realisable value
NYSE	New York Stock Exchange
OCI	other comprehensive income
OPAT	operating profit after tax
OTC	over the counter
P/E	price/earnings ratio
P2P	peer-to-peer lending
PBIT	profit before interest and tax
PFI	Private Finance Initiative
PI	profitability index
PPP	Public-Private Partnership
pu	per unit
PURP	provision for unrealised profit
PV	present value
RADR	risk-adjusted discount rate
RFR	risk-free rate
RM	market rate of return
RM	raw material
ROA	return on assets
ROCE	return on capital employed
ROE	return on equity
ROL	re-order level
SEC	Securities and Exchange Commission
SME	small and medium-sized enterprises
SML	security market line
SoFP	Statement of Financial Position

SOX	Sarbanes-Oxley Act
SPE	special purpose entity
SPV	special purpose vehicle
SVA	shareholder value analysis
SWOT	strengths, weaknesses, opportunities and threats
T-bill	Treasury bill
TPS	Toyota Production System
TSR	total shareholder return
TVM	time value of money
VED	vital, essential, desirable
WACC	weighted average cost of capital
WAVCO	weighted average cost
WCC	working capital cycle
WC ratio	working capital ratio
WDA	writing down allowances
WIP	work-in-progress

Part one

Chapter 1
The regulatory framework and the role of International Financial Reporting Standards

Chapter 2
The Conceptual Framework for Financial Reporting

The need to regulate financial reporting

Overview

Part one provides an overview of the frameworks of financial reporting, along with the reasons why the regulation of financial reporting is necessary. It discusses the role of the regulatory framework and the International Accounting Standards Board (IASB)'s Conceptual Framework in enhancing the usefulness of financial reporting for a wide range of financial decision makers.

Chapter 1 discusses the role of the regulatory framework in meeting the objectives of financial reporting and developing accounting standards that work to enhance the transparency and comparability of financial statements. It covers the various statutory frameworks and legal requirements that make up the regulatory environment of accounting. It looks at key concepts such as the principal–agent relationship and the differences between principles-based and rules-based approaches to reporting frameworks. It discusses the development of the International Financial Reporting Standards (IFRS) framework, its development, its role in global harmonisation of financial reporting and the key differences between IFRS and UK Generally Accepted Accounting Principles (GAAP).

Chapter 2 outlines the IASB's 2018 Conceptual Framework for Financial Reporting, which provides the generally accepted theoretical principles that set out the fundamental concepts for the preparation and presentation of financial statements. The Framework also provides the basis for the development and evaluation of new and existing accounting standards.

At the end of this Part, students will be able to:

- critically engage with the need to regulate financial reporting and discuss the benefits of accounting standards, as well as the arguments against standardisation;
- consider the various laws and regulations that make up the regulatory framework for financial reporting, as well as distinguish between principles-based and rules-based frameworks;
- link agency theory to the principles of corporate governance frameworks and external audit processes in enhancing financial reporting;
- explain the role of environmental reporting and corporate social responsibility (CSR) towards integrated reporting and understand recent developments;
- understand the development of the IFRS framework, its role in global harmonisation of financial reporting and the factors that act as barriers to global harmonisation;
- highlight key differences between UK GAAP and IFRS;
- demonstrate an understanding of the basic concepts and purpose of IASB's Conceptual Framework for Financial Reporting;
- understand the need for a business to prepare financial reports, explain the objective of general purpose financial reporting and identify the users of financial statements;
- discuss the underlying assumption (going concern) of financial statements and the qualitative characteristics (such as relevance, faithful representation, comparability,

timeliness, understandability and verifiability) that determine the usefulness of information in financial statements;
- distinguish between the elements of financial statements such as assets, liabilities, equity, income and expenses; and
- explain the concepts of capital and capital maintenance in accruals-based financial statements.

Chapter one
The regulatory framework and the role of International Financial Reporting Standards

Contents

1. Introduction
2. The need for a regulatory framework
3. Agency theory and the role of corporate governance
4. The role of financial reporting and accounting standards
5. Arguments against accounting regulation
6. National and company law
7. International Financial Reporting Standards
8. Barriers to global harmonisation
9. Principal differences between IFRS and UK GAAP
10. Environmental reporting
11. Social accounting

1 Introduction

The objective of financial reporting is to provide useful financial information about the reporting entity to shareholders, as well as other users of financial statements who use the information to make financial decisions.

This chapter will discuss the role of a regulatory framework in ensuring relevant and faithfully presented financial information, as well as providing a structure for regulatory bodies producing financial reporting and accounting standards. It will also look at the various legal and regulatory structures that make up the regulatory environment of accounting. These include:

corporate governance
the set of internal rules, policies and processes that determine how a company is directed.

- agency theory and the role of **corporate governance**
- national or company law
- financial reporting and accounting standards
- regulatory frameworks on corporate governance

- environmental reporting
- corporate social responsibility (CSR)

We will consider the **International Financial Reporting Standards (IFRS)** framework and its role in the global harmonisation of financial reporting. Global markets have witnessed an increasing volume of cross-border trade and cross-listing on the world's capital markets, resulting in greater demands for quality cross-border financial information. International Financial Reporting Standards attempt to provide a platform for global financial reporting. However, they have their own barriers and shortcomings which will be discussed in the later part of this chapter, along with a comparison of key differences between IFRS and the UK's **Generally Accepted Accounting Principles (GAAP)**.

2 The need for a regulatory framework

The regulatory framework plays a key role in ensuring financial information is reported consistently and objectively to provide relevant, reliable and faithfully represented information that enables shareholders and other stakeholders to make financial decisions.

Accounting standards guide the accounting treatment of statement of financial position items such as assets and liabilities and profit or loss items such as revenue and expenses. Although some of the content of financial statements is governed by law, laws are inflexible and take a long time to change.

The core responsibility has therefore devolved to accounting standards, which allows the framework to evolve in a structured way in response to changes in economic conditions and events such as corporate collapses of international companies.

The role of regulatory frameworks for the preparation of financial statements is:

- to ensure financial reporting is regulated through financial reporting standards such as IFRS, UK GAAP and US GAAP;
- to ensure financial information is reported objectively to provide relevant, reliable and faithfully represented information that enables users to make financial decisions;
- to provide an adequate minimum level of information for users of financial statements;
- to ensure financial information is comparable and consistent in the relevant economic arena (this is especially important with the growth in multinational companies and global investment);
- to ensure and improve transparency and credibility of financial reports, promoting users' confidence in the financial reporting process;
- to regulate the behaviour of companies and directors through the corporate governance framework; and
- to achieve desired social goals through environmental and CSR reporting.

International Financial Reporting Standards
IFRS (International Financial Reporting Standards) is the universal business language followed by companies across the globe. It is a set of accounting standards developed and issued by the International Accounting Standards Board (IASB).

Generally Accepted Accounting Principles
Generally Accepted Accounting Principles (GAAP) are the rules and regulations influenced by local issues that have given rise to particular accounting procedures.

2.1 Principles-based versus rules-based systems

There are two main approaches to regulatory frameworks.

A principles-based system (such as IFRS) uses a 'conceptual framework' to provide an underlying set of principles within which standards are developed. In the absence of such a framework, rules have to be designed to cover every eventuality. Some local or national GAAPs (such as the current US GAAP approach) are considered a more rules-based system of accounting.

One presumed advantage of rules-based systems is that the exercise of judgement is minimised and is preferred by auditors who fear litigation. However, they may lead to a large volume of regulatory measures, which do not always detect or prevent financial irregularities. It could be argued that a rules-based approach is more appropriate for controversial areas in accounting.

Stop and think 1.1

Think of reasons why a rules-based approach to reporting framework is preferred by many over a principles-based approach.

Test yourself 1.1

What is the role of a regulatory framework in the preparation of financial statements?

2.2 Statutory frameworks and legal requirements

There are many elements to the regulatory environment of accounting. A typical regulatory structure includes the following.

- **National or company law:** the legislation that regulates businesses in the UK is the Companies Act 2006 (CA2006).
- **A financial reporting standards body:** without a single body with overall responsibility for producing financial reporting standards, GAAP would be unable to evolve in a structured way in response to changes in economic conditions. The accounting standards are generally produced by independent private sector bodies who are given authority by legislation to set standards. The Financial Reporting Council (FRC) (expected to become the Audit, Reporting and Governance Authority (ARGA) by 2023) currently issues Financial Reporting Standards (FRS) in the UK.
- **Market regulations**: legislations from other jurisdictions may affect accountability in the global market. For example, compliance with the Sarbanes-Oxley Act (SOX) is important to all businesses with US listings. It was passed in 2002 to increase transparency in accounting practice

following the high-profile collapse of US giants such as Enron and WorldCom.

- **Industry-specific and securities exchange rules:** there are various industry-specific regulatory bodies and systems in place. For example, the Financial Conduct Authority (FCA) oversees the financial services industry in the UK. Similarly, the London Stock Exchange provides regulations for companies whose shares are quoted on its market.

- **Corporate governance frameworks:** these seek to enhance financial reporting by providing confidence to the users of accounting information. They aim to align the interests of directors, management and shareholders in pursuing the success of the company. The root of corporate governance frameworks in the UK was the Cadbury Report, titled *Financial Aspects of Corporate Governance*, which was published in December 1992. It was commissioned in response to continuing concern about standards of financial reporting and accountability, particularly heightened by the BCCI and Maxwell corporate scandals. It set out recommendations to raise standards of corporate governance and mitigate the related risks and failures. It has evolved into the FRC's current UK Corporate Governance Code, which sets out standards of good practice for listed companies on accountability, audit, board composition and development, remuneration and shareholder relations.

- **Environmental and sustainability reporting:** there are national and international standards for social, environmental and sustainability reporting, which are generally moving towards the goal of **integrated reporting**. Denmark, the Netherlands, Norway and Sweden all require environmental reports by law, particularly in environmentally sensitive industries.

integrated reporting
An integrated report is a holistic form of reporting about how an organisation's strategy, governance, performance and prospects lead to the creation of value over the short, medium and long term.

3 Agency theory and the role of corporate governance

3.1 Agency theory

Standard setting and theories around financial reporting have developed significantly throughout the past five decades.

One of the most notable developments is the concept of agency theory. This was developed by Jensen and Meckling (1976) and defines the characteristics of a public limited company (a company which may be listed on a capital market). The theory suggests that the modern corporation is based on the principal–agent relationship, where the owner (shareholder) is the principal and the manager is the agent. The two enter into a contract whereby the manager acts as the custodian over the assets of the firm and aims to maximise the owner's wealth.

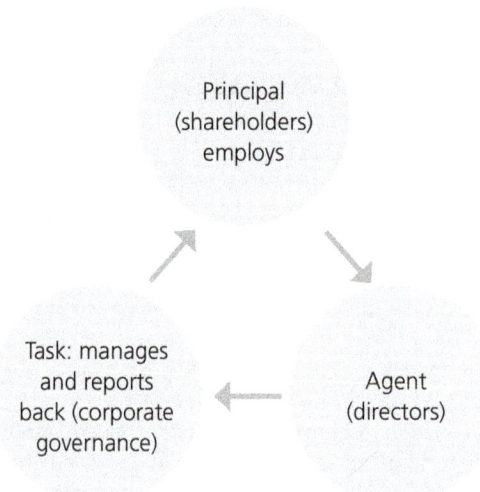

Figure 1.1 Agency theory (Stephen Ross and Barry Mitnick)

3.2 Agency problem

The idea of a conflict of interests between the principal and agent is the cornerstone of the agency theory. The manager or agent may pursue their own interests at the expense of the principal.

One particularly famous scandal that demonstrates the principal–agent problem is the 2009 Bernie Madoff affair. Madoff was criminally charged and convicted for creating a sham business that ultimately cost many small investors all of their savings, with a total worth of nearly $16.5 billion.

3.3 Solutions to the problem

The principal will incur **agency costs** to monitor the agent's activities and take corrective action where necessary. Agency costs are direct and indirect costs arising from the disagreement or the inefficiency of a relationship between shareholders and business managers. Examples of direct agency costs include use of company's resources for the agent's own benefit (such as excessive executive pay) and the monitoring costs such as fees payable to external auditors to assess the accuracy of the company's financial statements. The key objective of an **external audit** is to protect the interests of shareholders by independently reporting the state of a company's finances. The auditors ensure that the board receives accurate and reliable information and makes an assessment on the appropriateness of the accounting principles. An audit results in an audit opinion about whether the financial statements give a 'true and fair' view of the company's state of affairs and operations for the period.

Indirect agency costs refer to lost opportunities that arise out of the shareholder/management conflict but does not have a directly quantifiable value. To reduce the risk from conflicting interests and to minimise the agency cost, the contracting parties will seek to optimise their relationship.

---

agency cost
Agency costs are direct and indirect costs arising from the inefficiency of a relationship between shareholders and business managers. Examples of the direct agency costs include the monitoring costs such as fees payable to external auditors to assess the accuracy of the company's financial statements.

external audit
An independent audit opinion on whether the financial statements give a 'true and fair' view of the company's state of affairs and operations for the period. The auditors ensure that the board receives accurate and reliable information and assesses the appropriateness of the accounting principles used by a company.

3.4 The role of corporate governance

Corporate governance is a part of the monitoring process. It is an internally adopted mechanism by which control is exercised by the board of directors over the activities of the managers. Corporate governance refers to the set of internal rules, policies and processes that determine how a company is directed. The corporate governance framework can play an important role in helping boards gain a better understanding of their oversight role. It seeks to enhance financial reporting by providing a degree of confidence to the users of accounting information.

4 The role of financial reporting and accounting standards

The corporate collapse of international companies such as Enron (2001), WorldCom (2002), Parmalat (2003), Satyam (2009) and Carillion (2018) in large part was due to fraud, with irregularities in accounting procedures and misrepresentation of the financial state of affairs. These corporate failures necessitated the need for transparency in financial reporting through standardisation, harmonisation and convergence of accounting regulation.

In addition, stakeholders demand quality financial reports and accounting information due to the global nature of capital movement. Accounting standards require companies to disclose the accounting policies they have adopted as well as additional information that they might not disclose if the standards did not exist.

The key objectives of financial reporting and accounting standards are to:

- improve the transparency of financial reporting and make financial information reliable, relevant and easier to understand;
- reduce the risk of creative accounting;
- make the financial statements of different period or of different entities comparable;
- increase the credibility of financial statements by improving the uniformity of accounting treatment between companies; and
- provide quality financial reports and accounting information which can be relied upon for consistency, commonality and overall transparency.

Test yourself 1.2

List the key objectives of accounting standards.

5 Arguments against accounting regulation

There are also arguments against accounting regulation, some of which are listed below.

- A rigid accounting regulation could have a detrimental effect in the long term and the influence of political, economic and cultural climates of different countries is often ignored. One reporting regulation may not fit all countries when considering disclosure regulation (Bushman and Landsman, 2010).

- Frameworks apply to entities from various industries and the tendency to enforce standardisation may not be suitable for those on the margins. The choices provided by accounting standard setters, such as on the valuation of inventories, can be somewhat arbitrary. There would be considerable disagreement as to the method to be used, which could distort the comparability of companies' financial statements.

- There is a concern amongst some professionals that standards tend to remove the need for accountants to exercise their judgement. However, others argue there is still plenty of scope for this.

- A key criticism of standardisation is that it gives an illusion of precision and comparability. This is debatable and arguably not fully justified in view of the wide range of subjective decisions that have to be made.

- A final criticism of accounting regulation is that there are simply too many standards of increasing complexity.

6 National and company law

Most businesses prepare financial statements (or accounts as termed by CA2006) by following the applicable financial reporting and accounting standards. The requirements to prepare financial statements and follow the standards is enacted by company law. In the UK, CA2006 acknowledges that companies should follow financial reporting and accounting standards. The Companies Act 2006 has specified rules that requires companies to prepare accounts either:

- under IFRS as adopted for use in the EU; or
- under the UK's own FRS and more detailed legal requirements.

UK-listed companies and companies on **AIM** must follow IFRS in their **group financial statements**, but others have a choice between IFRS and UK FRS. The requirements to prepare proper accounts for unincorporated businesses such as partnerships and sole traders are often found in tax law. We will focus on CA2006.

The Companies Act 2006 sets out the statutory requirements for UK companies with the aim of:

AIM
AIM (formerly the Alternative Investment Market) is a sub-market of the London Stock Exchange designed to provide a platform for smaller companies to raise capital from the general public without going through the rigors of compliance requirements which must be satisfied to raise capital from the main platform.

group financial statements
Group or consolidated financial statements are a set of financial statements which combine the results of a parent and all its subsidiary undertakings. They eliminate all trading and balances between group members, thus presenting financial statements that report transactions and balances only with those outside the group.

- strengthening and simplifying regulation by reforming provisions for private and public companies;
- providing rules around the formation and running of a company;
- improving communication with shareholders and management by codifying common law principles such as those relating to directors' duties;
- enhancing a long-term investment culture;
- protecting the interests of consumers by increasing a company's disclosure requirements; and
- affording flexibility for the future.

Though CA2006 was developed from UK law, it has also implemented the requirements of European Union (EU) directives. Various EU accounting directives have developed a common approach to financial reporting which aims to facilitate the transparency, consistency and commonality of accounting information across EU member states. They include the Takeover and Transparency Obligations Directives (which imposes regulation in relation to financial reporting, disclosure of major acquisitions or disposal of shares), the Statutory Audit Directive and various older company law directives. These directives have created minimum reporting standards by providing accounting guidance on the preparation and reporting of accounting information.

However, concerns have been expressed that too much detail has been inserted in an attempt to cover every eventuality. In addition, CA2006 seems to have simplified certain aspects only at the margins while, in other areas, it appears to have complicated and confused previously settled law – making it harder for small companies to do business.

While many CA2006 provisions apply to all companies, others depend on the nature or size of the company. The main distinctions are as follows:

- Public interest entities (PIEs) or non-PIEs
- **Traded companies** or untraded companies
- **Quoted companies** or unquoted companies
- **Public companies** or private companies
- Micro, small, medium-sized or large companies

A company's size is a key issue in determining which accounting rules it can follow. There are three size classifications of company to consider when preparing financial statements: small, medium and large.

Table 1.1 shows current UK company size limits. A company must fulfil at least two of these conditions to fit into a category. Any companies that do not meet these criteria are counted as large companies.

traded company
A company with securities traded on a regulated market, such as the London Stock Exchange's main market.

quoted company
A company whose equity share capital is listed on a stock exchange such as the London Stock Exchange main market, the New York Stock Exchange or Nasdaq. AIM companies are not quoted.

public company
A company whose certificate of incorporation states it is a public company, or which has converted to public company status since incorporation and whose shares are traded freely on a stock exchange.

Category	Turnover	Balance sheet total	Employees
Micro (a subcategory of small)	£632,000	£316,000	10
Small	£10.2m	£5.1m	50
Medium-sized	£36m	£18m	250

Table 1.1 UK company size limits (revised in 2015) using terminology in CA2006

In effect, the smaller a company, the fewer and simpler the rules it has to follow. However, some companies in activities such as insurance or banking cannot follow simpler regimes. Companies can always choose to opt into a more complex regime if they intend to grow rapidly.

7 International Financial Reporting Standards

The International Accounting Standards Board (IASB) has developed IFRS with the objective of achieving comparable financial reporting across borders.

Scholars such as Hopwood (2000) have argued that the global adoption of IFRS will result in the achievement of comparable financial information about organisations in different countries, overcoming factors like environmental and cultural differences.

The adoption of IFRS continues to grow due to its significance in global business and the pressure to harmonise existing national GAAP systems to the IFRS system. At present, more than 120 countries have adopted IFRS as a framework to govern financial statements.

7.1 The IFRS Framework

The IASB's Conceptual Framework for Financial Reporting refers to a principles-based approach to developing a common set of financial reporting standards.

It provides a platform for accounting and financial reporting on the basis of existing International Accounting Standards (IAS) and IFRS. It also sets out the concepts that underlie the preparation and presentation of financial statements as outlined in the 'Framework for the Preparation and Presentation of Financial Statements'.

The former International Accounting Standards Committee (IASC) issued IAS. However, standards issued since the formation of the IASB in April 2001 are referred to as IFRS. IAS and IFRS are deemed to have equal status. International Financial Reporting Standards for public limited companies have been used in the UK and the EU since 2002.

The conceptual framework itself is not a standard. Its purpose is to help the IASB to develop new or revised accounting standards, to assist in the application of the accounting standards and to deal with any issues that the standards do not cover. The IASB conceptual framework covers:

- the objectives of financial reporting;
- the underlying assumptions;
- the qualitative characteristics;
- the elements of financial statements;
- the recognition (and derecognition) of the elements;
- the measurement of the elements; and
- the concepts of capital and capital maintenance.

The advantages and disadvantages of adopting IFRS (which also relate to the harmonisation of financial reporting and accounting standards) are widely debated. The main advantages and disadvantages are discussed below.

Advantages
- Financial statements presented under IFRS make global comparisons easier.
- Cross-border listing is facilitated, making it easier to raise funds and make investments abroad.
- Multinational companies with subsidiaries in foreign countries have a common, company-wide accounting language.
- Foreign companies can be more easily appraised for mergers and acquisitions.
- Multinational companies benefit for the following reasons:
    - preparation of group financial statements may be easier;
    - a reduction in audit costs might be achieved;
    - management control would be improved; and
    - transfer of accounting knowledge and expertise across national borders would be easier.

Disadvantages
- The cost of implementing IFRS.
- The lower level of detail in IFRS.
- International Financial Reporting Standards are principles-based standards which require the application of judgement. Many do not favour this approach. For example, US GAAPs are more rules-based standards. US accountants are subject to a high degree of litigation and their defence is usually that they complied with the relevant sections of detailed standards which make up US GAAP. They fear that adoption of IFRS will remove this defence.

- There are challenges in adopting IFRS in emerging economies, namely:
    - the economic environment;
    - incompatible legal and regulatory environments;
    - concern around SMEs;
    - level of preparedness; and
    - education needs of auditors.

Test yourself 1.3

What are the key arguments for adopting harmonisation of accounting standards across the world?

7.2 Convergence and harmonisation

The increasing global use of accounting and financial information has made it necessary to reduce the variation in financial information prepared and reported in different countries. Standard setters use two particular approaches to standards development to reduce accounting differences.

- Standardisation is the process by which rules are developed to set standards for similar items on a global basis and through which technical issues relating to accounting treatments are resolved. For example, earnings per share (EPS) is now consistently measured and stated at the foot of the statement of profit or loss and other comprehensive income (OCI) under IAS 33 (Earnings per Share).
- Harmonisation reconciles national differences and achieves a common set of accounting principles. It provides a common framework to deal with major issues in a similar manner.

The IASB and the US Financial Accounting Standards Board (FASB) signed the Norwalk Agreement in September 2002 as the starting point for a project to converge their respective sets of financial reporting standards. Both IASB and FASB stated their commitment to the development of high-quality, compatible accounting standards that are suitable for both domestic and cross-border financial reporting. The key objectives for the convergence included:

- making the existing accounting standards compatible
- maintaining compatibility once convergence had been achieved

Both IASB and FASB agreed and published a memorandum of understanding in February 2005 to identify short-term and long-term convergence projects. This was based on the following three principles:

- Convergence of accounting standards can best be achieved through the development of high quality, common standards over time.
- Trying to eliminate differences between two standards that are in need of significant improvement is not the best use of the FASB's and the IASB's

resources. Instead, a new common standard should be developed that improves the financial information reported to investors.

♦ Serving the needs of investors means that the boards should seek convergence by replacing standards in need of improvement with jointly developed new standards.

The two most recent IFRS (15 (Revenue from Contracts with Customers) and 16 (Leases)) were both developed jointly between the FASB and the IASB, although they took a long time from initial discussions to the Standards being issued.

7.3 The roles of the European Commission, UK GAAP and US GAAP

Countries in which the accounting profession has developed over a long period of time (such as the UK or the US) have generally led the evolution of accounting principles.

The European Commission

The European Commission has worked extensively to promote the quality, comparability and transparency of the financial reporting of companies through the adoption of IFRS, particularly among member states. For example, the Commission in 2005 made the use of IFRS obligatory for the consolidated financial statements of EU companies that are listed on the EU's stock markets. The UK's departure from the European Union is not expected to have any impact on financial reporting practice.

UK GAAP

In the UK, Financial Reporting Standards (FRS) are issued by the FRC. Given the abolition of Statements of Standard Accounting Practice (SSAP) and FRS 1–18, the FRC regime only contains FRS 100–105.

The Companies Act 2006 governs the principal reporting legislation in the UK. It dictates certain minimum reporting requirements for companies and incorporates the requirements of European law. As a result of European law, listed companies in the UK were required to adopt IFRS from 2005. Companies that were not listed had the option to report either under IFRS or under UK GAAP.

The FRC publication FRS 102 (The Financial Reporting Standard Applicable in the UK and Republic of Ireland), replaced UK GAAP with effect for periods beginning on or after 1 January 2015. FRS 102 is based on the IASB's IFRS for SMEs. The text of the IASB's standard has been amended in some significant respects in order to comply with CA2006. For micro-entities (see Table 1.1 for defining size criteria) the FRC has also published FRS 105 (The Financial Reporting Standard Applicable to the Micro-Entities Regime), which further simplifies reporting and disclosure requirements.

US GAAP

US Generally Accepted Accounting Principles are a set of accounting standards to help prepare and present financial reports for a range of entities, including public and private enterprises, non-profit organisations and government departments.

While US GAAP takes a rules-based approach to financial reporting, IFRS are principles-based standards. The Financial Accounting Standards Board (FASB) is an independent entity responsible for the standards of generally accepted accounting principles in the US.

Currently, the FASB is charged to establish GAAP for public and private companies, as well as for non-profit entities. Despite numerous attempts to adopt IFRS, the US has still not come on board. It is, however, making some slow progress towards convergence with the IASB.

There is also a call for the listing requirements of the US's Securities and Exchange Commission (SEC) for companies to follow IFRS. Continued global adoption and IFRS requirements elsewhere have already affected US companies through cross-border, merger and acquisition activity and the demand for IFRS reporting by non-US stakeholders.

8 Barriers to global harmonisation

National differences in accounting and corporate reporting continue despite the increasing adoption of IFRS globally.

The financial reporting system of a country is affected by the local laws and environment. As a result, it tends to reflect its political system, economic system, legal system and cultural environment. The speed of change in the global business environment, the pressure for change and convergence of national GAAP to the IFRS system have resulted in many countries adopting IFRS.

Nevertheless, national implementation of IFRS differs in the degree of convergence. In the past, the content of accounting standards was considered as one of the major factors that contributed to these differences. However, the process of convergence has highlighted that local forces may act as constraints in the globalisation of financial reporting.

Several models have been developed to assess the differences and areas of similarity between countries. This research considers country-level differences in accounting practices – both at a macro level (including cultural, colonial, economic and political factors) and at a micro level (including individuals, firms, companies and organisational culture). The individual attributes of professional accountants (including education, practical experience, motivation and ability) may also come into play.

Meek and Saudagaran (1990) identify the following five external environmental and institutional factors that can affect convergence.

- **Legal system:** this affects the accounting standardisation process – such as whether the legal system is based on common law or code law. The differences in the legal system can restrict the development of certain accounting practices.

- **Business financing and accounting practices:** decision-making processes regarding arrangement of funds may include accounting practices. Many countries do not have strong independent accountancy or business bodies which would press for higher standards and greater harmonisation.
- **Tax system:** a country's tax system is very influential, particularly in terms of its connection with accounting. In most countries, tax authorities may influence the accounting rules around recording of revenues and expenses.
- **Level of inflation:** this is likely to influence valuation methods for various types of assets.
- **Political and economic relationships:** while Commonwealth countries may share similarities in their accounting and tax systems, cultural differences may still result in accounting systems differing from country to country. In addition, developing countries may have less developed standards and principles, although this is not always the case. Some countries may be experiencing unusual circumstances (civil war, currency restrictions) which affect all aspects of everyday life. Others may resist the adoption of 'another country's standard' for nationalism reasons.

9 Principal differences between IFRS and UK GAAP

Despite the effort for global harmonisation, differences between IFRS and UK GAAP persist.

The convergence process between UK GAAP and IFRS originally began in 2003 but was subsequently paused. As a result of European law, listed companies in the UK were required to adopt IFRS from 2005. Companies that were not listed had the option to report either under IFRS or under UK GAAP.

The FRC decided that the optimum solution was a transition to an IFRS-based framework. Over the course of 2012 and 2013 it issued three new standards:

- FRS 100 (Application of Financial Reporting Requirements)
- FRS 101 (Reduced Disclosure Framework)
- FRS 102 (The Financial Reporting Standard Applicable in the United Kingdom and Republic of Ireland)

These standards are based on IFRS, with FRS 102 based on IFRS for SMEs. However, the text of these standards has been amended in some significant respects in order to comply with the Companies Act. Table 1.2 presents the principal differences between UK GAAP and IFRS.

	UK GAAP (FRS 102)	IFRS
Goodwill and intangibles	Goodwill is **amortised** annually. Intangible assets and goodwill have a **finite life** but not exceeding 10 years if no reliable estimate can be made.	Goodwill is **not amortised** but tested annually for impairment. (IFRS 3 (Business Combinations)) Intangibles under IFRS can exist indefinitely. (IAS 38 (Intangible Assets))
Negative goodwill (gain from a bargain purchase)	Negative goodwill is credited in the statement of profit or loss and OCI in the periods in which the non-monetary assets are recovered, with any excess recognised **over the period** expected to benefit.	Negative goodwill is credited in statement of profit or loss and OCI **immediately as it arises** (on the acquisition date) (IFRS 3).
Impairment	**All non-financial assets reviewed** for indicators of impairment where there is an indication of impairment.	All non-financial assets with **finite lives reviewed for indicators** of impairment where there is an indication of impairment. Goodwill and other intangibles with **indefinite lives are reviewed annually for impairment** and are not amortised (IAS 36 (Impairment of Assets)).
Investment property	Investment property is initially **measured at cost and subsequently measured at fair value** at the reporting date with any changes recognised in the statement of profit or loss and OCI.	Initially measured at cost and subsequently **a choice is provided** between fair value (through the statement of profit or loss and OCI) and the cost method (IAS 40 (Investment Property)).
Business combinations	**Transaction costs** are included as part of the acquisition cost. **Contingent consideration is included as acquisition cost** if it is probable that the amount will be paid and it can be measured reliably.	**Transaction costs are expensed. Contingent consideration is recognised,** regardless of the probability of payment (IFRS 3).
Investments in associates and joint ventures	In the consolidated financial statements, investments in associates are generally accounted for using the equity method. For an investor that is not a parent, **a choice is provided** between the cost model and the fair value model (with gains recognised either through other comprehensive income or through profit or loss).	Accounted for using the equity method. **The cost and fair value models are generally not permitted.**

	UK GAAP (FRS 102)	**IFRS**
Assets held for sale	**Not covered** by FRS 102. Provides no definition and required classification. The decision to sell an asset is assessed as an **indicator of impairment**.	**Covered** by IFRS 5 (Non-Current Assets Held for Sale and Discontinued Operations). Requires classification of items as held for sale if the carrying amount is recovered through sale rather than use.
Discontinued operations	Items are considered as discontinued when they are **sold or terminated**. Presented **line-by-line** on the face of the statement of profit or loss and OCI.	Defined differently with focus on **shift of operational focus**. Presented as a **single amount** on the face of the statement of profit or loss and OCI (IFRS 5).
Statement of cash flows	Qualifying entities may take advantage of **exemption from preparing a statement of cash flows** and related notes.	**No similar exemptions** (IAS 7 (Statement of Cash Flows)).
Financial instruments	**Basic financial instruments** (such as simple payables, receivables and bank loans) are mostly measured at amortised cost using the **effective interest method**. **Other or complex financial instruments** are generally measured at fair value through the statement of profit or loss and OCI or have the option of adopting the recognition and measurement criteria of IFRS.	**No such distinction** between basic and other financial instruments IFRS 9 (Financial Instruments) provides rules on the classification and measurement of financial assets and financial liabilities, impairment and hedging.
Development costs	Provides **choice to either expense** as they are incurred or capitalise and amortise them over the useful life of the asset.	**Capitalisation is mandatory** where the criteria for capitalisation are met (IAS 38).

Table 1.2 Differences between UK GAAP and IFRS

10 Environmental reporting

Businesses are now acknowledged to have a wider societal role than that expressed by the traditional 'maximising shareholder wealth' perspective.

Pressure on businesses to act responsibly in the same way as individual human citizens is increasing. Businesses should work to reduce any adverse impact on the environment to an absolute minimum. They have a duty to account for their environmental impacts using **environmental reporting**. There are also domestic requirements like mandatory greenhouse gas (GHG) emissions

environmental reporting
The process of externally communicating the environmental effects of an organisation's economic actions through the corporate annual report or a separate stand-alone publicly available environmental report.

reporting by quoted companies and environmental reporting in accordance with certain financial reporting and accounting standards. The quality and quantity of environmental reports depend on the nature of the business. For example, companies engaged in industries such as chemical, gas, petroleum and pharmaceuticals have the most to report on in relation to environmental issues.

Air pollution from industrial units necessitated environmental legislation due to the release of harmful substances in the air. The laws in the UK can be traced as far back as the 1860s; these eventually gave rise to the Environmental Protection Act 1990, which defines the fundamental structure and authority for waste management and control of emissions into the environment.

Environmental reporting is the process of communicating the environmental effects of an organisation's economic actions through the corporate annual report or a separate environmental report. The demand for environment-related information has led to pressures on corporations, requiring them to make a plethora of disclosures (such as information on policy, procedures and processes and the **environmental audit** report).

environmental audit
An assessment of the extent to which an organisation meets the set criteria or standards that help to minimise harm to the environment.

Environmental reporting does have economic implications as follows.

- **Risk management:** financial, legal and reputation implications.
- **Marketing advantages:** public image and brand enhancement by demonstrating environmental responsibilities. Businesses that are considered environmentally irresponsible are likely to lose market share.
- **Legal needs**: a business may be legally required to provide environmental reports. It is a legal requirement for quoted companies and those that carry on insurance market activity.
- **Competitive advantage:** it can improve relationships with key stakeholders such as investors, suppliers and the wider community. Improved environmental performance should lead to cost savings.
- **Ethics:** showing a commitment to accountability and transparency.
- **Compliance and accounting requirements:** the annual review is expected to include environmental matters, including the company's impact on the environment.
- **Green (ethical) investors:** companies with environmental disclosures are in a better position to be considered in investment decisions by trustees. For example, UK pension fund trustees must disclose how they have considered social, economic and environmental matters.
- **Employee interests:** applicants increasingly look at the environmental performance of a business.
- **Value-added reporting:** environmental key performance indicators are now used to report on environmental matters to add value to corporate reports and communicate to a wider range of stakeholders.
- **Integrated reporting**: a move towards integrated reporting on CSR and environmental issues that allows interactive web-based publication of such reports. Standalone environmental reporting is primarily web-based disclosure that is usually separate from a company's annual report.

10.1 Environmental management systems

An environmental management system (EMS) is a management system and database designed to implement and maintain policy for environmental protection. It integrates:

- organisational structure
- planning activities
- processes and procedures for training of personnel
- implementing, monitoring and maintaining of environmental policy
- reporting of specialised environmental performance to internal and external stakeholders

The most widely used standards on which EMSs are based is the International Organization for Standardization (ISO) Standard 14000 and the European Union's Eco-Management and Audit Scheme (EMAS).

Before 1992, organisations voluntarily constructed their own EMSs, making comparison between companies difficult. In March 1992, as part of a response to growing concerns about protecting the environment, BSI Group published the world's first environmental management systems standard, BS 7750. This supplied the template for the development of the ISO 14000 series in 1996.

ISO 14000 is an industry-led standard related to environmental management that requires companies to document and work towards reducing or eliminating pollution and processes that can be harmful to the environment. The requirements of ISO 14000 are an integral part of EMAS, although EMAS includes some additional requirements.

10.2 The EU Eco-Management and Audit Scheme

The Eco-Management and Audit Scheme is a voluntary environmental management tool specifically designed for eco-management audits. It was developed in 1993 by the European Commission. It allows a company to assess and identify the full extent of its environmental impact and continuously improve and manage its environmental performance. The scheme is globally applicable and open to all types of private and public organisations that meet the requirements of the EU EMAS regulation.

The EMAS tool requires the company to follow its legal and regulatory framework and existing environmental management practices and procedures. Key elements include:

- conducting an environmental review by considering all environmental aspects of the organisation's activities, products and services;
- adopting an environmental policy to comply with all relevant environmental legislation and hence improve environmental performance;
- establishment of an EMS aimed at achieving the organisation's environmental policy objectives including operational procedures, training needs, monitoring and communication systems;

- carrying out an internal environmental audit to check if the organisation is in conformity with the organisation's policy and programme and complying with relevant environmental regulatory requirements;
- preparing an environmental statement that lays down the results achieved against the environmental objectives and the future steps to be undertaken to improve its performance;
- independent verification of the environmental review, the EMS, the audit procedure and the environmental statement by an EMAS verifier: generally, an environmental audit involves the collection, collation, analysis, interpretation and presentation of information. This information is then used to
    - assess performance against pre-set targets of protecting the environment
    - evaluate and assess compliance with environmental legislation as well as corporate policies
    - measure performance against the requirements of an EMS standard
- registering with the appropriate EMAS competent body and making the validated statement publicly available; and
- using the validated environmental statement above to market its activities with the EMAS logo, assess suppliers against EMAS requirements and give preference to suppliers registered under EMAS.

The disclosures enable users of the report to understand a company's level of compliance with relevant legislation and its achievements in company environmental practice.

Test yourself 1.4

Why is there an ever-growing need for businesses to account for and report on environmental issues?

11 Social accounting

Corporate social responsibility, also called social accounting or sustainable development, is a commitment by business to behave ethically and contribute to economic development while remaining sensitive to the needs of all of the stakeholders. Stakeholders includes the company's workforce and their families, as well as the local community and society at large. Companies should make decisions based not only on financial factors, but also on the social and environmental consequences of their actions. Over the last decade, CSR has moved from a voluntary effort by individual companies to being the subject of mandatory schemes at regional, national and even transnational levels.

The wider community has a direct and indirect involvement in CSR and the behaviour of entities. For example, the impact of the Deepwater Horizon oil spillage in 2010 had more than just a financial impact upon BP. A variety of stakeholders have been and continue to be, affected. Some have lost their livelihoods, while others have had to move out of their homes.

Carroll's CSR Pyramid (Figure 1.2) is a model of CSR that shows how and why organisations should meet their social responsibilities.

CSR is built on the foundation of profit – profit must come first, followed by the need to comply with all laws and regulations. Before a business considers its philanthropic options, it also needs to meet its ethical duties

Philanthropic
Focus on doing 'what is desired'

Ethical
Focus on doing 'what is right'

Legal
Focus on compliance with the law

Economic
Focus on profitability

Figure 1.2 Carroll's CSR pyramid: the four responsibilities

The four responsibilities displayed on the pyramid are as follows.

- **Economic:** this is the responsibility of business to be profitable, to survive and to benefit society in the long term. Customers demand quality at a fair price. Creating shared value (CSV) provides the link between corporate success and social welfare. For society to thrive, profitable businesses must be developed to create income, provide jobs and tax revenue for society. In return, a business relies on a healthy, educated workforce and adept government to operate effectively.
- **Legal:** this is the observance of laws and regulations in the society, such as competition, employment and health and safety laws.
- **Ethical:** this relates to acting morally and ethically in issues such as treatment of employees and suppliers.
- **Philanthropic:** this is discretionary, but still important, behaviour to improve the lives of others. It includes charitable donations in areas such as the arts, education, housing, health, social welfare, non-profit organisations, communities and the environment. It excludes political contributions and commercial event sponsorship.

Case study 1.1

Yala plc is in the mining, oil and gas extraction industry. It seeks to create a balance between the company's business activities and its social and environmental responsibilities by recognising that it is directly or indirectly responsible for a variety of environmental, social and economic impacts, both positive and negative, from its operations.

It uses its CSR programme to manage these operational impacts and to earn the trust of various stakeholders. While it is an expense against the company's profits, it is also an investment in building up a strategic asset of goodwill among the local community.

It recognises its CSR by following three basic principles.

1. **Products:** throughout the three stages of each product's life (production, selling and usage), it aims to encourage ethically and environmentally responsible behaviour – such as by reducing factory emissions of poisons and pollutants.

2. **People:** it implements policies that entitles everyone who works at the company to a mix of benefits such as work–life balance and providing protections against ageism and other discrimination at work. This approach is also encouraged amongst the company's suppliers, franchisees and other business partners.

3. **Places:** The company recognises its obligations to the communities in which it trades. It recognises that successful mining, oil and gas extraction industries require economically healthy and sustainable communities. It also considers the demands and the rights of indigenous communities.

A regular evaluation is undertaken to verify organisational commitment to society through independent social audit, certification on standards and compliance and periodic reviews by independent persons or organisations. Social accounting adds value to a company's annual report by providing information about non-financial activities and the related costs of business behaviour in society. Using feedback from relevant stakeholders, a company can monitor, adjust and plan its activities to achieve an organisation's objectives.

While critics argue that CSR distracts from a company's economic role, it is generally considered to increase long-term profits through management control and accountability. Management exercises control over the resources and assets of a business. Social accounting can help management to facilitate internal corporate planning and objectives, thus allowing organisations to pursue profits as well as social objectives for a sustainable future.

On the one hand, the lack of uniformity in CSR can be exhausting. On the other hand, it enables companies to be flexible with a report that best applies to its circumstances, reflecting the vision, values and personality of the company.

Benchmarking of CSR policy, implementation and effectiveness involves reviewing competitor initiatives and how others perceive competitor CSR strategy, as well as evaluating the effectiveness of these policies on society and the environment.

Chapter summary

- The role of a regulatory framework is to ensure financial information is reported consistently and objectively to provide relevant, reliable and faithfully presented information which enables shareholders and other stakeholders to make financial decisions. Financial reporting and accounting standards allow the framework to evolve in a structured way in response to changes in economic conditions.
- A principles-based system with an underlying conceptual framework works within a set of laid-down principles, as opposed to a rules-based system that regulates issues as they arise.
- A typical regulatory structure includes:
    - National or company law
    - Financial reporting and accounting standards
    - Market regulations such as SOX
    - Industry-specific or securities exchange rules
    - Corporate governance frameworks
- Agency theory suggests that the modern corporation is based on the principal–agent relationship, where the owner (shareholder) is the principal and the manager is the agent. Corporate governance frameworks can play an important role in helping boards gain a better understanding of their oversight role. It seeks to enhance financial reporting by providing a degree of confidence to the users of accounting information.
- The role of financial reporting and accounting standards has been amplified after the high-profile collapse of corporates in recent years. This has necessitated the need for transparency in financial reporting through standardisation, harmonisation and convergence of accounting regulation. Financial reporting and accounting standards require companies to disclose the accounting policies they have adopted as well as additional information that they might not disclose if the standards did not exist.
- Arguments against accounting regulation includes the following criticisms:
    - accounting regulations are too rigid
    - standardisation is not suitable for those on the margins
    - they remove the need for accountants to exercise their judgement
    - they provide an illusion of precision and comparability
    - there are too many standards of increasing complexity
- National or company law sets out the requirements to prepare financial statements and follow financial reporting and accounting standards.

- The IFRS framework provides a platform for accounting and financial reporting on the basis of IAS and IFRS.
- The increasing use of global accounting and financial information has made it necessary to reduce the accounting differences of financial information prepared and reported in different countries. Standardisation is the process by which rules are developed to set standards for similar items on a global basis. Harmonisation reconciles national differences and achieves a common set of accounting principles.
- The barriers to global harmonisation include the following five external environmental and institutional factors:
  - legal systems
  - business and financial practices
  - tax systems
  - level of inflation
  - political and economic relationships
- Despite efforts towards global harmonisation, national differences in financial reporting practices continue, including between UK GAAP and IFRS.
- Environmental reporting is the process of communicating the environmental effects of an organisation's economic actions through the corporate annual report or a separate environmental report. The demand for environment-related information has led to pressure on corporations as a plethora of disclosures need to be made. The EMAS and EMS are voluntary environmental management tools specifically designed to implement, maintain and manage policy for environmental protection.
- Corporate social responsibility is a commitment by business to behave ethically and contribute to economic development while remaining sensitive to the needs of all of the stakeholders. Stakeholders include the workforce and their families as well as the local community and society at large.

Chapter two
The Conceptual Framework for Financial Reporting

Contents

1. Introduction
2. The need for a conceptual framework
3. The objective of general purpose financial reporting
4. Qualitative characteristics of useful financial information
5. Financial statements and and the reporting entity
6. The elements of financial statements
7. Recognition and derecognition of the elements of financial statements
8. Measuring the elements of financial statements
9. Presentation and disclosure
10. Concepts of capital and capital maintenance

1 Introduction

The objective of financial reporting is to provide useful financial information about the reporting entity to users of financial statements who use the information to make financial decisions. A conceptual framework for financial reporting is a statement of generally accepted theoretical principles that provide the basis for the development and evaluation of new and existing accounting standards.

In March 2018, the IASB published a revised version of its Conceptual Framework for Financial Reporting, replacing the 2010 version (see Figure 2.1). The document sets out the fundamental concepts of financial reporting, guiding the IASB in developing and revising IFRS. The framework helps all parties to understand and interpret IFRS. It helps preparers to develop consistent accounting policies, based on consistent concepts, for areas that are not covered by a standard or where there is choice of accounting policy.

Figure 2.1 IASB's conceptual framework for financial reporting

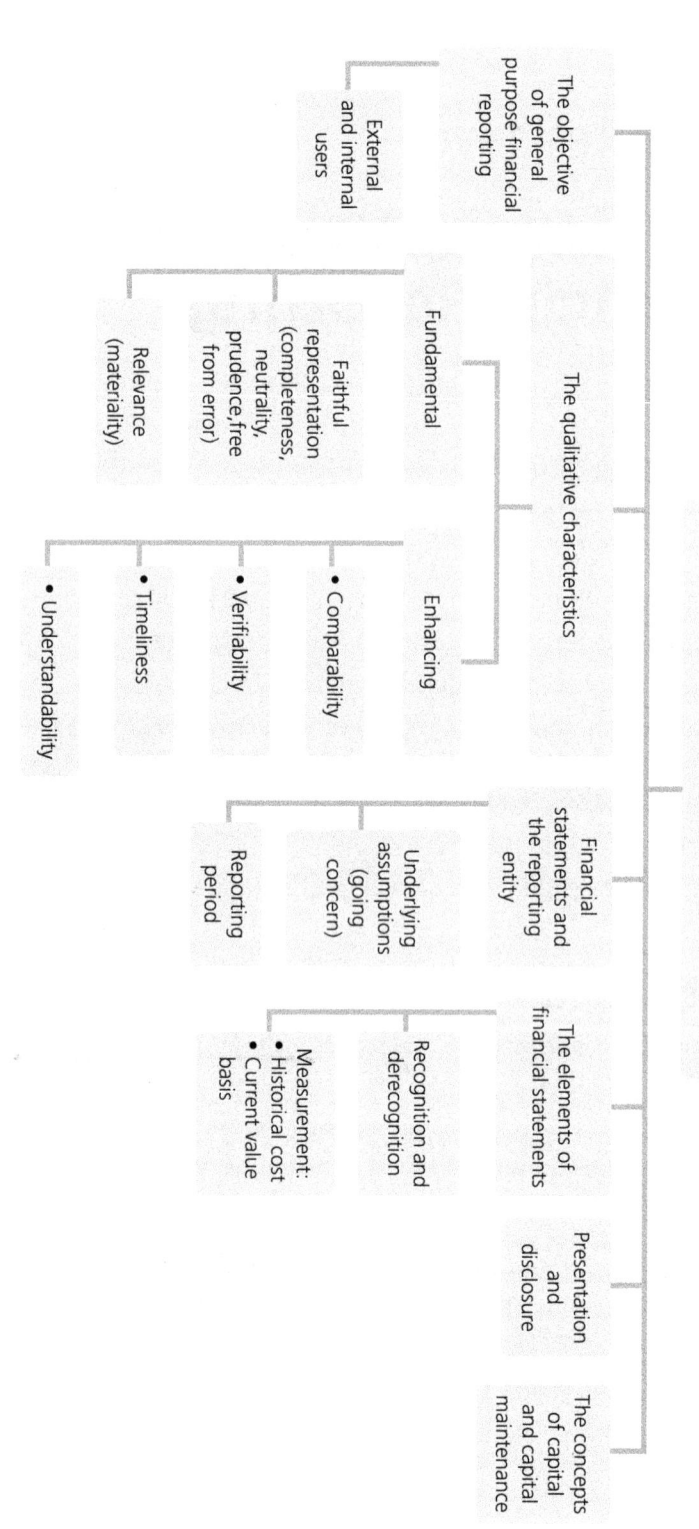

Conceptual Framework for Financial Reporting (Scope and Purpose)

- The objective of general purpose financial reporting
  - External and internal users
- The qualitative characteristics
  - Fundamental
    - Faithful representation (completeness, neutrality, prudence, free from error)
    - Relevance (materiality)
  - Enhancing
    - Comparability
    - Verifiability
    - Timeliness
    - Understandability
- Financial statements and the reporting entity
  - Underlying assumptions (going concern)
  - Reporting period
- The elements of financial statements
  - Recognition and derecognition
  - Measurement:
    - Historical cost
    - Current value basis
- Presentation and disclosure
- The concepts of capital and capital maintenance

In this chapter we will look at the key aspects of the IASB's Conceptual Framework that deals with:

- the objective of general purpose financial reporting
- qualitative characteristics of useful financial information
- financial statements and the reporting entity
- the definitions, recognition, derecognition and measurement of the elements of financial statements
- concepts and guidance relating to presentation and disclosure
- concepts of capital and capital maintenance

2 The need for a conceptual framework

2.1 Scope and purpose of a conceptual framework

A conceptual framework is a statement of generally accepted theoretical principles. It is the underlying basis of the framework for the preparation and presentation of financial statements, which in turn provide reliable and relevant information about the business.

These theoretical principles provide the basis for the development and evaluation of new and existing accounting standards. The framework forms the theoretical basis for determining which events should be accounted for, how they should be measured and how they should be communicated to users.

Accounting standards tend to be produced in a haphazard way in the absence of a conceptual framework, as demonstrated in the way some countries' standards have developed over recent years. Standards developed from a conceptual framework will be less open to criticism than national standards, which are subject to considerable political interference from interested parties. The document sets out the fundamental concepts of financial reporting, guiding the IASB in developing and revising IFRS.

2.2 Limitations of a conceptual framework

A strong and coherent conceptual framework is vital for the development and setting of the standards for accounting practices and principles, as well as the progression towards convergence in international financial reporting and accounting standards. However, there are some limitations.

- Financial statements devised based on a single conceptual framework may not suit all users given the diversity of user requirements.
- There may be a need for a variety of financial reporting and accounting standards with different concepts as a basis, each produced for a different purpose.
- It is not clear that a conceptual framework makes the standard-setting process any easier than without a framework.

2.3 The IASB's Conceptual Framework for Financial Reporting

The 2018 IASB Conceptual Framework provides updated definitions and recognition criteria for assets and liabilities. It also includes some new concepts to set standards and to help others to better understand and interpret the standards.

The Conceptual Framework deals with:

- the objective of general purpose financial reporting
- the qualitative characteristics that determine the usefulness of information in financial statements
- financial statements and the reporting entity
- the definitions, recognition, derecognition and measurement of the elements from which financial statements are constructed
- concepts and guidance related to presentation and disclosure
- concepts of capital and capital maintenance

The purpose of the Conceptual Framework is:

- to assist the IASB in the development of future IFRS and in its review of existing IFRS (and IAS);
- to provide a basis for reducing the number of alternative accounting treatments permitted by IFRS, thus assisting the harmonisation of regulations, accounting standards and procedures relating to financial reporting;
- to assist national standard setting bodies in developing national standards;
- to assist preparers of financial statements in applying IFRS, or when dealing with topics that are not covered by a standard or where there is choice of accounting policy;
- to assist auditors in forming an opinion as to whether financial statements comply with IFRS;
- to assist users of financial statements in interpreting the financial statements prepared in compliance with IFRS; and
- to provide those who are interested in the work of the IASB with information about its approach to the formulation of IFRS.

The IASB's Conceptual Framework should not be confused with IFRS. It does not define standards for any particular measurement or disclosure issue, nor does it override any individual IFRS. In the (rare) case of conflict between an IFRS and the Conceptual Framework, the IFRS will prevail (IASB, Conceptual Framework: Purpose and Status).

The number of cases of conflict between the Conceptual Framework and IFRS should diminish over time as the development of future IFRS are guided by the Conceptual Framework. It assists both the IASB and national standard setters in developing new standards, applying the existing ones and dealing with topics that have yet to form the subject of an IFRS.

Test yourself 2.1
What is the purpose of the IASB's Conceptual Framework?

3 The objective of general purpose financial reporting

The IASB Conceptual Framework states that 'the objective of general purpose financial reporting is to provide financial information about the reporting entity that is useful to present and potential equity investors, lenders and other users in making decisions about providing resources to the entity'. This is a key concept developed throughout this text.

Financial statements also help the stakeholders in assessing the stewardship of the management team who run the business and have control of the underlying assets of the entity. They provide information about:

- the economic resources
- the claims against those resources
- financial performance (the changes in its economic resources and claims) that indicates how efficiently and effectively such resources have been used by management

Information about a reporting entity's financial performance is helpful in predicting future returns. Financial statements highlight the strengths and weaknesses of the entity. They help users to assess the entity's liquidity and solvency and determine the prospects of the entity's future net cash flow, plus any needs for additional financing.

The Framework notes that general purpose financial results cannot provide all of the information that users may need to make economic decisions. They will need to consider pertinent information from other sources as well. The need for benchmarking, competitor analysis and industry analysis, developed later in this text, all clearly relate to this.

Stop and think 2.1
Why does a business need to prepare financial reports?

3.1 Users of general purpose financial reporting

Users of financial accounting information consist of external and internal users. External users include shareholders, creditors, customers, investors, governments and their agencies, lenders and the public. Internal users include employees, management or operational managers, lenders, suppliers and other trade creditors. The key benefits of preparing general purpose financial statements for users are as listed below.

- **Investors:** shareholders or proprietors are interested in the earning capacity of the business, its future prospects and the wellbeing of the business. Financial statements help investors to decide about buying, holding or selling shares. They also provide information about the level of dividend and the overall financial health of an entity. The statement of profit or loss and other comprehensive income (OCI) and statement of financial position and earnings per share (EPS) indicate the financial performance of the preceding year and whether the management has been running the company efficiently. They also help investors to see the company's prospects, present its liquidity position and how the company's shares compare with those of its competitors.
- **Employees and management:** company performance is related to the security of employment and future prospects for jobs in the company. Employees are interested in financial statements that reflect the company's job prospects and the growth of profit, usually for salary negotiations or bonus agreements with management. The financial position and performance helps management to manage the business, such as by preparing budgets and assessing the performance of various departmental heads.
- **Lenders:** the information in the financial statements helps lenders decide whether to lend to a company. This information is checked for adequacy of the value of security (if any) and the ability to make interest and capital repayments. This is also used to ensure financial restrictions or covenants (such as maximum debt/equity ratios) have not been breached.
- **Suppliers:** are interested in information to assess whether the company will be a good customer and pay its debts.
- **Customers:** the company should be in a good financial position to be able to continue producing and supplying goods or services.
- **Governments and their agencies:** are specifically concerned with the business's compliance with tax and company law, determining its tax liability, its ability to pay tax and its general contribution to the economy. Governments use financial information to formulate policies and regulations, including taxation policy.
- **The public:** All of the reasons stated above could be useful to the general public. Others, such as researchers, use the published financial reports to research business affairs and practices.

Test yourself 2.2

Why do businesses need to prepare financial statements for their users?

4 Qualitative characteristics of useful financial information

The IASB Conceptual Framework has a series of concepts, or certain 'qualitative characteristics', which a business must embody in order for its financial statements to be useful to the stakeholders. These are divided into fundamental qualitative concepts and enhancing qualitative concepts.

Fundamental qualitative characteristics
- relevance
- faithful representation

Enhancing qualitative characteristics:
- comparability
- verifiability
- timeliness
- understandability

4.1 Fundamental qualitative characteristics

If financial information is to be useful, it must be relevant and faithfully represent what it purports to represent.

The qualitative characteristics of 'relevant' and 'faithfully representative' are consistently conveyed in the Conceptual Framework to make the financial information more useful to the entity's various stakeholders.

Relevance
Financial information is regarded as relevant if it is capable of influencing the decisions of users.

In determining what is relevant to users, preparers of financial statements should consider whether information is material and the extent to which reliable information may be omitted. Information may be **material** or relevant simply because of its magnitude or because its omission from the financial statements could affect decision making.

materiality
As per the IASB Conceptual Framework, items (or transactions) are material if their omission or misstatement could influence the financial decisions of users taken on the basis of the financial statements.

Faithful representation
Faithful representation means that financial information must meet three criteria: completeness, neutrality and be free from error.

- **Completeness:** all information that users need to understand the item is given.
- **Neutral or unbiased:** there is no bias in the selection or presentation of information.
- **Free from error:** there are no omissions, errors or inaccuracies in the process to produce the information. This is something that cannot be completely eradicated, due to human error. Inaccuracies can arise,

particularly in cases of making estimates and judgements. The financial reporting and accounting standards expect that the estimates are made on a realistic basis, not arbitrarily and the information contained within the financial statements presents a fair view of the organisation.

The IASB's revised Conceptual Framework has reintroduced the concept of prudence. It clarifies that measurement uncertainty might have an influence on the faithful representation of an item.

- Prudence is the exercise of caution when making judgements under conditions of uncertainty. It supports neutrality of information by ensuring that assets and income are not overstated and liabilities and expenses are not understated.
- Measurement uncertainty is a factor that can affect faithful representation. For example, relevant information with a high level of measurement uncertainty may provide less useful information than less relevant information with a lower measurement uncertainty. It may be necessary to override the legal form of a transaction to portray the true economic position.

The idea of 'substance over form' is key for the faithful representation of financial information. For example, a lease might not transfer ownership of the leased property to the lessee. The lessee might nevertheless be required to record the leased item as an asset if the lessee receives most of the benefits of ownership and also carries most of the risks, for example in relation to obsolescence of the asset. Reporting the substance of transactions will be covered more in detail in Chapter 4.

Test yourself 2.3

Briefly explain the meaning of faithful representation.

4.2 Enhancing qualitative characteristics

Information that is relevant and faithfully represented can be enhanced by the application of other characteristics.

Comparability
The accounting methods, including the presentation and classification of items in the financial statements, must be applied consistently for similar situations. This facilitates comparison with similar information about other entities and with similar information about the same entity for another period.

The consistency concept is important because of the need for comparability of financial statements. This will be discussed in more detail in Chapter 3.

Verifiability
Verifiability means that the accounting information presented in financial statements must be checked or demonstrated to be true, accurate or justified. If information can be verified (such as by an independent accountant) this provides assurance to the users that it is both credible and reliable. If something is not verifiable, it is unlikely to be auditable; hence, its reliability and usefulness is diminished.

Timeliness
Timeliness of accounting information is important due to its usefulness and relevance to the decision-making needs of the users of financial statements. Local legislation and market regulations impose specific deadlines on certain entities. Timeliness is important to protect the users of the financial statements, such as potential investors, from outdated information or from delayed financial reporting.

Understandability
Information should be understandable through appropriate classification, characterisation and presentation of information. Some financial transactions are inherently complex and difficult to understand, but to omit such information would not give a fair representation of the financial statements. It is therefore important that the format and layout of the financial statements, the accounting policies applied, the terminology used and other statements made within the financial statements are clear and concise.

5 Financial statements and the reporting entity

5.1 Objective and scope of financial statements

The IASB Conceptual Framework addresses the scope and objectives of financial statements. The objective of financial statements is to provide information about the assets, liabilities, equity, income and expenses of the reporting entity. Financial statements are a particular form of financial report that provides useful information about the financial position, financial performance and cash flows of a reporting entity to a wide range of users. This enables those users to make rational investment decisions such as buying, selling or holding equity and debt instruments and credit decisions such as providing or settling loans and other forms of credit.

This information is provided in the statement of financial position and the statement(s) of financial performance, as well as in other statements and notes. A set of basic financial statements will be covered in Chapter 3.

International Accounting Standard 1 (Presentation of Financial Statements) sets out the overall objective for the preparation of financial statements and some important principles that apply across financial reporting. This will be further discussed in Chapter 3.

5.2 Reporting period and reporting entity

Financial statements are prepared for a specified period of time, referred to as a 'reporting period'. This will usually be one year. The statements will also provide comparative information and certain forward-looking information.

A reporting entity (not necessarily a legal entity) is any entity that is either required or choses to prepare financial statements. It can be either a single entity, a portion of an entity or can be comprised of more than one entity (for example, a group of companies).

Financial statements provide information about transactions and other events viewed from the perspective of the reporting entity as a whole. Consolidated, unconsolidated and combined financial statements are all acknowledged as forms of financial statements in the revised Conceptual Framework. Consolidated financial statements are generally considered to provide more useful information to users of financial statements than unconsolidated financial statements. Financial reporting by a group of companies will be covered in Chapter 6.

5.3 Going concern

The Conceptual Framework requires financial statements and their underlying information to be prepared on a going-concern basis. The Conceptual Framework notes that financial statements are normally prepared assuming the entity is a going concern and will continue in operation for the foreseeable future.

Financial statements are prepared on a going-concern basis unless management has significant concerns about the entity's ability to continue as a going concern (e.g. if they either intend to liquidate the entity, to curtail major operations or have no realistic alternative but to cease trading). International Accounting Standard 1 (Presentation of Financial Statements) provides further guidance on the going-concern assumption, its assessment and the disclosure requirement for entities not prepared on a going-concern basis.

6 The elements of financial statements

The IASB's Conceptual Framework defines the building blocks or elements from which the financial statements are constructed.

- Elements relating to the statement of financial position: assets, liabilities and equity.
- Elements relating to the statement of financial performance: income and expense.

The statement of cash flows reflect elements of both the statement of financial position (balance sheet) and the statement of profit or loss and OCI. In order to appropriately report the financial performance and position of a business the financial statements must summarise five key elements.

6.1 Assets

An asset is a present economic resource controlled by the entity as a result of past events. An economic resource is a right that has the potential to produce future economic benefits. For example, a property that is owned and controlled by an entity that is used to house operations and generate revenues would be classed as an asset.

6.2 Liabilities

A liability is a present obligation or duty of responsibility of the entity to transfer an economic resource as a result of past transactions or events that the entity has no practical ability to avoid. For example, a trade payable is a liability.

6.3 Equity

This is the 'residual interest' in the assets of the entity after deducting all its liabilities. It represents what is left when the business is wound up, all the assets are sold and all the outstanding liabilities are paid. It is effectively what is paid back to the owners (shareholders) when the business ceases to trade.

6.4 Income

Income is increases in assets or decreases in liabilities that result in an increase in equity, other than those relating to contributions from holders of equity claims. Sales revenue is a good example of income.

6.5 Expenses

Expenses are decreases in assets or increases in liabilities that result in a decrease in equity, other than those relating to distributions to holders of equity claims. The cost of goods or services is an example of an expense.

6.6 Categorisation of assets and liabilities

There are some additional rules that relate to the classification of assets and liabilities which depend on the length of time they will be employed in the business. These will be covered in Chapter 3.

Test yourself 2.4

Management commits to purchase assets in the future. Does this give rise to a liability?

7 Recognition and derecognition of the elements of financial statements

7.1 Recognition

As per the Conceptual Framework, an item needs to meet the definition of an asset, a liability or equity to be recognised in the statement of financial position. Likewise, an item needs to meet the definition of income or expenses to be recognised in the statement of profit or loss and OCI.

In addition to meeting the definition of an element, items are only recognised when their recognition provides users of financial statements with information that is both relevant and a faithful representation of the element being represented. This must be judged on the basis of the nature of the entity's environment and the evidence available when the financial statements are prepared.

The Conceptual Framework refers explicitly to the qualitative characteristics of useful information. It requires recognition of an item for inclusion in the statement of financial position or the statement of profit or loss and OCI, when it meets the definition of an asset, a liability, equity, income or expenses.

The general criteria for recognising these elements in financial statements are as follows.

Assets

An asset is a present economic resource controlled by the entity as a result of past events. An economic resource is further defined as a right that has the potential to produce future economic benefits.

For an economic resource to be an asset, it must possess both of the following inherent characteristics:

- a present economic resource with potential to produce future economic benefits
- its access or use is presently controlled by the entity

For example, the workforce of an entity certainly represents future economic benefits, but the entity does not hold any control over these employees as they may leave the organisation at any point in time and seek employment with a rival firm. Therefore, employees do not qualify as assets.

Recognition of an element as an asset is neither dependent upon its physical form nor its legal form. The key is substantial control over such element. An accounting concept popularly termed as 'substance over form' (which will be discussed in Chapter 4) implies that the transactions recorded in the financial statements must reflect their economic substance rather than their legal form alone. For example, patents and intellectual property are assets controlled by the entity and have future economic benefits although they do not have any physical form. Transactions or events that are expected to occur in the future do not, in themselves, give rise to assets. For example, merely an intention to purchase a building does not, in itself, meet the definition of an asset.

The criteria for recognising assets have also been mentioned specifically in IAS 2 (Inventories), IAS 16 (Property, Plant and Equipment), IAS 38 (Intangible Assets), IAS 32 (Financial Instruments: Presentation) and IFRS 9 (Financial Instruments).

Liability
A liability is a present obligation of the entity to transfer an economic resource or provide services to other entities as a result of past events. For example, accounts payable are present obligations to transfer an economic resource and thus are recognised as a liability.

The criteria for recognising liabilities have also been enumerated in IAS 1 (Presentation of Financial Statements), IAS 37 (Provisions, Contingent Liabilities and Contingent Assets), IAS 32 (Financial Instruments: Presentation) and IFRS 9 (Financial Instruments).

Equity
Equity is the residual interest in the assets of the entity after deducting all of its liabilities. The amount assigned to equity will be the excess of its assets over its liabilities, thus the criteria for the recognition of assets and liabilities provide the criteria for the recognition of equity.

An example of this lies in the 'owner's claim', which consists of items such as share capital and other components of equity.

Income
Income includes both revenue and gains, in the form of an increase in assets or reduction in liabilities of the entity, which results in an increase in equity, other than those relating to contributions from equity participants.

Revenue which arises in the normal course of business of an entity includes sales, fees, royalties = and rent received. Gains represent other items that may, or may not, arise in the course of the ordinary activities of an entity. Such gains include those on the disposal of non-current assets and finance income (dividends and interest).

The recognition of income occurs simultaneously with the recognition of increases in assets or decreases in liabilities. For example, when a sale is made, it results in a net increase in assets (cash or receivables) and is therefore recognised as revenue.

IFRS 15 (Revenue from Contracts with Customers) specifies the recognition and disclosure requirements and provides a single, principles-based five-step model to be applied to all contracts with customers. This will be discussed in Chapter 5.

Expenses
Expenses include both day-to-day expenses and the loss of future economic benefits, in the form of reductions in assets or increases in liabilities, that result

in a decrease in equity, other than those relating to distributions to holders of equity claims.

Recognition of expenses also occurs simultaneously with the recognition of an increase in liabilities or a decrease in assets. For example, **depreciation** of machinery will be recognised as an expense as it will result in reduction in the cost of assets.

Expenses that arise in the normal course of business include cost of sales, wages and depreciation charges. Losses may, or may not, arise in the course of the ordinary activities of the entity.

> **depreciation**
> The systematic spread of the cost to the entity of an asset over its useful life (period it will be used to generate benefit).

Test yourself 2.5

Explain how you would report a transaction that fails to satisfy the recognition criteria.

7.2 Derecognition

The Conceptual Framework provides new guidance on derecognition that discusses criteria on when to remove or derecognise assets and liabilities in financial statements. Derecognition is the removal of all or part of a recognised asset or liability from an entity's statement of financial position.

- **Asset:** derecognition of an asset occurs when the entity loses control of all or part of the recognised asset.
- **Liability:** derecognition of a liability occurs when the entity no longer has a present obligation for all or part of the recognised liability.

The derecognition guidance reflects the view that both the control approach and the risk-and-rewards approach to derecognition are valid, though it does not specify the use of one or the other. The IASB has adopted an approach that aims to faithfully represent both:

- the change in the entity's assets (resources) and liabilities (obligations) as a result of the derecognition transaction; and
- the assets and liabilities (if any) that are retained.

An entity should derecognise an asset or liability with appropriate presentation and disclosure.

In limited cases, it may be necessary to continue to recognise a transferred component of an asset or liability together with a liability or asset for the proceeds received or paid, with appropriate presentation and disclosure.

8 Measuring the elements of financial statements

Measurement is described as quantifying, in monetary terms, elements that are recognised in the financial statements. The objective of measurement is to contribute to the faithful representation of relevant information in the financial statements.

Measuring those elements requires the selection of a measurement basis. A single measurement basis for all elements may not provide the most relevant information for users of financial statements. For some elements, one basis may provide more useful information than the other.

There are varieties of measurement basis that are used extensively to different degrees and in varying combinations in financial statements. The Conceptual Framework provides guidance on measurement. It identifies two categories of measurement bases:

- Historical cost
- Current value basis (includes fair value, value in use/fulfilment value and current cost)

8.1 Historical cost

This is the historical price of the transaction or event that gave rise to the item being considered for measurement. It is the price paid or cost incurred to acquire or create an asset. For a liability, this would be the value of the consideration received pursuant to the incurrence of a liability.

Assets and liabilities presented at historical cost reflect the prices at the dates of transactions, rather than at the date of the financial statements. Consequently, amounts presented may reflect prices at multiple dates and may impede comparability between entities.

The historical cost of both an asset and a liability will be updated over time to depict its present condition. For example, the historical cost of assets is reduced to depict any consumption of the asset (depreciation) or if they become impaired. The historical cost of liabilities is increased if they become onerous.

An example of a historical cost measurement basis is to measure financial assets and financial liabilities at **amortised cost.** The guidelines for initial recognition of assets has been detailed in these standards:

- IAS 16 (Property, Plant and Equipment)
- IAS 38 (Intangible Assets)
- IAS 40 (Investment Property)

amortised cost
An accounting method which requires financial assets or financial liabilities to be measured at initial cost, less principal repayment, adjusted for amortisation of discount/premium and foreign exchange differences, less any reduction for impairment.

8.2 Current value basis

This is based on current monetary value, updated to reflect conditions at the measurement date. This method can be applied in circumstances in which a historical cost amount is not available, typically because the asset or liability did not arise from an exchange transaction. For example, the asset/liability can be measured using the cost of an equivalent asset/liability or the price paid to acquire an asset with equivalent service potential.

Measurement bases may include the following.

- **Fair value:** the price that would reflect market participants' current expectations of the amount to be received to sell an asset, or paid to transfer a liability, in an orderly transaction at the measurement date. The description of fair value in the revised Conceptual Framework is in line with IFRS 13 (Fair Value Measurement). For example, investment properties (IAS 40) are initially measured at cost and may be subsequently measured using a cost model or fair value model.
- **Value in use for assets and fulfilment value for liabilities:** the value that reflects entity-specific current expectations about the amount, timing and uncertainty of future cash flows. The descriptions of value in use and fulfilment value are derived from IAS 36 (Impairment of Assets). For example, an asset must not be carried in the financial statements at more than the highest amount to be recovered through its use or sale. If the **carrying amount** exceeds the recoverable amount, the asset is described as impaired. The entity must reduce the carrying amount of the asset to its recoverable amount and recognise an impairment loss.
- **Current cost:** reflects the current amount required to be paid to acquire an equivalent asset or received to settle an equivalent obligation or liability.

carrying amount
The recorded cost of an asset or a liability net of any accumulated depreciation or accumulated impairment losses. Also referred to as (net) book value.

Consideration of the factors and the cost constraint is likely to result in the selection of different measurement bases for different assets, liabilities, income and expenses. The factors to be considered in selecting a measurement basis are the two fundamental qualitative characteristics of useful information – relevance and faithful representation – because the aim is to provide information that is useful to investors, lenders and other creditors.

Test yourself 2.6

Explain the most commonly used measurement in financial statements.

9 Presentation and disclosure

All information about assets, liabilities, equity, income and expenses is communicated through presentation and disclosure in the financial statements.

The Conceptual Framework introduces concepts that describe how information should be presented and disclosed in financial statements. It provides guidance on including income and expenses in the statement of profit or loss and OCI. The key factor to consider is effective communication, so that the information in financial statements is relevant and contributes to the faithful representation of an entity's assets, liabilities, equity, income and expenses.

9.1 The statement of profit or loss and OCI

This provides information about an entity's financial performance for the reporting period. In principle, all income and expenses are classified and included in the statement of profit or loss. The revised Conceptual Framework introduces the term 'statement(s) of financial performance' to refer to the statement of profit or loss, together with the statement presenting OCI. Profit or loss could be a section of a single statement of financial performance or a separate statement.

9.2 Other comprehensive income

In exceptional circumstances, the IASB may decide to exclude some income or expenses from the statement of profit or loss and include it in OCI, to provide more relevant information or a more faithful representation. For example, items arising from a change in the current value of an asset (for example, a revaluation of property) or liability are included in OCI.

9.3 Recycling

Recycling is the term that the Conceptual Framework uses for the release of items in the OCI to the statement of profit or loss in a subsequent period. Income and expenses included in OCI should subsequently be 'recycled' (released) to the statement of profit or loss, provided that the recycling results in more relevant and faithfully representative information in the statement of profit or loss.

10 Concepts of capital and capital maintenance

Under the concept of capital maintenance, profit may be recognised only if the total value of all assets (net of all liabilities) at the end of the accounting period exceeds the value at the beginning of the accounting period (after excluding any distributions to and contributions from owners during the period). In other words, an organisation is said to be making a profit only if the net value of its assets increases.

The Conceptual Framework identifies two concepts of capital maintenance:

- financial capital maintenance
- physical capital maintenance

The Conceptual Framework does not indicate a preference for either of these concepts of capital maintenance.

The selection of a concept of capital maintenance (and of the measurement basis to be used) determines the accounting model used in preparation of the financial statements. The Conceptual Framework acknowledges that different accounting models exhibit different degrees of relevance and reliability and that preparers of financial statements should seek a balance between those characteristics.

10.1 The financial concept of capital maintenance

According to this concept, the capital of the entity is linked to the net assets, which is the equity of the entity. Profit is earned only if the financial or monetary value of the net assets at the end of the accounting period exceeds the monetary value of net assets at the beginning of the accounting period. This is adjusted for any distributions (such as dividends) to or contributions (such as equity capital raised) from the owners.

The financial statements can be viewed by users as:

Opening equity (net assets) + profit − distributions = closing equity (net assets)

Where: assets − liabilities = equity

The financial concept of capital maintenance can be further categorised as

- money financial capital maintenance
- real financial capital maintenance

The only difference between these two categories is that money financial capital maintenance considers the time value of money or the impact of inflation, whereas these are ignored in real financial capital maintenance.

A financial concept of capital is usually followed by an entity where the financial statements are referred to by its users in the context of purchasing power of the amount invested as capital or the maintenance of their invested capital.

10.2 Physical concept of capital maintenance

This concept works for an entity where the capital is regarded as its production capacity. Profit under this concept is earned only if the production capacity at the end of the year exceeds the production capacity of an entity at the beginning of the year, after excluding any distributions to or contributions from the owners.

This production capacity may be based on units of output. The main concern of users of these financial statements is with the maintenance of the operating capability of the entity. This method is usually followed if the users of the financial statements are mostly concerned with the operating capacity of the entity, as well as enhancing such operating capacity.

Most organisations use the financial concept of capital maintenance as it is easier to apply.

Worked example 2.1

Prerana Limited is established on 1 January 20X9 with 20,000 equity shares at £1 each.

It then buys £20,000 worth of inventory, which it sells during the year for £28,000.

There were no other transactions during the year.

At the end of the year the purchase price of the inventory had increased to £23,000.

Calculate retained profit using:

1. (a) the financial concept of capital maintenance.
2. (b) the physical concept of capital maintenance.

Solution:

1. If the financial capital maintenance concept is used, the profit for the year is £8,000 (£28,000 – £20,000). However, if the company paid out the £8,000 profit to shareholders, it would be unable to buy the same inventory again as the purchase price has risen.
2. If the physical maintenance concept is used, the profit for the year is £5,000 (£28,000 – £23,000). To keep the operating capability of the company the same, profit is measured as sales less the replacement cost of the goods sold.

Chapter summary

- The IASB's Conceptual Framework (revised in 2018) is a statement of generally accepted theoretical principles that provide the basis for the development and evaluation of new and existing financial reporting and accounting standards. It helps preparers to develop consistent accounting policies, based on consistent concepts.
- The Conceptual Framework deals with:
  - the objective of general purpose financial reporting;
  - the qualitative characteristics that determine the usefulness of information in financial statements;
  - financial statements and the reporting entity;
  - the definitions, recognition, derecognition and measurement of the elements of financial statements;
  - the concepts and guidance on presentation and disclosure; and
  - the concepts of capital and capital maintenance.

- The objective of general purpose financial statements is to provide useful information about the financial position, financial performance and cash flows of an entity to a wide range of users in making rational financial and investment decisions.
- Users of financial accounting information consist of external users and internal users. External users include investors, lenders, creditors, customers, the government and its agencies and the public. Internal users include employees, management or operational managers, lenders, suppliers and other trade creditors.
- There are certain qualitative characteristics which a business must embody in order for the financial statements to be useful to the stakeholders. These are divided into:
  - fundamental qualitative characteristics:
    - relevance (materiality)
    - faithful representation (completeness, neutrality, prudence and to be free from error)
  - enhancing qualitative characteristics:
    - comparability
    - verifiability
    - timeliness
    - understandability
- The objective of financial statements is to provide information about the assets, liabilities, equity, income and expenses of the reporting entity. This information is provided in the statement of financial position and the statement of profit or loss and OCI as well as in other statements and notes.
- Financial statements are prepared for a specified period of time, referred to as a 'reporting period'. They provide comparative information and, under certain circumstances, forward-looking information. A reporting entity is a single entity or a portion of an entity. It can comprise more than one entity that is required, or chooses, to prepare financial statements.
- The Conceptual Framework requires financial statements and the underlying information to be prepared on a going-concern basis.
- The Conceptual Framework defines the building blocks or elements from which the financial statements are constructed as follows:
  - elements relating to financial position – assets, liabilities and equity; and
  - elements relating to financial performance – income and expense.
- For an item to be recognised in the financial statements, it needs to meet the definition of an asset, a liability or equity and income or expenses. Items are only recognised when their recognition provides users of financial statements with information that is both relevant and faithfully represented.

- Derecognition is the removal of all or part of a recognised asset or liability from an entity's statement of financial position.
- Measurement is described as quantifying, in monetary terms, elements that are recognised in the financial statements. The objective of measurement is to contribute to the faithful representation of relevant information in the financial statements. The Conceptual Framework identifies two categories of measurement basis:
    - historical cost
    - current value basis (includes fair value, value in use/fulfilment value and current cost)
- The Conceptual Framework introduces concepts that describe how information should be presented and disclosed in financial statements and provides guidance on including income and expenses in the statement of profit or loss and OCI and other comprehensive income. The key factor to consider is effective communication, so that the information in financial statements is relevant and contributes to the faithful representation of an entity's assets, liabilities, equity, income and expenses.
- There are two concepts of capital maintenance: the financial concept of capital maintenance and the physical concept of capital maintenance.
- The fundamental qualitative characteristics of 'relevance' and 'faithful representation' are consistently conveyed in the Conceptual Framework to make the financial information more useful to the entity's various stakeholders.

Part two

Chapter 3
Presentation of single entity published financial statements

Chapter 4
Other contents and features of published financial statements

Chapter 5
Accounting policies based on IFRS

Chapter 6
Financial reporting by groups of companies

Chapter 7
Analysis of published financial statements

Understanding and interpreting financial statements and reports

Overview

Part two covers a wide range of financial reporting topics, from the preparation and presentation of single entity financial statements and the interpretation of IFRS-based accounting policies and published financial statements through to group reporting and the analysis of financial reports.

Chapter 3 looks at the requirements of International Accounting Standard 1 (Presentation of Financial Statements) which governs the preparation and presentation of single entity financial statements. It discusses and illustrates a complete set of financial statements, comprised of a statement of financial position, a statement of profit or loss and OCI, a statement of changes in equity and a statement of cash flows. It also looks at the requirements of IFRS 5 (Non-Current Assets Held for Sale and Discontinued Operations) regarding discontinued operations.

Chapter 4 introduces the interpretation of published financial statements within a company's annual report and financial statements (or accounts) which enable investors, other users and the public at large to understand the company's profitability, financial position, growth prospects and probable risks. It also discusses segment reporting and reporting the substance of transactions, as well as the limitations of published financial statements.

Chapter 5 covers some key accounting policies that govern the preparation and presentation of financial statements, including: accounting for inventories; accounting for property, plant and equipment; accounting for events after the end of a reporting period; revenue from contracts with customers; and provisions contingent liabilities and contingent assets.

Chapter 6 deals with group reporting, the requirements to prepare consolidated financial statements and the basic procedures required in consolidation. It discusses the different types of investment and influence that a parent (or investor) may have over other entities and how each is treated for accounting purposes. It also looks at the rules on exclusion of subsidiaries from consolidation and exemptions from preparing consolidated financial statements.

Chapter 7 looks at how financial reporting can be analysed and interpreted to evaluate financial performance. It will discuss how to interpret and analyse published financial statements using different tools, including fundamental analysis, trend analysis (horizontal and vertical) and ratio analysis. It also discusses the limitations of accounting ratios and the effect of accounting irregularities and creative accounting. The practical application of analysis and interpretation is explored in Chapter 16.

At the end of this Part, students will be able to:

- understand how financial statements are constructed and prepared in line with the relevant financial reporting and accounting standards (IFRS) to meet the objective of the general purpose financial statements;
- demonstrate an understanding of the overriding concepts of financial reporting such as going concern, the accruals basis of accounting, fair presentation, compliance with IFRS, materiality, the reporting period and offsetting;

- understand how a complete set of financial statements is prepared in accordance with the structure and content prescribed within IFRS and interpret the main components of a statement of financial position;
- understand how the statement of profit or loss and OCI is constructed to analyse the performance of a company;
- lay out the usual contents of the annual report and accounts;
- discuss the purpose and content of the strategic report, the directors' report and the notes to the financial statements;
- explain the importance of segmental information and interpret a segment report;
- discuss the limitations of published financial statements;
- understand the application of relevant IFRS when interpreting financial statements;
- demonstrate familiarity with the nature of accounting policies, including the criteria and impact of changing accounting policies;
- describe and apply the requirements of the relevant IFRS for accounting for inventories, accounting for property, plant and equipment and accounting for events arising after the end of the reporting period;
- explain how revenue is accounted for under IFRS 15 and apply the principles for the recognition and measurement of revenue;
- understand the different types of investment and influence a company may have in other businesses, broadly classified as subsidiaries, joint arrangements or associates and describe the difference between them;
- describe the concept of a group as a single economic unit, explain the objective of consolidated financial statements, explain when parent companies are required to prepare consolidated financial statements and discuss the control criteria for consolidation;
- explain the reporting requirements for consolidated financial statements;

- describe the circumstances when a group may claim exemption from the preparation of consolidated financial statements and the circumstances when subsidiaries are excluded from consolidation;
- discuss the significance of financial analysis and explain how it is used to interpret the profitability and financial soundness of a business from the perspectives of different stakeholders;
- explain key financial indicators used to analyse and evaluate entity's performance;
- explain what is meant by fundamental analysis, trend analysis (horizontal and vertical) and ratio analysis and demonstrate how they are used to evaluate company performance; and
- explain how creative accounting and accounting irregularities are used to manipulate figures for a desired result.

Chapter three
Presentation of single entity published financial statements

Contents

1. Introduction
2. The objective of financial statements
3. Presentation of financial statements
4. Fair presentation and compliance with IFRS
5. Overriding concepts of financial statements
6. Structure and content of financial statements
7. Statement of financial position
8. Statement of profit or loss and other comprehensive income
9. Statement of changes in equity
10. Statement of cash flows

1 Introduction

This chapter outlines the overall requirements of IAS 1 (Presentation of Financial Statements). IAS 1 was originally issued by the IASC in September 1997 and was the first comprehensive accounting standard to deal with the presentation of financial standards.

It was adopted by the IASB on its formation in 2001 and reissued in September 2007. International Accounting Standard 1 applies to all general-purpose financial statements that are prepared and presented in accordance with IFRS (which includes all existing International Accounting Standards). General purpose financial statements are a set of basic financial statements intended to serve a broad group of users for a range of activities, not tailored to any particular information needs. The objective of the financial statements is to provide financial information such as the financial position, financial performance and cash flows of an entity to help users in make financial decisions.

International Accounting Standard 1 sets out the overall requirements for the presentation of financial statements and prescribes the structure and minimum requirement for the content of financial statements, including overriding concepts such as going concern, the accruals basis of accounting and the current/non-current distinction. Standards for recognising, measuring and disclosing specific transactions are addressed in other standards and interpretations. International Accounting Standard 1 also sets out the different statements required to make up a complete set of financial statements of a single entity, the main components of each of the statements, their presentation and structure and what information must accompany them.

The standard requires a complete set of financial statements to comprise:

- a statement of financial position
- a statement of profit or loss and other comprehensive income
- a statement of changes in equity
- a statement of cash flows
- notes to the accounts

Figure 3.1 summarises the overall features and components of financial statements.

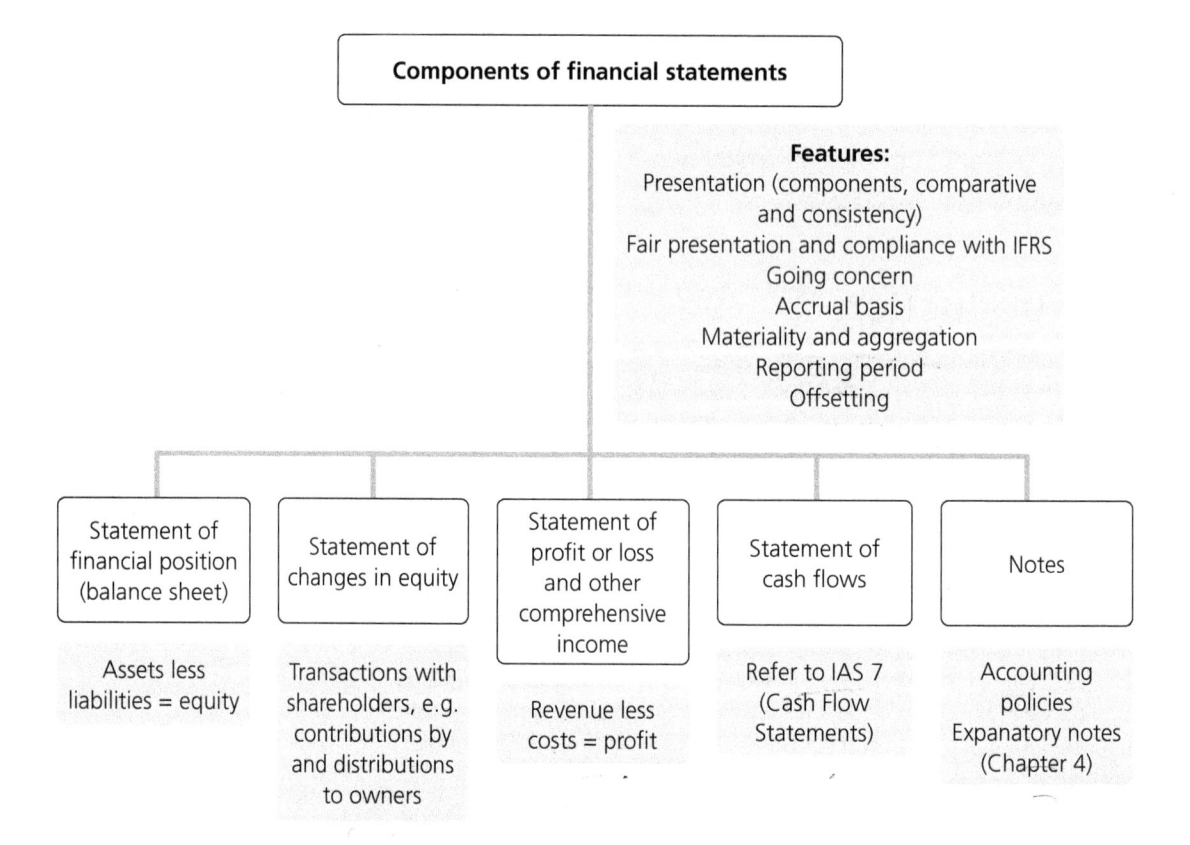

Components of financial statements

Features:
Presentation (components, comparative and consistency)
Fair presentation and compliance with IFRS
Going concern
Accrual basis
Materiality and aggregation
Reporting period
Offsetting

Statement of financial position (balance sheet)	Statement of changes in equity	Statement of profit or loss and other comprehensive income	Statement of cash flows	Notes
Assets less liabilities = equity	Transactions with shareholders, e.g. contributions by and distributions to owners	Revenue less costs = profit	Refer to IAS 7 (Cash Flow Statements)	Accounting policies Expanatory notes (Chapter 4)

Figure 3.1 Single entity financial statements

This chapter will focus on the disclosures which are within the scope of this syllabus and will provide a pro forma set of financial statements based on IAS 1.

2 The objective of financial statements

A commercial entity raises equity and borrows debt to set up business primarily to make a profit. It uses these funds to purchase resources, including tangible and intangible assets and finance its running costs, such as wages, rent and rates. From running its business, it generates profits (and cash flows) that are used to:

- service debt and equity holders through interest, dividends and repayments
- reinvest in the business to help the business grow

Financial statements are designed to capture this cycle. The purpose of financial statements is mainly to provide a report of the financial position (at a specific point in time) and financial performance (over a period) to show how an entity has performed. The financial information is useful to a wide range of users in making financial decisions.

In Chapter 2 we covered the IASB's Conceptual Framework for Financial Reporting, which addresses the objective of general purpose financial reporting in providing useful information about the financial position, financial performance and cash flows of an entity to a wide range of users to allow them to make financial decisions. International Accounting Standard 1 sets out the overall objective for the preparation of financial statements and some important principles that apply across financial reporting.

To meet the objective of general financial reporting, financial statements categorise the information presented into the following elements (discussed in Chapter 2):

- assets
- liabilities
- equity
- income (including gains)
- expenses (including losses)
- other changes in equity (contributions from and distributions to owners)
- cash flows

This information is provided in the statement of financial position and the statement(s) of financial performance, as well as in other statements and notes.

Financial statements highlight the strengths and weaknesses of the entity and help users to assess the entity's liquidity and solvency, plus any needs for additional financing. They are also used to predict future returns.

3 Presentation of financial statements

The objective of IAS 1 is to ensure comparability of financial statements, both with the entity's financial statements of previous periods and with the financial statements of other entities. Under IAS 1, an entity must present a complete set of financial statements (including prior period comparative information) on at least an annual basis. A complete set of financial statements comprises:

- a statement of financial position (also called a balance sheet)
- a statement of profit or loss and other comprehensive income (previously known as the income statement)
- a statement of changes in equity
- a statement of cash flows
- notes to the financial statements (discussed in Chapter 4)

An entity may use titles for the statements other than those stated above. The use of legacy terms such as balance sheet (rather than statement of financial position), income statement (rather than statement of profit or loss) and cash flow statement (rather than statement of cash flows) are likely to be found in practice. This study text uses the titles in IAS 1.

3.1 Comparative information

Although each statement serves a particular objective, all the statements are interconnected and must be looked at in totality to get the full impression of the business. All financial statements are required to be presented with equal prominence.

International Accounting Standard 1 requires that comparative information is provided in respect of the previous period for all amounts reported in the financial statements, both on the face of the financial statements and in the notes, unless another standard requires otherwise. Narrative and descriptive comparative information is also disclosed where it is relevant to understanding the financial statements of the current period. Various disclosures must be made if comparative figures are amended or reclassified due to a change in accounting policy.

3.2 Consistency

The presentation and classification of items in the financial statements should be same from one period to the next, unless a change is justified either by a change in circumstances or a requirement of a new IFRS. Consistency is important because of the need for comparability of financial statements. Any change justified either by a change in circumstances or a requirement of a new IFRS must be disclosed along with its effects on financial statements items. For instance, when a firm ceases to be a going concern, the application of the prior year's measurements methods would produce an inaccurate position. In such situations, the entity must provide in its financial report the reason(s) for the change, the nature of the change(s) and the effects of the change(s) on items in the financial statements.

4 Fair presentation and compliance with IFRS

International Accounting Standard 1 states that the financial statements must present the financial position, financial performance and cash flows of an entity fairly and accurately. A fair presentation is presumed to be achieved from compliance with IFRS, as well as ensuring transactions are fairly represented in accordance with the definitions and recognition criteria for assets, liabilities, income and expenses as set out in the Conceptual Framework. International Accounting Standard 1 requires an entity to explicitly disclose compliance with IFRS in the notes. All the requirements of IFRS must be followed if compliance with IFRS is disclosed.

A fair presentation of financial statements requires:

- selection and application of appropriate accounting policies and practices;
- presentation of information which is relevant, reliable, comparable and understandable; and
- additional disclosures where required to ensure that the financial statements give a fair representation of the results, financial position and cash flow.

International Accounting Standard 1 acknowledges that, in extremely rare circumstances, departure from IFRS is permitted where compliance with IFRS would conflict with the objective of financial statements, thus misleading the users of financial statements. Any departure from the IFRS requirement must be supported with detailed disclosure of the nature, reasons and impact of the departure. There must be good reasons for not following the principles as set out in the Conceptual Framework (see Chapter 2). The effect that would have been achieved by following IFRS should also be fully disclosed.

Use of an inappropriate accounting policies cannot be rectified either by disclosure of the accounting policies used, or by using notes and/or explanatory material.

5 Overriding concepts of financial statements

Some important principles and overriding concepts that apply in the preparation and presentation of financial statements include the following:

5.1 Going concern

The IASB's Conceptual Framework (discussed in Chapter 2) notes that financial statements are normally prepared on the assumption that the entity is a going concern and will continue in operation for the foreseeable future. IAS 1 requires management to make an assessment of an entity's ability to continue as a going concern.

The financial statements should not be prepared on a going-concern basis where there are material uncertainties over the entity's ability to continue to operate in the foreseeable future as a going concern. IAS 1 requires such uncertainties to be disclosed, including details of events that might threaten the future of the entity.

5.2 Accruals basis of accounting

The Framework states that financial performance is reflected by accruals-based accounting and this provides a better basis for assessing past and future performance than cash-based information. International Accounting Standard 1 requires financial statements, except for cash flow information, to be prepared using the accruals basis of accounting, not on a cash basis. The accruals concept is the most fundamental principle of accounting. It requires transactions to be accounted for in the period when income is earned or expenses are incurred, not when they are received and paid in cash.

The accruals concept is the basis for income, expense, asset and liability recognition that results in accurate reporting of the company's financial performance and financial position over different periods.

In Figure 3.2, a typical situation arises around the reporting year end of a company when a customer orders (and receives) goods and pays for them later. The revenue is recorded at the time it is earned no matter when payment is made: in this case, when the goods are delivered in November. It would be too late to record the revenue when payment is received in January as it had been earned much earlier. Cash accounting recognises economic events only when cash is exchanged, without indicating the true position of the business. Accruals-based accounting recognises revenue and expenses in the periods in which they are incurred.

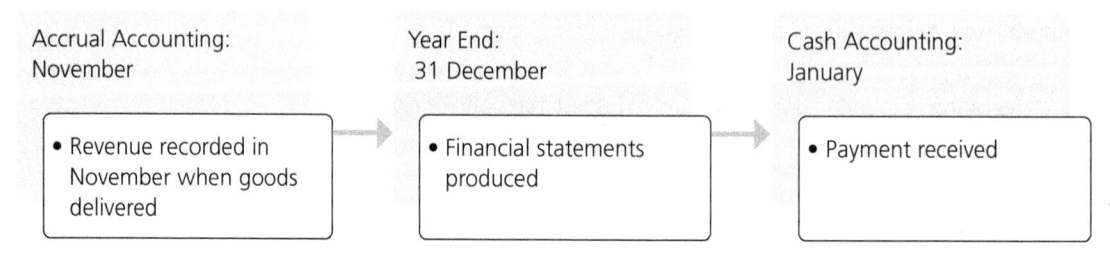

Accrual Accounting: November	Year End: 31 December	Cash Accounting: January
• Revenue recorded in November when goods delivered	• Financial statements produced	• Payment received

Figure 3.2 Accruals accounting

matching principle
An accounting concept in accruals-based accounting that requires expenses and the corresponding revenue to be recorded in the same period (whenever it is logical and feasible to do so).

The expressions **'matching principle'** and 'accruals basis of accounting' are often used interchangeably. Both require recognition of income and expenses in the accounting periods to which they relate. However, the matching principle is a further refinement of the accruals concept, requiring expenses and the corresponding revenue to be recorded in the same period (whenever it is logical and feasible to do so). The application of this principle will be further discussed in Chapter 5.

Stop and think 3.1

Refer to the latest published financial statements of a company of your choice and see whether they include a complete set of financial statements as required by IAS 1.

Test yourself 3.1

1. What is the key objective of financial statements?
2. What are the components of a complete set of financial statements as required by IAS 1?

5.3 Materiality and aggregation

The concept of materiality is important. International Accounting Standard 1 states that each material class of similar items should be presented separately and items that are dissimilar in terms of nature or function should be presented separately unless they are immaterial.

The concept of materiality is a key feature of financial reporting and its consideration applies to all parts of the financial statements and disclosures. Materiality depends on the nature or size of the item, or a combination of both and whether the non-disclosure thereof could influence the financial decisions of the users of financial statements. The decision about whether or not an item is material requires the application of judgement and its relative significance to the user of financial statements. Information may be material or relevant simply because of its magnitude or because its omission from the financial statements could affect decision making.

The most common examples are directors' remuneration and related party disclosures. They may be small in size compared to the company's overall net assets or profit but may be material due to its significance to the users of financial reports.

Financial information is capable of making a difference in decision making if it has predictive value, confirmatory value or both. The IASB gives the example of the revenue for a company for a particular year, which can be used to confirm previous predictions about revenue for the period, as well as being used to predict next year's revenue.

5.4 Reporting period

Entities should prepare financial statements at least annually, as per IAS 1. In unusual cases, where the end of an entity's reporting period is changed to less or more than one year, the entity should disclose:

- the reason for the change
- the fact that the comparative figures given are not entirely comparable

International Accounting Standard 1 allows some entities to use a period which approximates to a year, such as 52 or occasionally 53 weeks, for practical purposes as it will produce statements not materially different from those produced on an annual basis.

5.5 Offsetting

Assets and liabilities and income and expenses, shall not be offset unless required or permitted by a standard or an interpretation. The netting off of assets and liabilities, or items of income and expense, can disguise both transactions and the financial position and hence may not provide a true picture of the entity's assets and liabilities, or income and expenses. They should not be shown on a net basis unless required or permitted by an IFRS.

Common examples of treatments permitted by an IFRS are the netting off of the allowance for receivables from trade receivables and accumulated depreciation from the cost (or valuation) of non-current assets.

6 Structure and content of financial statements

6.1 Disclosure of items

International Accounting Standard 1 specifies particular disclosures of line items in the financial statements and in the notes. Some items must appear on the face of the statement of financial position or statement of profit or loss and OCI. Other items can appear in a note to the financial statements instead. Recommended (but not mandatory) formats are given in IAS 1 for entities, depending on their circumstances.

Disclosures specified by both IAS 1 and other IFRS may be made either on the face of the statement or in the notes, unless otherwise stated. For example, IAS 7 (Statement of Cash Flows) sets out the requirements for the presentation of cash flow information.

These disclosures cannot be made in an accompanying commentary or report. Judgement must be used in determining the best way of presenting such information. International Accounting Standard 1 suggests that the approach will be very different when the financial statements are communicated electronically. For example, separate pages are not always used when an entity presents the financial statements electronically, as long as the information included in the financial statements can be understood.

6.2 Identification of financial statements

An entity should clearly identify and distinguish the financial statements and related notes which are prepared under IFRS from other information published with them in the annual report. This is to enable readers of the annual report to differentiate between the parts of the report which are prepared using IFRS and those which are not. International Financial Reporting Standards apply only to the financial statements, not necessarily to other information presented in an annual report. International Accounting Standard 1 also requires repeated disclosure of the following information in a prominent manner wherever it is felt necessary:

- the name of the reporting entity and any change in name
- whether the statements are for an individual entity or for a group of entities
- the period end date or period covered by the financial statements
- the presentation currency as defined by IAS 21 (The Effects of Changes in Foreign Exchange Rates)
- the level of rounding used in presenting amounts (thousands, millions)

In this study text, all examples will use sterling (£) as the presentation currency.

The level of rounding is important and must be disclosed. Disclosing the level of rounding often makes financial statements more understandable, as long as the entity does not omit material information.

7 Statement of financial position

The statement of financial position, previously known as the balance sheet, presents the financial position of an entity at a given date. It is comprised of three main components: assets, liabilities and equity. It provides a snapshot or record of resources owned or controlled (assets) and obligations owed (liabilities) at a specific point in time: the end of the accounting period. However, this snapshot will change every time an accounting transaction takes place. The statement of financial position helps users to assess the financial soundness of an entity in terms of liquidity risk, financial risk, credit risk and business risk.

7.1 Line items

The following line items are specified by IAS 1 for disclosure on the face of the statement of financial position.

Assets
- property, plant and equipment
- investment property
- intangible assets
- financial assets (excluding amounts shown under (5), (8) and (9))
- investments accounted for using the equity method

- biological assets
- inventories
- trade and other receivables
- cash and cash equivalents
- assets held for sale

Liabilities
- trade and other payables
- provisions
- financial liabilities (excluding amounts shown under (1) and (2))
- current tax liabilities (or as a current tax asset)
- deferred tax liabilities (or as a deferred tax asset)
- liabilities included in disposal groups classified as held for sale

Equity
- issued share capital and other components of equity (attributable to owners of the parent in a consolidated statement of financial position)
- non-controlling interests (NCI) presented as part of equity (in a consolidated statement of financial position)
- non-controlling interest

Other equity interests in a subsidiary company in a situation where a parent company has control but owns less than 100% of the shareholding. Previously known as the minority interest.

7.2 Additional information

International Accounting Standard 1 only specifies the minimum line items that must be included on the face of the statement of financial position. Additional line items, headings with sub-classifications and subtotals may be needed for a fuller understanding of the entity's financial position. Any subtotals must be comprised of line items made up of amounts recognised and measured in accordance with IFRS.

7.3 Format of statement

International Accounting Standard 1 does not prescribe the format of the statement of financial position nor does it specify the order or format in which the items listed should be presented. It simply requires that items which are sufficiently different in nature or function are to be presented separately. An additional item must be presented separately based on judgements and on the basis of an assessment of the following factors:

- **Nature and liquidity of assets and their materiality**: monetary/non-monetary assets and current/non-current assets are presented separately.

Goodwill and assets arising from development expenditure (intangible assets) are also shown separately.

- **Function of assets within the entity:** operating and financial assets, inventories, receivables and cash and cash equivalents should be presented separately.
- **Amounts, nature and timing of liabilities:** interest-bearing and non-interest-bearing liabilities and provisions are classified. They are shown separately as current or non-current (see section 7.4).

A separate presentation is also required where different measurement bases are used for assets and liabilities which differ in nature or function. For example, certain items of property, plant and equipment can be presented at cost or at a revalued amount (according to IAS 16 (Property, Plant and Equipment)).

Line items are included when the size, nature or function of an item, or aggregation of similar items, is such that separate presentation is relevant and required to fairly present the entity's financial position. If needed, the descriptions or/and ordering of items, or aggregation of similar items, can be amended to provide relevant information for a better understanding of the entity's financial position. A financial institution, for instance, may reorder the above items and change their descriptions to provide information that is more relevant to its operations. The classification will depend upon the nature of the entity's operations.

Further sub-classifications of the line items listed above should be disclosed to provide more relevant information in the statement or in the notes. Sub-classification of each line item depends on its size, nature, function and the requirements of IFRS. For example, amounts payable to or receivable from any group company or other related party should be disclosed separately as per IFRS requirements.

The following disclosures are provided as examples by IAS 1.

- Property, plant and equipment are classified as per IAS 16 (Property, Plant and Equipment).
- Receivables are sub-classified into amounts receivable from trade customers, other members of the group, receivables from related parties, prepayments and other amounts.
- Inventories are sub-classified as per IAS 2 (Inventories). The item is analysed to show merchandise, production supplies, materials, work in progress and finished goods.
- Provisions are analysed, showing separate provisions for employee benefit costs and any other items classified in a manner appropriate to the entity's operations.
- Equity capital and other components of equity are analysed, showing the various classes of paid-in share capital, share premium and other components.

7.4 Current/non-current classification

A statement of financial position must normally present classifications separating current and non-current assets and current and non-current liabilities, unless presentation based on liquidity provides information that is reliable and more relevant.

These distinctions should give an indication of the extent when they can be realised. This is useful for an assessment of the financial position and solvency of an entity. Entities such as financial institutions, who do not supply goods or services within a clearly identifiable operating cycle, should present all assets and liabilities in order of liquidity in increasing or decreasing order.

In all cases, an entity shall disclose the amount for each assets and liabilities expected to be settled after the reporting date into the following separate classifications:

- less than 12 months after the reporting period (current); or
- more than 12 months after the reporting period (non-current).

These classifications provide useful information by distinguishing assets (or liabilities) that are expected to be realised (or settled) within the current operating cycle from those used in the long-term operations.

A long-term debt expected to be refinanced under an existing loan facility is classified as non-current, even if the liability would otherwise be due within 12 months. Likewise, if a liability has become payable on or before the reporting date because of a breach under a long-term loan agreement, the liability becomes current. However, the liability is non-current if the lender provides a grace period ending at least 12 months after the end of the reporting period, within which the entity can rectify the breach and during which the lender cannot demand immediate repayment.

The liquidity and solvency of an entity is assessed based on information about expected dates of realisation of assets and liabilities. IFRS 7 (Financial Instruments: Disclosures) requires disclosure of the maturity dates of financial assets, such as trade and other receivables and financial liabilities, including trade and other payables.

Current and non-current assets:
An asset is classified as current by IAS 1 when it is:

- expected to be realised (sold or consumed) in the entity's normal operating cycle;
- held primarily for the purpose of trading and expected to be realised within 12 months after the reporting date; or
- cash or a cash equivalent which is not restricted in its use.

Current assets include assets (such as inventories and trade receivables) that are sold, consumed or realised as part of the normal operating cycle, even when they are not expected to be realised within 12 months after the reporting date. They also include assets held primarily for the purpose of trading and the current portion of non-current financial assets. The normal operating cycle is the cash conversion cycle an entity takes to realise its purchases into cash or cash equivalents from customers. For example, the operating cycle for a manufacturer is the average time that it takes to convert its initial purchase of inventory to cash proceeds from the sale of its products. Normal operating cycle varies from business to business. It is normally assumed to be 12 months when it is not clearly identifiable.

All other assets should be classified as non-current assets. Non-current assets include tangible, intangible and financial assets of a long-term nature. The standard does not prohibit the use of alternative descriptions as long as the meaning is clear.

Current and non-current liabilities
A liability is classified as current by IAS 1 when it is:

- expected to be settled in the entity's normal operating cycle;
- held primarily for the purpose of trading;
- due to be settled within 12 months after the reporting date; or
- it does not have an unconditional right to defer settlement of the liability.

Liabilities not falling within the definitions of 'current' are classified as non-current. It should be noted that an entity shall not classify deferred tax assets (liabilities) as current assets (liabilities). Deferred tax is not covered in the syllabus.

7.5 Share capital and other components of equity

International Accounting Standard 1 requires the following disclosures regarding **issued share capital** and other components of equity (previously known as reserves), either on the face of the statement of financial position or in the notes.

Share capital for each class of share capital
- number of shares issued and fully paid and issued but not fully paid
- par or **nominal share value** per share (or that shares do not have a par value)
- reconciliation of the number of shares outstanding at the start and end of the period
- rights, preferences and restrictions attached to the shares
- shares in the entity held by the entity itself or by related group companies
- shares reserved for issuance under options and sales contracts
- a description of the nature and purpose of each reserve within equity

issued share capital
The nominal value of share capital issued to shareholders. The rights and voting powers of shares and the differences between the different classes of shares should be listed in the articles of association.

nominal share value
The book or face value of a share. In the UK, it is generally £1, 50p, 25p, 10p or 5p. The nominal value is also known as the par value.

Description of the nature and purpose of each component within equity

Other components of equity (or reserves) include share premium, revaluation surplus and retained earnings.

Additional disclosures are required in respect of entities without share capital, such as partnerships. Such entities should disclose the movement during the period in each category of equity interest and any rights, preferences or restrictions attached to each category of equity interest.

Worked example 3.1 shows a format for an entity's statement of financial position that covers most of the information that is expected to appear.

Worked example 3.1

The most recent (20X2) figures are shown first as these are providing the reader of the statement with new information.

Yala plc
Statement of financial position as at 31 December 20X2

	20X2 £m	20X1 £m
Assets		
Non-current assets		
Property, plant and equipment	195	180
Goodwill	45	45
Other intangible assets	90	75
Investments	20	15
Total non-current assets	350	315
Current assets		
Inventories	18	15
Trade receivables	37	45
Cash and cash equivalents	3	15
Total current assets	58	75
Non-current assets held for sale	9	NIL
Total assets	417	390
Equity and liabilities		
Equity		
Share capital	150	150
Revaluation surplus	22	15

Retained earnings	75	60
Total equity	247	225
Non-current liabilities		
Long-term borrowings	59	81
Long-term provisions	13	9
Total non-current liabilities	72	90
Current liabilities		
Trade and other payables	53	37
Short-term borrowings	15	12
Current portion of long-term borrowings	22	22
Current tax payable	8	4
Total current liabilities	98	75
Total liabilities	170	165
Total equity and liabilities	417	390

Test yourself 3.2

1. What is meant by a current asset, a non-current asset, a current liability and a non-current liability?
2. How does having an agreement to refinance and an unconditional right to defer settlement of the liability impact on an entity's current/non-current classification.

8 Statement of profit or loss and other comprehensive income

The statement of profit or loss and other comprehensive income (OCI) is the new name for the profit and loss account or income statement for IFRS-compliant entities.

It provides a significant indicator of the performance of the entity during the accounting period, as well as summarising revenues generated and costs incurred as a result of undertaking business activity. It is the review of overall performance as a result of the financial transactions that took place during the accounting period.

Users obtain the following information from the statement of profit or loss and OCI:

- the profit (or loss) made in the period
- the estimated amount of corporation tax payable
- the residual amount retained by the company (profit for the period)

The most common measurement of an entity's financial 'performance' is profit. Profit is the excess of income receivable over expenses incurred in the period. It is important to note that profit is not measured in cash terms, but on the basis of accounting entries and adjustments. Therefore, a separate statement of cash flows is also provided in accordance with IAS 7 (see section 10 on page 74). It is possible for a company to be making profit and still have difficulties in terms of cash flow, or even the other way round – incurring losses by selling off assets to raise cash. A statement of cash flows will provide information that reconciles profit and the change in cash for a period. Some decisions in a company are a balance between maximising profit and the timing of cash receipts. We will look at some of these issues in the sections on working capital management in Part three.

All items of income and expense recognised in a period must be included in the statement of profit or loss unless an IFRS requires otherwise. Other comprehensive income is income and expense items (including reclassification adjustments) that are not recognised in the statement of profit or loss as required or permitted by other IFRS. Total comprehensive income is defined as 'the change in equity during a period resulting from transactions and other events, other than those changes resulting from transactions with owners in their capacity as owners'.

> Total comprehensive income for the period = profit or loss for the period + other comprehensive income recognised in the period.

8.1 Presentation and basic requirements

International Accounting Standard 1 provides an entity a choice of presenting either:

- a single 'statement of comprehensive income' with profit or loss and other comprehensive income, presented in two sections; or
- a separate 'statement of profit or loss' showing the profit or loss for the period followed by a 'statement of other comprehensive income'.

The statement(s) must present profit or loss for the period, other comprehensive income, total comprehensive income for the period and (for consolidated statement(s)) an allocation of the final results between owners of the parent and any NCIs.

Worked example 3.2 provides a format that covers most of the information that is expected to appear in an entity's statement of profit or loss and OCI (previously known as an income statement). It is the most popular method of reporting the statement of profit or loss and OCI in the EU. It analyses expenses by function, although a more complex analysis by nature is also permitted.

In this example, gross profit is calculated by subtracting cost of sales (the term used in IAS 1) from revenue. The cost of sales is the accumulated total of all the costs used to create a product or service which has been sold in the period. If the company manufactures or sells goods, it will often be labelled as the cost of goods sold.

The various costs of sales fall into the general sub-categories of direct labour, direct materials and overheads. They may also be considered to include the cost of any direct commissions or royalties associated with a sale. Therefore, the accounting concepts of matching and accruals are key, as the cost of sales must directly relate to the revenue accounted for. The cost method used for accounting for inventory will affect the cost of goods sold, as this is where these various cost elements are reported. The calculations for different types of companies are as follows.

- Cost of goods sold for a **manufacturer** is the cost of its finished goods in its beginning inventory, plus the cost of goods manufactured during the accounting period, minus the cost of finished goods in ending inventory.
- Cost of goods sold for a **retailer** is the cost of merchandise in its beginning inventory, plus the net cost of merchandise purchased during the accounting period, minus the cost of merchandise in its ending inventory.
- Cost of sales for a **service company** cannot usually be based on inventory but is more likely to be based on the direct labour costs of providing services.

Worked example 3.2

Yala plc

Statement of profit or loss and other comprehensive income for the year ended 31 December 20X2

	20X2 £m	20X1 £m
Income from continuing operations		
Revenue	180	150
Cost of sales	(98)	(82)
Gross profit	82	68
Distribution costs	(15)	(12)
Administrative expenses	(27)	(24)
Operating profit	40	32
Investment income	25	18
Finance costs	(5)	(4)

Profit before tax	60	46
Income tax	(18)	(14)
Profit for the year from continuing operations	42	32
Discontinued operations		
Loss for the year from discontinued operations	(10)	
Other comprehensive income:		
Gain on revaluation (IAS 16)	7	3
Total comprehensive income for the year	39	35

8.2 Profit or loss

International Accounting Standard 1 lists the following as the minimum items to be presented in the profit or loss section:

- revenue
- finance costs
- share of profits and losses of associates and joint ventures accounted for using the equity method (see Chapter 6)
- a single amount for the total of discontinued operations
- tax expense
- a total for profit or loss for the period
- gains and losses from the derecognition of financial assets measured at amortised cost

Expenses recognised in profit or loss should be analysed either by nature (raw materials, staffing costs, depreciation and so on) or by function (cost of sales, distribution, administrative costs). Additional information on the nature of expenses should be disclosed in the notes (depreciation, amortisation, employee benefits and so on).

8.3 Other comprehensive income

Items must be classified by their nature in the OCI section and grouped according to whether they will be transferred (recycled) to the profit or loss section in subsequent periods. Items included in the OCI figure include:

- changes in the revaluation surplus on non-current assets
- actuarial gains and losses on the re-measurement of defined benefit plans
- exchange differences (gains and losses) arising from the translation of the financial statements of a foreign operation
- certain gains and losses relating to financial instruments, including on certain instruments used for hedging

- correction of prior period errors and the effect of changes in accounting policies

Not all of the items which would appear under OCI are included on the syllabus.

8.4 Other requirements

In order to give a fair presentation of results, IAS 1 requires disclosure of certain items to be made separately. These are material items of income and expense of such size, nature or incidence that they require disclosure either in the statement of comprehensive income or in the notes. These include:

- write down of inventories to net realisable value (NRV)
- write down of property, plant and equipment to recoverable amounts, as well as any reversal
- provisions for the costs of restructuring
- reversals of write downs and provisions
- gains/losses on disposal of non-current assets
- gains/losses on disposal of investments
- discontinued operations
- litigation settlements

Extraordinary items are clearly prohibited under IFRS. These were previously defined as items that were both unusual in nature and infrequent in occurrence. The classification of an item as extraordinary was often contentious and ruled on by standard setters. For example, a hurricane is not considered extraordinary, just unusual or infrequent.

extraordinary items
An extraordinary item is an event or transaction that is considered abnormal, not related to day-to-day business operations and unlikely to recur in the foreseeable future. Note that extraordinary items are no longer recognised by IFRS and under GAAP.

There are some additional requirements for listed companies, such as the splitting of their results between operating segments to give more insight into the make-up of their operations (see Chapter 4). In accordance with IAS 33, listed companies are also required to disclose earnings per share (EPS – a key market measure) and the bases used for the calculation of different EPS measures.

8.5 Discontinued operations

A discontinued operation must meet two criteria under IFRS 5 (Non-Current Assets Held for Sale and Discontinued Operations) requirements:

- the asset or component must be disposed of or reported as being held for sale
- the component must be a distinguishable separate area of business intentionally being removed from operation or a subsidiary of a component being held with the intention of selling

IFRS also permits equity method investments to be classified as held for sale. IFRS 5 requires non-current assets held for sale to be measured at the lower of its carrying amount and fair value, less costs to sell; such assets held for sale are not depreciated. These assets would be reported on the statement of financial position below current assets (see Worked example 3.1).

When discontinued operations occur – such as when the relevant assets or parts of the business are being sold or closed down or scrapped – IFRS 5 requires the results of any discontinued operation(s) to be disclosed separately. Any gain or loss from the sale of assets should be reported in a special section of the statement of profit or loss and OCI to provide users with a clear picture of which parts of an entity's business result will not be repeated (see Worked example 3.2).

An entity must, therefore, distinguish continuing operations from any discontinued operations. Discontinued operations are reported after the post-tax earnings from continuing operations. The total gain or loss from discontinued operations is reported, followed by any related income tax. The income tax is often a future tax benefit, as discontinued operations tend to result in losses. The gain or loss on discontinued operations is aggregated with the result of continuing operations to determine total profit or loss for the period.

The entity must also present the net cash flows attributable to the operating, investing and financing activities of discontinued operations in the statement of cash flows. Non-current asset assets and liabilities of a disposal group classified as held for sale must be presented separately from other assets and liabilities in the statement of financial position.

Test yourself 3.3

What is the key difference between 'profit or loss' and 'other comprehensive income' in a statement of profit or loss and other comprehensive income?

9 Statement of changes in equity

Equity is the residual interest in the assets of the entity after deducting its liabilities. Hence, its value equals the entity's net assets. International Accounting Standard 1 requires an entity to present a separate statement of changes in equity. The statement of changes in equity provides an analysis of the change in shareholders' equity over an accounting period.

The key components of equity include share capital or funds contributed by shareholders, **retained earnings** and other components such as a revaluation surplus. The statement must show:

- total comprehensive income for the period, showing separately amounts attributable to owners of the parent and to NCIs (in a consolidated statement);
- reconciliations between the balances at the beginning and the end of the period for each component of equity such as share capital, share premium, revaluation surplus and retained earnings. The closing balances represent

retained earnings
Earnings (or profits) not paid out as dividends (or other distributions) but retained by the company to be reinvested in its core business or to pay debt. It is recorded under shareholders' equity on the statement of financial position.

the balance of shareholders' equity at the end of the reporting period as reported in the statement of financial position.

Worked example 3.3 shows a statement of changes in equity prepared according to the format prescribed by IAS 1.

Worked example 3.3

Yala plc

Statement of changes in equity for the year ended 31 December 20X2

	Share capital £m	Revaluation surplus £m	Retained earnings £m	Total equity £m
Balances at 1 January 20X2	150	15	60	225
Changes in accounting policy (IAS 8)	–	–	–	–
Correction of prior period error (IAS 8)	–	–	–	–
Restated balances at 1 January 20X2	150	15	60	225
Changes in equity for the year 20X2				
Issue of share capital	–	–	–	–
Profit for the year from continuing operations	–	–	42	42
Loss for the period from discontinued operations	–	–	(10)	(10)
Other comprehensive income: revaluation gain	–	7		7
Dividends paid	–	–	(17)	(17)
Balances at 31 December 20X2	150	22	75	247

Movement in shareholders' equity over an accounting period typically includes the following elements.

- **Capital injections or withdrawals by the shareholders** shown as the issue or redemption of shares. The former includes **rights issues** and other new share issues; the latter includes **bonus issues** and companies

> **Rights issue of shares**
> An offer to existing shareholders to buy new shares in proportion to their existing shareholdings.
>
> **Bonus issue of shares**
> A bonus issue of shares, also known as a scrip issue, is additional free shares given to the current shareholders without any additional cost, based upon their existing number of shares, by transfer from other components of equity.

buying back their own shares (also known as treasury shares in the US). Any share issue below the market price dilutes share value.

- **Dividends** representing distribution of wealth attributable to the shareholders.
- **Prior period adjustments** if prior period mistakes or errors are material, the effects of any retrospective application of accounting policies or restatements are made in accordance with IAS 8 (Accounting Policies, Changes in Accounting Estimates and Errors). For example, a research and development expense wrongly capitalised will have a subsequent reducing impact on retained earnings and intangible assets.
- **Profit or loss attributable to shareholders** during the period, as reported in the statement of profit or loss and OCI.
- **Revaluation gains and losses** recognised during the period must be presented in the statement of changes in equity to the extent that they are recognised outside the statement of profit or loss.
- **Any other gains and losses** not recognised in the statement of profit or loss and OCI, such as actuarial gains and losses arising from the application of IAS 19 (Employee Benefit).
- **Transfer between components of equity** for example, when a revalued non-current asset is eventually disposed of, any gain held in the revaluation surplus will be transferred from the surplus to retained earnings (and so becomes distributable to shareholders). Another example would be a bonus issue of shares where share capital is increased as other components of equity are decreased.

10 Statement of cash flows

International Accounting Standard 7 (Statement of Cash Flows) governs the preparation and presentation of statements of cash flows. The statement of cash flows provides additional information to supplement the other primary financial statements, showing changes in cash and cash equivalents over the reporting period. Cash and cash equivalents generally consist of the following:

- Cash in hand
- Cash at bank
- Short-term investments that are highly liquid and involve very low risk of change in value (therefore this usually excludes investments in equity instruments)
- Bank overdrafts (a bank overdraft facility specifically negotiated for financing a shortfall in funds is classified under financing activities)

The statement of cash flows provides management with a way of measuring an organisation's effectiveness by listing all cash inflows and outflows during the reporting period under review. The statement reflects an entity's cash position to help assess the viability of a business in terms of liquidity, solvency and financial adaptability.

The statement of cash flows is based on 'hard cash' ('cash is a fact; profit is an opinion'). Unlike the statement of profit or loss and OCI, this is prepared on an accruals basis and is hence more susceptible to manipulation. It is necessary to adjust the amount extracted from the key financial statements for any non-cash items in order to present only the movement in cash inflows and outflows during a period.

The statement of cash flows should indicate any looming problems in the entity's capability of meeting its future financial obligations. For example, the statement of profit or loss and OCI may show a healthy figure for operating profit, but the statement of cash flows could show a gloomier picture of actual cash flow from operating activities. Similarly, the main financial statements may sometimes show a worse result than the statement of cash flows when they include large non-cash expenses such as write offs, depreciation charges, impairment losses and provisions for future obligations.

10.1 Structure of the statement of cash flows

Under IAS 7, cash flows are classified under operating, investing and financing activities.

Cash flows from operating activities

Operating activities are the principal revenue-producing activities of an entity, as well as other activities that are not part of its investing or financing activities.

International Accounting Standard 7 permits cash flows from operating activities to be shown on a direct or an indirect basis. Both lead to the same result: cash generated from operations. Even though IAS 7 clearly states that 'entities are encouraged to report cash flows from operating activities using the direct method', the indirect method is easier and is most commonly used because it derives substantially from the existing accruals-based accounting records.

The indirect method, also called the reconciliation method, starts with operating profit (or profit before tax), adds back non-cash expenses such as depreciation, then calculates changes in working capital items (such as inventories, receivables and payables). This method reconciles profit and cash generated from operations. The profit or loss is adjusted for the effects of transactions of a non-cash nature, such as any deferrals or accruals of past or future operating cash receipts or payments and items of income or expense associated with investing or financing cash flows. This results in a net cash flow from operating activities. The indirect method is illustrated in Worked examples 3.4 (part 2) and 3.5.

Examples of cash flows from operating activities are:

- cash receipts from the sale of goods and services
- cash receipts from royalties, fees, commissions and other revenue sources
- cash receipts from supplier refunds
- cash receipts from the settlement of lawsuit and insurance claims
- cash payments to suppliers for goods and services
- cash payments to and on behalf of employees

- cash payments or refunds of income taxes unless they can be specifically identified with financing and investing activities
- cash receipts and payments from contracts held for dealing or trading and interest paid on borrowings

Certain items such as the profit or loss on the sale of a non-current asset will also be included in profit or loss (this is an adjustment for any over-charged or under-charged depreciation). Even so, the cash flow from the sale will be classed as investing. Dividends and interest received and paid could be either operating or investing activities, depending on the business activities. They may be classified as operating activities provided the classification remains consistent from one reporting period to the next, although such presentation is restricted to financial institutions.

Cash flows from investing activities

Cash flows from investing activities show the extent of new investment in non-current assets which should generate future profit and cash flows. These include the acquisition and disposal of long-term assets, as well as cash flows arising from obtaining and losing control of subsidiaries and other investments. International Accounting Standard 7 gives the following examples of cash flows arising from investing activities:

- cash payments to acquire property, plant and equipment, intangibles and other non-current assets, including those relating to capitalised development costs and self-constructed property, plant and equipment
- cash receipts from sales of property, plant and equipment, intangibles and other non-current assets
- cash acquisitions and disposals of shares or **debentures** of other entities
- cash advances and loans made to other parties and repayments of such loans

debenture
A written acknowledgement of a debt used by large companies to borrow money at a fixed rate of interest.

Cash flows from financing activities

Financing activities include raising capital, repaying investors, adding or changing loans and other debt. This section is an indicator of likely future interest and dividend payments. International Accounting Standard 7 gives the following examples of cash flows arising from financing activities:

- Cash proceeds from issuing shares (this will not include a bonus issue of shares)
- Cash payments to owners to acquire or redeem the entity's shares
- Cash proceeds from issuing debentures, loans, notes, **bonds**, mortgages and other short-term or long-term borrowings
- Principal repayments of amounts borrowed under leases. The interest paid will be shown under operating activities

bond
A fixed income investment in which an investor loans money to an entity (private or government) for a defined period of time at a fixed interest rate. It is a general term for the various types of long-term loans to companies, including loan stock and debentures.

Dividends paid to equity holders are generally classified as financing activities.

International Accounting Standard 7 requires entities to disclose the components of cash and cash equivalents and to present a reconciliation of the amounts in its statement of cash flows with the equivalent items reported in the statement of financial position.

As required by IAS 1, the previous year's comparative figures should be provided for all disclosures.

Worked Example 3.4

Part 1

The following is an extract from the financial statements of Limbu plc. It provides an illustrative statement of cash flows presented according to the direct method suggested in IAS 7 (Statement of Cash Flows).

Limbu plc
Statement of cash flows for the year ended 31 December 20X9

	£m	£m
Cash flows from operating activities (direct method):		
Cash receipts from customers	135	
Cash paid to suppliers of goods and services	(70)	
Cash paid to employees	(45)	
Cash generated from operations	20	
Interest paid	(1)	
Income taxes paid	(4)	
Net cash from operating activities		15
Cash flows from investing activities:		
Acquisition of Rajkarnikar Ltd (Subsidiary)	(4)	
Purchase of property, plant and equipment	(2)	
Proceeds from sale of equipment	0	
Interest received	3	
Dividends received	1	
Net cash used in investing activities		(2)
Cash flows from financing activities:		
Proceeds from issue of share capital	1	
Proceeds from long-term loan raised	3	
Payment of lease obligations	(3)	
Dividends paid	(5)	
Net cash used in financing activities		(4)

	£m
Net increase in cash and cash equivalents	9
Cash and cash equivalents at beginning of the year	27
Cash and cash equivalents at end of the year	36

Part 2

The following is an extract from the financial statements of Limbu plc. It provides an illustrative statement of cash flows presented according to the indirect method suggested in IAS 7 (Statement of Cash Flows)

The main difference between the direct method and the indirect method involves presenting the cash flows from operating activities. There is no difference at all in how the cash flows from investing activities and financing activities are calculated under both methods.

Limbu plc

Statement of cash flows for the year ended 31 December 20X9

	£m	£m
Cash flows from operating activities (indirect method)		
Operating profit	14	
Depreciation	5	
(Increase)/decrease in trade and other receivables	(3)	
(Increase)/decrease in inventories	2	
Increase/(decrease) in trade and other payables	1	
Non-cash and other movements	1	
Cash generated from operations	20	
Interest paid	(1)	
Income taxes paid	(4)	
Net cash from operating activities		15

Regardless of whether the direct or indirect method is used, the cash generated from operations and the net cash from operating activities will be the same amount; the only difference is in the format in which these are presented.

The operating activities section starts with profit that has been calculated under accruals-based accounting and principles of matching and recognition. Therefore, this profit needs to be adjusted to remove all the non-cash items that were included.

Non-cash items such as depreciation and amortisation charges for a period, gains and losses from the disposal of non-current assets, provisions for future liabilities, impairment charges for a period, movement in deferred tax, etc. are added back to profit.

Next, profit is adjusted for changes in current assets and current liabilities appearing on the statement of financial position. An increase in the current asset accounts including inventories, trade receivables and prepaid expenses will have had a negative impact on cash flows and need to be subtracted from profit. An increase in the current liability accounts, including trade payables and accrued expenses (excluding tax and interest), will have had a positive impact on cash flows and need to be added to profit.

As Worked Example 3.5 shows, decreases in current assets and liabilities will have the opposite effect.

Worked example 3.5

Below are extracts from the financial statements of ABC plc for the year ended 31 December 20X1:

	£m
Revenue	450
Cost of sales (Note 1)	(335)
Gross profit	115
Administrative expenses (Note 1)	(43)
Distribution costs	(1)
Operating profit	71
Finance costs	(9)
Profit before tax	62
Income tax expense	(17)
Profit for the year	45
Other comprehensive income: revaluation gain	5
Total comprehensive income for the year	50

ABC plc

Statement of financial position as at 31 December 20X1

	20X1 £m	20X0 £m
Assets		
Non-current assets		
Property, plant and equipment at cost (Note 2)	175	167
Accumulated depreciation	(55)	(77)

Total non-current assets	120	90
Current assets		
Inventories	41	42
Trade and other receivables	27	34
Cash	22	5
Total current assets	90	81
Total assets	210	171
Equity and liabilities		
Equity share capital (Note 3)	60	50
Share premium (Note 3)	36	25
Revaluation surplus	10	5
Retained earnings	28	8
Total equity	134	88
Non-current liabilities		
Long-term borrowings	45	50
Total non-current liabilities	45	50
Current liabilities		
Trade and other payables	19	20
Bank overdraft	–	9
Current tax payable	12	4
Total current liabilities	31	33
Total liabilities	76	83
Total equity and liabilities	210	171

Additional notes

1. Depreciation during the year was charged to cost of sales and administrative expenses.
2. Non-current asset disposed of during the year:

Original cost	45
Accumulated depreciation	42
Cash received on disposal	11

3. A dividend of £25m was paid during the year. A cash issue of 10m £1 equity shares made during the year for £2.10 per share.

ABC plc
Statement of cash flows for the year ended 31 December 20X1

	Working	20X1 £	20X1 £
Cash flows from operating activities (indirect method)			
Operating profit			71
Adjustments for:			
Add depreciation charged during the year	Working 1		20
Less gain on disposal of non-current assets	Working 2		(8)
Working capital changes:			
Add: decrease in inventory (41 – 42)			1
Add: decrease in trade receivables (27 – 34)			7
Less: decrease in trade payables (20 – 19)			(1)
Cash generated from operations			90
Less: interest paid (= finance cost)			(9)
Less: income tax paid (= opening balance + tax expense – closing balance) (4 + 17 – 12)			(9)
Net cash from operating activities (A)			72
Cash flows from investing activities			
Cash used for purchases of non-current assets	Working 3		(48)
Proceeds from disposal of non-current assets	Note 2		11
Net cash used in investing activities (B)			(37)

Cash flows from financing activities

Issue of share capital (10,000 × £2.10)	Note 3	21
Dividends paid	Note 3	(25)
Repayment of borrowings (Closing balance less opening balance) (45,000 − 50,000)		(5)
Net cash from financing activities (C)		(9)
Net increase in cash and cash equivalents (A + B + C)		26
Cash and cash equivalents at start of the year	Working 4	(4)
Cash and cash equivalents at end of the year	Working 4	22

Working 1: depreciation charge	£m
Closing depreciation	55
Less: opening depreciation	(77)
Add back: depreciation on sale of asset	42
Depreciation charge	20

Working 2: gain/(loss) on disposal of non-current assets		£m
Cash received on disposal		11
Cost of disposed assets	45	
Less: accumulated depreciation of disposed assets	(42)	
Carrying amount of disposed assets		3
Gain on disposal of assets		8

Working 3: non-current assets purchased for cash		£m
Closing balance		175
Cost before revaluation:		
Opening balance	167	
Less disposal	(45)	
	122	

Interpreting Financial and Accounting Information

Deduct: cost before revaluation		(122)
Gain on revaluation:		
Closing revaluation surplus	10	
Less opening revaluation surplus	(5)	
	5	
Deduct: gain on revaluation		(5)
Non-current assets purchased for cash		48

Working 4: Cash and cash equivalents closing balances (20X2)	Opening balances (20X1)	Change	
	£m	£m	£m
Cash	22	5	17
Bank overdraft	NIL	(9)	9
Change in the year	(22)	(4)	26

Commentary on ABC plc

ABC plc made an operating profit of £71 million and a net profit of £45 million in the year ending 31 December 20x1. These are the most common measurements of an entity's financial performance. However, we must note that profit is not measured in cash terms. ABC generated £90 million in cash from its operating activities, having made an operating profit of £71 million. Therefore, every £1 of profit generated £1.27 of cash.

The separate statement of cash flows tells us what is happening to the company cash flows. ABC needs to retain sufficient cash to continue operating, but also make payments to shareholders by way of dividends and fund capital investments by the business.

From the statement of cash flows we can see:

- net cash from operating activities (A) of £72 million
- net cash used in investing activities (B) of £37 million
- net cash outflow from financing activities (C) of £9 million
- net increase in cash and cash equivalents of £26 million

These show us that ABC has retained £26 million of the cash it has generated in the year, improving its cash position. However, due to the overall level of cash generation from its operating activities, ABC has managed to invest a net £37 million in purchasing new non-current assets. ABC has also been able to pay £25 million in dividends to its shareholders and pay £5 million towards its long-term borrowings, while receiving £21 million from a shares issue.

This gives us a view of how ABC is able to invest in the future of the business and reward current shareholders, both of which require the expenditure of cash and both of which are fundamental to the success of the company.

Test yourself 3.4

What is the primary purpose of the statement of cash flows?

Chapter summary

- International Accounting Standard 1 governs the preparation and presentation of single entity financial statements. This includes structure, content and overriding concepts such as going concern, the accruals basis of accounting and the current/non-current distinction.
- The key objective of the financial statements is to provide and fairly represent the financial position, performance and cash flows of an entity in a way that is useful to a wide range of users in making financial decisions. A complete set of financial statements comprises:
    - a statement of financial position
    - a statement of profit or loss and other comprehensive income
    - a statement of changes in equity
    - a statement of cash flows
- It also includes narratives or notes to the financial statements which help to further explain numbers on the financial statements.
- International Accounting Standard 1 lays out the basic format of the statements and prescribes some basic information that should be disclosed about the reporting entity.
- Some overriding concepts applied in the preparation and presentation of financial statements include:
    - presentation (components, comparative and consistency)
    - fair presentation and compliance with IFRS
    - going concern
    - accruals basis
    - materiality and aggregation
    - reporting period
    - offsetting

- The statement of financial position, previously known as the balance sheet, presents the financial position of an entity at a given date. It is comprised of three main components: assets, liabilities and equity. It provides a snapshot or record of resources owned or controlled (assets) and obligations owed (liabilities) at a specific point in time (the end of the reporting period). A statement of financial position must normally present separate classifications separating current and non-current assets and current and non-current liabilities, unless presentation based on liquidity provides information that is reliable and more relevant. It also contains disclosures regarding issued share capital and other components of equity, either on the face of the statement of financial position or in the notes.
- The statement of profit or loss and OCI provides a review of overall performance as a result of the financial transactions that took place during the accounting period. It summarises revenues generated and costs incurred as a result of undertaking business activity.
- Total comprehensive income is defined as the change in equity during a period resulting from transactions and other events, other than those changes resulting from transactions with owners in their capacity as owners.
- In order to give a fair presentation of results, IAS 1 requires items of income and expense of such size, nature or incidence that are considered material to be disclosed separately either in the statement of profit or loss and other comprehensive income or in the notes.
- IFRS 5 requires the result of any discontinued operation(s) to be disclosed separately from the results of continuing operations so that the users' view of the financial statements is not skewed by results which will not be present in future years. Assets held for sale as a consequence of a discontinued operation should be shown on the statement of financial position below current assets.
- The statement of changes in equity provides an analysis of the changes in shareholders' equity over an accounting period. The key components of equity include share capital or funds contributed by shareholders, retained earnings and other components such as the revaluation surplus.
- International Accounting Standard 7 governs the preparation and presentation of statements of cash flows. The statement of cash flows supplements the primary financial statements by showing changes in cash and cash equivalents over the accounting period. It helps users to see the amount of cash generated and used during the period and to understand:
    - how much of the profits earned have been converted into cash
    - how much cash has been reinvested
    - how much cash has been used to service finance or has been paid out to shareholders
- Under IAS 7, cash flows are classified under operating, investing and financing activities. IAS 7 permits cash flows from operating activities to be shown on a direct or indirect basis. The presentation only differs in their reporting of cash generated from operating activities.

Chapter four
Other contents and features of published financial statements

Contents

1. Introduction
2. Content of the annual report and financial statements (or accounts)
3. The strategic report
4. The directors' report
5. Notes to the financial statements
6. Segment reporting
7. Reporting the substance of transactions
8. Limitations of published financial statements

1 Introduction

The financial statements of a company are published to enable the members, investors and the public at large to understand the company's profitability and financial position, its growth prospects and probable risks. In this chapter, we will look at the contents of published financial statements within a wider set of information, known as the annual report and financial statements (or accounts). The annual report includes:

- the strategic report or business review
- the directors' report
- the directors' remuneration report
- the corporate governance statement
- the auditor's report
- audited financial statements
- notes to the financial statements

We looked at the overriding concepts and elements of financial statements in earlier chapters. This chapter will focus on other features and reports of published financial statements. We will look at strategic and directors' reports and what they entail (the directors' remuneration report, corporate governance statement and auditor's report are not covered in this module). We will examine the information to be disclosed in the notes to the financial statements (governed by IAS 1), including their structure and contents.

We will then look at other key aspects in the interpretation of published financial statements, such as segment reporting (IFRS 8) and reporting the substance of transactions. The chapter will also cover the limitations of published financial statements.

```
                        Annual report
                        and accounts
    ┌──────────┬──────────┬─────┴──────┬──────────┬──────────┐
 Strategic  Directors'  Directors'   Corporate   Auditor's  Financial
  report     report    remuneration  governance   report    statements
                          report     statement              and notes
                              │
                    Segment reporting ── Substance of   Limitations of published
                        – IFRS 8          transactions    financial statements
```

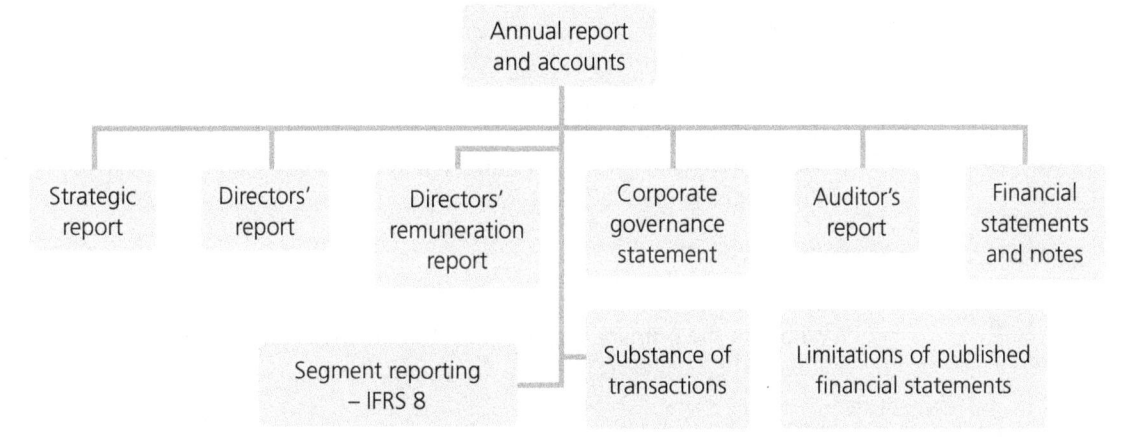

Figure 4.1 Annual report and financial statements

2 Content of the annual report and financial statements (or accounts)

Companies publish their financial statements within a wider set of information, known as the annual report and financial statements (or accounts). The annual report becomes the tool for 'voluntary disclosure'. The contents of this document are governed by law, IFRS, the relevant stock market rules for listed and AIM (previously known as Alternative Investment Market) companies. The report includes:

- the strategic report or business review
- the directors' report
- the directors' remuneration report
- the corporate governance statement
- the auditor's report
- audited financial statements (covered in Chapter 3), including:
    - statement of financial position
    - statement of profit or loss and OCI
    - statement of changes in equity
    - statement of cash flows
    - notes to the financial statements (covered in section 5 on page 93)

The annual report and financial statements (or accounts) provides information about the company's activities and financial performance throughout the preceding year. To some extent, it indicates the future prospects of the business.

Most jurisdictions require listed companies to prepare and disclose annual reports. Many require the annual report to be filed at the companies registry. Annual reports are a key element of communication with shareholders, the market and other interested parties such as bank lenders or suppliers. The published financial statements are used by investors and other parties to examine profitability, look at the trends of revenue and profits, assess the strength of its financial position and identify any potential risks.

The company may also disclose other information on a voluntary basis, such as information on CSR issues. Separate chair and chief executive officer (CEO) statements regarding company position may be included, although these are often placed in the strategic report.

Test yourself 4.1

What are the primary uses of published financial statements?

3 The strategic report

strategic report
A strategic report, also known as a business review, is a detailed report written in non-financial language to provide clear and coherent information about the company's activities, performance and position. It includes the strategic position of the business and probable risks attached with the business.

The **strategic report** or business review is a detailed report written in non-financial language. It provides clear and coherent information about the company's activities (such as what it does and why), performance, position, the strategic position of the business and probable risks attached with the business. It ensures information is accessible to a broad range of users, not just analysts and accountants who have sophisticated knowledge. It is prepared separately from the directors' report.

3.1 Duty to prepare the strategic report

All companies except small and micro companies (those that qualify for small company exemptions – see Chapter 1) must produce a strategic report.

In the UK, the Companies Act 2006 (Strategic Report and Director's Report) Regulations 2013 provide comprehensive guidelines about the strategic report's preparation, contents and structure, signing and approval. Companies which have more than 500 employees and meet the CA2006 definition of a 'traded company', 'banking company', 'authorised insurance company' or 'company carrying on an insurance market activity' have additional strategic reporting requirements as a result of the EU's Non-Financial Reporting Directive. Quoted companies in particular have enhanced requirements for the strategic report and directors' report.

The Financial Reporting Council (FRC) also provides guidance on the strategic report, arguing that the strategic report enhances a holistic and meaningful picture of an entity's business and encourages companies to consider wider stakeholders and broader matters that impact performance over the longer term. The 2018 revisions to the FRC Guidance on the Strategic Report and the recent changes to the FRC's Corporate Governance Code recognise the increasing importance of non-financial reporting. This will contribute to promoting integrity, trust and transparency in business.

It is the duty of the directors to prepare the strategic report for each financial year. In case of group financial statements, the strategic report must be a consolidated report (a 'group strategic report') prepared and signed by directors of the parent company. Failure to comply with the requirements of the strategic report will result in the directors being fined.

3.2 Purpose and contents of the strategic report

The purpose of the strategic report is to provide information to the members of the company and help them assess how the directors have performed their duties and functions. The strategic report must provide the following information.

Fair review
A fair review is a balanced and comprehensive analysis of the company's business for an understanding of the following.

- The performance and development of the company's business during the financial year, including analysis using financial key performance indicators (KPIs). Large companies should also include non-financial KPIs such as those relating to environmental and employee matters in their analysis, where appropriate.
- The position of the company's business at the end of that year.

Description of the principal risks and uncertainties the company faces
These may include any risks and uncertainties that have affected the company's business.

Going concern
If an event has affected the going concern assessment, this should be disclosed.

References to the financial statements
The strategic report should, where appropriate, include references to and additional explanations of, amounts included in the company's financial statements which the directors consider are of strategic importance to the company. For example, 'exceptional' or other items separately identified on the face of the primary statements could form part of these references.

Signing and approval of strategic report
The strategic report must be approved by the board of directors and signed on its behalf by a director or the company secretary.

Additional information for quoted companies

The strategic report of a quoted company must also include the following information:

- a description of the company's strategy
- a description of the company's business model
- information on environmental, employee and social issues, including human rights and gender diversity information when material

For example, the disclosure of greenhouse gas (GHG) emissions data should be disclosed as part of environmental issues. Gender diversity information must include a breakdown of directors, senior managers and employees by gender as at the end of the financial year.

Strategic report or business review

- Fair review
  - Performance, development and KPIs
  - Business position
- Principal risks and uncertainties
- Going concern
- References to annual accounts
- Approval of strategic report
- Additional information for quoted companies
  - Strategy
  - Business model
  - Environmental, employee and social issues, including human rights and gender diversity

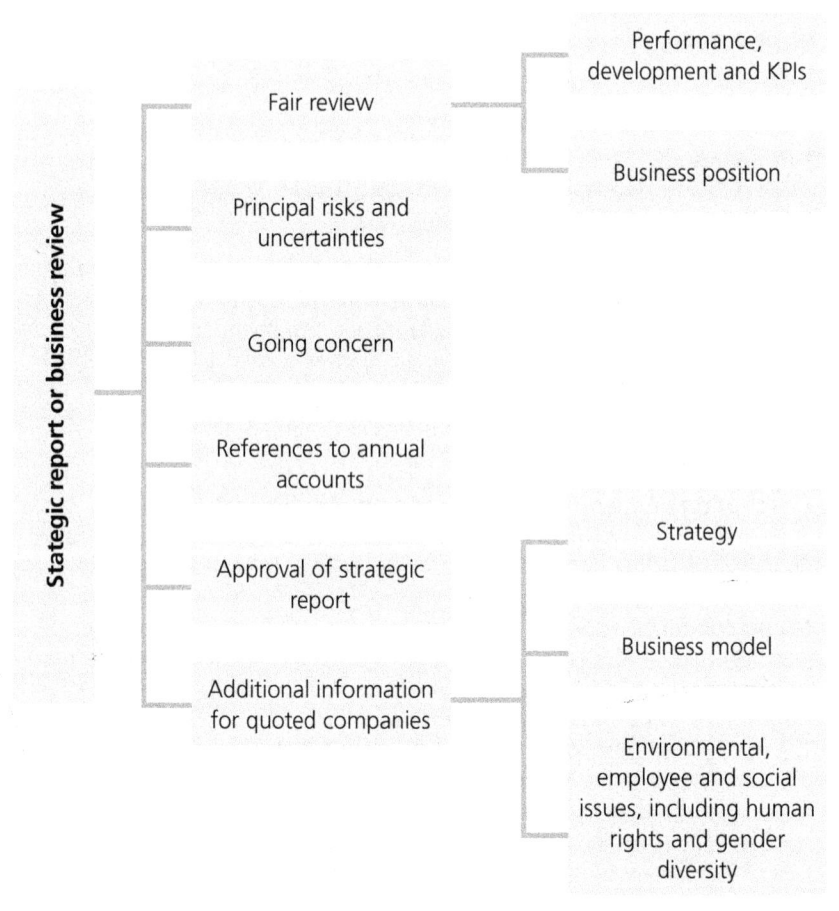

Figure 4.2: The strategic report or business review

The strategic report could also include a statement regarding the company's financial performance and position from the CEO. A company has the option to send the strategic report, along with certain supplementary material, to shareholders in place of the full annual report. Where this option is taken, the full strategic report must be sent to shareholders, including cross-references to the annual report. Shareholders retain the right to ask for the full annual report and financial statements (or accounts). The supplementary material must include information on the auditors' report, administrative particulars and provide a note on how to obtain a copy of the full annual report and financial statements (or accounts).

For quoted companies, the supplementary material must include selected excerpts from the directors' remuneration report. The supplementary material does not have to include any additional financial information, although directors could include financial information in the pack if they consider it appropriate.

Test yourself 4.2

What are the objectives of the strategic report?

4 The directors' report

The directors' report is a financial document prepared by the directors. Its purpose is to inform members of the company of the financial state of the company, as well as its compliance with financial reporting, accounting and CSR standards.

All companies must produce a directors' report, although there are certain exemptions available for small companies. The directors' report will generally be positioned after the strategic report in the annual report.

The preparation of the directors' report is governed by company law. In the UK, the directors of a company are required to prepare a directors' report at the end of each financial year under s. 415 of CA2006. This legislation is part of a general move for greater transparency in corporate governance.

4.1 Purpose and contents of the directors' report

The directors' report helps shareholders make informed decisions when casting their votes at the annual general meeting or other members' meetings. It provides information on:

- whether the company has good finances
- whether the business has the structural capacity to expand and grow
- how well it is performing within its market and market in general
- whether the company is complying with financial regulations, financial reporting and accounting standards (IFRS) and social responsibility requirements

The directors' report also serves as an important source of public information. These reports are used for credit checking, to assess investment worthiness, for social accounting and to gain background information on individual directors.

The directors' report must disclose the following information:

- the names of all directors during the financial year;
- a summary of the company's trading activities;
- a summary of future prospects;
- the principal activities of the company and, if relevant, the principal activities of its subsidiaries;
- the amount of dividend, if any, recommended by the directors for the reporting year;
- any financial events that occurred after the date on the statement of financial position, if these events could affect the company's finances;
- any significant changes to the company's non-current assets;
- a statement confirming that all relevant audit information has been provided to the company's auditor;
- a directors' statements of responsibilities, including:
  - that the directors have a responsibility to promote the success of the company, as per CA 2006 s. 172;
  - that the directors are responsible for preparing the annual report, remuneration report and the financial statements in accordance with applicable law and regulations and with the specific requirements of IFRS;
  - that the directors must not approve the financial statements unless they are satisfied that they give a true and fair view of the state of affairs of the company and of the profit or loss of the company for that period;
  - that the directors are required to properly select and apply accounting policies to provide relevant, reliable, comparable and understandable information;
  - that accounting estimates are based on reasonable and prudent judgement;
  - that the board recognises its responsibility to establish and maintain a sound system of internal control, which is regularly reviewed and monitored;
  - that the appointment of the chair and other members of the board, along with terms of their appointment and remuneration policy, is in line with the best prevailing practices of the country; and
  - that the directors are responsible for keeping proper accounting records, safeguarding the assets of the company and hence for taking reasonable steps for the prevention and detection of fraud and other irregularities;
- a record of all board and board committee meetings in a financial year with a directors' attendance record.

The directors' report must be approved by the board and signed on its behalf by a director or the company secretary.

Stop and think 4.1

Download the latest published annual report from your favourite retail company's website. Find the strategic report and the directors' report. Identify their key contents.

5 Notes to the financial statements

The notes to the financial statements provide information not presented elsewhere in the financial statements. These include:

- more detailed analysis of figures in the statements
- narrative information explaining figures in the statements
- additional information, for example, contingent liabilities and capital expenditure and lease commitments

International Accounting Standard 1 requires the notes to the financial statements to disclose the following key information:

- the basis for the preparation of financial statements, including the specific accounting policies chosen and applied to significant transactions/events
- information which is required by IFRS but not presented elsewhere in the financial statements
- any additional information that is relevant to understanding which is not shown elsewhere in the financial statements

The notes should be presented in a systematic manner and cross-referenced to the relevant item in the financial statements where appropriate. It may be necessary to vary the order of items within the notes in some circumstances. For example, an entity may combine notes relating to information on changes in fair value recognised in profit or loss with information on maturities of financial instruments that relate to the statement of financial position.

5.1 Structure and contents

The IASB's Conceptual Framework states that the objective of general purpose financial reporting is to provide financial information about the reporting entity that is useful for a wide range of users in making rational financial decisions. International Accounting Standard 1 suggests that notes are presented in the following order to assist users to understand the financial statements and to compare them with the published financial statements of other entities.

- Statement of compliance with IFRS.
- Statement of the measurement bases and a summary of the significant accounting policies applied in preparing the financial statements. The information on measurement bases (e.g. historical cost, current cost, net realisable value, fair value or recoverable amount) used in the preparation

of financial statements significantly affects users' analysis. Where more than one basis is used, such as when particular classes of assets are revalued, it should be stated to which assets each basis has been applied. Accounting policies are covered in Chapter 5.

♦ Supporting information for items presented in the statement of financial position, the statement of profit or loss and OCI, the separate statement of profit or loss (if presented) and the statements of changes in equity and of cash flows. This should be presented in the same order as each statement and each line item.

♦ Other disclosures, including:

- **contingent liabilities** (IAS 37) and unrecognised contractual commitments;

- non-financial disclosures that enables users of financial statements to evaluate the entity's financial risk management objectives and policies. International Financial Reporting Standard 7 (Financial Instruments: Disclosures) requires entities to provide disclosures that enable users to evaluate the significance of **financial instruments**, the nature and extent of risks arising from them and how those risks are managed. This includes a confirmation of whether capital requirements are met (for example, for financial institutions such as banks);

- dividends proposed or declared before the financial statements were authorised but not recognised and the related amount per share together with the amount of any cumulative preference dividends not recognised; and

- capital disclosures about an entity's objectives, policies and processes for managing its capital. For example, the description of the capital an entity manages and whether it has complied with external capital requirements (if any).

If not cited elsewhere in the financial statements – such as in the opening pages of the annual report and financial statements (or accounts) – the reporting entity should also include the following:

♦ the domicile and legal form of the business, its country of incorporation and its registered office address or, if different, principal place of business;

♦ a description of the nature of the entity's operations and principal activities;

♦ the name of its parent and the ultimate parent of the group;

♦ if it is a limited-life entity, information regarding the length of its life; and

♦ related parties disclosures (IAS 24) that require disclosures about transactions and outstanding balances with an entity's related parties.

contingent liabilities
A possible obligation that may occur depending on the outcome of an uncertain future event or a present obligation. not meeting the recognition criteria (payment is not probable or the amount cannot be measured reliably).

financial instrument
A legally enforceable (binding) agreement, between two or more parties that can be created, traded, modified and settled. International Financial Reporting Standards define a financial instrument as 'any contract that gives rise to a financial asset of one entity and a financial liability or equity instrument of another entity'.

Stop and think 4.2

Using the same annual report as in Stop and think 4.1, look at the notes to the financial statements and check to see if the items suggested by IAS 1 are available.

Test yourself 4.3

Briefly discuss the purpose of the notes to the financial statements in a published annual report.

6 Segment reporting

Segment reporting provides information regarding the financial performance and position of the identifiable operating segments of a company to users of its financial statements. It can be particularly useful when dealing with large entities that produce a diversified range of products and services and/or have a number of business lines and operations – often in different geographical areas or countries.

Segment reporting supplementing the statement of profit or loss and OCI, based on product or geographical areas, helps users to better understand and assess the following elements of an entity:

- past performance
- profit characteristics
- risks and returns
- potential for future growth
- more information about the entity as a whole

It is important to understand segment reporting and how to analyse what it reveals about a company (see Worked example 4.1 for an example of a segment report).

International Financial Reporting Standard 8 (Operating Segments) requires listed entities to disclose information that will allow users of the financial statements to evaluate the nature and effects of its operating activities and environments. It is helpful to understand the IFRS definitions, including which segments need to be included.

segment reporting
Segment reporting provides financial information regarding the financial performance and position of the key operating units of a company to users of the financial statements

6.1 International Financial Reporting Standard 8

International Financial Reporting Standard 8 defines reportable operating segments, providing the basis for financial disclosure of businesses based on segment activity. International Financial Reporting Standard 8 applies to both the individual and group financial statements of an entity whose debt or equity instruments are traded or are in the process of being traded in a public market (on a stock exchange).

The standard works on a 'management model': the segment analysis is reported as it would be reported internally to help management's decision making. It is applicable to both the annual and interim financial statements of an entity. An entity must disclose information that enables users of its financial statements to evaluate the nature and financial effects of the business activities in which it engages and the economic environments in which it operates.

Stop and think 4.3

Can you think of ways how IFRS 8 improves consistency between internal and external financial information?

6.2 Operating segments

International Financial Reporting Standard 8 defines an operating segment of an entity as a business component:

- from which it may earn revenue and incur expenses;
- whose operating results are regularly reviewed by the entity's chief operating decision maker (CODM) to make decisions about resources to be allocated to the segment and assess its performance; and
- for which discrete financial information is available.

The chief operating decision maker is a function (not necessarily a person) that makes strategic decisions about the entity's segments and is likely to vary from entity to entity. For example, the CODM may be the CEO, the chief operating officer, the senior management team or the board of directors.

6.3 IFRS 8 thresholds and reporting segments

Operating segments must be presented and reported separately, if they exceed any one of the following quantitative thresholds:

- reported revenue (both external and inter-segment sales or transfers), is more than 10% of overall gross revenue of all operating segments;
- the absolute amount of the segment's reported profit or loss is 10% or more of the greater, in absolute amount, of:
  - the combined reported profit of all operating segments that did not report a loss; and
  - the combined reported loss of all operating segments that reported a loss;
- the segment's assets are 10% or more of the combined assets of all operating segments.

Any operating segment representing over 10% of gross revenue, profits or assets of the entity must always be presented separately.

After determining the reportable segments, the entity should ensure that the total external revenue attributable to those reportable segments is at least 75% of the entity's total revenue. If they constitute less than 75% of the total revenue, additional reportable segments should be identified (even if they do not meet the 10% threshold), until at least 75% of the entity's revenue is included in reportable segments.

6.4 Disclosures for operating segments

Disclosures must include:

- how the entity has identified operating segments and their general nature;
- the information on operating segment assets and liabilities and profits and losses, if presented regularly to the CODM and measured in a different way to the primary or main statements;
- reconciliations of amounts disclosed by segments to the totals within the financial statements; and
- any change in the internal structure of the entity with the new and old segment information.

Worked example 4.1

Sherpa plc operates through segments M, N, O and P: each representing a product line. The simplified segment information for the year ending 31 December 20X9 is illustrated in the table (amounts in £m):

	M	N	O	P	Sherpa plc total
	£m	£m	£m	£m	£m
1. Segment revenue	800	100	100	90	1,090
2. Segment operating profit or loss	77	50	(5)	5	127
3. Segment assets less current liabilities	420	38	150	60	668

We know from the statement of profit or loss and OCI for Sherpa plc that it made a net profit of £127 million in the year ending 31 December 20X9. The **segment reporting** provides information regarding the financial performance and position of the identifiable operating segments of Sherpa plc to users of its financial statements.

One segment (O) made a small net loss. This loss on segment O would not be visible to users of the accounts from the aggregated information in the published financial statements. Therefore, segment reporting provides the user with another level of information about the financial performance of Sherpa plc.

We can perform some simple analysis of the financial performance that Sherpa plc is reporting on:

Profit margin % (Profit/revenue) x 100	9.6%	50.0%	−5.0%	5.6%	11.7%
Asset turnover (Revenue/assets)	1.9	2.6	0.7	1.5	1.6
Return on capital employed (Operating profit/assets)	18.3%	131.6%	−3.3%	8.3%	19.0%

Segment N has the highest profit margin, the highest asset turnover and the highest return on capital employed. Financially, this is clearly a successful segment. On the other hand, segment O has a net loss and negative ratios for the other two metrics as a result. As the users would know what the segments are and maybe even have some commentary on their performance, this starts to reveal further insight into company performance.

More detail on ratios is included in Chapters 7 and 16, including full explanations of the ratios used above and how analysis helps stakeholders understand a business better. This example illustrates how segment reporting can be an important part of that.

7 Reporting the substance of transactions

The 'substance of transactions' refers to the economic benefits or economic losses of any kind and the economic implications related to a transaction.

It includes an accounting concept popularly known as 'substance over form', which means the transactions recorded in the financial statements must reflect their economic (or commercial) substance rather than their legal form. It mandates that the financial statements and accompanying disclosures of an entity should reflect the underlying realities of accounting transactions.

It entails the use of judgement on the part of the preparers of the financial statements to derive the business sense from the transactions/events and to present them in a manner that best reflects their true commercial essence. Although legal aspects of transactions and events are of great importance, they may have to be disregarded at times in order to provide more useful and relevant information to the users of financial statements.

It is not always the case that the economic substance of a transaction will differ from its legal form. However, in some cases, the substance can be different from the form of the transaction. Some examples are as follows.

- **Sale and leaseback arrangements:** whereby a company sells an asset to another party and gets it back via a lease agreement. The company must first determine whether the transfer qualifies as a sale based on the requirements for satisfying a performance obligation in IFRS 15 (Revenue from Contracts with Customers). If the nature of the transaction is that of a lease, lease accounting is applied as per IFRS 16.
- **Consignment stock:** whereby the consignor (seller) ships goods to the consignee (buyer). The consignee acts as an agent of the consignor and holds the goods on behalf of the consignor with a view to selling the goods on behalf of the consignor, thereby earning a fee or a commission.
- **Debt factoring or invoice discounting:** a type of debtor finance in which a business sells (for cash) its trade receivables to a third party (called a factor) at a discount in exchange for the rights to cash collected from those receivables. Debt factoring is a widely used method of financing for many entities. Some factoring arrangements transfer substantially all the risk and rewards of the receivables. If substantially all the risks and rewards have been transferred, the asset is derecognised by the seller (IFRS 9 (Financial Instruments)).
- **Sale and repurchase arrangements:** a type of loan arrangement whereby the sale of an asset takes place between two parties with a view to subsequently repurchase the same asset at a higher price.

This area of accounting is somewhat subjective and entails considering the perspective of the preparer. To help preparers in better implementation of this concept, IASB has identified the relevant IFRS and IAS that provide detailed guidelines on disclosure of some key transactions:

- IAS 8 (Accounting Policies, Changes in Accounting Estimates and Errors)
- IFRS 15 (Revenue)
- IFRS 16 (Leases)

For example, IFRS 16 (which replaced IAS 17 from 1 January 2019) prescribes accounting policies for the recognition, measurement, presentation and disclosure of leases to provide relevant information that faithfully represents those transactions. The new standard provides a single lessee accounting model, requiring lessees to recognise assets (representing its right to use the assets) and liabilities (representing its obligation to make lease payments) for all leases with a term of more than 12 months, unless the underlying asset has a low value. For short-term and low value leases, a lessee expenses the lease payments on a straight-line basis over the lease term. Lessors continue to classify leases as operating or finance (as in IAS 17) and to account for those two types of leases differently.

Test yourself 4.4

A plc sold a property to B plc on terms that the property will be leased back to A plc under a lease agreement and A plc continues to occupy the property. How will this transaction be recorded in the financial statements of A plc?

8 Limitations of published financial statements

Published financial statements provide a lot of useful information about a business. However, they still do not provide the whole picture. While IFRS attempts to ensure optimum disclosure, published financial statements still have a few inherent drawbacks which can undermine the overall credibility and reliability of financial information.

8.1 Historical cost basis

Historical cost is the most widely used basis of measurement of assets, but its use presents various problems for the users of published financial statements as it fails to account for the change in price levels of assets over a period of time. For example, a price index in one year may differ from a price index in other years. This not only reduces the relevance of accounting information by presenting assets at amounts that may be far less than their realisable value, but also fails to account for the opportunity cost of using those assets. The published financial statements neither represent the value for which non-current assets can be sold nor the amount which will be required to replace those assets.

8.2 Creative accounting or earnings management

Creative accounting – popularly termed as 'earnings management' – is the presentation of an entity's financial statements in the best possible or most flattering way. It is a deliberate manipulation of financial statements which is geared towards achieving predetermined results. This occurs due to inherent weaknesses in the accounting system, accounting choices, accounting judgement and accounting transactions. It has been largely outlawed by:

- IAS 37, which aims to ensure proper accounting and disclosure of provisions, contingent liabilities and contingent assets.
- IAS 27, which ensures consolidation of financial statements of subsidiaries with that of parent entity.
- IFRS 16, which aims to ensure proper reporting of leased assets to curb the effect of any disguised loan or 'off-balance sheet' items (for example, where a lease agreement is framed to ensure the leased asset and the related liability are not reported on the statement of financial position).

A rigorous audit process will almost invariably identify areas where management may improve their controls or processes, further adding value to the company by enhancing the quality of its business processes. An audit underpins the trust and obligation of stewardship between those who manage a company and those who own it, or otherwise have a need for a clear and objective view. It requires both auditors' expertise (ability to detect errors or misstatements) and independence (ability to report these errors or misstatements). This topic will be further discussed in Chapter 7.

8.3 Intra-group transactions

An intra-group transaction occurs when one unit of an entity is involved in a transaction with other unit of the same entity. It is common for entities to carry on activities with or through subsidiaries and associates, or occasionally to engage in transactions with directors or their families.

There is a high possibility that such transactions have not been agreed at arm's-length prices or in the best interests of the entity itself. Such transactions might have been entered into in order to evade taxes. To curb such practices, IAS 24 (Related Party Disclosures) has been introduced to ensure adequate disclosure of all such transactions.

8.4 Ignoring non-financial matters

There are certain factors which have a bearing on the financial position and operating results of the business but they do not become a part of the financial statements because they cannot be measured in monetary terms. Such factors may include the reputation of the management, creditworthiness of the entity, cooperation and skills of the employees, environmental attentiveness or how well the business works with the local community. A business reporting excellent financial results might be weak in these areas.

8.5 Not forward looking

A prospective investor will be interested in knowing those developments that will affect the future prospects of an entity. It becomes very difficult for an investor to arrive at any decision by looking at the financial statements prepared on the basis of historical information. The strategic report can, however, provide some insights into the future prospects of the business.

8.6 Seasonality of trading

Many entities whose trade is seasonal in nature tend to report their results when the company is at its most solvent (for example, retailers often report after Christmas). This may distort reported results and particularly statement of financial position items as atypical compared to the rest of the year.

8.7 Not always comparable

Different entities use different accounting practices and accounting policies depending on their size, nature of business and conventions. It can be difficult to compare two different entities on the basis of their published financial statements.

8.8 Only covers a specific time period

A statement of financial position is prepared on a specified date and reflects the financial position on that date. The position may be different the day before or the day after. For example, a business may sell assets just before the end of the financial year to make it appear that the business is more liquid than it is. The timing of various transactions can be manipulated to influence the appearance of the financial statements.

Test yourself 4.5

1. **Outline the reasons why managers may engage in earnings management or creative accounting.**

Test yourself 4.6

1. **What are the key limitations of historical cost as a basis for the measurement of assets?**

Chapter summary

- Companies publish their annual financial statements within a wider set of information known as the annual report and financial statements (or accounts). The annual report provides information about the company's activities, financial performance and the future prospects of the business. The annual report includes:
    - the strategic report or business review
    - the directors' report
    - the directors' remuneration report
    - the corporate governance statement
    - the auditor's report
    - audited financial statements
    - notes to the financial statements
- The strategic report is a detailed report written in non-financial language that provides clear and coherent information about the company's activities, performance and position, including the strategic position and probable risks of the business. It contains:
    - a fair review of the company's business
    - a description of the principal risks and uncertainties

- the going concern assessment
- references to annual financial statements
- additional information for a quoted company including its strategy, business model and information on environmental, employee and social issues

◆ The directors' report helps shareholders make informed decisions when casting their votes at annual or other meetings. It provides information on the financial state of the company and its compliance with financial reporting, accounting and corporate social responsibility standards.

◆ IAS 1 provides guidance on the information to be disclosed in the notes to the financial statements, including their structure and contents. The notes to the financial statements provide information not presented elsewhere in the financial statements. This includes:
  - more detailed analysis of figures in the statements
  - narrative information explaining figures in the statements
  - additional information, such as contingent liabilities (IAS 37), capital expenditure commitments, IFRS 7 (Financial Instruments) disclosures and related party disclosures (IAS 24)

◆ Segment reporting provides financial information regarding the financial performance and position of the key operating units of a company. International Financial Reporting Standard 8 defines reportable and operating segments and provides the basis for financial disclosure of businesses based on segment activity.

◆ Substance of transactions refers to the economic benefits, economic losses or any kind of economic implications related to the transaction. It includes an accounting concept popularly termed as 'substance over form' which means the transactions recorded in the financial statements must reflect their economic (or commercial) substance rather than their legal form alone. It mandates that the financial statements and accompanying disclosures of an entity should reflect the underlying realities of accounting transactions.

◆ Some examples where the substance can be different from the form of the transaction include:
  - sale and leaseback arrangements
  - consignment stock
  - debt factoring

◆ This area of accounting is somewhat subjective. To help preparers, the IASB has identified the relevant IFRS/IAS that provide detailed guidelines on disclosure of some key transactions:
  - IAS 8 (Accounting Policies, Changes in Accounting Estimates and Errors)
  - IFRS 15 (Revenue)
  - IFRS 16 (Leases)

- Published financial statements have a few inherent limitations which can undermine the overall credibility and reliability of information contained in the annual report and financial statements (or accounts). These include:
    - historical cost basis
    - creative accounting or earnings management
    - intra-group transactions
    - ignores non-financial matters
    - non-forward looking
    - seasonality of trading
    - not always comparable
    - only covering a specific time period.

Chapter five
Accounting policies based on IFRS

Contents

1. Introduction
2. Accounting policies
3. Accounting for inventories
4. Accounting for property, plant and equipment
5. Accounting for events after the reporting period
6. Revenue from contracts with customers
7. Provisions, contingent liabilities and contingent assets
8. Accounting for leases

1 Introduction

In this chapter we will be covering several key accounting policies that are not captured elsewhere but are included in this syllabus. These include (along with the relevant international standard (IFRS or IAS)):

- accounting policies (IAS 8)
- accounting for inventories (IAS 2)
- accounting for property, plant and equipment (IAS 16)
- accounting for events after the reporting period (IAS 10)
- revenue from contracts with customers (IFRS 15)
- provisions, contingent liabilities and contingent assets (IAS 37)
- accounting for leases (IFRS 16)

Table 5.1 summarises all the current international standards. The standards covered within this text are identified in the final column.

Standard	Standard title	Relevant chapter
IAS 1	Presentation of financial statements	3
IAS 2	Inventories	5
IAS 7	Statement of cash flows	3
IAS 8	Accounting policies, changes in accounting estimates and errors	5
IAS 10	Events after the reporting period	5
IAS 12	Income taxes	*
IAS 16	Property, plant and equipment	5
IAS 19	Employee benefits	*
IAS 20	Accounting for government grants and disclosure of government assistance	*
IAS 21	The effects of changes in foreign exchange rates	*
IAS 23	Borrowing costs	*
IAS 24	Related party disclosures	4
IAS 26	Accounting and reporting by retirement benefit plans	*
IAS 27	Separate financial statements	6
IAS 28	Investments in associates and joint ventures	6
IAS 29	Financial reporting in hyperinflationary economies	*
IAS 32	Financial instruments: presentation	*
IAS 33	Earnings per share	7
IAS 34	Interim financial reporting	*
IAS 36	Impairment of assets	*
IAS 37	Provisions, contingent liabilities and contingent assets	5
IAS 38	Intangible assets	*
IAS 40	Investment property	*
IAS 41	Agriculture	*
IFRS 1	First time adoption of International Financial Reporting Standards	*
IFRS 2	Share-based payment	*

Chapter five Accounting policies based on IFRS

Standard	Standard title	Relevant chapter
IFRS 3	Business combinations	6
IFRS 4	Insurance contracts (Will be superseded by IFRS 17 from 2021)	*
IFRS 5	Non-current assets held for sale and discontinued operations	3
IFRS 6	Exploration for and evaluation of mineral resources	*
IFRS 7	Financial instruments: disclosures	*
IFRS 8	Operating segments	4
IFRS 9	Financial Instruments	*
IFRS 10	Consolidated financial statements	6
IFRS 11	Joint arrangements	6
IFRS 12	Disclosures of interests in other entities	6
IFRS 13	Fair value measurement	6
IFRS 14	Regulatory deferral	*
IFRS 15	Revenue from contracts with customers	5
IFRS 16	Leases (IFRS 16 replaced IAS 17 effective 1 January 2019)	5

* These standards are not examinable on this module

Table 5.1 International Accounting Standards and International Financial Reporting Standards

2 Accounting policies

Accounting policies may differ from company to company but published financial statements require compliance with IFRS which are relevant to the specific circumstances of the entity.

Accounting policies are the specific principles, rules and procedures applied by an entity to ensure that transactions are recorded properly and financial statements are prepared and presented correctly.

These policies are used to deal specifically with complicated or subjective accounting practices such as depreciation methods, recognition and treatment of goodwill, accounting for research and development costs, inventory valuation and the preparation of consolidated financial statements.

2.1 Objective of accounting policies and IAS 8

Accounting policies are defined in IAS 8 (Accounting Policies, Changes in Accounting Estimates and Errors) as 'the specific principles, bases, conventions, rules and practices applied by an entity in preparing and presenting financial statements'. Implicit in the definition is the need to provide useful financial information to the users of financial statements.

IAS 8 prescribes the criteria for selecting and changing accounting policies, together with the accounting treatment and disclosure of changes in accounting policies, changes in accounting estimates and correction of errors. The standard is intended to enhance the relevance and reliability of an entity's financial statements. It also aims to improve the comparability of those financial statements both over time and with the financial statements of other entities. The two major concerns governing the application of accounting policies are:

- selection and application
- consistency

2.2 Selection and application of accounting policies

International Accounting Standard 8 prescribes the criteria for the selection and application of the appropriate accounting policies. Across all IFRS there is guidance to assist entities in applying their requirements. Guidance that is an integral part of IFRS is mandatory, whereas guidance that is not an integral part of IFRS does not contain requirements for financial statements.

In the absence of an IFRS, or any guidance that specifically applies to the reporting of a transaction, item or activity, IAS 8 requires the entity's management to use its judgement in selecting accounting policies that are:

- relevant to the economic decision-making needs of the users
- reliable

When making their judgements, management should first refer to the requirements and guidance in IFRS dealing with similar issues; then take consideration of the definitions, recognition criteria and measurement concepts for assets, liabilities, income and expenses in the IASB's Conceptual Framework (see Chapter 2).

2.3 Consistency of accounting policies

An entity should select and apply its accounting policies consistently to promote comparability between financial statements of different accounting periods and for similar transactions, other events and conditions. The only exception is where IFRS specifically requires or permits item categorisation and the application of different policies. An appropriate accounting policy should be selected and applied consistently to each category. For example, non-current assets may be categorised and have a depreciation policy applied to each class, rather than a single policy applicable to all tangible non-current assets.

2.4 Changes in accounting policy

An entity should change an accounting policy only if the change is required by IFRS or if it results in the financial statements providing reliable and more relevant information.

As a general rule, a change in an accounting policy must be applied retrospectively in the financial statements – in other words, it should be applied to prior periods as though that policy had always been in place. This will require adjustment of:

- the opening balance(s) in the current year's statement of changes in equity (usually retained earnings)
- adjustment of all comparative amounts presented in the financial statements

International Accounting Standard 8 requires full disclosure of the following items at the end of the first accounting period in which the change was introduced:

- the IFRS that was responsible for the change;
- the nature of the change in policy;
- transitional provisions;
- for the current and each prior period presented, the amount of the adjustment to:
  - each line item affected
  - earnings per share
- the amount of the adjustment relating to prior periods not presented; and
- an explanation outlining how the change in policy was applied, if retrospective application is impracticable.

2.5 Accounting estimates

Often, there is little or no certainty about an activity or an item within the financial statements. The use of reasonable estimates, therefore, is an essential part of the preparation of financial statements. It does not undermine the reliability of financial statements. Changes in accounting estimates result from new developments or information and should not be confused as corrections of errors.

A common example of an accounting estimate is the allowance for receivables (doubtful debts). This is an estimated amount deducted from trade receivables, representing those who may be unable to meet their debt obligations. It is estimated based upon a combination of factors including professional judgement, historical behaviour and current analysis. Revising the allowance upwards or downwards is an example of a change in accounting estimate, not a change in accounting policy. A change that frequently causes misunderstanding is a change of depreciation method of a tangible non-current asset: this is a change of estimate, not policy, as the accounting policy is the asset continues to be depreciated. All that has changed is the estimated consumption of benefits from the asset.

The effect of a change in an accounting estimate is recognised prospectively by including it in the statement of profit or loss and OCI.

- If the change affects that period only, the effect is recognised in the period of the change.
- If the change affects both the period of the change and future periods, the effect is recognised in the current and future periods.

The disclosure requirements are less onerous than for a change in accounting policy. The only disclosure required is the nature and amount of change that has an effect in the current period (or is expected to have in future).

Stop and think 5.1

Think of a situation when an entity is required to make changes in its accounting estimates. How would such a change in an accounting estimate be accounted for?

2.6 Prior period errors

International Accounting Standard 8 defines prior period errors as omissions from and misstatements in the entity's financial statements for one or more prior periods arising from a failure to use, or misuse of, reliable information that:

- was available when the financial statements for those periods were authorised for issue; and
- could have been reasonably expected to be taken into account in the preparation and presentation of those financial statements.

Financial information may not be reliable for users because of material prior period errors. Omissions or misstatements of items are material if they could, individually or collectively, influence the financial decisions of users taken on the basis of the financial statements (discussed in Chapter 2).

Examples of a material prior period error include:

- a material over/understatement of revenue, inventory or other expenses due to mathematical mistakes;
- mistakes in applying accounting policies;
- oversights or misinterpretations of facts; and
- fraud.

Errors should be corrected retrospectively in the first set of financial statements after their discovery by:

- restating the comparative amounts for the prior period(s) presented in which the error occurred; or
- if the error occurred before the earliest prior period presented, the opening balances of assets, liabilities and equity for the earliest period presented should be restated.

In this set of financial statements, full disclosure of the following should be made at the end of the first accounting period in which a material prior period error was discovered:

- the nature of the prior period error;
- for each prior period presented, if practicable, disclose the correction to each line item affected and EPS; and
- the amount of the correction at the beginning of earliest period presented.

Table 5.2 provides a snapshot of the key points about accounting policies, accounting estimates and prior period errors.

	Accounting policies	Accounting estimates	Prior period errors
What is it?	Principles/measurement basis	Estimates/patterns based on professional judgement, historical behaviour and current analysis	Omissions and misstatements
Examples	Application of new accounting policy such as IFRS 16 on leases that replaced IAS 17 (effective from 1 Jan 2019) Change from historical cost to fair value	Estimated lifespan of a non-current asset, allowance for receivables or amounts based on fair value	Over/understatement of revenue, expenses or assets
Accounting	Retrospectively Full disclosure	Prospectively Disclosure of nature and amount of change	Retrospectively Full disclosure

Table 5.2 Accounting policies, accounting estimates and prior period errors

Worked example 5.1

During the audit of Bexley Ltd for the year ended 31 December 20X9, the auditor discovered the inventory was understated by £60,000 as at 31 December 20X8 due to clerical error.

A summary of the draft statement of profit or loss and OCI for the year ending 31 December 20X9 (and 20X8 comparative) is shown as follows:

	20X9 £'000	20X8 £'000
Revenue	1,500	975
Cost of goods sold	(645)	(525)
Gross profit	855	450
Operating expenses	(480)	(390)
Profit before tax	375	60
Tax expense (at 20%)	(75)	(12)
Profit for the year	300	48

Explain how the error should be corrected in the financial statements for 20X9.

Solution:

The error should be corrected retrospectively in the first set of financial statements after their discovery by:

- restating the comparative amounts for the prior period(s) presented, in which the error occurred; or
- if the error occurred before the earliest prior period presented, the opening balance of assets, liabilities and equity for the earliest period presented should be restated.

Since the error occurred in 20X8, a restated statement of financial position as at 31 December 20X8 should be prepared as the comparative in the financial statements for 31 December 20X9. The impact of correction in the statement of profit or loss and OCI (and 20X8 comparative) is illustrated below:

	20X9	Restated 20X8
	£'000	£'000
Revenue	1,500	975
Cost of goods sold	(705) = 645 + 60	(465) = 525 − 60
Gross profit	795	510
Operating expenses	(480)	(390)
Profit before tax	315	120
Tax expense (at 20%)	(63)	(24)
Profit for the year	252	96

(margin note: minus because it is added to a negative figure.)

The gross profit in the prior period has increased by the £60,000 understatement in the restated statement of profit or loss and OCI. This correction will also be reflected in the current year. The profit reported in 20X9 has decreased by £60,000 and the computed level of taxation has decreased proportionately. The profit reported has also decreased in 20X8 and the computed level of taxation has decreased proportionately. Taking the two years together, the company's results are unchanged, because profit before tax has gone up by £60,000 in 20X8 and down by £60,000 in 20X9.

This correction is needed because inventory is the key element in the calculation of the cost of goods sold (cost of sales). As per section 8.1 in Chapter 3:

- Cost of goods sold for a manufacturer is the cost of its finished goods in its beginning inventory plus the cost of goods manufactured during the accounting period minus the cost of finished goods in its ending inventory.

- Cost of goods sold for a retailer is the cost of merchandise in its beginning inventory plus the net cost of merchandise purchased during the accounting period minus the cost of merchandise in its ending inventory.

There will also be changes to the statement of financial position for Bexley Ltd. In 20X8 the closing balance for inventory would have been increased by £60,000 (to correct for the understatement), hence the adjustment to the cost of goods sold as you subtract the closing inventory. In 20X9, the opening balance for inventory would have been increased by £60,000, hence the adjustment to the cost of goods sold as you add the opening inventory.

Test yourself 5.1

How are changes in an accounting policy, the correction of material prior year errors and changes in accounting estimates applied in the financial statements in order to comply with IAS 8?

3 Accounting for inventories

Most businesses will hold inventories or stocks of some kind. International Accounting Standard 2 (Inventories) sets out the accounting treatment for inventories, including the determination of cost, the subsequent recognition of an expense and any write-downs to net realisable value.

3.1 Scope and objective of IAS 2

Inventories within the scope of IAS 2 are assets:

- held for sale in the ordinary course of business (finished goods)
- in the process of production in the ordinary course of business (work in progress)
- in the form of materials and supplies that are consumed in production (raw materials) or in the rendering of services

Assets that are excluded from the scope of IAS 2 include:

- work in progress arising under construction contracts
- financial instruments
- biological assets related to agricultural activity and agricultural produce at the point of harvest

Also, while the following are within the scope of IAS 2 it does not apply to the measurement of inventories held by:

- producers of agricultural and forest products and minerals and mineral products, both of which are measured at net realisable value in accordance with well-established practices in those industries
- commodity broker-traders who measure their inventories at fair value less costs to sell

International Accounting Standard 2 does not deal with initial recognition. Instead, the general rule applies – inventories will be recognised as an asset when the entity obtains control. The main concern in inventory accounting is the amount of cost to be recognised as an asset and carried forward until the related revenue is recognised. The aim of IAS 2 is to streamline the accounting method for inventories, providing guidance on the determination of cost and its subsequent recognition as an expense, including any write-down to net realisable value.

3.2 Measurement and cost of inventories

International Accounting Standard 2 requires inventories to be measured at the lower of cost and net realisable value (NRV). The cost of inventories comprises all costs of purchase, costs of conversion and other costs incurred in bringing the inventories to their present location and condition.

The cost of inventories comprises all costs of:

- purchase (including taxes, transport and handling), net of trade discounts received;
- costs of conversion (including fixed and variable manufacturing overheads); and
- other costs incurred in bringing the inventories to their present location and condition.

Inventory cost does not include:

- abnormal waste
- storage costs
- administrative overheads unrelated to production
- selling costs
- foreign exchange differences arising directly on the recent acquisition of inventories invoiced in a foreign currency
- interest cost when inventories are purchased with deferred settlement terms

International Accounting Standard 23 (Borrowing Costs) identifies some limited circumstances where borrowing costs (interest) can be included in the cost of inventories that meet the definition of a qualifying asset.

3.3 Methods of costing inventories

There are a number of methods of accounting for inventory cost. The standard cost and retail methods may be used for the measurement of cost, provided that the results approximate to actual cost.

Standard costing, usually associated with a manufacturing company, is the practice of assigning an expected or standard cost for an actual cost and periodically analysing variances between the expected and actual costs into various components (direct labour, direct material and overhead) to maintain productivity.

The **retail method**, used by retailers that resell merchandise, is a technique used to estimate the value of ending inventory using the cost-to-retail price ratio. The retail inventory method works when there is a clear relationship between the price purchased from a wholesaler and the price sold to customers and the mark-up is consistent across all products sold – such as if a retailer marks up every item by 80% of the wholesale price.

standard costing
The practice, usually associated with a manufacturing company, of assigning an expected or standard cost for an actual cost in the accounting records and periodically analysing variances between the expected and actual costs into various components (direct labour, direct material and overhead) to maintain productivity.

retail method
A technique used by retailers to estimate the value of ending inventory using the cost to retail price ratio.

first in, first out (FIFO)
A method used to account for inventory costs where the earliest produced or purchased inventory items are assumed and expensed as being sold first.

weighted average cost (WAVCO)
A method used to account for inventory costs that uses the average of the costs of the goods, such as dividing the cost of goods available for sale by the number of units available for sale.

For inventory items that are not interchangeable, specific costs are attributed to the individual items of inventory. For items that are interchangeable, IAS 2 allows the **'first in, first out'** (FIFO) or **weighted average cost** (WAVCO) formulas.

An entity should use the same cost formula for all inventories having a similar nature and use to the entity. For inventories with a different nature or use, different cost formulas may be justified.

3.3 Write-down to net realisable value

Net realisable value is the estimated selling price in the ordinary course of business, less the estimated cost of completion and the estimated costs necessary to make the sale. Any write-down to NRV should be recognised as an expense in the period in which the write-down occurs. Any reversal should be recognised in the statement of profit or loss and OCI in the period in which the reversal occurs. Assets should not be carried in excess of amounts expected to be realised from their sale or use.

3.4 The matching principle and expense recognition

When inventories are sold, the carrying amount of those inventories should be recognised as an expense in the period in which the related revenue is recognised, as per IFRS 15 (Revenue from Contracts with Customers). The amount of any write-down of inventories to NRV and all losses of inventories should be recognised as an expense in the period the write-down or loss occurs.

Inventories are usually written down to NRV item by item. However, it may be appropriate to group similar or related items in some circumstances.

3.5 Disclosure

International Accounting Standard 2 requires disclosure of:

- accounting policy for inventories;
- amount of any write-down of inventories recognised as an expense in the reporting period;
- cost of inventories recognised as expense (cost of goods sold or cost of sales);
- amount of any reversal of a write-down to NRV and the circumstances that led to such reversal; and
- separate disclosure of inventories carried as assets at the period end, including:
  - carrying amount, generally classified as merchandise, supplies, materials, work in progress and finished goods;
  - carrying amount of any inventories carried at fair value less costs to sell; and
  - carrying amount of inventories pledged as security for liabilities.

Test yourself 5.2

Konyak plc imports goods from Nepal and sells them in the local market. It uses the FIFO method to value its inventory. The following are the purchases and sales made by the company during the current year.

Purchases

- January: 10,000 units at £15 each
- March: 15,000 units at £20 each
- July: 10,000 units at £45 each

Sales

- May: 15,000 units
- November: 15,000 units

Based on the FIFO method, calculate the value of inventory at the end of May, September and December.

4 Accounting for plant, property and equipment   IAS 16

Most businesses require capital assets such as plant, property and equipment. International Accounting Standard 16 (Property, Plant and Equipment) sets out how entities should report their investment in property, plant and equipment.

4.1 Scope and objective of IAS 16

Property, plant and equipment are tangible items that:

- are held for use in the production or supply of goods or services, for rental basis, or for administrative purposes; and
- are expected to be used for more than one accounting period.

The objective of this standard is to deal with the accounting treatment of property, plant and equipment. It includes guidance on:

- recognition and measurement
- determination of carrying amount
- depreciation charges
- any impairment loss
- derecognition
- disclosure

International Accounting Standard 16 does not apply to:

- plant, property and equipment held for sale under IFRS 5 (see section 8.5, Chapter 3);
- biological assets related to agricultural activity accounted for under IAS 41 (Agriculture); and
- exploration and evaluation of mineral assets recognised in accordance with IFRS 6 and mineral rights and mineral reserves such as oil, natural gas and similar non-regenerative resources.

However, IAS 16 is applicable to the property, plant and equipment which are used to maintain or develop the above listed biological assets, as well as mineral rights and reserves and other non-regenerative resources.

4.2 Initial recognition and measurement

Under IAS 16, the cost of an item of property, plant and equipment shall be recognised as an asset if and only if, it is probable that future economic benefits associated with the item will flow to the entity and the cost of the item can be measured reliably.

Initial recognition
Property, plant and equipment shall be measured at its cost or the cash price equivalent at the recognition date. Cost includes:

- purchase price, including duties and non-refundable purchase taxes, after deducting trade discounts;
- costs directly attributable to bringing the asset to the location and condition necessary for it to operate in the manner intended by management; and
- the estimated costs of dismantling and removing the item and restoring the site on which it is located.

The capitalisation of costs should *cease* when the asset becomes available for operating use or intended use by the management.

International Accounting Standard 23 (Borrowing Costs) identifies some limited circumstances where borrowing costs (interest) can be included in cost of property, plant and equipment that meet the definition of a qualifying asset. This applies when the borrowing costs are directly attributable to the acquisition, construction or production of a qualifying asset.

4.3 Subsequent recognition and measurement

- Assets requiring the replacement of some component parts during the useful life (such as the spare parts of a plant or the roof of a building) will recognise the cost of replacement in the carrying amount of the relevant asset if it satisfies the recognition criteria.
- The cost of day-to-day or ongoing repair and maintenance will be charged to the statement of profit or loss and OCI as an expense.

- An asset requiring an inspection after a specified interval as per industry laws (such as in the airline industry) will recognise the cost of such inspection in the carrying amount of the related asset, if its economic benefits are for more than one accounting period.

Subsequent measurement

After recognition, an entity has two options to choose from for the accounting of property, plant and equipment at each reporting date.

- **Cost model:** after recognising an item of property, plant and equipment as an asset, it should be carried at cost less any accumulated depreciation/accumulated impairment losses (the carrying amount, previously known as (net) book value).
- **Revaluation model:** after recognition as an asset, an item of property, plant and equipment whose fair value can be measured reliably should be carried at the revalued amount (fair value at the date of the revaluation) less any subsequent accumulated depreciation/accumulated impairment losses (the carrying amount, previously known as (net) book value).

Revaluation increases are recognised under the heading of revaluation surplus in OCI and reported in the statement of changes in equity. The increase should only be recognised in the statement of profit or loss and OCI to the extent that it reverses a revaluation decrease of the same asset previously recognised in the statement of profit or loss and OCI. Revaluation decreases are recognised in the statement of profit or loss and OCI unless they reverse a previous revaluation increase.

Revaluations should be made with sufficient regularity to ensure that the carrying amount does not differ materially from that which would be determined using fair value at the end of the reporting period.

4.4 Depreciation

Depreciation is the systematic allocation of the depreciable amount of the asset over its useful life (the period it will be used to generate benefit).

The depreciable amount is the cost of an asset less its residual value. The depreciation charge for each period should be recognised in the statement of profit or loss and OCI. The depreciation method used should reflect the pattern in which the asset's future economic benefits are expected to be consumed by the entity. For example, in straight-line depreciation, the cost of an asset is allocated evenly over its useful life. If a piece of equipment that cost £10,000 has a useful life of eight years and an expected salvage value of £2,000, the annual depreciation charge will be £1,000 over its useful life.

The residual value of an asset is the estimated amount that an entity would obtain from disposal of the asset, after deducting the estimated costs of disposal, if the asset were at the end of its useful life.

> **depreciation**
> The systematic allocation of the depreciable amount of an asset over its useful life (the period it will be used to generate benefit).

4.5 Recoverability of the carrying amount and impairment

Property, plant and equipment requires impairment testing and, if necessary, recognition of an impairment loss. An item of property, plant, or equipment shall not be carried at more than its recoverable amount. The recoverable amount is the higher of an asset's fair value less costs to sell and its value in use.

The asset is impaired when an asset's carrying value exceeds its recoverable amount (the higher of fair value less costs of disposal and value in use). In IAS 36, companies are required to conduct impairment tests where there is an indication of the impairment of an asset. Goodwill and certain intangible assets are an exception to this, as they require an annual impairment test.

Indications of impairment might include external factors such a decline in market values, negative changes in the economy or in the legal environment and internal sources such as physical damage or if the asset is idle.

Any claim for compensation for impairment or damage of property, plant and equipment from third parties (such as an insurance company) is included in the statement of profit or loss and OCI when the claim becomes receivable.

4.6 Derecognition (retirements and disposals)

An asset should be removed from the statement of financial position on disposal or when it is withdrawn from use. The gain or loss on disposal is the difference between the proceeds and the carrying amount at that time and should be recognised in the statement of profit or loss and OCI.

4.7 Disclosure

International Accounting Standard 16 requires the following disclosures for each class of property, plant and equipment:

- the basis for measuring carrying amount;
- the depreciation methods to be used or used;
- useful lives or depreciation rates;
- the gross carrying amount (cost or valuation) and accumulated depreciation and impairment losses;
- a reconciliation of the carrying amount at the beginning and the end of the period, showing:
  - additions
  - disposals
  - acquisitions through business combinations
  - revaluation increases or decreases
  - impairment losses
  - reversals of impairment losses
  - depreciation
  - net foreign exchange differences on translation and
  - other movements

4.8 Additional disclosures

International Accounting Standard 16 also encourages additional disclosures for:

- restrictions on title and items pledged as security for liabilities;
- contractual commitments and expenditures to construct property, plant and equipment during the period; and
- compensation from third parties for items of property, plant and equipment that were impaired, lost or given up that is included in the statement of profit or loss and OCI.

4.9 Revalued property, plant and equipment

If property, plant and equipment is stated at revalued amounts, certain additional disclosures are required:

- the effective date of the revaluation;
- whether an independent valuer was involved;
- for each revalued class of property, the carrying amount that would have been recognised had the assets been carried under the cost model; and
- the revaluation surplus, including changes during the period and any restrictions on the distribution of the balance to shareholders.

Test yourself 5.3

1. Cuba Ltd acquired a new item of plant in exchange for land with a book value of £10 million (fair value amounted to £15 million), plus cash paid upfront of £5 million.
2. What will be the cost of the acquired plant in the financial statements of Cuba Ltd?
3. What are the criteria set out by IAS 16 for the recognition of the cost of an item of property, plant and equipment as an asset?

5 Accounting for events after the reporting period

5.1 Scope and objective of IAS 10

According to IAS 10 (Events after the Reporting Period) these are those events, favourable and unfavourable, that occur between the end of the reporting period and the date when the financial statements are authorised for issue.

The objective of this standard is to provide guidance to determine when an entity should adjust its financial statements for events after the reporting period. Two types of events after the reporting period can be identified.

5.2 Adjusting events

An adjustment is made to the financial statements when the condition existed at the end of the reporting period. Settlement of litigation in respect of events that occurred before the end of reporting period may be recorded as liability in the financial statements or adjusted in accordance with IAS 37 (Provisions, Contingent Liabilities and Contingent Assets). Discovery of errors in the financial statements may be adjusted in accordance with IAS 8 (Accounting Policies, Changes in Accounting Estimates and Errors).

5.3 Non-adjusting events

No adjustment is required for event or conditions that arose after the reporting period. For example:

- A dividend declared after the reporting period does not indicate a liability (there is no obligation until the dividend has been approved by the shareholders in a general meeting) at the reporting date and so is not recognised as a liability at the end of the reporting period.
- Any litigation charges against the company arising out of events that occurred after the reporting period do not indicate a liability at the reporting date and do not trigger the recognition of a liability.

If these events are material and could influence the financial decisions of users, the following disclosures are required for each material category of non-adjusting event after the reporting period:

- the nature of the event; and
- an estimate of its financial effect, or a statement that such an estimate cannot be made.

If events after the reporting period indicate that the going concern assumption is not appropriate, then an entity should not prepare its financial statements on a going-concern basis. An example of this would be if management intends to liquidate the entity or to cease trading, or that it has no realistic alternative but to do so.

Events after the reporting period – IAS 10

Adjusting events
(event or condition existed at the end of the reporting period). An adjustment is made to the financial statements

Non-adjusting events
(event or condition arose after the reporting period). No adjustment is made but disclosures are required for each material category of non-adjusting event

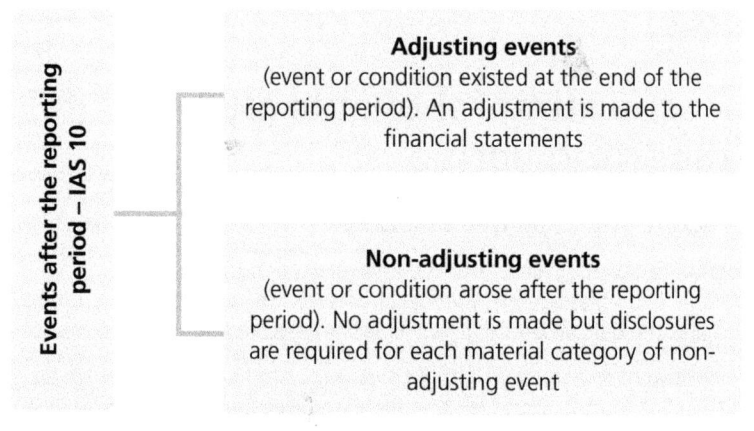

Figure 5.1 Events after the reporting period (IAS 10)

Worked example 5.2

Momo Ltd is preparing its financial statements for the year ended 31 Dec 20X8.

A fire explosion took place on 12 January 20X9, damaging the warehouse and inventories with carrying amounts of £10 million and £5 million respectively on this date. The company is only expected to recover up to a maximum of £8 million from its insurance cover. Operations were severely interrupted with losses expected in the coming years.

1. A long-outstanding receivable of Momo Ltd declared itself as bankrupt after the reporting date.

How will these events be reported in the financial statements and notes of Momo Ltd for the year ended 31 Dec 20X8?

Solution

Damage caused by the fire after the reporting date does not provide evidence of the conditions that existed at the reporting date. Therefore, IAS 10 requires an event which gives rise to loss due to a natural disaster, such as fire or flood, to be disclosed in the notes to the 20X8 financial statements as a non-adjusting event.

However, if events after the reporting period indicate that the going concern assumption is not appropriate, an entity should not prepare its financial statements on a going-concern basis. Instead, the entity will have to prepare its financial statements as per the **breakup value method**. The insurance claim will be disclosed as a contingent asset in the notes to the financial statements.

Declaration of bankruptcy by a long-outstanding receivable after the reporting date is treated as an adjusting event, as it may provide evidence of its non-recoverability (impaired value) at the reporting date. An adjustment is made in the financial statements by:

- recognising its impairment;
- reducing the amount of receivable to its recoverable amount (if any); and
- recognising the impairment loss in the statement of profit or loss and OCI.

breakup value method
Breakup value is based on net realisable value. It is calculated by taking the current market value of all assets of the business, then deducting the liabilities and reasonable liquidation fees. This method is used by an entity reporting on non-going concern basis that is based on cost/fair value (as per IFRS requirements).

Test yourself 5.4

1. Precipe Ltd recorded inventories at their cost of £500,000 in the statement of financial position as at 31 December 20X8. The entity sold 70% of these for £300,000 on 15 January 20X9. It also incurred a commission expense of 10% of the selling price of the inventory.

2. The financial statements for the year ended 31 December 20X8 were authorised for issue on 10 March 20X9. The government introduced tax changes on 31 March 20X9. As a result, the tax liability recorded by the entity at 31 December 20X8 increased by £400,000.

How will these events be reported in the financial statements of Precipe Ltd for the year ended 31 Dec 20X8?

6 Revenue from contracts with customers

The top-line revenue item in the statement of profit or loss and OCI shows the income figure from which expenses are subtracted to determine gross and operating profits. This drives the performance of the business and it is critical that it is properly accounted for.

The primary issue at the core of many well-known accounting scandals has been accounting for revenue. Revenue may be recognised and measured incorrectly in an attempt to inflate financial results. Studies have revealed that more than half of all financial statement frauds involved revenue manipulation.

- In the fraud case of Satyam Computer Services (2010), false invoices were used to record fictitious revenue amounting to $1.5 billion.
- In the case of Enron (2001), directors inflated the revenue from the 'agency' services by reporting the entire value rather than just the agency commission on the sale. In a bid to keep up with Enron's results, other energy companies adopted the same 'model' to report their revenue.
- In the scandal leading to the bankruptcy of WorldCom (2002), revenue had been overstated to meet revenue targets tied to executive bonuses. This was done by making dubious accounting adjustments.
- Tesco (2014) overstated its half-yearly profits by over £250 million, partly due to 'accelerated' revenue recognition.

International Financial Reporting Standard 15 was issued in May 2014 to tighten the rules relating to revenue. The new standard replaced two standards: IAS 18 (Revenue) and IAS 11 (Construction Contracts). It applies to annual reporting periods beginning on or after 1 January 2018.

International Financial Reporting Standard 15 specifies how and when revenue is recognised, as well as requiring entities to provide more informative, relevant disclosures to the users of financial statements. Under IFRS 15, revenue is recognised when it is probable that future economic benefits will flow to the entity and these benefits can be measured reliably.

6.1 Objective and scope of IFRS 15

International Financial Reporting Standard 15 establishes the principles that an entity should apply to report useful information to users of financial statements about the nature, amount, timing and uncertainty of revenue and cash flows arising from a contract with a customer.

Under IFRS 15, the transfer of goods and services is based upon the transfer of control (which is described as the ability to direct the use of and obtain substantially all of the remaining benefits from, the asset), rather than the transfer of risks and rewards as in IAS 18. IFRS 15 requires the recognition of revenue to reflect the consideration to which the entity expects to be entitled in exchange for those goods or services. IFRS 15 may make little impact for straightforward retail transactions, but it has resulted in changes in the amount and timing of revenue recognition for long-term service contracts.

The standard requires an entity to consider the terms of the contract. All relevant facts and circumstances must be applied consistently to portfolios of contracts with similar characteristics and in similar circumstances. The exceptions are contracts dealt with by other standards, such as lease agreements, insurance contracts and financial instruments.

Scope
The requirements of IFRS 15 apply to all contracts with customers except:

- lease agreements within the scope of IFRS 16 (Leases);
- insurance contracts within the scope of IFRS 4;
- financial instruments and other contractual rights and obligations within the scope of IFRS 9 (Financial Instruments), IFRS 10 (Consolidated Financial Statements), IFRS 11 (Joint Arrangements), IAS 27 (Separate Financial Statements) or IAS 28 (Investments in Associates and Joint Ventures); and
- non-monetary exchanges between entities in the same line of business.

When a contract is partially within the scope of IFRS 15 and partially within the scope of another standard (IAS or IFRS) which specifies how to separate and/or initially measure one or more parts of the contract, then those requirements are applied first. If no guidance is provided by other standards, IFRS 15 will be applied.

6.2 Recognition and measurement

The core principle of IFRS for revenue recognition is delivered in the five-step approach detailed in Figure 5.2.

Step 1: identify the contract with the customer
IFRS 15 does not rely on legal definitions, as the standard applies internationally across different legal systems. It lays out the following criteria for a contract to exist with a customer:

- the contract (written, verbal or implied) has been approved by the parties involved who are committed to carrying it out;

```
I
  P
    P
      A
        R
```

Identify the contract(s) with a customer — Step 1

Identify the performance obligations in the contract — Step 2

Determine the transaction price — Step 3

Allocate the transaction price to the performance obligation of the contract — Step 4

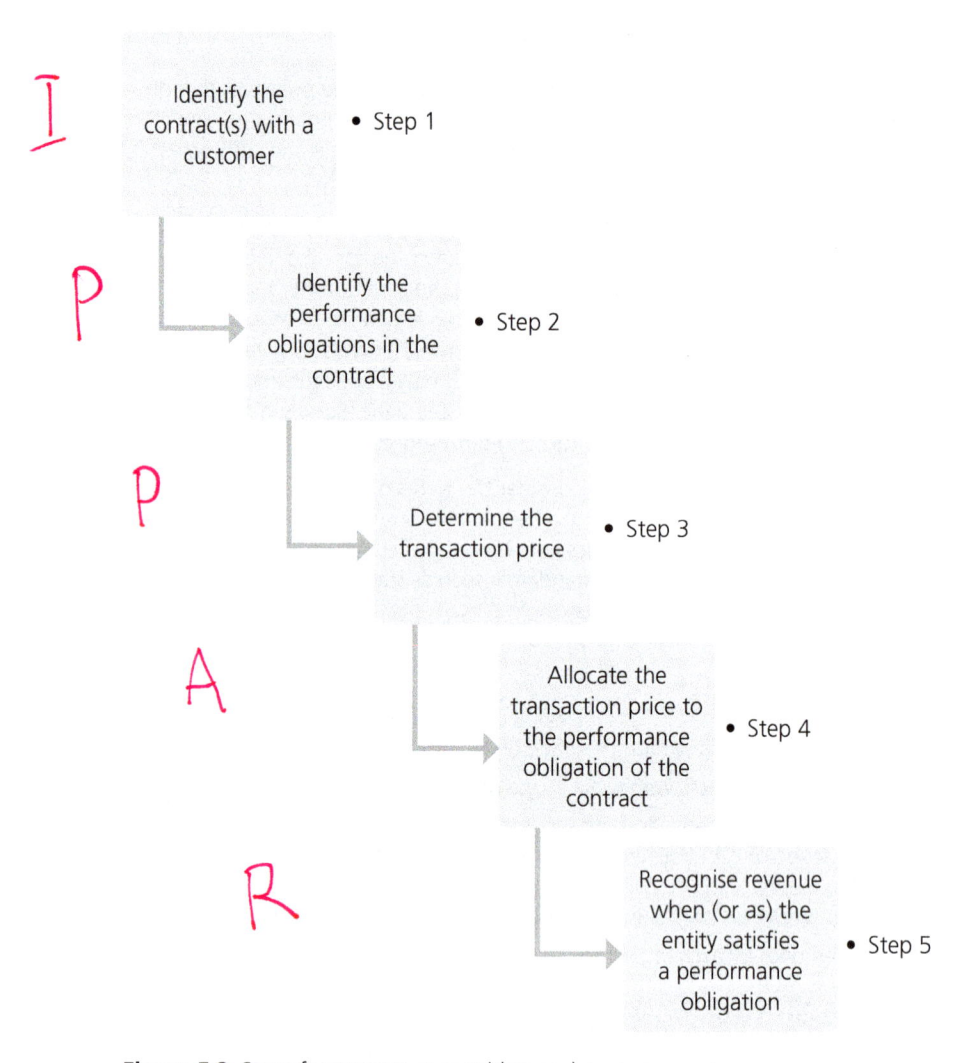

Recognise revenue when (or as) the entity satisfies a performance obligation — Step 5

Figure 5.2 Steps for revenue recognition and measurement

- the entity can identify each party's rights and payment terms regarding the goods or services to be transferred;
- the contract has commercial substance (the risk, timing or amount of the entity's future cash flows is expected to change as a result of the contract); and
- it is probable that the entity will collect the consideration to which it will be entitled.

Step 2: identify the performance obligations in the contract
IFRS 15 requires contracts with more than one performance obligation to be assessed separately. The goal is to separate the contract into parts or separate performance obligations when the promised good or service is distinct: for

example, if each part has a distinct function and a distinct profit margin and can be sold separately.

A distinct good or service is 'separately identifiable' from other promises in the contract. Examples include:

- a contract to supply a computer system and technical support for a specified period (the supply of the computer and the technical support are separate performance obligations); and
- a contract to supply, as a package, a 'free' mobile phone handset with a call package and insurance cover (the supply of the mobile phone, the call charges and the insurance premiums are separate performance obligations).

Step 3: determine the transaction price

The transaction price is the amount of consideration an entity expects from the customer in exchange for transferring goods or services. The consideration may include fixed amounts, variable amounts or both, in addition to the effects of the customer's credit risk and the time value of money (if material).

Variables such as settlement discounts, rebates, refunds, incentives and penalties are included where it is highly probable that there will not be a reversal of revenue when any uncertainty associated with the variable consideration is resolved.

Step 4: allocate the transaction price

An entity must allocate the transaction price to each separate performance obligation (with distinct goods or services) in proportion to the standalone selling price of the good or service underlying each performance obligation.

If an entity sells a bundle of goods and/or services (see examples above), each performance obligation is assessed as if it could be sold separately and revenue is allocated in proportion to those standalone selling prices. Using the second example above, some of the consideration for the contract should be allocated to the 'free' handset.

The standard allows other methods (such as similar market process) when such prices are not available, as long as they meet the overall objective of allocation.

Step 5: recognise revenue as obligations are performed

The standard provides guidance that governs the timing of revenue recognition. It states that an entity should recognise revenue when (or as) the entity satisfies a performance obligation by transferring a promised good or service (an asset) to the customer. An asset is transferred when (or as) the customer obtains control of that asset.

For example, handing over a car to a customer determines the timing of revenue recognition. For more complex contracts, such as those for construction assets (buildings, ships or roads), the performance obligation is satisfied when:

- the entity has the present right to payment for the asset;
- the customer has legal title to the asset;

- the entity has transferred physical possession of the asset;
- the customer has the significant risks and rewards of ownership of the asset; and
- the customer has accepted the asset.

Contracts for services (such as cleaning services or a training programme) are generally performed over a period of time. Where an entity transfers control of a good or service over time, it satisfies a performance obligation and recognises revenue over time.

Measurement

It must be possible to reasonably measure the outcome of a performance obligation before the related revenue can be recognised. Where it may not be possible to reasonably measure the outcome of a performance obligation, such as in the early stages of a contract, revenue is recognised only to the extent of costs incurred that the entity expects to recover. International Financial Reporting Standard 15 requires an entity to capitalise the incremental costs of obtaining a contract with a customer for revenue as an asset (if those costs will be recovered).

6.3 Presentation and disclosure

IFRS 15 requires any asset or liability arising from the difference between revenue recognised and measured under the standard and payments made by the customer, to be included in the statement of financial position. For example, any advance paid by the customer will be a liability; any customers in arrears will be an asset (subject to recoverability).

The standard also requires disclosures relating to key judgements made in applying the standard. This gives a clear picture of how the revenue line has been calculated.

Test yourself 5.5

Peter Telecom Ltd signs a mobile phone contract for two years with a customer. It provides a free handset as part of the contract. It also provides an option to insure the phone at an extra monthly cost. How are the performance obligations assessed, revenue allocated and at what point in time is revenue recognised as per IFRS 15?

7 Provisions, contingent liabilities and contingent assets

7.1 Objective and scope of IAS 37

The objective of IAS 37 is to ensure that appropriate recognition criteria and measurement bases are applied to provisions, contingent liabilities and contingent assets. It also aims to ensure that sufficient information is disclosed in the notes to the financial statements to enable users to understand their nature, timing and amount.

International Accounting Standard 37 excludes obligations and contingencies arising from:

- a non-onerous executory contract, under which no party has completed any part of its performance obligation or both parties have carried on their obligation in part to the same extent; and
- those covered by another standard, such as:
    - financial instruments including financial guarantees (IFRS 9);
    - income tax (IAS 12);
    - leases (IFRS 16); and
    - insurance contracts (IFRS 4).

Provisions made to adjust the value of an asset, such as provisions for depreciation or impairment, are not covered by IAS 37. However, the standard does apply to executory contracts which are onerous and lease contracts which have become onerous.

7.2 Provisions

A provision is defined as a liability of uncertain timing or amount. In IAS 37, a liability is defined as a present obligation of the entity arising from past events, settlement of which is expected to result in an outflow of resources. The provision should be used against the expenditure for which it was originally made. This is different to the Conceptual Framework definition of a liability, although the two definitions are similar.

Recognition

A provision should be recognised when all three of the following conditions are met:

- there is a present obligation (legal or constructive) as a result of a past event;
- it is probable that an outflow of economic resources will be required to settle the obligation; and
- the amount of the obligation can be estimated reliably.

Measurement

The amount recognised as a provision should be the best estimate of the expenditure required to settle the present obligation at the end of the reporting period.

Where a large population of items is being measured, the obligation is estimated by weighting all possible outcomes by their associated probabilities. When measuring a single obligation or liability, the individual most likely outcome may be the best estimate. The entity, however, should consider other possible outcomes in all cases, including:

- the use of expert opinion, legal advice or management's own judgement based on past experience;
- the use of the expected value method (discussed in Chapter 14) that uses the most probable outcome and the events which occur frequently for the measurement of one-off events;
- the effect of any related risk and uncertainties; and
- consideration of future events likely to occur that may affect the amount required to settle an obligation, such as future technology likely to reduce the value of provision.

If there is a material time difference for the settlement of a provision, the present value (PV) should be recognised using an appropriate pre-tax **discount rate** (also discussed in Chapter 14).

discount rate
The rate of return used in a discounted cash flow analysis to determine the current worth or present value of future cash flows.

Remeasurement of provisions

The entity should review and appropriately adjust all provisions at each reporting date. A provision should be reversed if circumstances indicate that the outflow of economic resources is no longer probable. Any change in a provision should be accounted for as a change in accounting estimate and will have prospective application (see IAS 8).

7.3 Contingent liability

A contingent liability is defined as:

- a possible obligation that arises from past events and whose existence depends upon the occurrence (or non-occurrence) of one or more uncertain future events which are not in the control of the entity; or
- a present obligation that arises from past events but is not recognised because either:
  - it is not probable that an outflow of economic benefits will be required to settle the obligation; or
  - a present obligation which arises from past events cannot be measured with sufficient reliability.

Examples include court cases where it is not clear whether the entity has a liability at the reporting date.

A contingent liability is not recognised in the financial statements (as an expense or a liability). It is disclosed as a contingent liability in the notes to financial statements unless the possibility of an outflow of economic benefits or resources is remote.

7.4 Contingent asset

A contingent asset is a possible asset that arises from a past transaction or event and whose existence depends upon the occurrence (or non-occurrence) of some uncertain future events not wholly within the entity's control. For example, compensation (an inflow of economic benefits) expected from the settlement of a court case where the outcome is not certain.

A contingent asset should not be recognised in the financial statements unless it is almost certain that the entity will be entitled to the inflow of economic benefits. However, if there is no certainty, the entity will disclose such a probable contingent asset in the notes to the financial statement.

Test yourself 5.6

A court case was filed against Goldwyns Ltd by its major customer for compensation for a loss caused by the supply of poor-quality products in the last consignment of goods.

At the reporting date of 31 December 20X7, the case was still pending with the value of the claim being disputed. The probability for the settlement of the loss was 'unlikely'.

However, based on new developments in the case, the company's lawyer has signalled that Goldwyns Ltd's liability to compensate for the loss was 'probable' at the reporting date of 31 December 20X8.

Discuss, as per the requirements of IAS 37, how the events will be accounted for in the financial statements of Goldwyns Ltd for the years to 31 December 20X7 and 31 December 20X8.

8 Accounting for leases

International Financial Reporting Standard 16 (which replaced IAS 17 from 1 January 2019) prescribes accounting policies for the recognition, measurement, presentation and disclosure of leases to provide relevant information that faithfully represents those transactions.

A lease agreement is a contract between two parties, the lessor and the lessee. The lessor is the legal owner of the asset, whereas the lessee obtains the right to use the asset in return for rental payments. Historically, assets that were used but not owned were not shown on the statement of financial position; any associated liability was also left out of the statement. This was known as 'off-balance sheet' finance and was a way for companies to reduce their liabilities, thus distorting gearing and other key financial ratios. This form of accounting did not faithfully represent the transaction. In reality, a company often effectively 'owned' these assets and 'owed a liability'.

Leases present a reporting issue and affect the interpretation of financial statements. International Financial Reporting Standard 16 aims to ensure proper reporting of leased assets (formerly operating leases for the lessee) to curb the effect of any disguised loan or 'off-balance sheet' items. This is intended to remove one route for creative accounting which could mislead any readers of the accounts.

The new standard provides a single lessee accounting model, requiring a lessee to recognise assets (representing its right to use the assets) and liabilities (representing its obligation to make lease payments) for all leases with a term of more than 12 months, unless the underlying asset has a low value. For short-term and low-value leases, the lessee expenses the lease payments on a straight-line basis over the lease term. Lessors continue to classify leases as operating or finance leases (as in IAS 17) and accounts for the two types of leases differently.

This is a good example of 'substance over form' as outlined in section 7 of Chapter 4 (page 98). 'Substance over form' implies that the transactions recorded in the financial statements must reflect their economic substance rather than their legal form alone.

In some cases, the substance can be different from the form of the transaction, such as in sale and leaseback arrangements. Sale and leaseback arrangements involves a company selling an asset to another party and getting it back via a lease agreement. The company must first determine whether the transfer qualifies as a sale based on the requirements for satisfying a performance obligation in IFRS 15 (Revenue from Contracts with Customers). If the nature of the transaction is that of a lease, lease accounting is applied as per IFRS 16.

Lease accounting throws up several other issues:

- **The treatment of assets 'controlled' by the lessee (and therefore depreciated):** leases are depreciated based on the time factor (the effluxion of time), even though the asset is not legally owned by the lessee.
- **Accounting for liabilities and cash flow (splitting interest and capital elements):** the principal repayments of amounts borrowed under leases will be shown as a cash flow from financing activities, whereas the cash flow from the interst paid will be shown under operating activities.
- **Short-term leases and low-value leases** benefit from a recognition exemption under IFRS 16. Preparers of financial statements can elect not to apply the initial and subsequent recognition and measurement requirements of IFRS 16 to leases for which the underlying asset is of 'low-value'. Instead, lessees can simply account for the cost of the lease by recognising the cost in equal amounts (straight-line basis) over the term of the lease.

Chapter summary

- The objective of IAS 8 is to prescribe the criteria for selecting and changing accounting policies, along with the accounting treatment and disclosure of changes in accounting policies, changes in accounting estimates and corrections of errors.
- International Accounting Standard 2 sets out the accounting treatment for inventories, including the determination of cost, the subsequent recognition of an expense and any write-downs to NRV. International Accounting Standard 2 also requires inventories to be measured at the lower of cost and NRV. The cost of inventories comprises all costs of

purchase, costs of conversion and other costs incurred in bringing the inventories to their present location and condition.
- International Accounting Standard 16 sets out how entities should report their investment in property, plant and equipment. This standard includes guidance on:
  - recognition and measurement
  - determination of carrying amount
  - depreciation charges
  - any impairment loss
  - derecognition and
  - disclosure
- International Accounting Standard 10 provides guidance on how an entity should adjust its financial statements for events after the reporting period:
  - adjusting events: an adjustment is made to the financial statements when the condition existed at the end of the reporting period.
  - non-adjusting events: no adjustment is required for event or conditions that arose after the reporting period.
- International Financial Reporting Standard 15 sets out the principles that an entity should apply to report the nature, amount, timing and uncertainty of revenue and cash flows arising from a contract with a customer. This core principle for revenue recognition is delivered in a five-step approach to revenue recognition and measurement:
  - identify the contract(s) with a customer
  - identify the performance obligations in the contract
  - determine the transaction price
  - allocate the transaction price to the performance obligation of the contract
  - recognise revenue when (or as) the entity satisfies a performance obligation
- The objective of IAS 37 is to ensure that appropriate recognition criteria and measurement bases are applied to provisions, contingent liabilities and contingent assets, as well as ensuring that sufficient information is disclosed in the notes to the financial statements to enable users to understand their natures, timings and amounts.
- International Financial Reporting Standard 16 prescribes accounting policies for the recognition, measurement, presentation and disclosure of leases, providing relevant information which faithfully represents those transactions.

Chapter six
Financial reporting by groups of companies

Contents

1. Introduction
2. Requirement to prepare consolidated financial statements
3. Principles for the consolidation of financial statements
4. Business combinations, fair value measurement and goodwill
5. Consolidated statement of financial position
6. Consolidated statement of profit or loss and OCI
7. Investments in associates and joint ventures
8. The IAS 28 equity method
9. A parent company's separate financial statements
10. Exemptions from preparing consolidated financial statements

parent company
An entity that controls one or more other entities. A company is a parent company of another company, its subsidiary, if it controls it through owning a majority of the voting shares, through having the power to appoint the board, through a control contract, by a power in the subsidiary's governing document or through other mechanisms specified in CA2006 or financial reporting and accounting standards.

subsidiary company
An entity controlled by another entity (parent company).

1 Introduction

A group of companies is an economic entity formed of a set of companies (or other entities) – usually a **parent company** and one or more **subsidiary companies**. There are many reasons for businesses to operate as groups or make an investment in other entities, such as the goodwill associated with names, tax or legal purposes, or the need to operate cross-border.

This chapter outlines the requirements to prepare consolidated financial statements and the basic procedures as follows.

- requirements for consolidation
- concepts and principles
- business combinations and acquisition accounting (IFRS 3)
- fair value measurement in consolidated financial statements (IFRS 13)
- goodwill impairment per IAS 36 (Impairment of Assets)
- preparation of consolidated financial statements
- accounting for associates and joint ventures (IAS 28)

- a parent company's separate financial statements (IAS 27)
- exemptions from preparing consolidated financial statements

The reporting requirements differ depending on the levels of investment and influence that a parent may have on other entities. The most important of these is the requirements around consolidation of a parent with its subsidiaries, which is guided by IFRS 10 (Consolidated Financial Statements) and IFRS 3 (Business Combinations).

There are also other entities where a company may have an investment interest and some influence, albeit less than a parent company would have. This includes jointly controlled investments and **associates** with significant influence. Joint operations and associates are not classified as members of a group. A simple shareholding with no significant influence is accounted for as a simple or trade investment.

> **associate**
> International Accounting Standard 28 defines an associate as 'an entity over which the investor has significant influence and that is neither a subsidiary nor an interest in a joint venture'.

The whole issue of consolidated financial statements, including what should be classed as a subsidiary, was revisited following the global financial crisis. The most complex aspects of this are beyond the scope of this text, but we will cover some of the key issues. Table 6.1 summarises the types of investment covered in this chapter and the relevant financial reporting and accounting standards.

Type of investment	Criteria	Share holding	Accounting method
Subsidiary	Control	>50%	Full consolidation (IFRS 10)
			Acquisition method (IFRS 3)
Associate or joint venture	Significant influence	20%–50%	Equity method (IAS 28)
Joint arrangement	Joint control	Equal	Depends on type (IFRS 11, IAS 28)
Other investments	Other	Other	Disclosures
			Depends on type (IFRS 9, IFRS 5)

Table 6.1 Financial reporting by groups of companies by investment type

2 Requirement to prepare consolidated financial statements

Many larger businesses operate through several entities for reasons relating to tax, liability limitation and regulation. From the point of view of the ultimate shareholders, who hold their investment in a parent entity, it would be inefficient to have to look at financial reports for each individual company in a group that is effectively operating as one business.

Even though tax and dividends are paid by reference to individual company financial statements, consolidated financial statements provide accountability to parent company shareholders for all activity in the group.

Although you need to understand the requirements and the theory of how consolidated financial statements are prepared, you will not be expected to prepare consolidated financial statements in the examination.

2.1 Laws, regulations and IFRS

International Financial Reporting Standard 10 (Consolidated Financial Statements) defines the principle of control. It outlines the requirements for the preparation and presentation of consolidated financial statements, requiring entities to consolidate the entities it controls. If one company controls another, then IFRS 10 requires that a single set of consolidated financial statements be prepared to reflect the financial performance and position of the group as one combined economic entity.

The requirements to prepare group financial statements (or accounts) are also set out by company law. The UK Companies Act 2006 requires all registered companies to prepare individual accounts. Where a business operates through more than one company, CA2006 requires group accounts to be prepared that give a clear picture of the total activities that the company controls. Small groups that can meet two out of three of size criteria relating to turnover, balance sheet total and employees (on a consolidated basis) are exempt from preparing group accounts (see Table 6.2).

Size criteria	Gross	Net
Aggregate turnover	£12.2 million	£10.2 million
Aggregate balance sheet total	£6.1 million	£5.1 million
Aggregate number of employees	50	50

Table 6.2 Small group size criteria for group account exemption

The net figures above are the same as for a small company (see Table 1.1 in Chapter 1). Company law and IFRS also provide exemptions for intermediate parent companies – a parent company that is itself a subsidiary of the ultimate parent company.

3 Principles for the consolidation of financial statements

3.1 Control concept

A group of companies is an economic entity made up of a set of companies where one entity (the parent) has control over another entity (the subsidiary). When assessing whether an investor controls an investee, more than one factor needs to be considered. In accordance with IFRS 10, 'control' of an investor over an investee consists of the following three elements: power, variable returns and the ability to use this power.

- Power over the investee is typically existing rights, normally exercised through most of voting rights (owning more than 50% of the equity shares).
- Exposure or rights to variable returns (a dividend) stems from the investor's involvement with the investee.
- A crucial determinant of the control is the ability to use power over the investee to affect the amount of investor returns.

Controlling a company means having the right to direct the relevant activities that significantly affect the investee's returns, such as having the power to appoint the majority of its directors.

Power over the investee

Rights to variable returns

Ability to use power over the investee

Figure 6.1 Control criteria

Stop and think 6.1

If P plc is the parent company of S Ltd, what are the 'control' criteria (under IFRS 10) that will require P plc to prepare consolidated financial statements?

3.2 Group structure

Control can be exercised in a variety of ways, most commonly by:

- control through direct and indirect voting rights
- via a contract
- through control of the board of directors
- through **de facto control**

In a simple group structure, a parent company has a direct interest in the shares of its subsidiary companies. Figure 6.2 demonstrates how direct or indirect control is achieved by a parent company:

de facto control
Control in fact, or 'de facto control', is a broader concept that focuses on influence rather than legal control. One party can have a substantial holding of voting rights and the remainder, while a majority, are held by a wide range of unconnected parties.

Direct Control

P plc
|
60%
|
S Ltd

Indirect Control

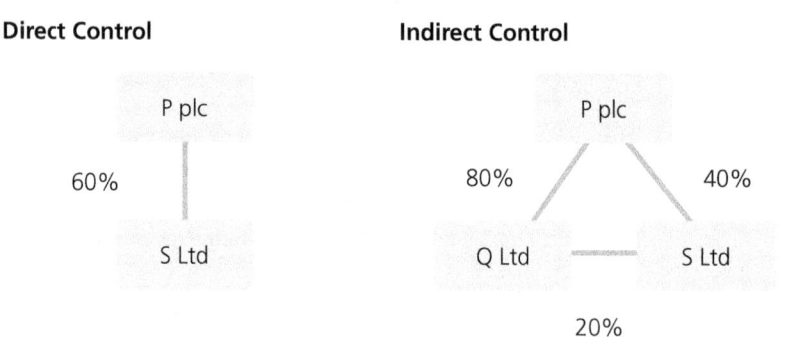

P plc
/   \
80%   40%
/   \
Q Ltd ——— S Ltd
      20%

Figure 6.2 Direct and indirect control

Under the direct control model, the parent company (P plc) has direct control of the subsidiary company (S Ltd) via the 60% majority shareholding (equity shares).

Under the indirect control model, the parent company (P plc) has indirect control over S Ltd through its direct shareholding of 40%, plus the indirect shareholding of its subsidiary Q Ltd (which also has a 20% stake in S Ltd). This gives P plc an effective majority shareholding of 56% (40% + (80% x 20%)) in S Ltd.

Test yourself 6.1

Tea Limited is a new company which formed on 1 January 20X4. At the date of its formation, the issued share capital of Tea Ltd consists of 100,000 equity shares of £1 each with equal voting rights. The directors of Tea Ltd retained 49,000 equity shares and Tea Ltd sold 51,000 equity shares to Ilam Ltd on 1 January 20X4 for the par value of the shares.

Does Ilam Ltd meet the criteria of a parent company?

3.3 The basic method of consolidation

When a parent company controls a subsidiary company, the parent must produce consolidated financial statements which effectively add together the results of the parent and its subsidiary. The consolidated financial statements must present their assets, liabilities, equity, income, expenses and cash flows as those of a single economic entity.

A parent may control its subsidiaries through direct or indirect voting rights. If subsidiaries are controlled by the parent, they must be consolidated irrespective of where subsidiaries are based (for example, they can be registered in another country) or what legal form they take.

The first step is to establish whether there is a parent-subsidiary relationship. It is important to consider all aspects of control, as well the percentage shareholding of the parent and any non-controlling interest (NCI). The NCI is the equity in the subsidiary not attributable, directly or indirectly, to the parent. It is also important to be aware of the date control was achieved or ceased.

When a parent has worked out which of its investments are subsidiaries, the parent's and subsidiaries' financial statements are simply added up line-by-line to create total figures for the group. The consolidated financial statements include everything controlled by the parent on a 100% basis.

There are a number of other factors that need to be considered.

- To avoid double counting, intra-group items including all transactions, balances and unrealised profits and losses arising from intra-group trading must be eliminated. Intra-group items include purchase and sales of inventories and other assets between parent and subsidiary. The consolidated totals should only consist of transactions, balances and profits and losses created through transactions with parties outside the group.
- The parent's investment in the subsidiaries, carried as investments in its own statement of financial position, are also eliminated through the process of consolidation (specifically through the calculation of goodwill).
- The accounting policies of all group companies must be aligned, so that like items are treated in the same way for the group as a whole. Subsidiaries (such as those based overseas) that follow local accounting rules will need to be adjusted just for the consolidation process.
- Subsidiaries should have same reporting date as that of the parent company. Where impracticable, the most recent financial statements of the subsidiary are used with adjustments made for significant transactions between the reporting dates of the subsidiary and the consolidated financial statements. The difference between the date of the subsidiary's financial statements and that of the consolidated financial statements shall be no more than three months. Special accounts will need to be prepared for the consolidation if the difference is more than three months.
- Any share of a subsidiary's results or equity that belong to any NCI (previously known as the minority interest) must be disclosed at the foot of each consolidated financial statement.
- Consolidation will cease from the date the parent loses control of a subsidiary. If the control ceases or the subsidiary is acquired part way through the year, the financial results must be time-apportioned during the consolidation process.

3.4 Content of consolidated financial statements

A group has no separate (legal) existence, except for accounting purposes. A separate set of consolidated financial statements gives a picture of the group's total activities by combining the information contained in the separate financial statements of the parent and its subsidiaries as if they were the financial statements of a single economic entity.

Most parent companies present their individual and consolidated financial statements in a single package. Consolidated financial statements include:

- a consolidated statement of financial position
- a consolidated statement of profit or loss and other comprehensive income
- a consolidated statement of changes in equity
- a consolidated statement of cash flows
- notes to the consolidated financial statements

Depending on local or national regulations, it may not be necessary to publish all of the parent company's financial statements.

4 Business combinations, fair value measurement and goodwill

When an acquirer obtains control of a business (such as through an acquisition or a merger), IFRS 3 requires business combinations to be accounted using the 'acquisition method'. This generally requires assets and liabilities of the investee to be measured at their fair values at the acquisition date.

IFRS 3 requires the reporting entity to:

- identify the acquirer (for example, when an acquirer entity buys another using cash or its own shares as currency);
- determine the acquisition date (the date control passes to the acquirer);
- recognise and measure the identifiable assets acquired, the liabilities assumed and any NCI in the acquiree; and
- recognise and measure goodwill (positive or negative).

There are two main methods for NCI valuation:

- the fair value method
- the proportion of net assets method

Under the fair value method, the fair value of the controlling interest is usually the consideration paid by the parent company for this interest. There is no parallel consideration transferred available to value the NCI. Therefore, the parent has to use other valuation methods, often using market share trading prices in the weeks before and after the purchase to evidence a valuation.

Under the proportion of net assets method, used in the remainder of this chapter, the value of the controlling interest (and the NCI) is valued as the proportion of equity acquired (or retained), multiplied by the net assets of the acquired company at the date of the purchase. This provides a valuation methodology for the controlling interest and the NCI. It is based directly on available accounting information and is therefore the most commonly used method.

4.1 Goodwill

The price paid for a company at acquisition (to gain control) will normally exceed the fair market value of its net assets or equity. The difference is purchased goodwill. This represents the additional amount paid for factors such as the reputation of the business, the experience of employees, the customer base and the brand of the business.

Purchased goodwill is the difference between the value of an acquired entity (including any NCI) and the net assets of that entity's identifiable assets and liabilities

Negative goodwill

Goodwill can be negative when the aggregate of the fair values of the separable net assets acquired may exceed what the parent company paid for them. IFRS 3 refers to it as a 'gain on a bargain purchase'.

For negative goodwill, an entity should reassess by measuring both the cost of the combination and the acquiree's identifiable net assets to identify any errors. Any excess remaining after such reassessment should be recognised (credited) immediately in the statement of profit or loss and OCI.

4.2 Impairment of goodwill

Goodwill should be capitalised in the consolidated statement of financial position and reviewed for impairment every year as per IAS 36 (Impairment of Assets). Although IAS 36 requires an impairment review for all assets where there is an indication of impairment, goodwill (and certain intangible assets) is tested for impairment annually even if there is no impairment indicator.

To test for impairment, IAS 36 requires goodwill to be allocated to a cash-generating unit (CGU) or a group of CGUs. A CGU is the smallest identifiable group of assets that benefits from the business combination and generates cash inflows independently from other assets. However, impairment is performed at a level no larger than an operating segment as defined in IFRS 8 (Operating Segments) (covered in Chapter 4).

The asset is impaired when an asset's carrying value exceeds its recoverable amount (the higher of fair value less costs of disposal and value in use). The concepts of value in use and the principles of impairment were discussed in section 4.5 of Chapter 5, while fair value is discussed in the next section.

Some triggering events that may cause the fair market value of a goodwill asset to drop below its carrying amount (impairment indicators) are:

- adverse economic conditions
- increased competition
- legal implications
- loss of key personnel
- declining revenue
- market value

An impairment is recognised as loss in the statement of profit or loss and OCI and as a reduction in the carrying amount of goodwill in statement of financial position.

For example, Nayu Ltd acquires a 100% equity shareholding In Nehi Ltd for £50 million, valuing its net assets at £40 million and recognising goodwill of £10 million. As per the requirement of IAS 36, Nayu Ltd tests its net assets for impairment after a year. Due to adverse market conditions and fierce competition from its rival, Nehi Ltd's revenue has been declining significantly. As a result, the current value of Nehi Ltd's net assets has decreased or been impaired by £3 million, thus dropping the value of the asset of goodwill to £7 million. The impact on the consolidated financial statements is recorded as:

- **Consolidated statement of financial position:** goodwill reduces from £10 million to £7 million.
- **Consolidated statement of profit or loss and OCI:** an impairment charge of £3 million is recorded as a loss. The impairment review is based on the requirement of IAS 36 that seeks to ensure that an entity's assets are not carried at more than their recoverable amount (the higher of fair value less costs of disposal and value in use).

4.3 Fair value measurement in consolidated financial statements

IFRS 13 defines fair value as 'the price that would be received to sell an asset or paid to transfer a liability in an orderly transaction between market participants at the measurement date'. The fair value method is used when calculating goodwill (and NCIs).

Goodwill is the difference between:

- the amount paid (measured at fair value) to acquire a shareholding and the fair value of any NCI; and
- the fair value of the net assets acquired.

The fair value of the identifiable assets and liabilities acquired may not reflect their value reported in the subsidiary's statement of financial position, which is often at their historical cost (less accumulated depreciation for non-current assets).

Consolidated financial statements are prepared from the perspective of the group and must reflect their cost to the group (to the parent), not the original cost to the subsidiary. The carrying amounts of the subsidiary's assets and liabilities are largely irrelevant in the consolidated financial statements. The cost to the group is the fair value of the acquired assets and liabilities at the date of acquisition. Fair values are therefore used to calculate the value of goodwill.

4.4 Purchase consideration

To ensure that an accurate figure is calculated for goodwill, the consideration paid for a subsidiary must also be measured at fair value (valued in today's monetary terms). Not all consideration is for cash or due immediately on acquisition. Any non-cash elements (such as share exchanges) must be valued at fair value. In general, the consideration given by the parent entity can be split into four categories:

- cash
- shares in the parent company
- deferred consideration
- contingent consideration

Cash is the most straightforward form of consideration. In large companies, shares are often purchased for cash plus deferred payments (often contingent upon achieving certain performance targets). For any deferred payments, the present value of the amount payable should be recorded as part of the consideration transferred at the date of acquisition. Where the part of the purchase consideration is settled in shares, the consideration is valued at the market value of the parent entity's shares at the date of acquisition. Direct costs of the acquisition, such as legal and other consultancy fees, are expensed and not treated as part of the purchase consideration.

Deferred consideration is the amount payable at a future date by an acquirer to the acquiree in a business combination after a pre-defined time period, often linked to post-acquisition performance targets. It tends to be driven primarily by tax and accounting considerations. The present value of the amount payable is recorded as the part of the consideration at the date of acquisition. Interest normally accrues on the deferred consideration.

Contingent consideration is an uncertain amount, that is payable at a future date by an acquirer to the acquiree in a business combination, which is linked to a specified future event or condition met within a pre-defined time period, such as financial performance of the acquiree.

For example, P plc acquired a 100% equity shareholding in S Ltd, with a fixed portion of the consideration of £1 million and a promise to pay £200,000 if S Ltd meets both the revenue and the profit targets specified for the next two years. The probability of meeting the targets is 50%.

Total consideration at the acquisition date is therefore calculated as:

Fixed portion of £1 million + expected value of £100,000 (£200,000 × 50%)

The contingent consideration payable at the end of the second year must be discounted back and recognised at its present value. The discounting technique for future cash flows will be discussed in Chapters 13 and 14.

The contingent consideration is recognised as a liability and periodically adjusted to its updated fair value. The associated gain or loss is recognised in the statement of profit or loss and OCI.

Under IFRS 3, consideration must be included on the acquisition date at its fair value as either an equity or a liability. It is recorded as an equity when it is expected to be settled in a fixed number of shares. A contingent consideration recognised as equity is not adjusted for changes in fair value, unlike consideration recognised as a liability.

Future events may also entitle the acquirer to negative contingent consideration when some of the previously paid consideration is returned to the acquirer.

deferred consideration
Amount payable at a future date by an acquirer to the acquiree in a business combination after a predefined time period, often linked to performance targets post acquisition.

contingent consideration
An uncertain amount that is payable at a future date by an acquirer to the acquiree in a business combination which is linked to a specified future event or condition met within a pre-defined time period, such as financial performance of the acquiree.

4.5 Net assets

Net assets are usually calculated by totalling the assets reported and deducting reported liabilities. The fair value of all assets and liabilities must be determined to reflect their market value. The carrying amount of assets is not always the same as their current market values, particularly in the case of plant, property and equipment. For example, property often appreciates in value, whereas it may be stated at historic depreciated cost in some companies.

Test yourself 6.2

Why are the subsidiary's identifiable assets and liabilities included at their fair values in the consolidated financial statements?

Worked example 6.1

Ealing plc acquired 100% of the equity shares in Woolwich plc on 31 December 20X1, when the draft statements of financial position of each company were as follows.

Ealing plc – Statement of financial position as at 31 December 20X1

	£m
Assets	
Non-current asset	
Investment in 50 million shares of Woolwich at cost	120
Current assets	60
Total assets	180
Equity and liabilities	
Equity shares	112
Retained earnings	68
Total equity and liabilities	180

Woolwich plc – statement of financial position as at 31 December 20X1

	£m
Current assets	90
Equity	
50 million equity shares of £1 each	50
Retained earnings	40
Total equity and liabilities	90

1. Calculate the goodwill that Ealing will have to report on the acquisition of 100% of the equity shares of Woolwich with a cash payment of £120 million, as set out in the worked example above.

Now consider the following variations on the worked example above. In each of the following scenarios, calculate the goodwill that Ealing will have to report on the acquisition of shares of Woolwich if:

2. Ealing acquired less than 100% of the shares of Woolwich, with Ealing paying £105 million for 35 million shares.
3. Ealing acquired 35 million shares, paying £55m at the date of purchase with £50 million of consideration deferred for 12 months. Ealing has a cost of capital of 10%.
4. Ealing acquired 35 million shares, paid by giving shareholders in Woolwich one share in Ealing for each two shares they held in Woolwich. Ealing shares are currently worth £5 per share.
5. Ealing acquired 35 million shares, paying £105 million, knowing that the current assets of Woolwich included freehold land with a fair value of £50 million, but which had a net realisable value of £70 million.

Solutions

1			£m
Consideration		100%	120
Net assets acquired as represented by:			
Equity share capital		50	
Retained earnings at acquisition		40	
			(90)
Goodwill			30

2		£
Consideration transferred		105
(for 70% or 35 million shares in Woolwich)		
NCI (90 million at 30%)		27
Net assets of subsidiary at acquisition (90 million)		(90)
Goodwill		42

See how the calculation considers all of the net assets of Woolwich, but effectively removes 30% of these as a NCI. This is because Ealing has only purchased 70% of the shares.

3

	£m
Consideration transferred	55
(for 70% or 35 million shares in Woolwich)	
Deferred consideration	45.5
(50 million ÷ 1.10) *cost of capital*	
NCI (90 million at 30%)	27
Net assets of subsidiary at acquisition (90 million)	(90)
Goodwill	37.5

The consideration is paid 12 months later, so it is discounted by Ealing's cost of capital, a factor which takes account of risk, inflation and investment potential. This is because £50 million in one year is worth less than £50 million today. There is more information on the cost of capital and discounting in Parts three and four.

4

	£m
Fair value of shares in Ealing	87.5
(70% or 35 million shares in Woolwich equates to 17.5 million shares in Ealing at £5 each)	
NCI (90 million at 30%)	27
Net assets of subsidiary at acquisition (90 million)	(90)
Goodwill	24.5

5

	£
Consideration transferred	105
(for 70% or 35 million shares in Woolwich)	
NCI ($90 million + $20 million fair value adjustment at 30%)	33
Net assets of subsidiary at acquisition ($90 million + $20 million fair value adjustment)	(110)
Goodwill	28

Test yourself 6.3

1. Sandra plc purchased 100% of the equity shares of Hayden plc for consideration of £500,000 cash and 100,000 shares in Sandra plc. The market value of Sandra plc's equity shares was £5 per share on the date of acquisition. The total fair value of Hayden plc's assets

and liabilities at the date of acquisition was £700,000. Calculate the goodwill that Sandra plc will include in its consolidated financial statements at the time of acquisition.

2. Explain why it is necessary to use the fair values of a subsidiary's identifiable assets and liabilities when preparing consolidated financial statements.

5 Consolidated statement of financial position

The consolidated statement of financial position shows all of the assets and liabilities under the control of the parent entity.

Once a parent-subsidiary relationship is established, along with the percentage shareholding of the parent and any NCI, the assets and liabilities of the parent and the subsidiary are added together on a line-by-line basis with the following adjustments.

5.1 Investment

The investment in the subsidiary shown in the parent's own statement of financial position is replaced by a goodwill figure. Only the share capital and share premium balances related to the parent are used in the consolidated statement of financial position. The total of share capital and share premium from a subsidiary's statement of financial position will remain unchanged at both the date of acquisition and any subsequent reporting date.

5.2 Intra-group items

Intra-group items (sales, purchases, unrealised profit and balances) are eliminated on consolidation to avoid double counting.

5.3 Profits

The group share of the subsidiary's profit earned after acquisition is calculated and added to overall group retained earnings.

Pre-acquisition profits are the retained earnings of the subsidiary which exist at the date when it is acquired. The subsidiary's pre-acquisition profits are excluded from group retained earnings as they belong to the previous shareholders, were earned under their ownership and are represented by part of the net assets used in the goodwill calculation.

Post-acquisition profits are profits recognised in retained earnings by the subsidiary at the year end but earned under the ownership of the new parent. Hence, the parent's percentage ownership is recognised in group retained earnings (see Table 6.3)

Group retained earnings	
	£
Parent's retained earnings (100%)	X
Parent's percentage share of subsidiary's post-acquisition retained earnings	X
Balance of consolidated (group) retained earnings at the consolidation date	X

Table 6.3 Group retained earnings

5.4 Non-controlling interest

Where the parent owns less than 100% of the equity share capital of a subsidiary, the amount attributable to NCI is calculated and shown separately on the face of the consolidated statement of financial position (see Figure 6.3)

Non-controlling interest:	
	£
NCI's percentage share of subsidiary's post-acquisition retained earnings	X
Retained earnings prior to the acquisition are not consolidated.	

Figure 6.3 Non-controlling interests

Figure 6.4 summarises the steps taken for preparing the consolidated statement of financial position (SoFP)

5.5 Dividends paid by a subsidiary

The retained earnings are consolidated after accounting for dividends paid by a subsidiary. The dividend paid to the parent company is cancelled on consolidation (it has become an intra-group transaction).

Test yourself 6.4

1. Why are pre-acquisition profits of a subsidiary not included in the consolidated financial statements?
2. Gorkha plc acquired Ye Ltd on 1 January 20X0. Their retained earnings at 1 January 20X0 amounted to £500,000 and £800,000 respectively. Explain how the retained earnings of Ye Ltd at 1 January 20X1 would be treated in the consolidated financial statements.

```
Parent          Subsidiary
SoFP            SoFP
         ↓
Combine line-by-line
         ↓
Eliminate investment in the subsidiaries.
Calculate and include goodwill.
         ↓
Eliminate intra-group items (sales, purchases,
unrealised profit and balances)
         ↓
Eliminate share capital and share premium balances of
subsidiaries.
Group Share Capital = Parent only
         ↓
Eliminate pre-acquisition profit of subsidiaries. Group
retained earnings = Parent's retained earnings (100%)
+ Parent's % of Subsidiary's post-acquisition earnings
(after consolidation adjustments)
         ↓
Disclose NCI at the foot of the SoFP
NCI = FV of NCI at acquisition + NCI share of post
acquisition earnings/reserve
         ↓
Consolidated
SoFP
```

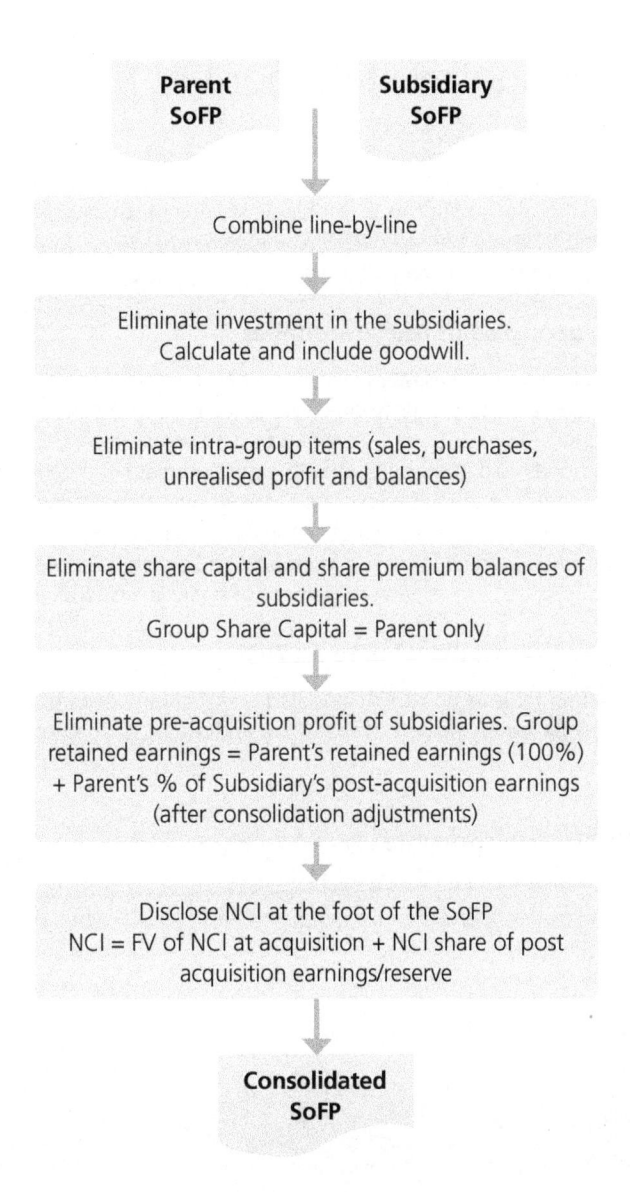

Figure 6.4 Steps for the consolidated statement of financial position (SoFP)

3. What are non-controlling interests? How are they accounted for in consolidated financial statements?

4. How is an investment of the parent in a subsidiary accounted for in the parent's separate financial statements? How is it accounted for in the consolidated financial statements?

6 Consolidated statement of profit or loss and OCI

The consolidated statement of profit or loss and OCI presents the financial performance of group companies in one single statement. Consolidation involves adding together the revenues (income) and expenses of the parent and the subsidiary with the following adjustments.

6.1 Intra-group sales and purchases

Intra-group sales and purchases are eliminated. The consolidated figures should represent sales to and purchases from, customers and suppliers outside the group. Any unrealised profits on intra-group trading should be excluded. This occurs when goods sold at a profit within the group remain in the inventory at the reporting date. The unrealised profit on unsold inventories of the purchasing company is therefore calculated to reduce the consolidated gross profit. The unrealised profit from the intra-group sales will also be eliminated against the inventory figure in the consolidated statement of financial position.

6.2 Net profits attributable to an NCI

Net profits attributable to an NCI is calculated and split between amounts attributable to the equity holders of the group and the NCIs. This is calculated as:

	£
NCI percentage share × subsidiary's profit for the period	X
Less:	
NCI percentage share × provision for unrealised profit (PURP) when the subsidiary is the seller	(X)
	–
Profit attributable to the NCI	X

A similar split is required for total comprehensive income (if there is any OCI for the subsidiary).

Test yourself 6.5

During the year ended 31 December 20X1, the parent company (P plc) sells goods to its subsidiary (S Ltd) at cost plus a mark-up of 15%. Explain the accounting treatment of the intra-group trading and the profit arising from the sales.

7 Investments in associates and joint ventures

As well as controlling other entities, businesses often conduct part of their activities through investments in associates and joint ventures in which they have acquired an equity interest of less than 50%. This avoids consolidation requirements.

The objective of IAS 28 is to prescribe the accounting for investments in associates. It also sets out the requirements for the application of the equity method when accounting for investments in associates and **joint ventures**.

joint ventures
A business arrangement whereby the parties that have joint control of the arrangement agree to pool their resources for the purpose of accomplishing a specific task.

7.1 Associates

An entity over which the investor has significant influence and which is neither a subsidiary nor an interest in a joint venture, is classed as a associate and is dealt with in IAS 28 (Investments in Associates and Joint Ventures).

The key criterion here is 'significant influence' which is defined as the 'power to participate in the financial and operating policy decisions of the investee, but not to control or have joint control over those policies'. Significant influence is assumed with a shareholding of 20% to 50%. In IAS 28, significant influence is evidenced in one or more of the following ways:

- representation on the board of directors (or equivalent) of the investee
- participation in the policy-making process
- material transactions between investor and investee
- interchange of management personnel
- provision of essential technical information

7.2 Joint ventures

Businesses often go into partnership with other businesses on profit-raising ventures under joint ventures, which are dealt with in IFRS 11 (Joint Arrangements). A joint venture is a business arrangement whereby the parties that have joint control of the arrangement agree to pool their resources and expertise to achieve a particular goal. They have joint rights to the assets and obligations for the liabilities relating to the arrangement. The risks and rewards of the enterprise are also shared.

Reasons behind the formation of a joint venture often include:

- business expansion
- development of new products
- moving into new markets, such as those overseas

The parties to a joint venture must recognise their interest in a joint venture as an investment and account for it using the equity method in accordance with IAS 28.

8 The IAS 28 equity method

International Accounting Standard 28 sets out the requirements for the application of the equity method when accounting for investments in associates and joint ventures.

The equity method initially recognises the investment in an associate or a joint venture in the investor's statement of financial position at cost. It adjusts the carrying amount thereafter with the change in the investor's share of the post-acquisition profit (or loss) of the investee.

8.1 Basic principles

The equity method of accounting is similar to the IFRS consolidation procedures in many ways, including the concepts underlying the procedures used in accounting for the acquisition of a subsidiary.

The equity method is sometimes called a 'one-line consolidation'. International Accounting Standard 28 requires the use of the equity method of accounting for investments in associates and joint ventures (the investee), whereby the investment is initially recorded at cost and adjusted thereafter for the post-acquisition change in the investor's share of the profit (or loss) of the investee. The value of the investment is cost plus the group's share of the investee's post-acquisition profits or losses.

Distributions received from an investee reduce the carrying amount of the investment, as these are cash inflows. Changes in the investee's OCI that have not been included in profit or loss, such as a revaluation, may also require adjustments to the carrying amount of the investment.

The value of the investor's share of the investee's profit or loss for the period is recognised in the investor's profit or loss. However, dividends are excluded from the statement of profit or loss and OCI as this would be double counting.

The carrying amount of the investment in an associate or joint venture is calculated as follows:

	£
Cost of investment	X
Group percentage share of post-acquisition profits or losses and other comprehensive income (since acquisition)	X
Less: impairment losses	(X)
Less: Group percentage share of unrealised profits (when the investor is the seller)	(X)
	X

As associates and joint ventures are not controlled, their financial statements may be prepared to a different date to that of the investor. IAS 28 allows some latitude for differences in year ends, but only up to a three-month difference. If the year-end dates are further apart than three months, special accounts would be required from the associate or joint venture.

Any transactions such as sales or purchases between group companies and the associate or joint ventures are not normally eliminated: they will remain part of the consolidated figures in the consolidated statement of profit or loss and OCI. It is normal practice to adjust for the group share of any unrealised profit in inventory.

As per IAS 28, the equity method is discontinued when significant influence or joint control is lost or if the investor's interest changes to achieve control. At this point, the associate or joint venture will become a subsidiary.

A loss-making associate or joint venture will have a negative impact in the investor's statement of financial position. Any additional losses after the investor's interest is reduced to zero are provided for and a liability is recognised, only to the extent that the entity has incurred legal or constructive obligations or made payments on behalf of the associate or joint venture. If the associate or joint venture subsequently reports profits, the investor will resume recognising its share of those profits only after its share of the profits equals the share of losses not recognised.

Stop and think 6.2

Think of a situation when a business may prefer the equity method over the acquisition method for accounting for its investments and vice versa.

Test yourself 6.6

How does the difference between the equity method and the full consolidation method affect the decisions of investing entities if the investee were a highly geared entity?

9 A parent company's separate financial statements

A parent company should produce its own single company financial statements as per IAS 27 requirements. Where an entity invests in a 'simple' or 'trade' investment, with neither control nor significant influence, it is carried as a non-current asset and any dividends received are recognised in the statement of profit or loss and OCI.

Investments in subsidiaries, associates and jointly controlled entities are accounted for either:

- at cost;
- In accordance with IFRS 9 (Financial Instruments); or
- using the equity method for investments in associates and joint ventures.

Where subsidiaries are classified as held for sale in accordance with IFRS 5, they should be accounted for in accordance with IFRS 5 (Non-Current Assets Held for Sale and Discontinued Operations) (see section 8.5 of Chapter 3 on page 71).

When separate financial statements are prepared in addition to consolidated financial statements, they must disclose:

- the fact that the statements are separate financial statements and the reasons why they have been prepared if not required by law; and
- information about investments and the method used to account for them.

10 Exemptions from preparing consolidated financial statements

A parent is exempted from presenting consolidated financial statements if all the following apply:

- when the parent is itself a wholly owned subsidiary or a partially owned subsidiary and the NCIs do not object;
- when its **securities** are not publicly traded nor in the process of trading in public securities markets; and
- when its ultimate or intermediate parent publishes IFRS-compliant financial statements.

securities
Tradable financial assets traded on a secondary market. Examples include debt securities (bank notes, bonds and debentures) equity securities (common stocks) and derivatives (forwards, futures, options and swaps).

Where a parent chooses to take advantage of the exemptions from preparing consolidated financial statements, it must comply with the IAS 27 requirements on separate financial statements by disclosing:

- the fact that the exemption from consolidation has been used, the name and country of incorporation of the entity whose consolidated financial statements that comply with IFRS have been published and the address where those are obtainable;
- a list of significant investments in subsidiaries, jointly controlled entities and associates, including the name, country of incorporation, proportion of ownership interest and, if different, proportion of voting power held; and
- the method used to account for its investments.

10.1 Exclusion of a subsidiary from consolidation

The rules on exclusion of subsidiaries from consolidation are strict because entities may use them to manipulate their results. For example, a subsidiary with a large amount of debt increases the gearing of the group as a whole.

Excluding the debts of a subsidiary would take that debt out of the consolidated statement of financial position.

Two exclusions originally allowed by IAS 27 (where control is intended to be temporary or where the subsidiary operates under severe long-term restrictions) have been removed. Instead, subsidiaries held for sale are accounted for in accordance with IFRS 5 (Non-Current Assets Held for Sale and Discontinued Operations) and the control must actually be lost for exclusion to occur.

International Financial Reporting Standard 10 also rejects the argument for exclusion on the grounds of dissimilar activities. More relevant information must be provided about such subsidiaries by consolidating their results and providing additional information about the different business activities of the subsidiary.

Test yourself 6.7

1. **When is a parent exempted from preparing consolidated financial statements?**
2. **When does IFRS allow subsidiary undertakings to be excluded from consolidation? Can they be excluded on the grounds of dissimilar activities?**

Chapter summary

- Many large businesses increasingly operate through a group structure. The reporting requirements depend on different levels of investment and influence that a parent company may have on other entities.
- International Financial Reporting Standard 10 (Consolidated Financial Statements) outlines the requirements for a parent company to present consolidated financial statements when it owns the majority or all of the voting shares in the other companies, called subsidiaries. Under IFRS 10, control of an investor over an investee consists of the following three basic elements: power, variable returns and the ability to use this power.
- When an acquirer obtains control of a business (such as through an acquisition or a merger), IFRS 3 requires business combinations to be accounted using the 'acquisition method'. This generally requires assets and liabilities of the investee to be measured at their fair values at the acquisition date.
- International Financial Reporting Standard 10 lays out the basic procedures for preparing consolidated financial statements. Consolidated financial statements are prepared by adding together the results of the parent and its subsidiary(ies) and presenting their assets, liabilities, equity, income, expenses and cash flows as those of a single economic entity. When a parent has worked out which of its investments are subsidiaries, the parent and subsidiary financial statements are simply added up line-by-line,

followed by adjustments required to create total figures for the group. The consolidation adjustments include:
- elimination of intra-group transactions and balances;
- elimination of unrealised profit from intra-group trading;
- alignment of accounting policies;
- recognition of goodwill which is the excess of the amount transferred plus the amount of NCIs over the fair value of the net assets of the subsidiary; and
- distinguishing and presenting any non-controlling interests (NCIs) at the foot of each consolidated financial statement.

◆ Goodwill should be capitalised in the consolidated statement of financial position and reviewed for impairment every year as per IAS 36 (Impairment of Assets).

◆ As well as controlling other entities, businesses often conduct part of their activities through investments in associates and joint ventures in which they have acquired an equity interest of less than 50% and which, consequently, escapes consolidation requirements. A simple holding with no significant influence is accounted as a simple or trade investment.

◆ Businesses often go into partnership with other businesses on profit-raising ventures under joint ventures. These are dealt with in IFRS 11 (Joint Arrangements).

◆ International Accounting Standard 28 (Investments in Associates and Joint Ventures) sets out the requirements for the application of the equity method when accounting for investments in associates and joint ventures. The equity method initially recognises the investment in an associate or a joint venture in the investor's statement of financial position at cost. It subsequently adjusts the carrying amount with the change in the investor's share of the post-acquisition profit or loss of the investee.

◆ The rules on exclusion of subsidiaries from consolidation are strict because entities could use them to manipulate their results. Where a parent chooses to take advantage of the exemptions from preparing consolidated financial statements, it must comply with the IAS 27 requirements on separate financial statements.

Chapter seven
Analysis of published financial statements

Contents

1. Introduction
2. The need for financial analysis
3. Fundamental analysis
4. Economic analysis
5. Industry analysis
6. Company analysis
7. Trend analysis
8. Ratio analysis
9. Profitability ratios
10. Limitations of ratio analysis
11. Accounting irregularities and creative accounting

1 Introduction

Financial statements are prepared and presented in accordance with GAAP to give readers an overview of the financial results and condition of a company. However, it is the analysis of financial statements that gives a true representation of what is going on inside the company. It is necessary to analyse the numbers in the statements to get a true and clear picture of the company. The financial statements are analysed with the help of different tools such as comparative statements, common size statements, ratio analysis, trend analysis and cash flow analysis.

Stakeholders – including current and potential investors, creditors, customers, employees, government, bankers and stock exchanges – all have an interest in the financial performance (and other aspects) of a company. For example, financiers and credit providers are concerned about the financial performance and creditworthiness of a company, especially before providing any loans or securities. Stakeholders will have enhanced confidence in a company if it has strong ratios compared to the market. Valuation of a company is based on its financial performance and earnings ratios.

Changes in company law and amendments to IFRS have emphasised presenting more detailed financial statements to provide more transparency and detailed information about a company to stakeholders. This chapter will focus on the analysis of financial statements and the methods used.

The analysis and interpretation of financial statements assesses the financial strengths and weaknesses of the company. The key measures used are as follows.

Fundamental analysis
- economic analysis
- industry analysis
- company analysis

Trend analysis
- vertical analysis
- trend or horizontal analysis

Ratio analysis
- profitability
- efficiency
- liquidity
- gearing
- activity
- investment performance

The chapter will conclude by analysing the impact of accounting ratios, accounting irregularities and earnings management (creative accounting).

2 The need for financial analysis

Published financial statements are prepared for decision-making purposes. Good decision making is driven by effective analysis and interpretation of financial statements (also referred to as financial analysis). Analysis provides meaningful conclusions by drawing a meaningful relationship between the various items of the two financial statements:

- the statement of profit or loss and OCI (or income statement)
- the statement of financial position (or balance sheet)

These provide the indicators of profitability and financial soundness of a company (business entity) for a given period.

2.1 Interested parties and stewardship of managers

Different parties are interested in financial statements and their analysis for various reasons. As discussed in Chapter 2, financial statements provide useful financial information to external and internal users in making financial decisions.

For example, investors want to know the earning capacity of the company, the wellbeing of the company and its future prospects. Understanding the company's financial position and recent performance helps management direct the company's operations and future strategy.

Stewardship refers to the traditional approach of accounting, under which the owners of a company (the shareholders) entrust the management to manage the company on their behalf. Shareholders entrust the board of directors with the responsibility for managing the resources entrusted to them by giving it direction and providing both control and strategy. The board employs managers to implement their strategic vision and to help ensure the investments of owners are maximised. Owners put mechanisms in place to monitor managerial behaviour. For example, the UK Corporate Governance Code (2018) provides guidelines that require directors to conduct business with integrity, responsibility and accountability. An obligation of stewards or the directors is to provide relevant and reliable financial information, including analysis of financial statements using various techniques.

2.2 Key financial indicators

The purpose of financial analysis is to assess the financial strength and weakness of a company by assessing its efficiency and performance. The key measures in determining the financial strength of a company are as listed below.

- **Profitability**: the main objective of a company and its management (the agent) is to earn a satisfactory return on the funds invested by the investors or shareholders (the principal). Financial analysis ascertains whether adequate profits are being earned on the capital invested. It is also useful to understand the earning capacity of a company, its wellbeing and its prospects, including the capacity to pay the interest and dividends.
- **Trend of achievements:** analysis can be done through the comparison of financial statements with previous years – especially in relation to trends regarding various expenses, sales/revenue, gross profits and operating profit. Users can compare the value of assets and liabilities and forecast the future prospects of a company.
- **Growth potential of a company:** financial analysis indicates the growth potential of a company.
- **Comparative position in relation to similar companies or businesses**: financial analysis help the management to study the competitive position of their company in respect of sales/revenue, expenses, profitability and capital utilisation.
- **Overall financial strength and solvency of a company:** analysis helps users make decisions by determining whether funds required for the purchase of new equipment and other assets are provided from internal sources or received from external sources and whether the company has sufficient funds to meet its short-term and long-term liabilities.

Test yourself 7.1

1. What is meant by stewardship accounting?
2. Who are the interested parties and how do they benefit from the analysis of financial statements?

3 Fundamental analysis

Fundamental analysis is a systematic approach to evaluating company performance based on the analysis of its published financial statements. It is an in-depth study of the underlying forces that drive a company's performance, which considers the overall state of the economy in which the company operates, the industry which it belongs to and other factors, including:

- interest rates
- production
- earnings
- employment
- gross domestic product (GDP)
- housing
- manufacturing
- management

The combination of qualitative and quantitative data depicts a holistic picture of the company. The end goal of this analysis is to generate insights and forecasts about the company's future performance. There are several other objectives, including:

- valuing the company
- evaluating the performance of company management and auditing business decisions
- determining the company's intrinsic value and its growth prospects
- benchmarking the performance of the company against its industry and the wider economy

Fundamental analysis includes:

- economic analysis
- industry analysis
- company analysis

Economic Analysis

Analysis of:
- GDP
- interest rates
- employment
- foreign exchange
- manufacturing

Industry Analysis

Analysis of:
- competitors
- state of industry
- Porter's five forces for the industry

Company Analysis

Analysis of:
- the business's assets
- liabilities
- earnings

Figure 7.1 Fundamental analysis

4 Economic analysis

The performance of the company mirrors the performance of the economy in which it operates. Different companies and industries perform differently during the various stages of an economic cycle.

The economic or business cycle is the periodic up-and-down movement in economic activity, measured by fluctuations in the growth of real GDP and other macroeconomic variables such as employment, interest rates and consumer spending. According to the UK's National Bureau of Economic Research (NBER), there are four stages of economic cycle: recovery (expansion), boom (peak), recession (contraction) and depression (trough). Economists note, however, that complete business cycles vary in length.

Analysts usually study the relevant variables of the economy which are impacting the company and its industry. Table 7.1 examines how each variable behaves across economic cycles.

	Recovery (expansion)	Boom (peak)	Recession (contraction)	Depression (trough)
Meaning	After reaching bottom, the slow growth starts to kick in under the expansion phase. This is characterised by gradual recovery, with increasing employment, economic growth and upward	Post-recovery, the growth in business activity reaches a peak (the highest point of the business cycle). In this phase, the real national output is rising at a faster rate than the average growth rate and the economy is producing at maximum allowable output.	After reaching a peak, business activity remains stagnant with a significant decline in economic activity spread across the economy, lasting more than a few months. It is normally	In this phase, business activity is declining with output reaching its lowest point. The economy has hit bottom, from which the next phase of expansion and positive sentiments starts to kick in.

	Recovery (expansion)	**Boom (peak)**	**Recession (contraction)**	**Depression (trough)**
Meaning (continued)	pressure on prices, wages, profits, demand and supply of products.		visible in real GDP, real income, employment, industrial production and retail sales.	Essentially, this phase is a combination of negative and positive sentiments.
Gross Domestic Product (GDP)	The growth in GDP starts to pick up.	GDP rises in this phase due to an increase in economic activity. Government tax revenues rise as spending increases.	A continuous fall in GDP is noted for two or more consecutive quarters. The government spends more on social benefits in order to revive the economy.	Real GDP decreases by more than 10% from its peak.
Consumer and business sentiments	Consumer sentiments are positive and the consumption is rising after a trough.	The growth in consumption reaches a peak, taking cues from surge in real incomes. Inflationary pressures on prices are evident.	Consumption declines with low business confidence. The savings rate goes up in the expectation of bottom, resulting in little to no investment.	Consumer confidence is at its worst and industrial production is at an all-time low in this phase.
Employment rate	Unemployment levels of less than 5% are consistent with full employment and are indicative of economic expansion.	Employment is at or above full employment. Lots of jobs are created, backed by more investment in business activity. Following a peak, the economy typically enters into a correction which is characterised by a contraction where growth slows, employment declines (unemployment increases) and pricing pressures subside.	Employment declines and the unemployment rate increases as little/no investment is made in business.	The unemployment rate reaches peak in this phase.

	Recovery (expansion)	Boom (peak)	Recession (contraction)	Depression (trough)
Interest rates	Interest rates are at the bottom with the yield curve getting steeper.	Interest rates rise rapidly with a flattening yield curve.	Interest rates are at their peak and the yield curve is flat or even inverted.	Interest rates are falling and the yield curve is normal.

Table 7.1 Economic cycles (NBER) and their impact

5 Industry analysis

Companies operate within an industrial context. It is important to conduct industry research while assessing company performance and formulating strategic plans for future growth. Industry analysis refers to an evaluation of the relative strengths and weakness of particular industries. It facilitates a company's understanding of its position relative to other companies that produce similar products or services.

An industry goes through stages during the course of its lifecycle. Each stage offers a different set of growth prospects and challenges. According to Julius Grodinsky's industry life cycle theory, the life of an industry can be segregated into four stages.

- **Pioneer stage:** this is the first stage of a new industry where products and technology are newly introduced and have not reached a state of perfection – such as new mobile applications and the software industry. There is an opportunity for rapid growth and profit – and high risk.
- **Expansion stage:** this is the second stage of expansion of those that survived the pioneering stage. Companies grow larger and are quite attractive for investment purposes.
- **Stagnation stage:** growth stabilises and sales grow at a slower rate than that experienced by competitive industries or by the overall economy.
- **Decay stage:** the industry becomes obsolete and ceases to exist with the arrival of new products and new technologies (for example, the black-and-white television industry).

In general, industry analysis includes an assessment of the strengths, weakness, opportunities and threats (SWOT analysis) for the industry. It requires businesses to take an objective view of the underlying forces, attractiveness and success factors that determine the structure of the industry. It consists of three aspects.

5.1 Underlying forces that drive the industry

In 1980, Michael Porter proposed a standard approach to industry analysis, known as 'Porter's five forces'. These help to identify the weaknesses and strength of the industry. According to Porter, the following five forces collectively determine the long-term profit potential of the industry.

- **Barriers to entry for new players to enter the market**: this refers to how difficult or easy it is for a new player to enter the industry. In an industry with little-to-no barrier to entry, new players have a competitive advantage while existing suppliers constantly face a new set of competitors. Barriers to entry include heavy capital requirement, significant differentiation via technology, regulation challenges and poor distribution channels.
- **Bargaining power of customers:** a strong buyer can make an industry more competitive and can push existing businesses to lower their or offer additional services in comparison to its competitors. Customers now have more bargaining power as they can switch between suppliers.
- **Bargaining power of suppliers:** suppliers in a strong bargaining position can choose to reduce the quantity of the product available. If there are few close substitutes, buyers can switch as and when the switching cost to new suppliers is too high. The suppliers hold the power to influence the customers and establish competitive advantage. Suppliers are also in a strong position if the product or service they supply is an essential component of the end product.
- **Availability of substitute goods:** product substitution occurs when customers can switch easily between competitors. If all players are producing similar products with little to no differentiation, pricing is fixed. However, businesses can work against this by adding significant product differentiation with a clear focus on consumer requirements.
- **Competitors and nature of competition**: the rivalry among players places significant barriers to the industry. This rivalry can result in price wars, constant innovation in product offerings and new product launches, leading to lower profits. In the long term, it increases fixed costs for businesses, lowers growth rates for the industry and stagnates company performance.

5.2 Attractiveness of the industry

The detailed analysis of the Porter's five forces reveals the existence of each of the industry forces. Based on this, the overall attractiveness of the industry can be analysed more effectively. Factors such as rivalry among players, availability of substitutes, barriers to entry or customer power may make an industry unattractive from an investment perspective.

5.3 Success factors required for the company's survival

Success factors are those pre-requisite qualities that determine whether a company is successful or not. Companies must focus on identifying that edge which will provide success in the long term. The edge could be product quality, better service, fair prices, cost advantages, or management with a good track record.

This type of detailed industry analysis results in an accurate assessment of a company's position with regard to its competitors.

6 Company analysis

Company analysis evaluates information relating to the company's profile, products and services as well as its profitability and financial position. During the process of company analysis, an investor also considers factors that have contributed to shaping the company. Different companiess from the selected industry are usually analysed and evaluated so that the most attractive company can be identified. Elements of a company analysis include the following.

- **An overview of the company:** the most important points about the company, like its mission statement, legal structure, goals and values, history, management team and location. Other useful information includes the company's service performance, product lifecycle stages, competitive strategy, sales and marketing practice, management track record and its future prospects.
- **Analysis of competitive strategies:** broadly, the company will either have a low-cost approach or a product/service differentiation approach when combating competition. There may be a hybrid approach in certain situations. This will help when understanding product positioning.
- **Analysis of financial statements:** conducted using trend analysis, financial ratios and other financial statistics.

Test yourself 7.2

What are the key objectives of fundamental analysis and its components?

7 Trend analysis

Trend analysis is the process of analysing financial data to identify any consistent results or trends. The trend can be horizontal or vertical. Horizontal analysis compares line items in a company's financial statements or financial ratios over multiple time periods, while vertical analysis is the proportional analysis of line items as a percentage of a base item. Trend analysis is useful when evaluating the true picture of a company.

For example, if a company booked a one-off loss of £10,000 in the statement of profit or loss and OCI by selling its equipment, its profit will decrease by £10,000. The profit for the year many not reflect the true picture of the company's average profit over a number of years. However, trend analysis that shows the average profit over the last five years generates meaningful insights into the financial statement.

Changes can be measured in percentage terms or absolute numbers. Periods may be measured in months, quarters, or years. Trend analysis is helpful in:

- analysing revenue patterns across products, geography, or customers
- checking the impact of any unusual one-off expenditure in a period
- preparing financial projections for the company
- comparing results from multiple company's in the same industry

7.1 Horizontal analysis: between periods

Horizontal analysis tracks the history and progress of a company's performance by comparing line items in a company's financial statements or financial ratios over multiple reporting periods. The formula for calculating change in a line item is as follows.

Change (in amount) = Current period amount − Base period amount

For example, Noric Ltd had the following revenue and operating profit in the years ended 31 December 20X8 and FY20X9.

Year ended 31 December	20X9	20X8	Change
	£m	£m	£m
Revenue	100,232	90,322	100,232 − 90,322 = 9,910
Operating profit	6,782	5,792	6,782 − 5,792 = 990

The change shows that revenue has increased by £9,910 million in 20X9, with the corresponding increase in operating profit of £990 million.

A better trend analysis is provided by the change in percentage, calculated as:

Percentage change = (Current period amount − Base period amount) ÷ Base period amount

Percentage change for Noric Ltd is as follows.

Year ended 31 December	20X9	20X8	Change	Percentage change
	£m	£m	£m	
Revenue	100,232	90,322	9,910	9,910 ÷ 90,322 = 11.0%
Operating profit	6,782	5,792	990	990 ÷ 5,792 = 17.1%

The above calculations that revenue has increased by 11% from 20X8 to 20X9, whereas operating profit increased by over 17%. This requires further investigation.

Worked example 7.1

Disco Ltd has finalised its results for the year ended 31 December 20X8. The statement of profit or loss and OCI is below. Can you determine the horizontal trends?

Year ended 31 December 20X8	20X7	
	£'000	£'000
Revenue	731	500
Cost of goods sold	(532)	(354)
Gross profit	199	146
Sales and administrative expenses	(50)	(23)
Marketing expenses	(32)	(21)
Other operating expenses	(32)	(12)
Operating profit	85	90
Finance costs	(56)	(30)
Profit before tax	29	60
Income tax	(6)	(12)
Profit for the year (Net profit)	23	48

Solution

Year ended 31 December	20X8	20X7	Change	Percentage change	Trend
	£'000	£'000	£'000		
Revenue	731	500	231	46%	Uptrend
Cost of goods sold	(532)	(354)	178	50%	Uptrend
Gross profit	199	146	53	36%	Uptrend
Sales and administrative expenses	(50)	(23)	27	117%	Uptrend
Marketing expenses	(32)	(21)	11	52%	Uptrend
Other operating expenses	(32)	(12)	20	167%	Uptrend
Operating profit	85	90	(5)	(6%)	Downtrend
Finance costs	(56)	(30)	26	87%	Uptrend
Profit before tax	29	60	(31)	(52%)	Downtrend
Income tax	(6)	(12)	(6)	(50%)	Downtrend
Profit for the year (Net profit)	23	48	(25)	(52%)	Downtrend

The analysis shows an upward trend in revenue by £231,000 (a 46% increase) and gross profit by £53,000 (a 36% increase). However, the expenses have increased by greater percentages: cost of goods sold increased by 50%, sales and administrative expenses increased by 117%, operating expenses increased by 167%, finance costs increased by 87% and tax increased by 50%. This has resulted in a downward trend of the overall operating profit and profit for the year.

Expressing the increase in revenue of £231,000 (monetary terms) as a percentage (46%) provides more useful information for readers.

Worked example 7.2

Disco Ltd prepared its statement of financial position as at 31 December 2018. Can you determine the trend with the help of its historical numbers?

Year Ended 31 December	20X8	20X7
	£'000	£'000
Assets		
Non-current assets		
Property, plant and machinery	55	50
Intangible assets	2	4
Long-term investments	3	2
Total non-current assets	60	56
Current assets		
Inventory	21	31
Receivables	42	21
Cash and cash equivalents	134	102
Total current assets	197	154
Total assets	257	210
Equity and liabilities		
Equity		
Share capital	123	100
Retained earnings	101	77
Total shareholders' equity	224	177
Current liabilities		
Payables	33	32
Other current liabilities	NIL	1
Total current liabilities	33	33
Total equity and liabilities	257	210

Solution

Year Ended 31 December	20X8	20X7	Change	Percentage change
	£'000	£'000	£000	%
Assets				
Non-current assets				
Property, plant and machinery	55	50	5	10%
Intangible assets	2	4	(2)	(50%) ✶
Long-term investments	3	2	1	50%
Total non-current assets	60	56	4	7%
Current assets				
Inventory	21	31	(10)	(325) ✶
Receivables	42	21	21	100%
Cash and cash equivalents	134	102	32	31%
Total current assets	197	154	43	28%
Total assets	257	210	47	22%
Equity and liabilities				
Equity				
Share capital	123	100	23	23%
Retained earnings	101	77	24	31%
Total shareholders' equity	224	177	47	27%
Current liabilities				
Payables	33	32	1	3%
Other current liabilities	NIL	1	(1)	(100%)
Total current liabilities	33	33	0	0%
Total equity and liabilities	257	210	47	22%

The trend analysis shows a 10% increase in property, plant and machinery. This is a material increase and shows that Disco Ltd has invested materially in tangible non-current assets in the year. This would normally be with a view to increasing future profitability and cash flows, so analysts would want to know more about this. It also shows a 50% increase in long-term investments and a 50% decrease in intangible assets, which could be due to impairment.

The trend analysis shows that the total current assets increased by £43,000 (28%). Changes were contributed to by the increase in receivables (up by £21,000 or 100%) and cash (up by £32,000 or 31%) but was partly offset by the downward trend in inventory of £10,000 (down by 32%).

The changes in absolute monetary terms may not provide a true scale of the periodic change. Changes are therefore expressed in percentage terms to ascertain the scale of periodic changes between two or more accounting periods. The increase of £43,000 in total current assets represents an increase of 28%. The expression in percentage terms provides more useful information for readers.

The balance to these increases in assets, is significant increases in share capital (23%) and retained earnings (31%). The increase in share capital could mean there was a share issue during the year and this would be covered in the annual report of the company. The retained earnings increase means that the company made a material surplus in the year and retained a good amount of that in the business, rather than distributing it all to shareholders.

7.2 Vertical analysis: common-sized analysis

Vertical analysis is a proportional analysis where each item in a financial statement is shown as a percentage of a base item. Usually, line items in the statement of profit or loss and OCI are shown as a percentage of revenue, while line items in the statement of financial position sheet are shown as a percentage of the total assets. It helps to provide a greater understanding of how revenue is being used within the company, thus requiring further investigation if the level of activity is not as expected. Vertical analysis is always done for a single reporting period rather than over multiple periods.

This analysis is useful for seeing changes in line items over a period, such as a five-year period. For example, if receivables has a trend of being 26% of total assets in each of the last five years, then a new percentage of 31% would be a concern for management.

Worked example 7.3

Let us continue the example of Disco Ltd. The company has finalised its annual results for 20X8. The team has also included the previous years' financials. The common size statement is prepared as follows:

Year ended 31 December_20X8	20X7	20X8	20X7	
	£'000	£'000	% of revenue	% of revenue
Revenue	731	500	100%	100%
Cost of goods sold	(532)	(354)	(72.8%)	(70.8%)

Gross profit	199	146	27.2%	29.2%
Sales and administrative expenses	(50)	(23)	(6.8%)	(4.6%)
Marketing expenses	(32)	(21)	(4.4%)	(4.2%)
Other operating expenses	(32)	(12)	(4.4%)	(2.4%)
Operating profit	85	90	11.6%	18.0%
Finance costs	(56)	(30)	(7.6%)	(6.0%)
Profit before tax	29	60	4.0%	12.0%
Income tax	(6)	(12)	0.8%	2.4%
Profit for the year (Net profit)	23	48	3.2%	9.6%

Remember to allow for the effects of rounding when working to decimal places of percentages.

Vertical analysis reveals that, although actual revenue was up in 20X8 from £500,000 to £731,000, the ratio of gross profit to revenue fell from 29.2% to 27.2% in 20X8. This is due to the increase in cost of goods (relative to revenue) from 70.8% to 72.8% in 20X8. This should trigger an investigation – for example, it could be that material was more expensive in 20X8.

Similarly, operating profit and the quarter's profit after tax both fell in relation to revenue – mainly compounded by the increase in sales and administrative expenses, operating expenses and non-operating expenses. All of these changes should warrant further investigation.

Vertical analysis also includes analysis of ratios such as the profitability ratio, turnover ratio, liquidity ratio and gearing ratio.

8 Ratio analysis

Ratio analysis is one of the most powerful tools to gauge the performance of a company. Ratios are mathematical indicators and are calculated by dividing one variable by another, such as revenue divided by number of stores, or revenue divided by operating profit. Ratio analysis is helpful when predicting future performance. Ratios are most relevant when they are analysed in conjunction with similar company's or previous periods.

Financial ratios help a company's owner and investors to check the overall health of the company as they help identify trends in their early stages. Ratios are also used by lenders and analysts to determine a company's financial stability and standing.

Ratio analysis enables comparison across companies which differ in size, stage and geography. By comparing a particular ratio for one company with that of the industry as a whole, a company can learn much about where its business stands in comparison with the industry average. For example, a hotel owner can compare its occupancy rate ratio with the average for all hotel properties in the UK in order to determine if it is within a competitive range.

Financial ratios can be divided into five categories:

- profitability ratios (summarised in Table 7.2 and covered in section 9 of this chapter)
- efficiency or turnover ratios (covered further in Chapter 8)
- liquidity or solvency ratios (covered in Chapter 8)
- gearing or debt ratios (covered in Chapter 12)
- investment or market value ratios (covered in Chapter 15)

Profitability ratios	
Return on capital employed (ROCE) (%) or accounting rate of return (ARR) (see Chapter 13, section 6)	(Operating profit x 100) ÷ (equity + non-current liabilities (debt))
OR: Return on total assets (ROA) (%)	(Operating profit x 100) ÷ total assets
Return on shareholders' equity (ROE) (%)	(Net profit (profit for period) x 100) ÷ total shareholders' equity
Operating profit margin (%)	(Operating profit ÷ revenue) x 100
Gross profit margin (%)	(Gross profit ÷ revenue) x 100
Net profit margin (%)	(Net profit ÷ revenue) x 100

Table 7.2 Profitability ratios

9 Profitability ratios

Profitability ratios measure the capability of the company to generate profit compared to revenue, expenses, assets and shareholders' equity. They indicate the effectiveness of the capital and asset utilisation. There are various types of profitability ratios which are used by companies and analysts. These ratios are broadly divided into two categories.

Margin ratios

These represent the company's ability to convert revenue into profit. Commonly used margin ratios include:

- gross profit margin ratio
- operating profit margin ratio
- net profit margin ratio

Return ratios

These represent the company's ability to generate returns to its investors (including) shareholders. Commonly used return ratios include:

- Return on assets ratio
- Return on capital employed (ROCE) ratio
- Return on shareholders' equity (ROE) ratio

9.1 Gross profit margin ratio

Gross profit margin calculates the ratio of gross profit to revenue. Gross profit refers to the margin that company charges above cost of goods sold. It indicates how much the company is earning considering the required costs to produce its goods and services. The underlying drivers behind this ratio are selling prices, product mix, purchase costs, production costs and inventory valuations.

The formula for calculating gross profit margin ratio is as follows.

(Gross profit ÷ revenue) × 100

Where gross profit = revenue − cost of goods sold.

The higher the ratio, the more favourable it is for the company.

9.2 Operating profit margin ratio

Operating profit margin calculates the ratio of operating margin to revenue. Essentially, it is the percentage of profit remaining after accounting for operating expenses. Companies with higher operating profit margins can comfortably cover their fixed costs including interest charges. Several factors such as employment policy, depreciation methods, write-offs of bad debts, selling and marketing expenses may impact on this ratio.

The formula for calculating operating profit margin ratio is as follows.

(Operating profit ÷ revenue) × 100

Where operating profit = revenue − cost of goods sold − operating expenses

The higher the ratio, the more favourable it is for the company.

9.3 Net profit margin ratio

Like the operating profit margin ratio, net profit margin ratio evaluates the company's ability to generate earnings after taxes. This ratio reflects the strength of the management, since visionary management strives to improve the profitability of a company above all its costs. It also checks how effectively the company has administered the process.

The formula for calculating net profit margin ratio is as follows.

(Net profit ÷ revenue) × 100

Where net profit = revenue − cost of goods sold − operating expenses − non-operating expenses + non-operating income − income tax.

As an alternative, the net profit margin ratio may use profit before tax. The higher the ratio, the more favourable it is for the company.

Worked example 7.4

Disco Ltd has provided its financial information for the year ended 31 December 20X7, 20X8 and now 20X9. Provide an interpretation of the current financial versus historical performance.

Statements of profit or loss

Year ended 31 December	20X9	20X8	20X7
	£'000	£'000	£'000
Revenue	742	731	500
Cost of goods sold	(601)	(532)	(354)
Gross profit	141	199	146
Sales and administrative expenses	(45)	(50)	(23)
Marketing expenses	(9)	(32)	(21)
Other operating expenses	(25)	(32)	(12)
Operating profit	62	85	90
Finance costs	(9)	(56)	(30)
Profit before tax	53	29	60
Income tax	NIL	(6)	(12)
Profit for the year (Net profit)	53	23	48

Solution

Based on the historical numbers, profitability ratios and trend analysis are as follows.

Year ended 31 December	20X9	20X8	20X7
Revenue growth rate	2%	46%	–
Gross profit growth rate	(29%)	36%	–
Operating profit growth rate	(27%)	(6%)	–
Net profit growth rate	130%	(52%)	–
	(see 7.3)	(see 7.3)	
Gross profit margin	19%	27%	29%
((Gross profit ÷ revenue) × 100)			
Operating profit margin	8%	12%	18%
((Operating profit ÷ revenue) × 100)			
Net profit margin	7%	3%	10%
((Net profit ÷ revenue) × 100)			

Performance commentary:

- Revenue grew a mere 2% in 20X9, compared to previous period's growth rate of 46%. The revenue growth rate could have slowed down for reasons such as a new competitor in the market offering product/services at competitive prices, loss of key employees, a stagnant market, low productivity and so on.

- Gross profit and operating profit declined dramatically in 20X9 due to an increase in cost of goods sold and ongoing incremental sales and marketing expenses. However, the company has managed to reduce non-operating expenses during the period, resulting in a net profit that has nearly doubled in 20X9. There is also possibility of a one-off non-operating expense being recorded in 201X8

- In terms of margins, revenue continues to rise but profitability is falling over the three years. Gross profit margin has reduced again in 20X9. This could be a result of various factors such as an increase in labour or raw material prices, regulatory challenges, changes in accounting policy or changes in sales mix.

- While both the operating margin and net profit margin declined in 20X8, net profit margin improved in 20X9. The trend could have been influenced by multiple factors as discussed above.

In summary, ratios are the first step towards your investigation of the company financials. One needs to study the performance in the light of other data and information available.

Test yourself 7.3

Ray plc and Kevin plc prepared their statements of profit or loss for the year ended 31 December 20X8, including the comparative figures relating to the year ended 31 December 20X7. Both companies are in the same industry but operate in two different countries, namely France and Italy. What is your opinion on the performance of both companies?

Ray plc – France	20X8	20X7
	£m	£m
Revenue	130	120
Cost of goods sold	(60)	(50)
Gross profit	70	70
Sales and administrative expenses	(20)	(10)

Kevin plc – Italy	20X8	20X7
	£m	£m
Revenue	350	230
Cost of goods sold	(240)	(150)
Gross profit	110	80
Sales and administrative expenses	(60)	(20)

Marketing expenses	(10)	(20)	Marketing expenses	(10)	(10)
Other operating expenses	(10)	(10)	Other operating expenses	(10)	(10)
Operating profit	30	30	Operating profit	30	40
Finance costs	(10)	NIL	Finance costs	(10)	(10)
Profit before tax	20	30	Profit before tax	20	30
Income tax	NIL	(10)	Income tax	NIL	(20)
Profit for the year (Net profit)	20	20	Profit for the year (Net profit)	20	10

9.4 Return on assets ratio

The return on assets (ROA) ratio evaluates how effectively the assets of the company are used in comparison to the profit earned. Economies of scale help in improving this ratio.

The formula for calculating return on assets ratio is as follows.

(Operating profit x 100) ÷ total assets

Where operating profit = revenue – cost of goods sold – operating expenses – non-operating expenses

This ratio uses operating profit before tax, recognising the inevitability that current liabilities are financing part of these assets. The higher the ratio, more favourable it is for the company.

9.5 Return on equity ratio

The return on equity (ROE) ratio measures the company's ability to provide returns to its equity holders. The formula for calculating the ROE ratio is as follows.

(Net profit (profit for period) x 100) ÷ total shareholders' equity

Where net profit = revenue – cost of goods sold – operating expenses – non-operating expenses – income tax

The higher the ratio, more favourable it is for the company.

9.6 Return on capital employed ratio

The return on capital employed (ROCE) ratio is a measure of return generated by all sources of capital, including equity and debt. It is similar to the ROE ratio but includes debt holders as well. The formula for calculating the ROCE ratio is as follows.

(Operating profit x 100) ÷ (equity + non-current liabilities (debt))

The higher the ratio, more favourable it is for the company.

Worked example 7.5

A summary of the financial statements of Disco Ltd is given below. Calculate the profitability return ratios.

	20X9	20X8
	£'000	£'000
Profit for the year (net profit)	53	23

Statement of financial position as at 31 December 20X9

	20X9	20X8
	£'000	£'000
Assets		
Non-current assets		
Property, plant and equipment	65	55
Intangible assets	1	2
Long-term investments	12	3
Total non-current assets	78	60
Current assets		
Inventory	1	21
Receivables	31	42
Cash and cash equivalents	130	134
Total current assets	162	197
Total assets	240	257
Equity and liabilities		
Share capital	123	123
Retained earnings	106	101
Total shareholders' equity	229	224
Current liabilities		
Payables	11	33
Total equity and liabilities	240	257

Based on the historical numbers, the profitability return ratios would be:

Return on assets

	20X9	20X8
ROA = net profit ÷ total assets	22%	9%
	(53 ÷ 240)	(23 ÷ 257)

The net profit relative to the total assets has gone up from 9% to 22%, implying that the assets of the company are being used more effectively in comparison to the income earned. Economies of scale help in improving this ratio.

Return on equity

ROE = net profit ÷ total (shareholders') equity   23%   10%
                                                (53 ÷ 229) (23 ÷ 224)

The ROE ratio measures the company's ability to provide returns to its equity holders. The net profit has gone up in 20X9, mainly due to favourable conditions such as significant savings in non-operating expenses, thereby also increasing the ROE to 23%.

Return on capital employed

ROCE = EBIT ÷ (total equity + long-term debt)   23%   10%
                                              (53 ÷ 229 + 0) (23 ÷ 224 + 0)

The ROCE ratio is a measure of pre-tax income available to all investors and not just to shareholders. The profit figure used is the operating profit (before any deductions for interest charges) In this case the profit available to investors has gone up in 20X9. As a consequence, the ROCE increased to 23%.

Test yourself 7.4

The financial statements of Ray plc and Kevin plc are below (continuing from Test yourself 7.3). Calculate the profitability return ratios.

Statements of profit or loss and OCI for the years ending 31 December 20X7 and 20X8

Ray plc (France)	20X8	20X7
	£m	£m
Operating profit	3	3
Non-operating expense	(1)	NIL
Profit before tax	2	3
Income tax	NIL	(1)
Profit for the year (Net profit)	2	2

Kevin plc (Italy)	20X8	20X7
	£m	£m
Operating profit	3	4
Non-operating expense	(1)	(1)
Profit before tax	2	3
Income tax	NIL	(2)
Profit for the year (Net profit)	2	1

Statements of financial position as at 31 December 20X7 and 20X8

Ray plc (France)

	20X8	20X7
	£m	£m
Assets		
Non-current assets		
Property, plant and equipment	1	2
Long-term investments	6	3
Total non-current assets	7	5

Current assets		
Receivables	8	11
Cash and cash equivalents	6	2
Total current assets	14	13
Total assets	21	18

Equity and liabilities		
Share capital	8	8
Retained earnings	8	7
Total shareholders' equity	16	15

Non-current liabilities	1	NIL
Current liabilities (payables)	4	3

Kevin plc (Italy)

	20X8	20X7
	£m	£m
Assets		
Non-current assets		
Property, plant and equipment	25	18
Long-term investments	2	1
Total non-current assets	27	19

Current assets		
Receivables	8	5
Cash and cash equivalents	12	5
Total current assets	20	10
Total assets	47	29

Equity and liabilities		
Share capital	10	7
Retained earnings	14	9
Total shareholders' equity	24	16

Non-current liabilities	8	4
Current liabilities (payables)	15	9

Total liabilities	5	3
Total equity and liabilities	21	18

Total liabilities	23	13
Total equity and liabilities	47	29

10 Limitations of ratio analysis

Ratio analysis provides company (or business) owners with trend or time-series analysis and trends within their industry, called industry or cross-sectional analysis. While ratio analysis is useful, it does have its limitations.

- Ratio analysis is only the first step towards financial statement analysis. Final conclusions cannot be drawn based on mere percentages shown by the ratios, as they may not reflect the holistic picture about a company's situation. One needs to be vigilant while conducting research on the company.
- Mathematical calculation does not work when the base figure is zero or negative, as it may not reflect the true picture. For example, if bad debts for the base period and the current period are zero and £500, respectively, one cannot calculate the change as a percentage.
- Company projections based on trend and ratio analysis are not adequate as the trend is a reflection of historical actions which may or may not be applicable in the future. Moreover, ratios are purely based on accounting data. An accurate business forecast depends on economic and industry performance, management plans, supply and demand situations, competitor analysis and so on.
- Benchmarking focuses on company-to-company comparisons of how products and services perform against their toughest competitors, or those companies recognised as leaders in their industry. The benchmark used for financial ratios may not always be the most appropriate.
- A time-series analysis that makes use of historical financial information may be distorted with inflation or seasonal factors.
- Ratios are meaningless without a comparison against trend data or industry data and without looking at the causation factors.
- There may be **window dressing** intended to manipulate financial statements.

window dressing
Transactions made at the end of a company's year-end or quarter-end to improve the appearance of its financial statements.

11 Accounting irregularities and creative accounting

The major scandals that have affected the accounting profession have usually been as a result of fraud. It is therefore important for auditors and directors to understand their role in the prevention and detection of fraud. Accounting irregularities are not formally defined in GAAP.

In order to maintain confidence in the profession, International Standard on Auditing (ISA) 240 (the Auditor's Responsibilities Relating to Fraud in an Audit of Financial Statements) recognises that misstatement in the financial statements can arise from either fraud or error (unintentional misstatement).

Fraud can be further split into two types:

- fraudulent financial reporting (intentional misstatement)
- misappropriation of assets (theft)

Auditors must be aware of the impact of both fraud and error on the accuracy of financial statements. Fraud is a criminal activity and it is the responsibility of a country's legal system, not the auditor, to determine whether this has actually occurred.

11.1 Errors

Errors are considered to be unintentional misstatement in financial statements, or the lowest level of accounting irregularity. These are non-fraudulent discrepancies in financial documentation and are corrected by those preparing the next financial statements. Examples of accounting errors include:

- a mistake in the processing of data (such as data entry error) from which financial statements are prepared;
- an incorrect accounting estimate arising from oversight or misinterpretation of facts; or
- a mistake in the application of accounting principles relating to measurement, recognition, classification, presentation or disclosure.

11.2 Fraudulent financial reporting

Fraudulent financial reporting is the most severe type of accounting irregularity, usually involving intentional misstatement or omission of amounts or disclosures in financial statements to deceive or mislead the users of the financial information. It generally involves accounting irregularities, such as:

- manipulation, falsification or alteration of accounting records or supporting documents;
- misrepresentation in, or intentional omission from, the financial statements of events, transactions or other significant information; or
- misapplication of accounting principles relating to amounts, classification, manner of presentation or disclosure.

This is one of the two types of accounting irregularities that are of most concern to auditors (the other one being theft).

11.3 Misappropriation of assets (theft)

The other type of fraud is asset misappropriation. This involves theft of a corporation's assets. It generally involves misstatements due to accounting irregularities, such as:

- stealing tangible or intangible assets;
- embezzling receipts; or
- making payment for the purchase of non-existent goods and services.

Misappropriation of assets is usually supplemented by false documents in order to conceal the fact that the assets are missing, thus causing accounting irregularities in financial statements.

11.4 Creative accounting

Chapter 4 briefly looked into creative accounting as one of the limitations of published financial statements. Creative accounting is the deliberate manipulation of figures for a desired result. The major consideration for the directors or employees who manipulate results is usually the effect the results will have on the share price of the company.

Creative accounting presents the financial statements of an entity in the best possible or most flattering way. It is a deliberate manipulation of financial statements which is geared towards achieving predetermined results. This occurs due to inherent weaknesses in accounting systems, accounting choices, accounting judgment and accounting transactions.

A key aspect of improving the appearance of the statement of financial position is keeping gearing as low as possible. Investors know that interest payments reduce the amount available for distribution. Potential lenders will be less willing to lend to a company which is already highly geared.

Creative accounting takes many forms.

off-balance sheet financing
A form of financing in which large capital expenditures and the associated liability (such as leases and partnerships) are kept off a company's statement of financial position. It impacts a company's level of debt and gearing and has serious implications.

- **Off-balance sheet financing:** is a form of financing in which large capital expenditures and the associated liability (such as leases and partnerships) are kept out of a company's statement of financial position. It impacts a company's level of debt and gearing and has serious implications.
- **Cut-off manipulation:** a company may delay invoicing in order to move revenue into the following year.
- **Revaluation of non-current assets:** this is a practice open to manipulation. It can have a significant impact on a company's statement of financial position.
- **Window dressing:** transactions are passed through the books at the year-end to make figures look better, often to be reversed after the year-end. An example is a loan repaid just before the year-end and taken out again at the beginning of the next year.
- **Change of accounting policies:** this is done as a last resort because companies which change accounting policies know they will not be able to do so again for some time. The effect in the year of change can be substantial. Potential areas open for such treatment are depreciation, inventory valuation, changes from historical cost to revaluations and the treatment of foreign currency gains and losses.

- **Manipulation of accruals, prepayments and contingencies:** this can be very subjective, particularly in relation to contingencies as a contingent liability (for example, the outcome of a pending lawsuit) is difficult to estimate. In such cases, companies will often only disclose the possibility of such a liability, even though the eventual costs may be substantial.

11.5 Regulations to prevent creative accounting

A number of creative accounting measures are aimed at manipulating the numbers but regulation is increasingly catching up. Some examples are listed below.

- International Accounting Standard 27 ensures consolidation of financial statements of subsidiaries with that of parent company. In the past, parent companies could exclude highly geared subsidiaries from the consolidation and obtain loans via such 'quasi-subsidiaries', so that the loan never appeared in the consolidated statement of financial position. This loophole was effectively closed by IAS 27.
- International Financial Reporting Standard 16 ensures proper disclosure of leased assets, which makes it very difficult to keep liabilities off the statement of financial position (balance sheet). Assets could be 'sold' under a sale and leaseback agreement – in effect a disguised loan – and leased back under a series of short-term leases in order to keep the asset and the liability off the statement of financial position.
- International Accounting Standard 37 aims to ensure proper accounting and disclosure of provisions, contingent liabilities and contingent assets.

Last-minute window dressing can still be undertaken: for instance, where cheques are written to creditors, entered in the cash book, but not sent out until well after the year-end.

These issues can be resolved to a great extent by resorting to audit. An audit underpins the trust and obligation of stewardship between those who manage a company and those who own it. A rigorous audit process may also identify areas where management may improve their controls or processes, further adding value to the company by enhancing the quality of its business processes. It requires both auditors' expertise (ability to detect errors or misstatements) and independence (ability to report these errors or misstatements).

Chapter summary

- Financial statements are prepared to aid decision making, which is underpinned by effective analysis and interpretation of financial statements. Financial analysis draws meaningful relationships between items on the two financial statements:
    - the statement of profit or loss and OCI (or income statement)
    - the statement of financial position (or balance sheet)

- They are the indicators of profitability and financial soundness of a business entity for a given period.
- The purpose of financial analysis is to assess the financial strength and weaknesses of a company by assessing its efficiency and performance. The key measures in determining the financial strength of a company are:
  - profitability
  - trend of achievements
  - growth potential of the company
  - comparative position in relation to similar company's or businesses
  - overall financial strength and solvency of the company
- The analysis and interpretation of financial statements assesses the financial strengths and weaknesses of a company. The key measures used are:
  - **fundamental analysis:** economic analysis, industry analysis and company analysis;
  - **trend analysis:** vertical analysis and horizontal analysis; and
  - **ratio analysis:** profitability ratios, asset efficiency or turnover ratios, liquidity or solvency ratios, gearing or debt ratios and investment or market value ratios.
- Fundamental analysis is a systematic approach to evaluating company performance based on the analysis of its financial statements. It is an in-depth study of underlying forces that drive a company's performance which considers the overall state of the economy in which a company operates, the industry which it belongs to and factors including interest rates, production, earnings, employment, GDP and so on. Fundamental analysis includes:
  - **economic analysis:** different companies/industries perform differently during the different stages of an economic cycle;
  - **industry analysis:** based on the four stages of the industry lifecycle; and
  - **company analysis:** evaluating information relating to the company's profile, products and services as well as its profitability and financial position.
- Trend analysis is the process of analysing financial data to identify any consistent results or trends. The trend can be:
  - horizontal: comparing line items in a company's financial statements or financial ratios over multiple reporting periods; or
  - vertical: the proportional analysis of line items as a percentage of base items.
- Ratio analysis provides businesses owners with trend or time-series analysis and trends within their industry, called industry or cross-sectional analysis.
- Profitability ratios measure the capability of the company to generate profit compared to revenue, expenses, assets and shareholders' equity.

It indicates the effectiveness of the capital invested and asset utilisation. These ratios are broadly divided into two categories:

- **margin ratios:** these represent a company's ability to convert sales into profits and include the gross profit margin ratio, the operating margin ratio and the net profit margin ratio; and
- **return ratios:** these represent a company's ability to generate returns to its shareholders and include the ROA ratio, the ROE ratio and the ROCE ratio.

◆ While ratio analysis is useful, it has its limitations. For example, mere percentages may not reflect a holistic picture about a situation, trends are a reflection of historical performance and do not consider inflation or seasonal factors, or window dressing which may be manipulating the financial statements.

◆ International Standard on Auditing 240 (the Auditor's Responsibilities Relating to Fraud in an Audit of Financial Statements) recognises that misstatement in the financial statements can arise from either fraud or error (unintentional misstatement).

◆ Fraud can be further split into two types: fraudulent financial reporting (intentional misstatement) and misappropriation of assets (theft).

◆ Creative accounting is the deliberate manipulation of figures for a desired result. This occurs due to inherent weaknesses in accounting systems, accounting choices, accounting judgment and accounting transactions. A number of creative accounting measures are aimed at manipulating the numbers, but regulation is increasingly catching up.

Part three

Chapter 8
Working capital management

Chapter 9
Sources of short-term finance

Chapter 10
Financial markets and the identification of financing needs

Chapter 11
Sources of long-term finance

Sources of finance, their associated risks and returns

Overview

Part three starts by discussing the management of working capital before examining the financial markets, discussing how financing needs of a business are assessed and looking at the importance of cash and cash management. It also looks at various sources of finance and their associated advantages and disadvantages.

Chapter 8 discusses the central role of working capital and the management of its key components: inventories, trade receivables and trade payables. It examines the impact of working capital ratios, the working capital or cash cycle, the trade-off between profitability and liquidity and the interpretation of liquidity and efficiency ratios.

Chapter 9 considers the sources of short-term financing, both internal and external and their associated benefits and risks.

Chapter 10 introduces the concept of financial markets, the principles underpinning different forms of market efficiency, the roles of different types of markets and the roles of key market players. It also considers how funding requirements are assessed through planning, budgeting and forecasting, before looking at cash and cash management.

Chapter 11 examines different sources of raising long-term finance and critically analyses the advantages and disadvantages associated with each of these sources of finance. Key long-term sources of finance include equity finance and debt finance.

At the end of this Part, students will be able to:

- demonstrate how working capital is estimated from the working capital cycle;
- calculate and interpret liquidity and efficiency ratios;
- demonstrate an understanding of inventory management and the use of relevant techniques;
- discuss the management of trade receivables and trade payables;
- explain the role of financial markets in providing finance, explain the characteristics of various types of financial markets and discuss the role of key market players;
- discuss the features and the roles of different institutional investors in the operation of private markets;
- explain how an organisation anticipates and monitors its funding requirements to meet its strategic goals and objectives through planning, budgeting and forecasting;
- explain the importance of cash management and apply relevant techniques;
- identify the sources of long-term finance;
- demonstrate a sound understanding of the factors financial managers consider in choosing the best way to raise funds by evaluating their advantages and disadvantages;
- understand the external and internal methods to raise equity finance and critically evaluate their advantages and disadvantages;

- evaluate the features, advantages and disadvantages of various sources of debt finance including preference shares, bonds and debentures, loans, leasing, securitisation of assets, private finance initiatives and government assistance;
- identity the external sources of short-term finance and evaluate the following sources: bank and institutional loans, overdrafts, bills of exchange or trade drafts, debt factoring and invoice discounting and alternative financing;
- discuss internal sources of short-term finance and demonstrate how cash benefits can be obtained through reduction or efficient management of working capital; and
- consider factors in choosing the right balance of working capital, including the trade-off between liquidity and profitability.

Chapter eight
Working capital management

Contents

1. Introduction
2. The nature and purpose of working capital
3. The working capital cycle
4. Working capital management: profitability versus liquidity
5. Working capital ratios
6. The management of inventories
7. The management of trade receivables
8. The management of trade payables

1 Introduction

This chapter looks at ways in which companies can manage their working capital.

Working capital includes inventories, trade receivables, cash and cash equivalents (which would include a bank overdraft) less trade payables. All of these are available for day-to-day operating activities. This chapter will look at the working capital cycle – also known as the cash operating cycle – and how to manage working capital to achieve a balance between profitability and liquidity.

The chapter will look at working capital ratios and their limitations, including liquidity and efficiency ratios. Finally, it will discuss the management of inventories, trade receivables and trade payables (cash management is covered in Chapter 10). The main ratios covered in this chapter are:

Figure 8.1 Working capital

Efficiency ratios	
Asset turnover (times)	Revenue ÷ capital employed
OR: Total asset turnover (times)	Revenue ÷ total assets
Non-current asset turnover (times)	Revenue ÷ non-current assets
Inventories turnover (times)	Cost of goods sold ÷ inventory
OR: Inventory holding period (days)	Inventory x 365 ÷ cost of goods sold
Rate of collection of trade receivables (days)	Trade receivables × 365 ÷ credit sales (or revenue)
Rate of payment of trade payables (days)	Trade payables × 365 ÷ credit purchases (or cost of goods sold)
Working capital cycle (days)	Inventory holding (or storage) period + trade receivables collection period − trade payables payment period
Current ratio (X:1)	Current assets ÷ current liabilities
Quick ratio (X:1)	(Current assets − inventory) ÷ current liabilities

Note: average figures may be used instead of year-end figures for these ratios.

Table 8.1 Efficiency ratios

2 The nature and purpose of working capital

Working capital is the difference between current assets and current liabilities. An asset expected to be realised, consumed or sold within the normal operating cycle of the business is referred to as a current asset. In the same manner, a liability is treated as a current liability if it is due to be settled within the normal operating cycle of the business.

Working capital is the total amount of capital tied up in current assets and current liabilities. This normally includes inventories, trade receivables, cash and cash equivalents less trade payables – all of which are available for day-to-day operating activities.

> Working capital = inventory + trade receivables + cash and cash equivalents – trade payables.

Working capital can be regarded as the lifeblood of an organisation. A company cannot survive without working capital funds, although theoretically it can survive without making a profit. The finance needed to fund a firm's required level of working capital can be either short term (such as an overdraft or a delay of payment to suppliers) or long term (such as a long-term loan or the issue of shares).

For **permanent working capital**, the overall level of working capital remains fixed and should be financed by long-term sources of finance. **Temporary working capital** fluctuates day-to-day above this level of permanent working capital: it should be financed by short-term sources of finance. The permanent working capital is the minimum level of working capital required to continue uninterrupted day-to-day business activities. Temporary working capital is the additional financial requirement that arises out of events such as seasonal demand for products or business activity.

permanent working capital
The permanent or fixed working capital is the minimum level of working capital required to continue uninterrupted day-to-day business activities.

temporary working capital
Additional financial requirements that arise out of events such as seasonal demand of the product or a higher level of business activity.

3 The working capital cycle

The working capital cycle (WCC), or cash operating cycle, refers to the time taken by an organisation to convert its net current assets (current assets less current liabilities) into cash. It can be determined by adding together the number of days required to complete each stage in the cycle.

In the case of manufacturing entities, the cycle starts from the placement of an order for raw materials; for service providers it starts from hiring employees. The working capital cycle ends when the customer makes payment. The duration of working capital cycles differs from industry to industry. The cash operating cycle of a service provider, for example, will be shorter than that of a manufacturer – as demonstrated in Figure 8.2.

The length of the cycle depends on:

- the balancing act between liquidity and profitability
- efficiency of management

- terms of trade
- the nature of the industry

3.1 Working capital cycle and the nature of the industry

The manufacturing sector (for example, motor manufacturers) has a long cycle with significant current assets. It tends to reduce inventory holding through just in time (JIT) systems. Suppliers deliver precise quantities, significantly reducing the manufacturer's holdings of raw materials and components.

The distributive sector, particularly retail, tends to have a shorter cycle with few credit customers, high finished goods inventory and long payment periods. Retailers tend to purchase from manufacturers and wholesalers on credit.

The service sector (for example, recruitment agencies or schools) does not hold any finished goods. Current liabilities will include less significant suppliers (such as stationery suppliers). Trade receivables could include amounts owed from students and customers.

Product provider or manufacturer

Cash → Purchase inventory → Supplier payment → Work in progress → Finished goods → Sales → Receivables → Cash

Service provider

Cash → Revenue → Trade receivables → Cash

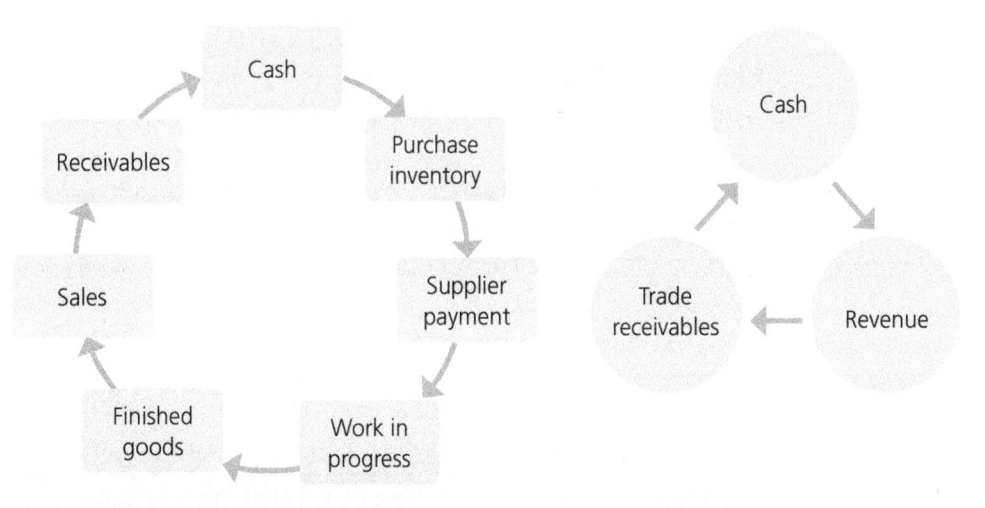

Figure 8.2 Working capital cycle of a product provider versus a service provider.

Test yourself 8.1

What factors determine working capital requirements?

3.2 Calculating the working capital cycle

Working capital consists of four components: inventory, trade receivables, cash and cash equivalents (including a bank overdraft) and trade payables. Inventory is further classified into raw materials (RM), work in progress (WIP) and finished goods (FG). The WCC (calculated in whole days) is the time between buying the goods to manufacture products and generation of cash receipts from selling the products.

>WCC = inventory holding (or storage) period + trade receivables collection period − trade payables payment period

The inventory holding period is the average number of days taken to process or sell inventory. It can be further broken down into the following stages.

>Raw material holding period = inventory of raw material (RM) ÷ cost of RM consumed per day

>WIP holding period = WIP inventory ÷ cost of production per day

>Finished goods storage period = inventory of FG ÷ cost of goods sold per day

The trade receivables collection period is the average number of days taken to receive payment from customers for goods or services sold to them on credit.

>The rate of collection of trade receivables = (trade receivables x 365) ÷ credit sales

The trade payables payment period is the average number days taken to make payment to suppliers for goods purchased on credit.

>The rate of payment of trade payables = (trade payables x 365) ÷ credit purchases.

Assuming 365 days in a year, the WCC is the sum of the following:

1.	Inventory holding (days)	
	(a) Finished goods	[FG ÷ cost of goods sold] × 365
	(b) Work in progress	[WIP ÷ cost of production*] × 365
	(c) Raw materials	[RM ÷ RM consumed] × 365
2.	Rate of collection of trade receivables (days)	Trade receivables × 365
		Credit sales (or revenue)
3.	Less: Rate of payment of trade payables (days)	Trade payables × 365
		Credit purchases (or cost of goods sold)

There is an important assumption to be aware of regarding the calculation of inventory holding (days), trade receivables collection (days) and trade payables payment (days). Average numbers are required to calculate these components correctly: therefore, opening and closing balances from the statement of financial position are required. This requires two statements of financial position (or the key numbers from them). This is different from the other ratios in this text, which can be calculated from a single statement of financial position.

In addition, the year-end figures will not be typical of the year for a seasonal business, when there are likely to be material shifts in these figures. This makes the calculation of an average figure based on two year-end figures of limited value to management or external stakeholders.

Therefore, in this study text (and the examination) the preferred approach will be to use the year-end figures, not an average. This will be the case unless it is clearly stated or otherwise specified.

4 Working capital management: profitability versus liquidity

4.1 A balancing act

Every company should have adequate or optimum working capital to run its operations efficiently and effectively, but without holding too much working capital. Holding high levels of working capital means the entity has idle funds with unnecessary cost implications – a phenomenon known as **overcapitalisation**.

A low level of working capital can result in a situation where the company is not able to meet its day-to-day demands (such as paying bills – including salaries and wages – when they arise) and may lead to insolvency. **Overtrading** is usually associated with a rapid increase in revenue that is not supported by sufficient working capital. The signs of overtrading are:

- a rapid increase in revenue and the volume of current assets
- most of the increase in assets being financed by credit
- a dramatic drop in liquidity ratios

Companies need working capital to keep the business running. For example, a company which has sufficient working capital will be able to make the usual payments of salaries, wages and other day-to-day obligations. Meeting these obligations might raise the morale of its employees, increase their effectiveness, decrease wastage, save costs and increase profits.

The main objective of working capital management is to get the balance of current assets and current liabilities right.

An aggressive approach that chooses to have a lower level of working capital (cash, receivables and inventory) will result in higher profitability and higher risk, while a conservative approach that chooses to have a higher level of working capital will result in lower profitability, lower risk, will require more cash and will 'tie up' cash.

overcapitalisation
Overcapitalisation is where the overall level of working capital is too high. Holding a high level of working capital means the company is holding idle funds with unnecessary cost implications.

overtrading
Overtrading (or under-capitalisation) is where the level of working capital is too low. It is associated with a rapid increase in revenue and current assets that is not supported by sufficient working capital.

A moderate working capital policy is the balance between the two, where the risk and return balance is maintained by using funds in an efficient and effective manner.

A conservative approach
Higher level of working capital
Higher liquidity
Cash tied up
Lower profitability
Lower risk

An aggressive approach
Lower level working capital
Lower liquidity
Cash savings
Higher profitability
Higher risk

Figure 8.3 Working capital management – a balancing act

Management decides on the optimal level and proper management of working capital that results in no idle cash or unused inventory, but also does not put a strain on liquid resources needed for the daily running of the business. The company faces a trade-off between profitability and liquidity.

Test yourself 8.2

Why is working capital needed in a business? What is the optimal level of working capital?

5 Working capital ratios

5.1 Liquidity ratios

Financial managers use liquidity or working capital (WC) ratios to control and monitor working capital. Two main ratios are employed. The first is the current ratio or the WC ratio, calculated as:

Current assets ÷ current liabilities

A current ratio of less than one could indicate liquidity problems. While there is a general target current ratio of 2:1, the acceptability of the ratio will depend on the nature of the business and how it compares with those of a similar type.

The second ratio is the quick ratio (also referred to as the liquidity or acid test ratio)

(Current assets − inventory) ÷ current liabilities

The quick ratio excludes inventory which cannot easily and quickly be converted into cash. Although the general target is 1:1, an ideal ratio depends on industry practice. Liquidity ratios and their application are covered in more detail in Chapter 16.

5.2 Efficiency ratios

Efficiency ratios measure how efficiently a company uses its assets to generate revenues and manage its liabilities. There are four main efficiency ratios.

Asset turnover
This measures the ability of a company to generate sales or revenues from its assets.

Asset turnover = revenue ÷ net assets or total assets (non-current and current assets).

Inventory turnover
Inventory turnover measures the effectiveness of inventory management. It indicates how quickly inventory is being sold or used during the period. Effectively, the inventory holding days – calculated as per section 3.2 – is inverted to arrive at inventory turnover (for example how many times a company has sold and replaced inventory in a year).

Inventory turnover = annual cost of goods sold ÷ inventory

Trade receivables collection
This measures how quickly customer debts are being collected (calculated as per section 3.2)

Trade payables payment
This measures how quickly trade payables (suppliers) are being paid (calculated as per section 3.2).

Worked example 8.1

You have been given the following information for Dhaka Fabrics plc.

Statements of financial position as at 31 December 20X8 and 20X9

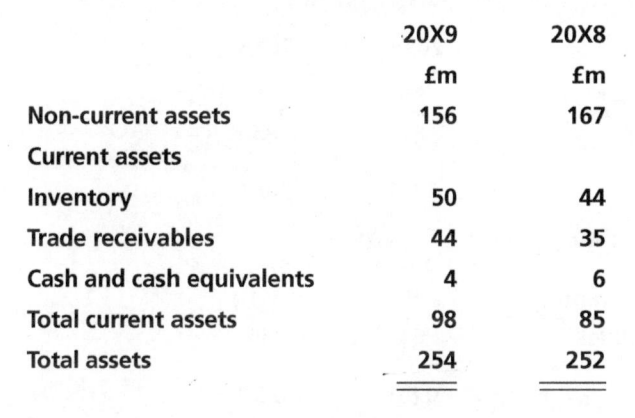

	20X9 £m	20X8 £m
Non-current assets	156	167
Current assets		
Inventory	50	44
Trade receivables	44	35
Cash and cash equivalents	4	6
Total current assets	98	85
Total assets	254	252

Equity and liabilities		
Equity		
Equity shares	42	42
Share premium	20	20
Revaluation surplus	13	1
Retained earnings	37	26
Total equity	**112**	**89**
Non-current liabilities		
Long-term loan	45	48
Preference shares	33	30
Total non-current liabilities	**78**	**78**
Current liabilities		
Trade payables	52	73
Taxation	12	12
Total current liabilities	**64**	**85**
Total equity and liabilities	**254**	**252**

1. The revenue for Dhaka Fabrics plc was £250 million in 20X9 and £235 million in 20X8, generating gross profits of £62 million and £54 million respectively.

2. Assuming all sales were made on credit terms and there are 365 days in a year, calculate the liquidity ratios and the length of the working capital cycle in 20X8 and 20X9.

3. There were trade purchases of £194 million in 20X9 and £191 million in 20X8. These were all made on a credit basis.

4. Comment on your results and the efficiency of the company's working capital management.

Solution

	20X9	20X8
Current ratio:		
$\dfrac{\text{Current assets}}{\text{Current liabilities}} =$	$\dfrac{98}{64}$	$\dfrac{85}{85}$
	1.5:1	1.0:1
Quick (or acid test) ratio:		
$\dfrac{\text{Current assets} - \text{inventory}}{\text{Current liabilities}} =$	$\dfrac{48}{64}$	$\dfrac{41}{85}$
	0.8:1	0.5:1

The liquidity ratios have improved in 20X9. We would normally expect the current ratio to be greater than one. A current ratio of less than one could indicate liquidity problems.

The quick ratio excludes inventory which cannot easily and quickly be converted into cash. Although the target is 1:1, an ideal ratio depends on industry practice.

In 20X9, current liabilities were well covered by current assets at a 1.5:1 ratio. Seventy per cent of the current liabilities were covered by liquid assets (including cash and trade receivables but excluding inventory).

The extent of the change in the liquidity ratios between the two years needs further explanation, which can be provided by looking at individual components of working capital or the WCC:

			20X9	20X8
			Days	Days
1. Inventory holding (days)	Inventory ÷ Cost of sales	× 365 =	97 (50 ÷ 250 − 62) × 365	68 (44 ÷ 235) × 365
2. Rate of collection of trade receivables (days)	Trade receivables ÷ Credit sales *Revenue*		64 (44 ÷ 250) × 365	84 (54) ÷ 235) × 365
Less:				
3. Rate of collection of trade payables (days)	Trade payables ÷ Credit purchases	× 365 =	(98) (52 ÷ 194) × 365	(140) (73 ÷ 191) × 365
Working capital cycle (WCC)			63	12

You would not be expected to calculate these last three ratios in any compulsory Section B question.

The overall WCC has lengthened from plus-12 to plus-63 days. The shorter the working capital cycle period, the more savings in interest expenses. The factors that impacted the overall WCC include the following.

Inventory holding period (days)

Inventory period has worsened from 68 to 97 days, resulting in more costs tied up in holding the inventory. Inventory that takes longer than three months to sell is normally not very liquid. The current ratio that includes inventory in the current asset may not be as optimistic as it looks. It is better to focus on the acid test ratio.

Rate of collection of trade receivables (days)

This has improved in 20X9 from 84 to 64 days. The company policy on credit allowed must be considered to be working. If 64 days is still significantly more than its normal credit period, then it could flag issues such as delays in sending out invoices, debt collection problems or poor screening of new customers. The acid test ratio ignores inventory (that takes a long time to convert into cash) but assumes trade receivables are liquid. If collection of trade receivables is an issue, the company could struggle to pay its current liabilities.

Rate of payment of trade payables (days)

The payment period has reduced significantly from 140 days to 98 days, thus increasing its opportunity costs. By using trade payables for financing, a company saves on interest on alternative financing such as bank overdrafts. However, any breach of the normal credit terms (such as suppliers requesting payment within 30 days) could result in default – resulting in the potential loss of any available discounts, the facility to pay on credit, increased prices or even the loss of suppliers.

Test yourself 8.3

The following are extracts from the financial statements of Kenya Ltd for the year ended 31 March 20X8.

Statement of financial position as at 31 March 20X8

	£'000
Non-current assets	800
Current asserts	
Inventories	600
Trade receivables	950
Cash and cash equivalents	50
Total assets	2,400
Equity shares	700
Retained earnings	400
Total equity	1,100
Non-current liabilities	
11% preference shares	300
12% debentures	700
Total non-current liabilities	1,000
Trade payables	300
Total equity and liabilities	2,400

Statement of profit or loss and OCI for the year ended 31 March 20X8

	£'000
Revenue	3,527
(credit sales = 3,500)	
Cost of goods sold	(2,500)
(credit purchases 2,537)	
Gross profit	1,027
Administrative expenses	(300)
Rent	(75)
Selling expenses	(100)
Depreciation	(80)
Operating profit	472
Interest charges	(72)
Profit before tax	400

Calculate:

1. Inventory holding period (days)
2. Rate of collection of trade receivables (days)
3. Rate of payment of trade payables (days)
4. Asset turnover ratio

How would you interpret the results?

Test yourself 8.4

How is working capital estimated from the working capital cycle?

Calculate the working capital requirement for Global Ltd from the following information:

	Cost per unit (£)
Raw materials	250
Direct labour	60
Overheads	140
Total cost	450
Profit	100
Selling price	550

- Raw materials are held in inventory for one month on average.
- Materials are in the process of manufacture for 20 days on average.
- Finished goods are held in inventory for 30 days on average.
- Average credit allowed by suppliers is 30 days and average credit allowed to customers is 45 days.
- Credit sales are 50% of total sales.
- Cash and cash equivalents are expected to be £120,000.
- The expected level of production will be 126,000 units for a year of 360 days.

6 The management of inventories

Inventory management is a key aspect of working capital management. It is crucial for businesses as it has a direct impact on profitability. The main objective of inventory management is to achieve maximum profits by maintaining adequate inventory levels for smooth business operations, while also monitoring the levels to minimise the costs of inventory holding. Holding too much inventory can result in the company's cash being tied up in purchasing, storing, insuring and managing inventory. It may also result in product obsolescence or waste, especially if the inventory is perishable.

By holding too little inventory, the business faces liquidity issues and costs of stock-outs, including re-order costs, setup costs and lost quantity discounts. The key task of inventory management – striking a balance between holding costs and costs of stock-out – involves determining:

- the optimum re-order level
- the optimum re-order quantity

Re-order level
Companies need to identify the level of inventory that must be reached before an order is placed. This is known as the re-order level (ROL). It indicates how much inventory to re-order and when to re-order.

In reality, demand will vary from period to period. When demand and lead time are known with certainty, ROL equals the demand in the lead time. Lead time is the time taken to receive inventory after it is ordered.

When demand and lead times are not known with certainty, inventory must include an optimum level of buffer (safety) inventory to minimise the costs of stock-outs. This depends on the level of demand, holding costs and the cost of stock-outs.

Inventory is a major investment for many companies and may take different forms. Manufacturing companies can easily be carrying inventory equivalent to between 50% and 100% of their revenue, (consisting of raw materials, work in progress and finished goods). In the case of retailers, inventory typically is made up of finished goods only.

6.1 Inventory management techniques

The balancing act between liquidity and profitability is key to good inventory management.

Inventory management techniques that help in efficient inventory management include:

- economic order quantity
- ABC inventory control
- just-in-time systems
- fixing the inventory levels
- vital, essential and desirable analysis

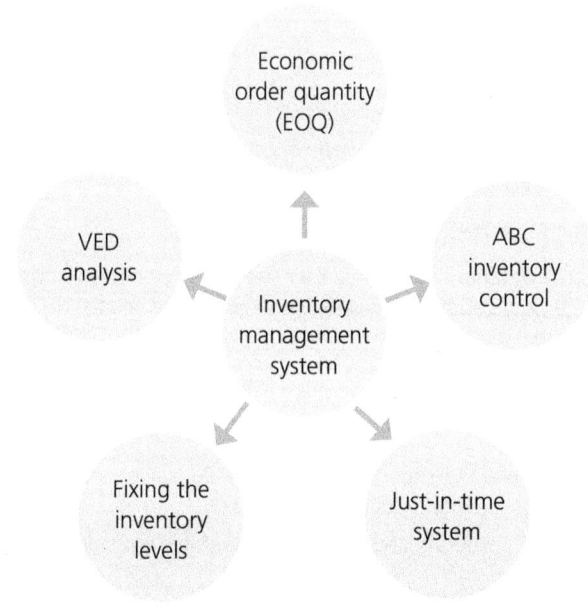

Figure 8.4 Inventory management techniques

6.2 Economic order quantity

The economic order quantity (EOQ) focuses on maintaining an optimum order quantity for inventory items. The aim of the EOQ model is to balance the relevant costs by minimising the total cost of holding and ordering inventory. The model makes following assumptions relating to its relevant costs.

Holding costs

The model assumes that it costs a certain amount to hold a unit of inventory for a year. The variable cost of holding the inventory is referred to as the holding cost. As the average level of inventory increases, so too will the annual holding costs. The annual holding cost is calculated as:

> Holding cost per unit × average inventory

Ordering costs

Ordering costs are the fixed costs of placing the order, incurred every time an order is placed. These include costs of transportation, inspections and so on. As the order quantity increases, the total ordering cost reduces. The annual ordering cost is calculated as:

> Order cost per order × no of orders per annum

Calculation of EOQ

The EOQ can be calculated using the formula:

$$EOQ = \sqrt{2 \times c \times d \div h}$$

Where:

d = annual demand,

c = ordering cost per order

h = holding cost per unit for one year

This provides the optimum inventory order size based on the annual inventory requirement, for which both the ordering cost and carrying cost are kept at minimum.

Assumptions and drawbacks

The model assumes that:

- demand and lead time are constant: this model will be ineffective for the business whose demand fluctuates frequently;
- purchase price, ordering and holding costs remain constant;
- no buffer inventory is held or needed;
- seasonal fluctuations can be ignored; and
- inventory levels are continuously monitored.

Quantity discounts

Economic order quantity must be compared with the quantity needed for quantity discounts. Companies must consider whether the order size should be increased above the EOQ to get the benefit of quantity discounts if the overall inventory cost is lower.

6.3 Determining inventory levels

The key to inventory management is to identify the correct level of inventory to hold. The level of inventory can be categorised into four levels.

Minimum level
This is the lowest balance that should be maintained by the company at all times. This level ensures that production will not be suspended due to lack of raw materials. While fixing the minimum level of inventory, one should keep in mind the time required for delivery and daily consumption.

Re-order level
This is the level of inventory at which the company should make a new order for supply. It is between the minimum level and the maximum level. When determining the re-order level, the minimum level and rate of consumption have to be considered.

Re-order level = minimum level + (rate of consumption × re-order period).

Maximum level
This is the maximum inventory level that the company can hold at any point of time. The inventory should not be more than the maximum level. If the level of inventory exceeds the maximum level, it increases the carrying costs and it is treated as overstocking.

Maximum level = re-order level + re-order quantity − (minimum rate of consumption × minimum re-order period).

Danger level
This level is fixed below minimum level. The inventory reaches this level when the normal issue of raw material is stopped and issued only in case of emergency. An immediate action must be taken by the company when the inventory reaches danger level.

Danger level = rate of consumption × maximum re-order period in case of emergency.

6.4 Just in time systems

The just in time (JIT) system is a series of manufacturing and supply chain techniques that aim to reduce inventory to an absolute minimum or eliminate it altogether by manufacturing at the exact time customers require, in the exact quantities they need and at competitive prices.

The JIT system, also known as the Toyota Production System (TPS), was developed in Japan in the 1960s and 1970s, particularly at Toyota. The key objective is to reduce flow times within the production system as well as response times from suppliers and to customers. It was defined by Monden Yasuhiro as a methodology used in 'producing the necessary items, in the necessary quantity at the necessary time'. Reducing the level of inventory not only reduces the carrying costs but, by using this technique, manufacturers also get more control over their manufacturing processes – making it easier to respond quickly when the needs of customers change.

JIT attempts to eliminate waste, capital being tied up in inventory and activities that do not add value by ensuring a smooth flow of work at every stage of the manufacturing and the production process. This also reduces storage and labour costs. Examples of waste include:

- capital and storage tied up in RM, WIP and FG
- materials handling costs
- rejects and reworks from poor quality
- queues and delays
- long raw material and customer lead times
- unnecessary clerical and accounting procedures

Relationships with suppliers are an important aspect of the JIT system. If the supplier does not deliver the raw materials in time, it could become very expensive for the business. A JIT manufacturer prefers a reliable, local supplier to meet the small but frequent orders at short notice, in return for a long-term business relationship. JIT has very low inventory holding costs (close to zero): however, inventory ordering costs are high.

Figure 8.5 Benefits of the JIT system

Despite the magnitude of the preceding advantages, there are also some drawbacks associated with the JIT system.

- Since the manufacturer does not maintain high levels of inventoy, any price fluctuations in raw materials could make the JIT system costlier.

- This model may not be helpful in cases of excess and unexpected demand, since it means few or no inventories of finished goods are held.
- Production is highly reliant on suppliers. If raw materials are not delivered on time, it could become very expensive for the business.
- It may need an investment in technology that links the information systems of the company and its suppliers.

6.5 ABC inventory control

ABC inventory control is an analytical approach for classifying inventory items based on the items' consumption values. Under this method of inventory management, materials are divided into three categories.

- **A category items** require high investment but only represent small amounts in terms of inventory items. Generally, these items represent only 15% to 20% of inventory items but have a relatively high consumption (also referred to as the 80/20 rule by the 'Pareto approach' where 80% of the output is determined by 20% of the input). Due to the high value associated with A category items and the greatest potential to reduce costs or losses, these are closely monitored and controlled to ensure these items are not over- or under-stocked.
- **B category items** represent 30% to 35% of inventory items by item type and about 20% of the value of consumption. B category items are relatively less important than A items. However, these will be maintained with good records and regular attention.
- **C category items** are the remaining items of inventory with a relatively low value of consumption. Usually they only make up to 10% of the total value of consumption. C category items are ordered on a half-yearly or yearly basis. It is not usually cost-effective to deploy tight inventory controls, as the value at risk of significant loss is relatively low.

Better control over high-value inventory improves efficiency and improves overall profitability. For example, inventory management resources can be dedicated to higher valued categories to save time and money. This method is mainly based on the monetary value of inventory items. It helps to focus inventory control and monitoring over costly items. However, it could ignore other factors which may be important to business. It requires keeping track of all inventory items and will be successful only if there is proper standardisation of inventories.

6.6 VED analysis

VED stands for vital, essential and desirable. It is a popular technique, especially with companies at the start-up stage who are working with limited resources and small budgets. Under-ordering can reduce the revenue stream while over-ordering can lead to capital being tied up.

The key objective of VED analysis is to identify the criticality of inventory items that the business cannot operate without. Inventory items are classed based on the degree of criticality.

- **Vital:** these are the vital items without which the production activities of the company would come to halt. These inventories should always be kept in hand.
- **Essential:** these are essential spare parts but whose non-availability may not adversely affect production. Such spare parts may be available from multiple sources within the country and the procurement lead time may not be long.
- **Desirable:** desirable items are those items whose stock-out or shortage causes only a minor disruption for a short duration in the production schedule. The cost incurred is very nominal.

Test yourself 8.5

1. How does the JIT system help a company to improve its relationships with customers and suppliers?
2. What are the key features of ABC inventory control?

7 The management of trade receivables

There are a number of ways in which companies may manage trade receivables more efficiently and reduce the level of working capital.

In highly competitive industries, companies often use credit sales as a promotional tool. Trade receivables are debts owed to a company by its customers for goods or services sold on credit. The management of trade receivables is a key aspect of working capital management, as a substantial amount of cash is tied up in trade receivables. The ultimate goal of trade receivables management is to maintain an optimum level of trade receivables by achieving a trade-off between:

- profitability from credit sales
- liquidity (reducing the cost of credit allowed)

The main purpose of managing trade receivables is to meet competition and to increase sales and profits, as long as the costs of funding the additional credit do not exceed the returns. The objectives of trade receivables management are:

- to control the costs associated with the collection and management of trade receivables: administrative costs associated with trade receivables include maintenance of records, collection costs, defaulting costs and writing off bad debts;
- to achieve and maintain an optimum level of trade receivables in accordance with the company's credit policies; and
- to achieve an optimum level of sales.

7.1 Factors affecting the size of trade receivables

- **Size of credit sales:** the primary factor in determining the volume of trade receivables is the level of credit sales made by the company. Trade receivables will increase with any increase in credit sales.
- **Terms of trade:** sometimes, companies make credit sales at higher prices than the usual cash sales price. This gives them an opportunity to make extra profit over and above the normal profit. If the company allows a customer a longer credit period than normal, then the trade receivables amount will also increase.
- **Credit policies**: credit policies are another major determinant in deciding the size of trade receivables. A liberal credit policy will create more trade receivables while the conservative or strict credit policy will reduce trade receivables.
- **Collection policies:** a company should have a strong and well-equipped credit collection system. Periodical reminders should be sent to the customers to reduce the trade receivables outstanding amounts. If proper attention is not paid to this, it will create potential issues such as additional cost on follow-ups or even the need to write off bad debts.
- **Expansion plans:** companies looking to expand their business encourage credit sales to attract customers. In the early stages of expansion, trade receivables are therefore usually at a high level. As the company becomes established, it may start reducing the credit period allowed.

7.2 Credit policy

A company's credit policy is important as it influences marketing policy and its value. The following factors need to be considered while developing a credit policy:

- level of credit sales required to optimise profits
- market conditions
- competition
- credit period
- terms of trade
- trade and settlement discounts
- efficiency in record keeping

A company needs to consider and evaluate the benefits and costs of different options to establish an optimal credit policy. The key elements or variants of credit policy that should be considered include the following.

Terms of credit
Terms of credit are the stipulations recognised by the company for making credit sales to its customers. They provide an agreement between a seller and buyer regarding the timing and amount of payments the buyer will make. It also covers other aspects, such as early cash settlement discounts.

Credit limits should be set for each customer and monitored on a regular basis. A longer credit period increases the working capital or cash operating cycle, thus increasing costs. However, customers prefer a generous credit period. The optimum policy formulates a trade-off between cost and profitability.

Assessing creditworthiness

A company should investigate the creditworthiness of all its new customers by checking their previous track record or credit files. This should be reviewed and monitored at regular intervals. Alterations to the credit terms should be made if necessary. Businesses use corporate credit rating agencies such as Dun & Bradstreet to assess the creditworthiness of their customers.

Collection policies

A credit period only begins once an invoice is issued to the customer. Prompt invoicing is essential. The risk of default increases if debts are allowed to go overdue: therefore, a system of follow-up procedures is required. A stringent collection procedure is expensive for the company because of high costs but it reduces bad debts. A lenient collection process attracts customers, but it has a higher risk of bad debt write-offs. An optimum collection policy can be formulated by balancing the cost and benefits. A collection process can be costly due to the lengthy steps involved. Most companies typically follow a collection procedure as demonstrated in Figure 8.6.

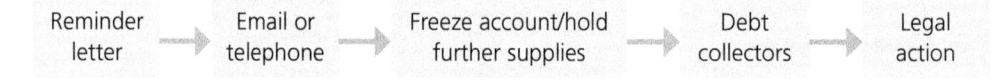

Reminder letter → Email or telephone → Freeze account/hold further supplies → Debt collectors → Legal action

Figure 8.6 Collection steps

Test yourself 8.6

What are the objectives of trade receivables management?

8 The management of trade payables

Managing trade payables is a key part of working capital management. The objectives of the management of trade payables are to ascertain the optimum level of trade credit to be given and to support mutually beneficial relationships with suppliers.

Deciding on the level of credit to accept is a balancing act between liquidity and profitability. Companies must consider the following factors in making the decision for the optimum level of trade payables and for the effective management of trade payables.

- Maintaining good relations with regular suppliers is important to ensure continuing supplies as and when required.
- The flexibility of available credit should be considered as it can be used as short-term finance when the company has a cashflow shortfall.
- Trade credit is the simplest and most important source of short-term finance for many companies. By delaying payment to suppliers, companies can reduce the level of working capital required. However, by delaying payments, a company risks its credit status with the supplier could result in supplies being stopped. It could also lose the benefit of any early settlement discount offered by the supplier for early payment.
- All other factors that could impact the overall cost of delaying payments must be considered: for example, whether interest is charged on overdue supplier accounts.
- Early settlement discounts should be taken up where possible. The discount is given when payables are promptly paid within the specified terms. However, a company might wish to maximise the use of the credit period allowed by suppliers if the firm is short of funds, regardless of any settlement discounts offered. When a choice of discount is given, the annual cost of a discount must be compared with the additional interest cost of paying the debt early (see Chapter 9).
- Management can use the trade payable days to control and to help monitor the level of trade payables.
- Companies should have sufficient liquidity to guarantee that trade payables can be paid off when they fall due. The current and quick ratios and the trade payables payment period ratio are all helpful in analysing the efficiency of management of trade payables.

Test yourself 8.7

What are the risks of delaying payment to suppliers?

Chapter summary

- Working capital is the total amount of capital tied up in current assets and current liabilities, which normally include inventories, trade receivables, cash and cash equivalents (less trade payables). It can be regarded as the lifeblood of an organisation. All of these are available for day-to-day operating activities.
- The working capital cycle (WCC) or cash operating cycle refers to the time taken by the organisation to convert its net current assets and current liabilities into cash. It can be determined by adding the number of days

required to complete each stage in the cycle. Length of the cycle depends on:
- the balancing act between liquidity and profitability
- efficiency of management
- terms of trade
- nature of the industry

- Working capital management is a balancing act between profitability and liquidity. Every business should have adequate or optimum working capital to run its operations efficiently and effectively but without holding levels of working capital that are too high or too low.
- Holding a high level of working capital can result in overcapitalisation, which means the entity is carrying idle funds with unnecessary cost implications.
- Low working capital can result in overtrading, which means the entity is not able to meet its day-to-day demands. This could lead to insolvency.
- Liquidity ratios or working capital (WC) ratios are used to control and monitor working capital. Two key WC ratios are the current ratio and the quick (or acid test) ratio.
- Efficiency ratios measure a company's ability to use its assets and manage its liabilities effectively. Key efficiency ratios are:
  - asset turnover
  - inventory turnover
  - rate of collection of trade receivables
  - rate of payment of trade payables
- Ratio analysis provides business owners with trend or time-series analysis, as well as trends within their industry. However, there are certain limitations to ratio analysis.
- The main objective of inventory management is to achieve maximum profits by maintaining adequate inventory levels for smooth business operations, while also monitoring the levels to minimise the costs of inventory holding. The key task of inventory management – striking a balance between holding costs and costs of stock-out – involves determining the optimum re-order level and the optimum re-order quantity.
- Popular inventory management techniques include:
  - economic order quantity (EOQ)
  - ABC inventory control
  - the just in time (JIT) system
  - fixing inventory levels
  - vital, essential, desirable (VED) analysis

- The management of trade receivables is a key aspect of working capital management as a substantial amount of cash is tied up in trade receivables. The ultimate goal of trade receivables management is to maintain an optimum level of trade receivables by achieving a trade-off between:
    - profitability from credit sales
    - liquidity (reducing the cost of allowed credit).
- The objectives of the management of trade payables are to ascertain the optimum level of trade credit and to support mutually beneficial relationships with suppliers. Deciding on the level of credit to accept is a balancing act between liquidity and profitability.

Chapter nine
Sources of short-term finance

Contents

1. Introduction
2. External sources of short-term finance
3. Bank and institutional loans
4. Overdrafts
5. Debt factoring
6. Invoice discounting
7. Alternative finance and online innovations
8. Internal sources of short-term finance
9. Controlling working capital
10. Reducing inventory levels
11. Tighter credit control
12. Delaying payments to trade payables
13. Sale of redundant assets
14. Retained earnings

1 Introduction

This chapter outlines sources of short-term finance and evaluates their associated risks and returns.

Short-term finance, also called working capital financing, is used to fund business requirements for working capital. It is normally repayable within one year of the year end. Its prompt availability enables businesses to seize business opportunities and run their day-to-day operations. There are various sources of short-term finance available which require varying levels of collateral and interest rate expense. Short-term finance may be either internal or external.

The main sources of finance are external – raised from outside the business – and include bank and institutional loans, overdrafts and debt factoring. Internal sources of short-term finance are internally generated, such as financing through reducing or better controlling working capital and using retained earnings. This chapter will provide an overview of each of these sources, along with the advantages, disadvantages and degree of risk attached to each source.

2 External sources of short-term finance

Companies cannot rely solely on reinvested profits to finance their expansion. The main sources of finance are external (raised from outside the business). External sources of short-term finance available to businesses include:

- bank and institutional loans
- overdrafts
- debt factoring
- invoice discounting
- alternative financing, such as crowdfunding and other online innovations

Stop and think 9.1

Identify the external sources of short-term finance available to your business.

3 Bank and institutional loans

Bank and institutional loans are the most popular type of finance. Bank loans are generally a quick and straightforward option for raising short-term business finance. They are usually provided over a fixed period of time and can be short term or long term, depending on the purpose of the loan. Lending to companies for less than one year is considered to be a short-term loan.

Loans can be negotiable, whereby the rate of interest, repayment dates and security for the capital offered must be agreed depending on the risk and credit standing of the company. Short-term loans are less risky than loans with longer terms and may be the only type of loan available to new businesses.

3.1 Secured versus unsecured loans

Secured loans
Banks and other finance companies often require security for a short-term loan just as they do for a long-term loan. Security for short-term loans usually consists of trade receivables, inventories or both. For example, invoice financing uses trade receivables. If the business fails to repay, the lender may take action to seize the security and take legal proceedings against the company. Company directors may also be personally liable, depending on how the loan was arranged.

Unsecured loans

The most common way to finance a cash deficit is to arrange a short-term, unsecured bank loan. Unsecured loans are normally taken for smaller amounts and take place over a shorter period of time. Businesses generally pay more interest with unsecured loans as they are not backed up by an asset. There is a higher risk for the lender, as they have no guarantee of getting their money back. Firms who use short-term bank loans often arrange a line of credit – an agreement between a bank and a customer that establishes a maximum loan balance that the lender permits the borrower to access or maintain. To ensure that the line is used for short-term purposes, it works as a revolving account. The borrower can spend, repay it and spend it again, in a virtually never-ending, revolving cycle. Examples of unsecured lending include unsecured bank loans and (in a consumer context) credit cards.

3.2 Loan covenant

A term loan is conditional on a **loan covenant**. A loan covenant places a restrictive clause in a loan agreement that places certain constraints on the borrower, with reference to:

- **financial reporting**: requiring lenders to submit management reporting, including cash flow and forecasts, on a regular basis (such as every quarter);
- **financial ratios:** getting debt or liquidity ratios within an agreed range or requiring working capital to be maintained at a minimum level;
- **regulatory reporting:** requiring the statutory financial statements to be audited annually; or
- **debt covenants:** restricting the borrower's ability to take on more debt without prior consent of the lender or forbidding it from undertaking certain activities.

loan covenant
A loan covenant places a restrictive clause in a loan agreement that places certain constraints on the borrower, such as forbidding the borrower from undertaking certain activities, restricting its ability to take on more debt without the prior consent of the lender or requiring working capital to be maintained at a minimum level.

3.3 Advantages

- Loans can be set up in a short space of time, providing access to money quickly.
- Businesses normally prefer unsecured loans as they are considered less risky than loans with longer terms.
- They are good for budgeting as they require set repayments spread over a period of time.
- Loans have more flexible terms than some other sources of short-term finance. For example, they may provide the option for interest-only payments with the balance of the loan to be paid off at a later date.
- Banks do not put as much emphasis on the credit history of the business as they do for longer-term loans.
- Loans do not require giving up control of or a share of the business.
- Interest and arrangement fees are normally tax deductible.
- They are usually not repayable on demand unless defaulted.

3.4 Disadvantages

- Short-term loans usually have higher interest rates than long-term loans.
- Loans can compound debt problems if a business cannot obtain cheaper long-term finance.
- Defaulting on repayment can damage credit status.
- A term loan is conditional on a loan covenant. The bank can demand repayment of the loan if the business defaults.
- There is normally an extra charge for early repayment.

4 Overdrafts

An overdraft is a pre-agreed facility provided by banks and financial institutions that allows a withdrawal of money in excess of the account's credit balance. It is a common way of financing small and medium entities (SMEs) and is often used as a back-up form of financing to ease pressures on working capital.

Overdrafts are ideal for those with fluctuating finance requirements, particularly when a company has to provide for unexpected expenditure such as paying for repairs and maintenance. They are either provided over a fixed period of time or as a rolling facility with no end date. There is no penalty for repayment of an overdraft, unlike the early repayment of a loan.

However, business overdrafts are normally provided at a cost of an annual arrangement or maintenance fee, plus interest. Interest rates on overdrafts are charged on a daily basis on the overdrawn amount and are usually high, but they vary depending on the risk of default. The interest rate of an overdraft is normally variable (a margin over base rate or the Bank of England base rate).

4.1 Advantages

- Overdrafts are easy and quick to arrange with immediate access to funds.
- Unlike many loans, an overdraft can normally be cleared anytime without an early repayment penalty.
- They serve as backup against unexpected expenditure.
- The bank normally allows for an interest-free period with interest paid only on the overdrawn balance.
- They do not require giving up control of or a share of the business, unlike equity financing arrangements.
- Interest and arrangement fees are normally tax deductible.
- Due to its short-term nature, an overdraft balance is not normally included in the calculation of the business's financial gearing.

4.2 Disadvantages

- Interest is unpredictable as it depends on a variable interest rate and on the amount overdrawn on each day of the charging period.

- Overdrafts are repayable on demand without prior notice, although this is unlikely unless the business experiences financial difficulties.
- A higher rate of interest is charged for using the unauthorised facility.
- Banks often charge an annual arrangement or maintenance fee for providing an overdraft facility.
- Larger facilities will often need to be secured, depending on the lender and the business's level of risk.
- Failure to pay the interest charges or going back into credit on a regular basis can lead to a fall in credit score.

Stop and think 9.2

What are the advantages of an overdraft over a loan? Should your business get a loan or an overdraft?

5 Debt factoring

debt factoring
A financial arrangement whereby a business sells all or selected trade receivables at a price lower than the realisable value to a third party, known as the factor, who takes responsibility for collecting money from the customers. Also known as invoice factoring.

Debt factoring, or invoice factoring, is a financial arrangement whereby a business sells all or selected trade receivables at a price lower than the realisable value to a third party, known as the factor, who takes responsibility for collecting money from the customers. The arrangement provides an immediate source of cash to the business selling its trade receivables.

There are two types of factoring.

- **With recourse:** the borrower maintains control over the trade receivables and collects from customers. The factor assumes no responsibility for bad debts. Credit risk of non-payment by the debtor is borne by the borrower and trade receivables are essentially used as collateral. This approach is least visible to customers and allows borrowers to keep customers from knowing about any factoring arrangements.

- **Without recourse:** the factor maintains control and bears the responsibility for bad debts and any risk of non-payment, subject to the payment of an additional fee. The lender advances a certain percentage, normally around 80% of the value of the debt, within two or three days of the factoring arrangement. Besides the assured cash flow, the administrative burden of the supervision of trade credit is reduced, which may be important for small and growing businesses. The lender monitors all trade receivables due from the customers of the borrower and has payments sent to the lender's designated location. The factor subsequently pays over the balance, less its administration costs, to the company.

5.1 Advantages

- Debt factoring provides an immediate source of finance.
- It is particularly useful to companies that are expanding rapidly, as it will leave other lines of credit open for use elsewhere in the business.
- Start-up businesses and SMEs can benefit from factoring when they cannot gain access to other forms of cheaper finance.
- Debt collection, when outsourced, can increase cash by providing savings in credit management and certainty in cash flows.
- The factor's credit control system can be used to assess the creditworthiness of both new and existing customers.
- Reduces the probability of bad debts for the company.
- Non-recourse factoring allows for insurance against bad debts.

5.2 Disadvantages

- Factoring can be expensive, with costs normally running at between 2% and 4% of sales revenue.
- Debt collection, when outsourced, raises fears about its viability. This may endanger the company's trading relationships with customers who may not wish to deal with a factor.
- The company risks losing control over its trade receivables and granting credit to its customers.
- The company still bears the risk of non-payment in factoring (with recourse) where credit risk of non-payment by the debtor is borne by the business.

6 Invoice discounting

Invoice discounting and factoring are both ways of speeding up the collection of funds from trade receivables. However, unlike factoring, **invoice discounting** does not use the sales ledger administration services of a factor.

Invoice discounting, also referred as 'bills discounting' or 'purchase of bills', is a short-term borrowing arrangement whereby a company can borrow cash from financial institutions against invoices raised with customers. The company uses unpaid trade receivables as collateral.

Generally, a company can use up to 80% of the value of all invoices which are at less than 90 days to borrow within 24 hours. The finance company relies on a spread of trade receivables among many customers. The actual percentage and duration may vary. While specialist invoice discounting providers exist, this is a service also provided by a factoring company.

Invoice discounting is a quick way to improve cash flow but may cause management to lose focus from the administrative and compliance aspect. Invoice discounting should be used as an additional facility. The key focus should be on improving credit control to improve the working capital cycle and liquidity.

> **invoice discounting**
> Invoice discounting, also referred as 'bills discounting' or 'purchase of bills', is a short-term borrowing arrangement whereby a company can borrow cash from financial institutions against invoices raised with customers.

6.1 Advantages

- Invoice discounting is a quicker method to procure cash than through loans and overdrafts (which often require a credit check).
- It provides significantly more cash than a traditional bank.
- It accelerates cash flow from customers, since generally up to 80% of the invoices can be converted into cash.
- No non-current assets are required as collateral – borrowings are against sales invoices.
- Invoice discounting allows more room for credit sales by making such sales more liquid.
- The borrowers maintains control over the trade receivables.
- Confidentiality of the arrangement can be maintained.
- The company can obtain the cash it needs while also allowing the normal credit period to its customers.

6.2 Disadvantages

- The additional fees charged by the discounting providers decrease the company's profit margin.
- Excessive reliance on invoice discounting may not be taken very positively by all stakeholders. It can give the appearance of the borrower struggling with finances.
- As it is available only on commercial invoices, payments owed from the general public may not be eligible for invoice discounting.
- When a business relies heavily on invoice discounting, it may cause management to lose its focus from strengthening its credit norms.

Stop and think 9.3

Can you think of situations where factoring may be more appropriate than invoice discounting and vice versa?

7 Alternative finance and online innovations

Alternative finance has grown into a considerable global industry in recent years following the financial crisis that engulfed global markets in 2008. Traditional finance providers demonstrate a high resistance to risk, often requiring tangible assets such as plant and machinery as collateral. A sizeable number of businesses, including SMEs, continue to struggle to secure funding through traditional routes. Continuing challenges include uncertainty in the wake of the UK's withdrawal from the European Union (Brexit) and financial impact from the Covid-19 pandemic, meaning some of those declined by banks may have to look elsewhere for financial support.

Alternative finance provides financial channels that are not as rigid as the traditional finance system. It is the 21st-century internet alternative to traditional banks. Consumers are increasingly going online to access finance that traditional lenders are not prepared to offer, or only offer at a high cost. Figures from *Pushing Boundaries: The 2015 UK Alternative Finance Industry Report* for 2015 revealed that the alternative finance industry in the UK was worth £3.2 billion. Part of its appeal is its efficiency and flexibility: rather than waiting several weeks, alternative finance can authorise finance within days and with fewer restrictions than the traditional lenders.

This new breed of alternative finance includes:

- reward-based **crowdfunding**
- peer-to-peer (P2P) lending
- invoice trading third-party payment platforms.

New rules came into force in 2014 for the regulation of alternative finance activities such as equity crowdfunding and P2P lending. The regulations require that platforms operating in the sector must be licensed and conform to standards set out by the FCA. The rules were introduced to provide sufficient protection for investors while continuing to allow consumers and businesses access to these methods of funding.

crowdfunding
A practice of raising money, most commonly via the internet, to support a business venture, project, or local initiative. The investors will sometimes receive shares in the business. More often, they will receive a reward such as early receipt of the product being produced and/or a discount on the price of the product.

7.1 Crowdfunding

Crowdfunding is not a source of debt finance but a practice of raising money, most commonly via the internet, to support a business venture, project or local initiative. The investors will sometimes receive shares in the business; more often, they will receive a reward such as early receipt of a product and/or a discount on the price of the product.

Crowdfunding usually takes place on a website platform such as Kickstarter, Indiegogo or GoFundMe. It uses social media to raise money alongside traditional networks of friends, family and work acquaintances.

Consumers may find it rewarding to be involved in the crowdfunding projects. In 2015, nearly 80,000 people put up more than $20 million on Kickstarter for a company that developed a smartwatch alternative to the Apple Watch (see Case study 9.1). More recently, Sono Motors raised nearly $60 million for the design and manufacture of Sion, a vehicle that can be charged by solar panels integrated into its outer skin.

If crowdfunding continues to grow while retaining its distinctiveness, it has the potential to increase entrepreneurship by expanding the pool of investors beyond the traditional dominance of bank finance to individuals with smaller resources. Crowdfunding platforms may offer higher returns than those available from other financial products, though there are usually greater risks and new challenges.

As the market is still evolving, new types of platforms that carry a different level of risk will continue to emerge. Campaigns and projects funded can fail. Investors face a high risk of losing their principal or sometimes being exposed to scams. As the market becomes more complex and competitive, it gets harder to accurately report performance and capture sensible data for businesses to make sound judgements and for governmental bodies to act upon.

Case study 9.1: Pebble Watch and Kickstarter

The most famous crowdfunded product, the Pebble Watch, showed how crowdfunding worked at its best.

Pebble wanted to release a reasonably priced smart watch that interacted with people's smartphones. With no luck from traditional investors, the founders marketed the watches by putting a video on the crowdfunding website Kickstarter. They first set a goal of $100,000 in order to develop their product. They took pre-orders in Kickstarter by promising watches from the first production run to investors putting up more than $115.

The funding target exceeded their expectations: they raised more than $1 million within 27 hours and over $10 million by the end of their 30-day run.

7.2 Peer-to-peer lending

Peer-to-peer (P2P) lending, sometimes referred to as crowdlending, is a business borrowing from a collection of private investors, usually through an online platform such as Funding Circle, RateSetter, ThinCats and Assetz Capital.

The P2P lending business facilitates the arrangement by matching lenders with borrowers and credit-checking the borrowers. P2P lending is debt finance that generally operates online, therefore operating with lower overheads and providing a lower cost service than traditional lenders. As a result, both the lenders and the borrowers expect to get a better rate than they would through banks. Businesses or individuals needing to borrow money apply online and the software determines the credit risk and the rate of interest to be charged.

Peer-to-peer loans are normally unsecured, although some of the largest amounts are lent to businesses. Secured loans are sometimes offered by using luxury assets and other business assets as collateral. They are made to an individual, company or charity. There is a risk of the borrower defaulting on the loans taken out from P2P websites.

7.3 Invoice trading third-party payment

Peer-to-peer invoice trading is a new type of invoice finance where businesses (usually SMEs) auction their outstanding invoices via centralised online platforms such as MarketInvoice and Platform Black to obtain immediate cash to boost their working capital.

It provides an online solution that connects businesses selling invoices with investors lending against those invoices for an attractive return. The platform charges a fee from both the businesses and the investors for the service provided. It provides finance more cheaply and quickly than from traditional providers. Like factoring, businesses receive funds against invoices without having to wait for the invoices to be settled.

Unlike factoring, invoice-trading platforms provide finance against individual invoices rather than signing clients up for long-term contracts. There are no setup or termination fees. The business is in control of the number of invoices they sell on a pay-as-you-go basis. Funds can be accessed the same day, with easy applications and online administration.

7.4 Advantages

- Alternative finance provides quick access to money with online applications.
- It provides new and innovative ways to connect borrowers and investors via the internet.
- It can save businesses from unexpected financing distress.
- It provides access to funds previously unavailable by use of non-traditional forms of determining credit worthiness, often in conjunction with credit reports.

7.5 Disadvantages

- Alternative financing is not subject to regulatory reporting requirements in many jurisdictions.
- It costs significantly more than annualised rates associated with conventional financing – anywhere from 30% to 50%.
- The amount of money that can be borrowed is quite limited (typically less than £100,000).
- Small businesses simply may prefer working with more established, well-recognised institutions.
- Lenders are subject to increased risk losses due to fraud.
- The market is still evolving with new platforms carrying the different level of risk for both lenders and borrowers.

Stop and think 9.4

What are the risks and returns of alternative finance sources?

8 Internal sources of short-term finance

Internal sources of short-term finance are funds generated internally by the business in its normal course of operations. For example, the business can raise short-term finance through cash improvements gained by reducing the level of or improving control of working capital. Similarly, it can sell assets that are no longer needed to free up cash or use its internally generated retained earnings.

Internal sources of short-term finance mainly include:

- Reducing or controlling working capital
  - reducing inventories
  - tighter credit control
  - delaying payments to suppliers
- sale of redundant assets
- retained earnings

9 Controlling working capital

Chapter 8 looked at ways in which companies manage their inventories, trade receivables and trade payables more efficiently, thus better controlling (which normally means reducing) the level of working capital. This chapter demonstrates how the reduction of working capital helps release funds that can be re-invested in the business as a source of short-term finance.

Working capital has the following components:

- current assets: inventory, trade receivables and cash
- current liabilities: trade payables and bank overdraft

A reduction in working capital can be achieved either by speeding up the cycle of inventory and trade receivables, or by lengthening the cycle of trade payables. In essence either approach, or a combination of both, will reduce the level of funds invested in working capital.

Normally, a business requires two types of finance: long-term finance for capital expenditure and working capital finance for everyday costs (wages, bills and paying suppliers). As discussed in Chapter 8, the permanent or fixed working capital is the minimum level of working capital required to continue uninterrupted day-to-day business activities. It is usually funded from long-term finance.

A higher level of working capital represents a large commitment of finance and a significant opportunity cost. Efficiency savings generated through the efficient management of trade receivables, inventory, cash and trade payables can reduce the bank overdraft and interest charges, as well as increasing cash balances that can be re-invested elsewhere in the business.

Every business should have adequate or optimum working capital to run its operations efficiently and effectively, but without holding too much working capital. A sensible working capital policy is the balancing act between the two, where the risk and return balance is maintained by using funds in an efficient and effective manner.

A conservative approach	**An aggressive approach**
Higher level of working capital	Lower level working capital
Higher liquidity	Lower liquidity
Cash tied up	Cash savings
Lower profitability	Higher profitability
Lower risk	Higher risk

Figure 9.1 Working capital management – a balancing act

Stop and think 9.5

How can increasing working capital management efficiency or reducing working capital to a minimal level be a source of internal finance?

Test yourself 9.1

What are internal sources of short-term finance? How can increasing working capital management efficiency be a good source of short-term internal finance?

10 Reducing inventory levels

The cost of holding inventory includes purchasing goods, storing, insuring and managing them once they are in inventory. For most businesses, carrying inventory involves a major working capital investment and uses large amounts of finance that could be used elsewhere in the business. We should note that some companies, such as service companies, may hold little or no inventory. Inventory levels need to be tightly controlled while retaining the capacity to meet future demand. Inventory management is balancing those two opposing factors for optimum profitability and cash savings. Methods for reducing and controlling inventories are discussed in Chapter 8.

10.1 Advantages

- Carrying low inventory reduces carrying costs of storage (rent, insurance and interest charges).
- It frees up money tied up in inventories.
- It reduces the risk of deterioration, obsolescence and theft.

10.2 Disadvantages

- Reducing inventories risks the possibility of stock-outs and dissatisfied customers.
- A higher risk of loss of production time.
- Bulk purchase discounts may not be available.

Worked example 9.1 demonstrates the amount of cash savings that can be released by reducing inventory levels as a result of applying inventory management principles.

Worked example 9.1

Takura Ltd is a manufacturing company with the following figures from the latest annual statement of profit or loss and OCI.

	£'000
Revenue	1,700
Cost of goods sold	(700)
Gross profit	1,000
Administrative expenses	(500)
Marketing expenses	(260)
Operating profit	240

The company's annual consumption of raw materials is £350,000 (50% of cost of goods sold).

The company introduces **just in time** (JIT) processes as a measure to control inventory. As a result:

- Takura Ltd will be able to reduce its raw materials cost from 209 to 45 days consumption and finished goods inventory from 78 to 50 days cost of goods sold. Takura Ltd is targeting a significant reduction in the inventory days ratio, as outlined in Chapter 8. It is targeting this improvement both to release cash and improve profitability.

- As there will be less inventory, the carrying costs (warehouse storage charges, insurance, etc.) will be reduced by 3% of the administrative expenses. Takura Ltd is also looking to reduce its overdraft as this is incurring a 15% per annum interest charge.

The potential financial benefit of these changes is as follows.

Workings

	Monetary figures in £'000	Current £'000	Monetary figures in £'000	Reduced £'000
Raw materials	(209 ÷ 365) × 350 = 200	200	Target = (45 ÷ 365) × 350	43
Finished goods	(78 ÷ 365) × 700 = 150	150	Target = (50 ÷ 365) × 700	96
		350		139

In terms of inventory days, Takura Ltd is targeting a reduction of its raw materials from 209 days to 45 days consumption and finished goods inventory from 78 days to 50 days cost of goods sold.

Financial benefit	£'000
Cash released from reduced inventory levels (350 – 139)	211
Cash release from reduced general administrative expenses (3% × 500)	15
Total cash released	226
Saving in interest charges at 15% per annum by reducing overdraft	34

The reduction in inventory levels would release cash that can be used to reduce the company's overdraft significantly, saving £34,000 per year in interest charges.

Inventory reductions, due to the application of sound inventory management principles, would also help the business to be more profitable by lowering the cost of goods sold and the related administrative expenses.

Stop and think 9.6

How would a business carrying too much inventory tie up money that could be used elsewhere?

Test yourself 9.2

Kathmandu Ltd is a retail store that sells Himalayan trekking equipment. Figures from its latest annual financial statements are as follows.

Statement of profit or loss and OCI

	£'000
Revenue	2,700
Cost of goods sold	(900)
Gross profit	1,800
Administrative expenses	(400)
Marketing expenses	(640)
Operating profit	760

Statement of financial position

- Raw materials: £100,000
- Finished goods: £350,000

The annual raw materials consumed were £200,000 and the annual cost of goods sold was £900,000. The company introduces a JIT process as a measure to control inventory. As a result, Kathmandu Ltd will be able to reduce its raw materials to 40 days consumption and its finished goods inventory to 45 days cost of goods sold.

The rate of interest charged on its overdraft is 10%. Calculate the reduction in raw materials and finished goods and the overall financial impact.

11 Tighter credit control

tighter credit control
A strategy employed by businesses, particularly in manufacturing and retailing to ensure sales are promptly realised as cash or liquid resources.

Tighter credit control is a strategy employed by businesses, particularly in manufacturing and retailing, to ensure customers pay promptly, so that cash is received by businesses as quickly as possible.

This control will increase cash sales and decrease bad debts written off, improving a company's cash flow and profit. Management of trade receivables is discussed in Chapter 8, which looked at ways in which companies may manage trade receivables more efficiently and thus reduce the level of working capital.

Efficient collection of income from credit customers releases funds which can be reinvested in the business as a source of short-term finance. Settlement discounts may be offered to encourage prompt payment. The higher the level of trade receivables, the larger the commitment of finance – and the more cost for the company in terms of opportunity cost in interest and the greater risk of losses through bad debts.

Businesses with too much credit could experience cash flow problems. Those not offering enough credit would risk losing customers with detrimental consequences on sales and profitability. The key is to choose the right mix of credit and cash flow for the business.

11.1 Advantages

- Tighter credit control frees up cash.
- It creates savings in opportunity cost in interest.
- It reduces the cost of credit control and the risk of losses through bad debts.

11.2 Disadvantages

- Tighter credit control risks losing the competitive edge over businesses providing credit, thus resulting in a potential loss of customers.
- Loss of customers could result in reduced sales and reduced profit.

Stop and think 9.7

If a company's revenue is mainly derived from credit sales, is it worth reducing average trade receivables days by increasing the use of loans and overdrafts?

12 Delaying payments to trade payables

Chapter 8 discussed the methods and principles applicable for effective management of trade payables. Companies often use trade payables as a cheap form of short-term finance by using the full credit period before payment. However, delaying payment beyond the agreed credit period would be dangerous. This is because a company risks losing its credit status with its suppliers and this could result in supplies being stopped. Additionally, the company could risk the possibility of not being able to buy on credit in the future and/or lose the benefit of any settlement discount offered by the supplier for early payment.

The annual effective cost of refusing early payment discounts can be calculated and compared with the cost of financing working capital to help make financing decisions in the short term.

12.1 Advantages

- Delaying payment to trade payables helps cash retention that can be used for other purposes.
- Trade payables are often viewed as a source of 'free credit' and a cheap form of short-term finance.

- 'Buy now, pay later': the if the business can sell the goods first and pay for them later, there are savings on opportunity costs if trade payables are paid within the agreed time.

12.2 Disadvantages

- There may be a reputational cost from loss of goodwill that could damage the company's credit status.
- Potential loss of suppliers due to breach of the terms of credit and default if their suppliers aren't paid on time.
- Suppliers may increase prices in future.
- Loss of benefits from suppliers who provide incentives such as settlement discounts on early payments.

Test yourself 9.3

If a company is risk-averse, why might it be more likely to choose a higher level of working capital? What are the factors to consider in choosing the right balance of working capital?

13 Sale of redundant assets

Businesses can raise funds by selling off their unused assets. It can work as a source of short-term or long-term finance, depending on the assets. Selling equipment or motor vehicles, for example, can cater to short-term and small finance needs. Selling land, buildings or machinery can cater to long-term, larger finance needs. This method can be used as a 'one off' source of finance to free up cash for other business needs. The future operating capability of the business should always be a consideration if this option is being undertaken as the assets can only be sold once. Routine replacement of non-current assets should always happen as part of day-to-day operations.

13.1 Advantages

- It raises finance from assets that are no longer needed – as long as this is clearly identified as being the case.
- No interest charges or dilution of control are associated with this, unlike debt or equity financing.

13.2 Disadvantages

- Businesses do not always have surplus assets available for sale.
- Selling off redundant assets is a 'one off' source of finance.
- It may not be easy to find potential buyers and can be a slow method of raising finance.

14 Retained earnings

Most business investments come from reinvested profit. Though it is normally considered long-term finance, it can also be used for financing working capital. Retained earnings as a source of financing is discussed in Chapter 11.

Chapter summary

- The main sources of finance are external (raised from outside the business). External sources of short-term finance available to businesses include:
    - bank and institutional loans;
    - overdrafts: pre-agreed facilities provided by banks and financial institutions that allows a withdrawal of money in excess of the account's credit balance;
    - debt factoring: a financial arrangement whereby a business sells trade receivables at a price lower than the realisable value to a third party, known as the factor, who provides an immediate cash fund and takes responsibility for collecting money from the customers;
    - invoice discounting: whereby a company can borrow cash from financial institutions against the invoices raised;
    - alternative finance and online innovation: provides a 21st-century alternative to traditional banks; it includes reward-based crowdfunding, peer-to-peer lending and invoice trading third-party payment platforms.
- Internal sources of short-term finance mainly include the reduction or controlling of working capital – efficiency savings generated through efficient management of trade receivables, inventory, cash and trade payables. These include:
    - reducing inventories
    - tighter credit control
    - delaying payments to suppliers
    - sale of redundant assets
- Retained profits can be used as both long-term and short-term finance.

Chapter ten
Financial markets and the identification of financing needs

Contents

1. Introduction
2. Identification of financing needs: budgeting and forecasting
3. The need for cash and cash management
4. Financial markets
5. Private versus public markets
6. The role of the stock exchange
7. Efficient market hypothesis
8. AIM
9. Other sources of finance from the private market

1 Introduction

This chapter looks at how a company's financing needs are identified through planning, budgeting and forecasting. It looks at the need for cash – the lifeblood of any company – and how this is managed using different models of cash management. It provides an overview of financial markets and covers the different types of markets, including:

- capital versus money markets
- primary versus secondary markets
- private versus public markets

This chapter examines the different market participants, including investors, borrowers, intermediaries, banks and regulators and explores the principles underpinning market efficiency in the form of the efficient market hypothesis.

2 Identification of financing needs: budgeting and forecasting

All organisations need finance to survive. The financial needs of an organisation can be grouped into the following categories:

- long-term financing needs (covered in Chapter 11)
- short-term financing needs (covered in Chapter 9)

The distinguishing factors between these needs are the time period, purpose, cost and means of finance. An organisation anticipates and monitors its funding requirements to meet strategic goals and objectives through planning, budgeting and forecasting.

2.1 Planning, budgeting and forecasting

Financial planning is a continuous process of directing and allocating financial resources and determining how an organisation will meet its strategic goals and objectives.

Budgeting is an outline of a company's financial plans, normally drawn up for the next full trading year. It is the process of creating a plan, also referred to as a financial budget, to project incomes and outflows for the next full year. It creates a baseline to compare actual results with the expected performance.

Financial forecasting is the projection of a company's future financial outcomes over a longer time period by examining its historical and current financial data. A long-term financial forecast will take a view of the possible financial performance of the company over several years. It is a financial model of potential future company performance, especially in the light of the strategy of the company and likely market and economic conditions over a longer time period. The first year of a financial forecast over years is likely to be based on the annual budget.

A financial budget establishes a picture of a company's financial health, anticipates its funding requirements and presents a strategy for managing its assets, cash flow, income and expenses. It provides an overview of spending relative to revenues. Budgets are an important tool to identify, allocate and manage the resources as they are needed. Budgeting also helps in motivating employees by setting the objectives of the company. Budgets may also be linked to rewards where targets are met. By formalising objectives through a budget, utilisation of resources is improved.

A budget assigns financial resources for a task for a specified period of time. Budgets can be prepared for a specific section of the company. Examples include a purchases budget (outlining expected purchases of raw materials or products for anticipated sales), a revenue budget (showing expected sales) or an IT department budget (allocating IT costs).

One of the most important budgets is a **cash budget.** A cash budget sets out the cash inflows and outflows for a company over a specific period of time

budgeting
Budgeting is an outline of a company's financial plans, normally drawn for the full year. It is the process of creating a plan, also referred to as a financial budget, to project incomes and outflows.

financial forecasting
The projection of a company's future financial outcomes over several years, by examining its historical and current financial data.

cash budget
A cash budget sets out the cash inflows and outflows for a company over a specific period of time. It ensures there is enough cash within the company to operate.

to ensure that there is enough cash within the company to operate and avoid financial embarrassment. See section 2.4 on page 235 for more detail.

The **master budget** shows how all the budgets work together to project combined incomes and outflows for the company. Each of these budgets will be controlled by a budget holder, managing a specific section of the company.

master budget
The master budget shows how all the budgets (such as purchases budget, sales budget and cash budget) work together to project combined incomes and outflows for the company.

Budgeting represents a company's goals, financial position, profit and cash flows. Budgets are presented mostly in the form of budgeted financial statements (profit or loss, financial position and cash flows). Detailed budgets include sales forecasts, production forecasts and other estimates that shows whether the company is heading in the right direction.

forecast
The revised estimate of company financial performance in a year (or other time period), given a review of current performance In the year against the budget.

While a budget is a plan for what a company wants to achieve, a **forecast** is the prediction of what will actually be achieved. Forecasting allows management to take immediate action in the short term and feeds the development of a sound budget in the long term.

Performance against the budget is monitored and updated on a regular basis, ideally each month. This enables company managers to frequently analyse monthly actual results and forecast revenues and expenses for the remaining months of the year based on their real-time observations of the current market conditions – therefore revising the forecast. See section 2.4 for more detail.

While budgeting and forecasting are different functions, they are not mutually exclusive. Both make sure the company is heading in the right direction. While budgeting quantifies the expectations or targets (in terms of revenue, cost allocation, savings and so on) by outlining what a company wants to achieve, company always needs a forecast to reveal the actual circumstances and numbers that will be achieved. Both rely on similar financial assumptions like revenue and expenses.

2.2 Flexible versus static budgets

There are two types of budgets: flexible budgets and static budgets.

The most common type of budget is a static budget that projects a fixed level of expected input, output and costs. It remains unchanged irrespective of the changes in volume or activity. The actual results at the end of the budget period very often vary from the static budgets.

A flexible budget, also known as variable budget, is one that adjusts with changes in volume or activity. It allows the budget to be adjusted throughout the year as company conditions change. The change can be due to delay in activity, change in volume or adding new activity. The budget will include a variable rate per unit of activity instead of one fixed total amount.

A flexible budget is often more useful than a static budget. For example, a company makes a static budget that has budgeted the cost of running its machinery at £100,000 per month irrespective of the machine hours used. However, in a flexible budget, the company can budget the running cost based on the average fixed cost of £34,000 + £6 per machine hour. In a flexible budget, the values change to reflect changes in activity or output, allowing managers to adjust to the needs of the business. The flexible budget offers a better opportunity for planning and controlling than a static budget.

2.3 Budgetary control

Once a budget is prepared, financial managers use budgetary control to control and monitor the actual results against the budgeted figure. The detailed analysis of variance (difference) is conducted to evaluate the performance of the project or budget area. It allows costs and performance to be reviewed and adjusted where needed.

Controlling the budget is a critical responsibility of the budget holder or the project manager. It helps management to set financial and performance goals (such as sales or spending goals), then evaluate progress by comparing and analysing the actual costs and performance results with the budgeted goals. It allows managers to focus on poorly performing areas and strengthen the favourable ones. The actual results are then compared with the budgeted performance over the entire period. A key element of budgetary control is providing a revised forecast of financial performance. Lastly, management will work to improve the under-performing areas and develop a plan to fix them in the next period.

2.4 Cash budget

A cash budget is a projection of cash receipts and payments for a future period to help determine any excessive idle cash or cash shortage that is expected during the period. The budget is linked to both the strategic and company plans. It is used by managers to signify if any action is necessary to bring the forecast in line with the overall company plan, such as arranging a bank overdraft.

A **cash forecast** is an estimate of cash receipts and payments for a future period that includes all the projected inflows and outflows under existing conditions. A forecast period normally covers the next 12 months; however, it can also cover a short-term period such as a month or a quarter.

Cash budgets are used to control and monitor the actual cash receipts and cash payments against the budgeted figures. On mapping of receipts and payments, a monthly cash surplus or cash deficit can be identified. An example of a cash budget statement is shown in Table 10.1.

The preparation of this statement gives an early warning of the future cash position. This will help the finance manager consider the timing of important decisions that will impact cash flows. You will not be expected to prepare a cash budget statement in the examination, but understanding how they are prepared will help with answering any questions on analysing what a cash budget statement might tell you about a company's financial performance.

cash forecast
A cash forecast is an estimate of cash receipts and payments for a future period, including all the projected inflows and outflows under existing conditions.

Month	January	February	March	Total
Amount	£	£	£	£
Opening cash balance (A)	xxx	xxx	xxx	xxx
Cash inflows/receipts				
Customer receipts	xxx	xxx	xxx	xxx
Receipts on repayment of loans	xxx	xxx	xxx	xxx
Total inflows (B)	xxx	xxx	xxx	xxx
Cash outflows/payments				
Purchase of materials	xxx	xxx	xxx	xxx
Salaries and wages	xxx	xxx	xxx	xxx
Interest payment on loans	xxx	xxx	xxx	xxx
Other overheads	xxx	xxx	xxx	xxx
Total outflows (C)	xxx	xxx	xxx	xxx
Net cash inflow/(outflow) (B − C)	xxx	xxx	xxx	xxx
Closing cash balance to be carried forward to next month (A + B − C)	xxx	xxx	xxx	xxx

Table 10.1 Cash budget statement for the period January to March 20X1

Worked example 10.1

Avahana Ltd provides you with the following forecast and the related information for you to help prepare a monthly cash budget for the six months ending 30 September 20X8.

The forecasts are as follows.

Month	Sales (£'000)	Purchases (£'000)	Wages and overheads (£'000)
February 20X8	30,000	15,000	4,200
March 20X8	25,000	16,200	4,300
April 20X8	20,000	18,000	4,500
May 20X8	24,000	15,000	4,600
June 20X8	26,000	15,600	4,600
July 20X8	27,000	20,000	4,600
August 20X8	29,000	21,000	4,600
September 20X8	31,000	19,000	4,650

1. The cash balance on 1 April 20X8 is £5,000,000
2. Sales are 50% on a cash basis and 50% on a credit basis. Credit sales are collected in the month following the sale. No bad debts are expected.
3. Credit allowed by suppliers is two months but invoices are normally paid a month in arrears.
4. Wages are paid in the same month.
5. There is a capital payment of £17,500,000 due in June 20X8 for the purchase of some additional land.

Solution

Cash budget statement for the 6 months ending 30 September 20X8

Particulars	April 20X8 £'000	May 20X8 £'000	June 20X8 £'000	July 20X8 £'000	August 20X8 £'000	September 20X8 £'000
Opening cash balance (A)	5,000	6,800	6,200	(3,900)	2,400	5,800
Inflows						
Cash sales	10,000	12,000	13,000	13,500	14,500	15,500
Receipts from receivables	12,500	10,000	12,000	13,000	13,500	14,500
Total inflows (B)	22,500	22,000	27,000	26,500	28,000	30,000
Outflows						
Purchases	16,200	18,000	15,000	15,600	20,000	21,000
Wages and overheads	4,500	4,600	4,600	4,600	4,600	4,650
Capital	0	0	17,500	0	0	0
Total payments (C)	20,700	22,600	37,100	20,200	24,600	25,650
Net cash inflow/ (outflow) (B – C)	1,800	(600)	(10,100)	6,300	3,400	4,350
Closing Cash Balance (A + B – C)	6,800	6,200	(3,900)	2,400	5,800	10,150

The cash budget statements shows cash inflows in four of the six months, but cash outflows in May 20X8 and June 20X8. The cash outflow in May 20X8 is £600,000, leaving a month end cash balance of £6.2 million. It should be noted that cash balances do not usually increase or decrease steadily during a month and the worst-case scenario is that all of the outflows take place before any inflows, so that there could be a lower cash balance during the month.

However, in June 20X8 there is a major capital payment of £17.5 million and this leads to a net cash outflow of £10.1 million. It also leaves a closing cash balance of minus £3.9 million. Avahana Ltd would need an overdraft agreement with its bank for this to be allowed to happen. Alternatively, it could consider some additional form of finance for this capital payment.

By the end of September 20X8, the balance is £10.15 million. Avahana Ltd may have organisational policies around minimum cash balances and investing any surplus cash balances.

Across the whole six-month period, the cash balance for Avahana Ltd increases by £5.15 million in spite of the £17.5 million capital payment. The company is generating a good level of surplus cash from its operations.

Test yourself 10.1

Port Louis Limited provides you with the following details.

£

Month/Year	Sales	Materials	Wages	Overheads
Apr-17	42,000	20,000	16,000	4,500
May-17	45,000	21,000	16,000	4,000
Jun-17	50,000	26,000	16,500	3,800
Jul-17	49,000	28,200	16,500	3,750
Aug-17	54,000	28,000	16,500	6,080
Sep-17	61,000	31,000	17,000	5,200

Other information

- Sales are 20% on a cash basis and 80% on a credit basis. 50% of the credit sales are collected within one month following the sale and the remainder within two months.
- Credit allowed by suppliers is two months.
- Wages and overheads are paid a month in arrears.
- Dividends on investments amounting to £25,000 are expected to be received in the month of June 2017.
- New machinery costing £400,000 is to be installed in June 2017. This is payable in 20 instalments starting from July 2017.
- The cash balance on 1 April 2017 is £45,000.

Prepare a monthly cash budget statement for the six-month period (April to September) on the basis of the above information.

3 The need for cash and cash management

Cash is the lifeblood of any company. It is the most liquid asset to help companies survive and meet their organisational goals. Cash management is the process of collecting and managing payments. It also involves payments of cash to third parties such as suppliers, contractors and banks. The primary responsibility of managing cash lies with the finance managers. The key objective of cash management is to avoid either a surplus or a deficit of cash by ensuring:

- there are adequate cash balances in times of need;
- surplus cash is invested or used to repay the existing debt to maximise the returns for the company; and
- there should not be a situation where there is deficit of cash due to unnecessary shortage of funds.

Cash management is a trade-off between liquidity and costs.

3.1 Need for cash

Every transaction results in an inflow or outflow of cash. These inflows and outflows may not be synchronised. Sometimes, the inflows are more than the outflows or vice versa. The primary motive of holding cash is to maintain a financial position in situations of certainty as well as uncertainty. According to Keynes' general theory of economics (1936), there are three basic motives for holding cash.

- **The transaction motive:** maintaining enough cash to meet the day-to-day operations such as payments to vendors, petty expenditure and salaries. Cash is received in the ordinary course of company from debtors (trade receivables) or investments. Often these inflows and outflows do not match, hence cash is required to meet these mismatches.
- **The precautionary motive:** holding cash to meet contingencies and unexpected situations, such as providing a safety net for unexpected events.
- **The speculative motive:** using cash to take advantage of profitable investment opportunities. For example, holding money will allow cheaper bonds or shares to be bought in the future.

3.2 Methods of dealing with cash surpluses and cash deficits

Cash surplus
An entity has a cash surplus if it has enough money to cover at least a couple of months of overheads in an emergency. A finance manager has to make the most of such a cash surplus. It can be used to either repay existing debts or to invest in opportunities which will give returns to the entity. Repayment of debt is usually the first option preferred by the organisation, as investment in short-term investments may not yield the savings that one may get on repayment of debt.

Cash deficit
When an organisation cannot meet its day-to-day cash expenditure, it experiences a cash deficit. Cash deficits arise due to unnecessary shortages of funds. When a situation of a cash deficit arises, the organisation may have to sell its assets, cut down its inventory levels, chase customers for payment or delay payments to employees and suppliers.

4 Financial markets

financial market
A marketplace where financial wealth or assets (such as equities, bonds, currencies and derivatives) of individuals, institutions, government and so on are traded.

stocks
Stocks refers to the overall ownership in one or more companies. The similar term 'shares' refers to the ownership certificates of a particular company.

A **financial market** is a marketplace where the financial wealth or assets (such as **stocks** or equities, bonds, currencies and derivatives) of individuals, institutions, governments and so on are traded. Trade is often conducted via a middleman called a broker or intermediary.

Like any other market, financial markets' primary participants are borrowers (those in need of finance) and investors (those with financial resources). The main factors that determine the prices of financial assets that trade in the market are the supply and demand of the trading assets. A company which has identified cash or financing needs might access a financial market in order to secure the funding it requires.

4.1 Financial market participants

There are a large number of participants in the financial market. Funds flow from one group (investors) to another group (borrowers). The link is often provided by market intermediaries such as investment bankers, brokers, mutual funds, leasing and finance companies. Key participants include the following.

Investors and lenders
An investor is a person or entity who invests or commits capital into an entity with the expectation of financial returns, either by subscribing to the shares of the entity or by purchasing its bonds or debentures. Any individual, company or other institution who owns at least one share of the company is considered to be a shareholder.

A lender is an individual, a public or private group, or a financial institution that lends money with the expectation that it will be repaid with interest.

Borrowers
A borrower is a person or entity who obtains funds (loans, bonds or debentures) from a company or individual for a specified period of time upon condition of promising to repay the loan. The terms of the loan are spelled out in a written document that is signed by both the lender and the borrower.

Banks
A bank is a financial institution licensed to receive deposits and make loans. Banks play a major role in managing the liquidity in the economy.

Regulators
A **financial regulator** is an institution that supervises and controls a financial system to protect the interest of investors and to guarantee fair and efficient markets and financial stability. For example, the London Stock Exchange (LSE) is regulated by the Financial Conduct Authority (FCA) and the New York Stock Exchange (NYSE) is regulated by the Securities and Exchange Commission (SEC).

Intermediaries
Intermediaries are service providers in the market who facilitate connections between investors and the users of funds. They include investment bankers or investment managers, registrars, brokers, mutual funds, leasing and finance companies.

4.2 Types of financial markets

There are various types of financial markets where different classes of assets are traded.

Capital markets
A **capital market** is a market where finance products with maturities of more than one year are traded. These include long-term debt, bonds or equity-backed securities. This type of market is composed of both primary and secondary markets. Broadly, a stock market, derivatives market and a bond market could be collectively called a capital market.

- **stock market:** for the trading of shares
- **bond market:** for the trading of bonds/debentures of various companies or the government
- **derivatives market:** for the trading of complex financial instruments such as futures, forwards, options and so on (not covered in this module)

Capital markets can be divided into the following types.

- **Primary market:** new shares and bonds are issued to the public for the first time to raise funds on these markets. An initial public offering (IPO) takes place on a primary market. An IPO is underwritten by one or more investment banks, who also arrange for the shares to be listed on one or more stock markets.
- **Secondary market:** existing securities – shares, stocks and **loan stock** – are traded after the company has sold all the stocks and bonds offered on the primary market. Markets such as NYSE and LSE have secondary markets.

Money markets
A money market is where instruments with high liquidity and very short maturity (less than one year) are traded, typically for the financing of working capital and meeting short-term liabilities. These instruments include treasury bills and commercial paper. They are regarded as being as safe as bank deposits yet provide a higher yield.

---

financial regulator
An institution that supervises and controls a financial system to protect the interest of investors and to guarantee fair and efficient markets and financial stability.

intermediaries
Intermediaries are service providers in the market who establish a link between the investors and the users of funds. They include investment bankers or investment managers, registrars, brokers, mutual funds, leasing and finance companies.

capital market
A capital market is where finance products with maturities of more than one year are traded. These include long-term debt or bonds (over a year) or equity-backed securities.

Treasury Bills (T-bills) are short-term debt instruments issued and backed by government (such as the US Treasury Department). It is essentially money lent to the government and hence considered safe. They have a maturity of less than one year with no interest payable. They are sold at a discount to their face value but pay the full face value at maturity.

Commercial paper is an unsecured, short-term debt instrument issued and backed by an issuing bank or company. It is essentially money lent to the issuing company or bank. They are sold at a discount but pay the full face amount on the maturity date of no more than 270 days from the date it was issued.

Trading in money markets is done over the counter (OTC) and is wholesale (traded by financial institutions in large quantities). An OTC market is decentralised, meaning assets are traded through private securities dealers rather than through a centralised, formal exchange.

Other markets
Other markets include:

- currency markets, where currencies of various countries are traded
- commodities markets, where agricultural, base metals and energy commodities are traded

These markets are not covered in this module.

Test yourself 10.2
How does a primary market differ from a secondary market?

5 Private versus public markets
Financial markets can be divided into private markets and public markets.

5.1 Private markets
This is where transactions are held and executed OTC through private securities dealers. The buyer and seller personally negotiate and execute the transaction, with no intermediary between the buyer and the seller. Instruments are not publicly traded and hence, the liquidity in such instruments is reduced comparatively. They are not as regulated as the public markets, mainly because the general public is not affected. Participants normally include:

- banks
- venture capitalists
- private equity investors
- hedge funds

The investments in private markets carry greater risk than public market investments. Hence, the investors would expect greater returns from such investments. Investments are not affected by movements in public market investments.

Advantages of private markets
- Selective access to investors and less competition.
- Normally no intermediary between the buyer and the seller.
- Not tightly regulated and hence less compliance costs for the investee.
- Greater probability of providing higher returns.

Disadvantages of private markets
- Investors usually do not have complete information at hand.
- Cannot be sold or purchased easily, making the investments less liquid than public markets.
- Highly risky, as they are essentially unregulated.

5.2 Public markets

A public market is a market in which the general public can participate. A typical example of a public market is a **stock exchange**, a public market in which securities (shares and loan stocks) are bought and sold (see section 6). A person with as little as £10 can participate in such a market. Public markets are highly regulated as the exposure to the general public is greater. They also offer greater liquidity, thereby enabling a smooth purchase or sale. However, the returns from investing in a public market may not be as exorbitant as the returns from the private market.

stock exchange
Public markets in which securities (shares and loan stocks) are bought and sold.

Issuing financial instruments in public markets requires companies to issue a prospectus and other documents that the regulator may prescribe. The risk profile of public markets is relatively small because of regulation, transparency and monitoring by seasoned investors and regulators.

Advantages of public markets
- No qualification or net worth criteria need to be fulfilled to enter the market.
- Highly regulated and transparent market, thereby reducing risk.
- Highly liquid investments.

Disadvantages of public markets
- Moderate returns.
- Regulated, with a high compliance burden on companies.
- Highly speculative market.

Test yourself 10.3

What are the key advantages of a public market over a private market?

6 The role of the stock exchange

Stock exchanges are public markets in which securities (shares and loan stocks) are issued, bought and sold. Most countries have some form of stock market which provides a primary market that brings together organisations wishing to raise capital and investors with capital to invest. A well-functioning stock market is essential for the progress of a nation. The index of the stock exchange could be used as a barometer of the performance of the economy.

There are stock markets with differing levels of sophistication, with major markets based in London, New York and Tokyo. The London Stock Exchange, for example, functions as both a primary market, a secondary market and as the market for dealing in gilts (government securities).

A company needs to be listed on a stock exchange in order to issue shares and raise capital through the primary market function of the stock exchange. Companies issue shares in the stock market to:

- raise funds for company requirements
- comply with the requirement of a stock exchange flotation where a minimum proportion of shares must be made available to the public.

Shares are bought and sold through a broker or market maker, who acts as an agent between sellers and sellers. Share prices are determined by the balance of supply and demand in the market, with higher demand pushing up the price. A perfect market responds immediately to the information made available to it.

Stock exchanges also provide services other than listing of securities, such as checks on unfair trade practices, providing research reports to the investors and regulating companies, brokers and other intermediaries. Stock exchanges also regulate listed companies in respect to disclosure of material financial and non-financial information. They could be seen as an information bank for investors.

A stock exchange also enables investors to value companies, as the stock exchanges provide a bid-offer quote (comprising of the highest price offered by an investor and the lowest price accepted by the seller) as well as the last traded price of the stock. It also provides a transparent mechanism for the transfer of stocks between the investors thereby protecting the investors from frauds, forgery and so on.

Test yourself 10.4

1. **Why do companies list their shares on a stock exchange?**
2. **What are the key functions of a stock exchange?**

7 Efficient market hypothesis

The efficient market hypothesis (EMH) theory was developed by Eugene Fama in the 1960s. It states that it is impossible to 'beat the market' if markets are efficient. This is because the market prices fully reflect the available information and the stocks are therefore always trading at fair values.

In an efficient and perfect market, quoted share prices are as fair as possible because they accurately and quickly reflect a company's financial position, as well as its current and future profitability. An efficient market ensures that the market price of all securities traded on it reflects all the available information. A perfect market responds immediately to the information made available to it.

According to EMH, the market price of the share is reflective of an unbiased **intrinsic value.** This is also referred to as fundamental value, which can be determined through fundamental analysis without taking its market value into consideration.

The market price can deviate from an intrinsic value, but these deviations are not based upon any specific variant. These deviations are random and cannot be correlated with any specific conditions. Based on this hypothesis, it would not be possible for investors or valuation experts to identify any overpriced or underpriced securities and take advantage of the market movements. This provides an equal opportunity to everyone in the stock markets.

intrinsic value
Intrinsic value refers to the inherent or perceived worth of a share which may deviate from its market value. It is also referred to as fundamental value, which is determined through fundamental analysis without taking its market value into consideration.

7.1 Levels of market efficiency

The EMH considers whether market prices reflect all information about the company. Fama identified three levels of market efficiency:

Weak form
Market prices are reflective of all historical information contained in the record of past prices. Share prices will follow a 'random walk', moving up or down depending on the next piece of information about the company that reaches the market. The weak form implies that it is impossible to predict future prices by reference to past share price movements.

Semi-strong form
Market prices reflect not just the past and historical data but all information which is currently publicly available. Investors are unable to gain abnormal returns by analysing publicly available information after it has been released. Prices will alter only when new information is published. With this level of efficiency, share prices can be predicted only if unpublished information were known. This would be known as **insider dealing**. Trading based on insider information to one's own advantage, through having access to confidential information, is illegal in most countries.

insider dealing
Trading on the stock exchange to one's own advantage through having access to confidential information. In most countries, trading based on insider information is illegal.

Strong form
Share prices reflect all available relevant information, published and unpublished, including insider information. This implies that even insiders

are unable to make abnormal returns as the market price already reflects all information.

Evidence suggests that insiders can still gain from such dealing in most markets. For example, insiders such as directors have access to unpublished information. If the market was 'strong form', share prices would not move with the news of potential takeover. However, in practice, share prices tend to rise on the announcement of a takeover which implies that most markets are 'semi-strong form' at best.

Strong
(reflects all information, public and private)

Semi-strong
(reflects all public information)

Weak
(reflects market prices and data)

Figure 10.1 EMH market efficiency

Stop and think 10.1

Consider the relevance of efficient market hypothesis in the share price of any listed company.

Test yourself 10.5

1. What are the three forms of market efficiency?
2. In what form of market efficiency can money be made by insider dealing?
3. Provide an example of exceptions when a sudden price change is not triggered by new information about the company reaching the market.

8 AIM

AIM (formerly the Alternative Investment Market) is a sub-market of the London Stock Exchange that was launched in 1995 to provide a platform for smaller companies. It is designed to allow companies to raise capital from the general public without going through the rigours of compliance requirements which needed to be satisfied to raise capital from the main platform. The London Stock Exchange regulates AIM. It is touted to be the most successful growth market in the world. Initially, AIM began operating with 10 listed companies with a combined market capitalisation of £82.2 million. Currently, more than 850 companies are listed with a combined market capitalisation of £104 billion.

AIM works on a principles-based, 'comply or explain' regulation model, where companies either comply with the regulations or explain why they have deviated from following any regulation. Its balanced approach is well-suited to smaller companies. Considering that the companies listed on AIM are small, typically only institutional or wealthy investors look to participate. Investing in AIM listed companies may provide high return but commensurately higher risk.

AIM provides an opportunity for small companies looking for growth capital to obtain the benefits of listing and expand the company without incurring high compliance costs. AIM is a source of finance for smaller companies looking to raise long-term finance with limited resources. A company looking to join AIM is required to carry out some due diligence, such as analysis of financial reports and the key aspects of the company activity and strategy.

Stop and think 10.2

Think of the key reasons why AIM was launched.

9 Other sources of finance from the private market

9.1 Institutional investors

An institutional investor is a person or an entity which pools money to purchase securities and other investments that provide sufficient returns and security to satisfy their stakeholders. There are several different types of institutional investor.

9.2 Private equity

Private equity finance is not publicly traded but raised through private investors – typically large institutional investors, university endowments, or wealthy individuals. It is also referred to as an investment fund that is organised through the mediation of a venture capital company or private equity company. Raising private equity finance does not expose the company to the same level of scrutiny and regulation as listing on a stock market.

private equity
Capital raised through private investors who are typically large institutional investors, university endowments or wealthy individuals. It is not publicly traded in a public exchange.

placing
A way of raising equity capital by selling shares directly to third-party investors (usually a merchant bank).

Investing through private equity is perceived to be relatively high risk. Investors provide finance through placing as they yield higher returns than they would from a market-listed company. **Placing** is a way of raising equity capital by selling shares directly to third-party investors (usually a merchant bank). Company angels (see below) are also a source of private equity finance for start-up and early-stage companies in return for a share of the their equity.

9.3 Venture capital

In the last few decades, investment from private firms and individuals has become a major source of finance for companies. For a new company or a small company, it may be difficult to get loans from customary lenders like banks and financial institutions. For such companies, which have potential for high future growth, private individuals and firms provide start-up capital and other technical assistance for a few years until they are self-sufficient or profitable.

company angels
Wealthy, private investors who provide their personal wealth to start-up and early-stage companies in return for a share of their equity. While venture capitalists use pooled money, company angels usually invest their own funds.

Venture capital financing is a method of raising money via high net worth individuals who are looking at diverse investment opportunities. These individuals are often known as **company angels**, as they act as benevolent mentors to help build the company. Company angels are a diverse group of individuals who have amassed their wealth through a variety of sources. They tend to be entrepreneurs themselves or have recently retired from the company empires they have built. Most company angels look for companies that are well-managed, have a good company plan and have growth potential. These investors prefer to support ventures that are in similar company sectors or categories with which they are familiar. They provide the company with much-needed capital to sustain company in exchange for shares or ownership in the company in the future.

9.4 Pledge funds

A pledge fund is a form of private equity investment but, unlike a traditional committed private equity fund, a pledge fund is not a 'blind pool'. It instead allows investors to provide capital on a deal-by-deal basis, contributing a sum of money toward a specific, predetermined goal. Not all pledge fund investors will participate in each deal.

It is a specific type of venture capital investment in which an individual can finance for a specific investment goal by making defined contributions over a period of time. Using a pledge fund format, an investor is not forced to follow the majority decision but will have the freedom to elect whether to take part in an investment opportunity on a case-by-case basis. Due to the nature of a pledge fund, investments are made on a per-deal basis and members may find it easier to raise funds, compared with other types of investment platforms.

The design and structure of a pledge fund resembles a conventional private equity fund to a certain extent. However, there is a greater control over how and where projects are funded. A pledge fund offers more control over deals compared to open investments which takes funding from investors but does not have a specific objective for the funding.

There are potential drawbacks to a pledge fund. For instance, more time may be needed to assess and evaluate investment opportunities, its objectives and impacts. It may also be harder to find additional investment in the future as the pledge funds have limitations on how the money can be used.

9.5 Unit trusts

A **unit trust** is a form of collective investment bought in units to allow small investors to hold a diversified portfolio of investments. There is no limit to how many people can invest in it or how much can be invested. The portfolio is managed on behalf of investors by a unit trust company which deducts management expenses from the income of the portfolio before they are paid out. Each investor holds a sub-unit or stake in the portfolio that can be traded at a price determined by the underlying value of the securities included within them. The investment fund is set up under a trust deed.

> **unit trust**
> A unit trust is a form of collective investment which is bought in units to allow small investors to hold a diversified portfolio of investments.

9.6 The Enterprise Investment Scheme

The Enterprise Investment Scheme (EIS) is a company expansion scheme launched in the UK in 1994 to encourage investments in small unquoted companies.

Investment in unquoted companies carries a high risk of loss of capital and low market liquidity. This scheme provides some incentives to counterbalance those risks. It provides a series of UK tax reliefs up to a maximum investment of £1 million in each tax year. It also offers exemptions from capital gains tax and inheritance tax.

9.7 Pension funds

A pension fund, known as a superannuation fund in some countries, is a fund from which pensions are paid.

Pension funds typically have large amounts of money to invest in both listed and private companies. Pensions are accumulated from contributions from employers, employees or both. In most pension funds there is a surplus of incoming funds from contributions over outgoings as pension payments. This surplus is invested to maximise the best possible return while maintaining the security of the funds.

The pension fund manager often spreads the investment between gilts, equity and property. Pension funds, along with insurance companies, make up a large portion of institutional investors that dominate stock markets.

9.8 Banks

There are different types of banks specialising in different areas. They are normally categorised into four main groups.

- **Retail banks** focus on the general public/consumers by operating with multiple branch locations. Services offered include providing current and saving accounts and issuing credit cards, mortgages and loans.

- **Commercial banks** focus on company customers by accepting deposits, offering checking (current) and saving accounts and providing company loans. They also support companies by offering additional services such as basic investment products, accepting payments from customers and providing letters of credit to companies overseas. Banks such as Barclays and HSBC provide retail and commercial banking.
- **Investment banks** such as JP Morgan, Deutsche Bank and Morgan Stanley help startup or expanding companies by issuing stocks or bonds to investors in financial markets. They help companies 'go public' or sell debt by locating interested investors. Similarly, corporations use investment bankers to negotiate the terms of a merger or acquisition.
- **Central banks,** also referred to as reserve banks (such as the US Federal Reserve Bank and the Bank of England), manage the monetary system for a government, including the state's currency, money supply and interest rates. They also usually oversee the commercial banking system of their respective countries. These institutions are usually in charge of overseeing the commercial banking sector within their jurisdictions.

Bank and institutional loans are the most popular type of finance. Bank loans are generally a quick and straightforward option for company finance. These are covered in Chapter 9.

Test yourself 10.6

How can companies raise finance from the following institutional investors?

1. **Private equity**
2. **Pension funds**

Chapter summary

- Financial planning is the continuous process of directing and allocating financial resources and determining how an organisation will meet its strategic goals and objectives.
- Budgeting is the process of creating a plan, also referred to as a financial budget, to project incomes and outflows for the long term as well as the short term. Financial forecasting is the projection of a company's future financial outcomes by examining its historical and current financial data.
- One of the most important budgets is a cash budget. This sets out the cash inflows and outflows for a company over a specific period of time to ensure that there is enough cash within the company to operate.
- Cash management is a process of collecting and managing payments in the due course of company. The key objective of cash management is to maintain the balance between surpluses and deficits of cash.

- A financial market is a marketplace where the financial wealth or assets (such as stocks or equities, bonds, currencies and derivatives) of individuals, institutions, government and so on are traded.
- There are a large number of participants in financial markets, including:
  - investors and lenders
  - borrowers
  - banks
  - regulators
  - intermediaries
- There are various types of financial markets where different classes of assets are traded, including:
  - capital markets
  - money markets
  - others (currency, commodities)
- The financial markets can be divided into private markets and public markets. Private markets are where transactions are held and executed 'over the counter' – a decentralised market where assets are traded through private securities dealers rather than through a centralised, formal exchange. Public markets are markets in which the general public can participate. A typical example of a public market is a stock exchange.
- The term 'stock exchange' refers to a public market in which securities (shares and loan stocks) are issued, bought and sold. Share prices are determined by the balance of demand and supply in the market, with higher demand pushing up prices. A perfect market responds immediately to the information made available to it.
- An efficient market ensures that the market price of all securities traded on it reflects all the available information. There are three levels of market efficiency: weak, semi-strong and strong.
- AIM is a sub-market of the London Stock Exchange that was launched to provide a platform for smaller companies to raise capital from the general public.
- Other sources of finance from the private market include institutional investors such as:
  - private equity
  - venture capital
  - pledge funds
  - unit trusts
  - the Enterprise Investment Scheme
  - pension funds
  - banks (retail, commercial, investment and reserve banks)

Chapter eleven
Sources of long-term finance

Contents

1. Introduction
2. Equity or ordinary shares
3. Retained earnings
4. Preference shares
5. Bonds and debentures
6. Bank and institutional loans
7. Leasing
8. Securitisation of assets
9. Private finance initiatives
10. Government grants and assistance

1 Introduction

Finance is important for any company which requires capital to finance long-term investments and overall working capital. As a company grows and expands, it needs additional capital to purchase non-current assets such as land, buildings and machinery to expand its production capacity, develop and market new products and enter new markets. Even a proportion of working capital, which is required to meet day-to-day expenses, is of a permanent nature and requires long-term capital.

Long-term finance is typically defined as a type of financing that is obtained for a period of more than a year. Some companies divide finance into three categories: less than one year as short term, one to five years as medium term and five years and longer as long term. For our purposes, we will consider any finance longer than one year as long-term finance. A company can look at various sources to fulfil these long-term financial requirements.

In general, companies must choose between **equity finance** and **debt finance**. Equity finance refers to the finance relating to the owners or equity shareholders of the company who jointly exercise ultimate control through their

equity finance
The finance relating to the owners or equity shareholders of the company who jointly exercise ultimate control through their voting rights. Equity finance is represented by the issued equity or ordinary share capital plus other components such as retained earnings.

debt finance
Borrowed money to be paid back at a future date with interest. It could be in the form of a secured as well as an unsecured loan.

voting rights. Equity finance is represented by the issued equity or ordinary share capital plus other components of equity (such as share premium and retained earnings). Debt finance is the main alternative to equity that involves the payment of interest. It can be used for both short-term and long-term purposes and may or may not be secured.

Depending upon the nature of finance, it could be for a fixed period of time (a five-year loan) or have no expiry date (equity shares). Financial managers must look at the best way to raise the capital.

This chapter looks at the different ways of raising long-term finance, considering their advantages and disadvantages as sources of finance. In addition, Chapter 12 will cover the choice between equity versus debt financing in the context of the overall risk that determines the rate of return an investor demands.

Some of the most common types of long-term finance under equity and debt finance are:

- equity finance
    - equity or ordinary shares
    - retained earnings or internally generated funds
- debt finance
    - preference shares
    - debentures (bonds or loan stocks)
    - bank and institutional loans
    - leasing
    - securitisation of assets and use of special purpose vehicles
    - private finance initiatives (PFIs)

2 Equity or ordinary shares

Equity shares are permanent capital and a long-term source of finance. It is not returned to the shareholders in most circumstances other than in the event of liquidation. Shareholders are collectively referred to as the owners of the company.

Ownership means that the equity shareholders bear the greatest risk. The equity shareholders receive dividends only after the payments of debts and dividends to preference shareholders have been made. To protect the interests of creditors, a company may declare a dividend only if it has sufficient profit available for the purpose.

Authorised share capital is the maximum amount of share capital that a company may issue, as detailed in the company's Memorandum of Association. Shares are issued to shareholders to show their ownership of a company at a nominal share value (the book or face value). In the UK, this is generally £1, 50p, 25p, 10p or 5p. The market price is the price at which shares are sold. The shares are said to be at par value, if the market value and the nominal value are the same. A successful company will be able to issue equity shares at a price in excess of their par value: this is recorded separately as the share premium.

The issued share capital is the nominal value of share capital issued to shareholders. The rights and voting powers of shares and the differentials between the different classes of shares are listed in the company's Articles of Association.

2.1 Advantages

- Equity shareholders are paid the residual funds (in the form of dividends) or the leftover funds in the event of liquidation, after all other lenders and creditors are paid.
- From an investor's liquidity point of view, equity shares of a quoted company can be easily traded in the stock market.
- A company which raises capital from issuing equity shares may provide a positive outlook for the company.
- It delivers greater confidence amongst investors and creditors.

2.2 Disadvantages

- In return for accepting the risk of ownership, equity shares carry voting rights through which equity shareholders jointly control the company.
- The equity shareholders have greater say in the management of the company, although managerial control may be limited.
- The issue of additional equity shares may be unfavourable to the existing shareholders, as it will dilute their existing voting rights.
- It may affect future dividends.

> **Stop and think 11.1**
>
> As a finance manager, would you advise a company to issue equity shares to fund its new capital projects if the existing shareholders preferred greater control?

2.3 Raising of equity shares

Exercises to raise equity shares can be categorised as new share issues, rights issues or scrip issues, depending upon the way in which they are raised. Quoted companies can issue new shares and make rights issues. However, an unquoted company can only raise its finance by rights issues and private placings due to its restricted access to the public. Statutory restrictions in the UK mean only public limited companies may offer shares to the general public.

The order of preference for share issues is generally a rights issue, a placing and then an offer for sale to the general public. The next source is used as available funds are consumed.

Setting the price correctly is the most difficult area for all share issues. For a public issue, there is a danger of undersubscription if the price is set too high, unlike placing which is pre-agreed and negotiated to be attractive enough to the subscribing institutions. A rights issue bypasses the price problem since the shares are offered to existing shareholders at an attractive price. For unquoted companies, pricing is more complex as they cannot refer to an existing market price.

New shares: public issue

Shares are offered to the general public by inviting the public to apply for shares in a company at a fixed price or by tender based upon information contained in a prospectus. A public listing increases the marketability of the company's shares to raise further equity finance.

However, listing a company is a time-consuming process that incurs costs. Once listed, the company also has to face a higher level of regulation and public scrutiny. There is also a greater threat of dilution of control and takeover.

New shares: placing

A company can use a placing to raise equity capital for the company by selling shares directly to third-party investors (usually a merchant bank). Examples include private equity, venture capital and pledge funds (see Chapter 10).

New shares: rights issue

A rights issue offers existing shareholders the right to buy new shares in proportion to their existing shareholdings. A rights issue enables shareholders to retain their existing share of voting rights. Shareholders also have an option to sell their rights on the stock market.

For example, a one-for-four rights issue means that a shareholder is entitled to buy one new share for every four shares currently held. Usually the price at which the new shares are issued by way of rights issue are offered at a discount to the current share price (that is, less than the current share price). If shareholders don't want to buy the shares, they can sell their rights in the market.

Bonus share or scrip issue

Bonus shares, also known as a scrip issues, are additional free shares given to the current shareholders based upon their existing number of shares. This is achieved by a transfer from one or more components of equity-to-equity share capital and does not raise any funds for the company.

Test yourself 11.1

1. What are the advantages of issuing equity shares from a company perspective?
2. How can companies raise finance from a rights issue?

3 Retained earnings

retained earnings
funds or equity finance in the form of undistributed profits attributable to equity or ordinary shareholders.

Retained earnings are equity finance in the form of undistributed profits attributable to equity shareholders. The proportion of the profits which is not distributed among the shareholders, but retained to be used in the growth of a company, are reported as retained earnings.

Retained earnings are the most common and important source of finance, for both short-term and long-term purposes. Use of retained earnings is also the most preferred method of financing over other sources of finance. However, retained earnings are that element of profit not distributed, so they are not a cash amount. The cash generated in relation to these profits may have been spent – on a capital project, for example – and yet the retained earnings figure would remain on the statement of financial position.

3.1 Advantages

- Since these are internally generated funds, they are the cheapest source of capital in that there are no issue costs. Companies save on expenses related to issuing shares or bonds such as marketing, publicity, printing and other administrative costs.
- The cash is immediately available (if it has not already been spent).
- There is no obligation on the part of the company to either pay interest or pay back the earnings.
- The management have more flexibility to decide how or where this money can be used.
- Retained earnings are part of equity. Therefore, the company is able to better face adverse conditions during depressions and economic downturns, thus building up its internally generated goodwill.
- Shareholders may also benefit from the use of retained earnings as they may be able to receive dividends out of them representing profits not distributed from previous years, even if the company does not earn enough profit for that year, provided that the company has sufficient cash to pay a dividend. Investors are also likely to view a company with sufficient retained earnings as favourable, thus appreciating its share value. The existing shareholders may profit from the rise in share prices.

3.2 Disadvantages

- Internally generated funds may not be sufficient for financing purposes – especially in new companies that require a lot of investment.
- The investment requirements might not match the availability and the timing of the funds. A company runs the risk of missing company opportunities.
- If no suitable investments are available, shareholders' money is being tied up in the company. This incurs an opportunity cost by having their money kept in the company. Large companies such as privatised utilities and

demutualised building societies have made special dividend payments for this reason in the recent years.
- The excessive 'ploughing back' of profits or accumulated retained earnings may result in overcapitalisation.
- Excessive savings may be misused against the interest of the shareholders.
- The money is not made available to those in the company who can use it. Devoting too much profit to growth may starve the company of the cash it needs to fund ongoing operations.

Stop and think 11.2
Consider reasons why retained earnings are cheaper than other types of finance.

Test yourself 11.2
What factors should you consider when choosing between sources of finance?

4 Preference shares

Preference shares are shares which carry preferential rights over equity shares on profits available for distribution (in the form of dividends) and on the leftover funds in the event of liquidation.

Although legally equity, they may be treated as debt rather than equity for accounting purposes as they carry a fixed rate of dividend, unlike equity shares where the dividend can fluctuate. From an investor's point of view, investment in these shares is safer as they get regular dividends and have lower risk. However, preference shareholders do not have a say/voting rights in the management of the company.

4.1 Types of preference share

Cumulative and non-cumulative
A cumulative preference share accrues or accumulates its annual fixed rate dividend in the following year if it cannot be paid in any year. If dividends are not paid due to insufficient distributable profits (usually denoted by retained earnings), the right to dividend for that year is carried forward to the next year and paid before any dividend is paid to equity shares. In case of non-cumulative preference shares, the right to dividend for that year is lost.

Normally preference shares are considered cumulative unless specifically mentioned otherwise.

Redeemable and irredeemable
Redeemable preference shares are those shares which can be purchased back (redeemed) by the company within the lifetime of the company, subject to the terms of the issue. These shares can be redeemed at a future date and the investment amount returned to the owner. Irredeemable preference shares are not redeemable or paid back except when the company goes into liquidation.

Participating and non-participating
Participating preference shares are entitled to a fixed rate of dividend and a share in surplus profits which remain after dividend has been paid to equity shareholders. The surplus profits are distributed in a certain agreed ratio between the participating preference shareholders and equity shareholders. Non-participating preference shares are entitled to only the fixed rate of dividend.

Convertible and non-convertible
The holder of convertible preference shares enjoys the right to convert the preference shares into equity shares at a future date. This gives the investor the benefit of receiving a regular fixed dividend as well as an option to gain further benefit by converting the preference shares to equity shares. The holder of non-convertible preference shares does not enjoy this right.

4.2 Advantages

- Unlike fixed interest for debt financing, dividends are only payable if there are sufficient distributable profits available for the purpose.
- There is no loss of control, as preference shares do not carry voting rights.
- Unlike debt, dividends do not have to be paid if there are not enough profits. The right to dividend for that year is lost except for cumulative preference shares (the right to dividend is carried forward).
- Unlike debt, the shares are not secured on the company's assets.

4.3 Disadvantages

- Unlike debt interest, dividends are not tax allowable. The use of preference shares is quite rare nowadays given the tax advantages of debt.
- Preference shares pay a higher rate of interest than debt because of the extra risk for shareholders.
- On liquidation of a company, preference shares rank before equity or ordinary shareholders.

5 Bonds and debentures

Long-term debt is an effective way to get immediate funds to finance company operations. For example, it is a way to obtain substantial initial funds to invest in capital items such as plant and machinery, as well as funds to pay for the running expenses, such as wages, insurance, legal fees and advertising.

A bond is a general term for various types of long-term loans to companies, including loan stock and debentures. Bonds are used by companies, municipalities, states and sovereign governments to raise money and finance a variety of projects and activities. Owners of bonds are accounted for as creditors of the issuing company. They may issue bonds directly to investors instead of obtaining loans from a bank. The company issues a bond with a fixed interest rate (coupon rate) and the duration of the loan, which must be repaid at the maturity date. The issue price of a bond is typically set at par, usually £100 ($1,000 in the US) face value per individual bond. The actual market price depends upon the expected yield and the performance of the company compared to the market environment at the time.

Debentures are the most common form of long-term loan used by large companies. A debenture is a written acknowledgement of a debt, most commonly used by large companies to borrow money at a fixed rate of interest. Debentures are written in a legal agreement or contract called 'indenture', which acknowledges the long-term debt raised by a company. Debentures can be traded on a stock exchange, normally in units. They carry a fixed rate of interest expressed as a percentage of nominal value. These loans are repayable on a fixed date and pay a fixed rate of interest. A company makes these interest payments prior to paying out dividends to its shareholders.

Loan stock refers to shares of common or preferred stock that are used as collateral to secure a loan from another party. The loan is provided at a fixed interest rate, much like a standard loan and can be secured or unsecured. Loan stock is valued higher if the company is publicly traded and unrestricted, since these loan stock shares can be easier to sell if the borrower is unable to repay the loan. Lenders will have control of the shares' loan stock until the borrower pays off the loan. Once the loan term expires, the shares would be returned to the borrower, as they are no longer needed as collateral.

5.1 Types of bonds and debentures

Secured and unsecured
Bonds or debentures are either unsecured or secured against collateral. Secured debts or debenture holders have first charge on the assets that are used as security if the company goes into liquidation. A company with a fixed charge debenture is restricted from selling the assets used as security until the loan is repaid in full. With a floating charge, it is free to dispose of its assets in the ordinary course of business. Unsecured debentures are backed only by the reputation and trust of the issuer.

Bond buyers generally purchase debentures based on the belief that the bond issuer is unlikely to default on the repayment. Private and government institutions frequently issue this type of bond to secure capital. Some examples of a government debentures would be government-issued Treasury bonds (T-bond) or Treasury bills (T-bill). They are generally considered risk free because governments are assumed not to default on payments. Unsecured debentures do not have this benefit and charge a higher rate of interest to compensate the risk.

Redeemable and irredeemable

Debentures can be either redeemable or irredeemable. Redeemable debentures are debentures which the company has issued for a limited period of time. Debentures which are never repaid are irredeemable (also known as perpetual debentures). They tend to be rare nowadays.

Redeemable debentures are usually repaid at their nominal value (at par) but may be issued as repayable at a premium on nominal value. They are repayable at a fixed date (or during a fixed period) in the future.

Convertible and non-convertible

Convertible debentures or convertible loan stock have the option to convert into equity shares at a time and in a ratio decided by the company when issued. Non-convertible debentures cannot be converted into equity shares.

Worked example 11.1

A company issues 10% convertible loan stock which can be converted into equity shares in three years' time at the rate of 25 shares per £100 nominal of loan stock. The share price at the time of issue is £2.

Calculate:

- **the conversion ratio: this is the number (or ratio) of equity shares received at the time of conversion for each loan stock**
- **the conversion price: this is the price per share at which loan stock can be converted into equity shares**
- **the conversion premium: this is the amount that would be yielded if loan stock is converted into equity shares**

Solution

- **Conversion ratio = 25 shares/£100 = 0.25 share/£1 of loan stock**
- **Conversion price = £100/25 = £4**
- **Conversion premium = £4 − £2 = £2**

5.2 Advantages

- These loans are repayable on a fixed date and pay a fixed rate of interest. The interest paid is usually less than the dividend paid to shareholders, as debentures are considered less risky than shares by investors.
- Debentures are advantageous to the issuer because they have a fixed repayment date.
- Unlike dividends, the interest paid is tax allowable, reducing the net cost to the company.
- Unlike shares, there are no restrictions contained in company law regarding the terms of issue of debentures.

- Debenture holders typically have no right to vote or have a voice in the management. They are preferred as a source of finance if any dilution of control is not desirable.

5.3 Disadvantages

- Debenture holders are creditors of a company. Secured debenture holders have first charge on the assets that are used as security if the company goes into liquidation.
- Debenture holders receive interest payments regardless of the amount of profit or loss at the stipulated time. The interest payments are due prior to paying out dividends to shareholders.
- The risk for an investor of investing in debentures and other loans is less than the risk of investing in shares but there is still a risk of default. The higher the amount of debt finance, the higher the debt or gearing ratio. This may make the company more volatile and could lead to insolvency.

Stop and think 11.3

Why would you prefer to buy debentures or loan stock rather than equity shares if you were risk averse?

5.4 Bonds with fixed interest (coupon)

A company can issue bonds of a certain face value or par value (normally in multiples of £100) for a fixed amount of time that promise to pay interest annually or semi-annually.

For example, a company could issue a 10-year bond with a coupon (interest) of 10% and par value of £100. This means that the company will pay interest of £10 per annum for 10 years and will pay £100 at the end of 10 years to buy back the bond from the lender.

The market price of such bonds depends upon the yield required or the rate of return expected by the investor. The market value of the bond is determined by calculating the present value of the cash flows arising from the bond (see Chapters 13 and 15).

5.5 Deep discount and zero-coupon bonds

These are bonds or debentures issued at a large discount in comparison to their nominal or face value but are redeemable at par on maturity.

The interest is either low (for deep discount bonds) or there is no interest (zero coupon bonds). Investors will receive a large 'bonus' on maturity. Some investors may prefer zero coupon bonds because of the tax implications. As these bonds do not pay any interest, investors may save on tax payments by holding the bond.

Growing companies can particularly benefit from these bonds because they pay low (or nil) interest during the life of the bonds or debentures. The company could also possibly issue more conventional debentures to finance the redemption when the time comes to redeem the original debentures.

For example, a company may issue straight 10% bonds with a face value of £100 and a maturity of five years. Interest of 10% (or £10) is payable each year. Zero coupon bonds are issued at a discount price in comparison with their face value with 0% interest per year. Hence, the company would issue 0% bonds for less than a face value of £100 (say £80). The earnings for the investor come from the difference between the payment price and the face value at which the bonds are redeemed.

Deep discount bonds are issued at deep or significant discounts (say £70) against the face value of £100 and carry a low rate of interest. On the maturity date, the issuer must pay the bondholder the face value of £100.

5.6 Eurobonds

A Eurobond is a bond issued for international investors. They are normally issued in a currency other than the home currency. The term Eurobond only means that the bond was issued outside of its home country; it does not mean the bond was issued in Europe or denominated in the Euro currency.

Commonly used Eurobonds are Eurodollar (issued in the dollar denominations) or Euroyen (issued in yen denominations). Issuance is usually handled by an international financial institution on behalf of the borrower. Eurobonds are popular as they offer issuers the ability to choose the country of issuance based on the regulatory market, interest rates and activity of the market. They are also attractive to investors because they usually have low par values and high liquidity.

5.7 Share warrants (options)

Warrants are rights given to lenders allowing them to buy new shares in a company at a future date at a fixed, given price.

Warrants are normally attached to a bond or a preference share to make it attractive for the investor by giving them the potential to earn a profit in the future. The price at which they can buy the share in the future is called the exercise price. If the current share price is less than the exercise price, the theoretical value of the warrant is zero, since the investor will be better off buying the shares in the market. If the current share price is higher than the exercise price, then the warrant holder has a potential to make a profit by getting the shares at a cheaper exercise price in the future.

Generally, if the company has good prospects, then the warrants will be quoted at the warrant conversion premium. This is calculated by comparing the cost of purchasing a share using the warrant and the current share price.

Test yourself 11.3

Why would investors be interested in preference shares with warrants attached?

6 Bank and institutional loans

Bank and institutional loans are the most popular type of finance. Bank loans are generally a quick and straightforward option. They are usually provided over a fixed period of time and can be short term or long term, depending on the purpose of the loan. Lending to companies for more than one year is considered a long-term loan. Loans can be negotiable: the rate of interest, repayment dates and security for the capital offered must be agreed depending on the risk and credit standing of the company.

Long-term loans are more stringent and may only be offered to established companies with a good credit profile. They are repaid in regular payments over a set period of time. The payment includes the principal and interest repayments. Term loans usually last between one and ten years, but some may last as long as 30 years.

A covenant is a promise in any debt agreement that a company will remain within a determined range of financial measures and performance. Normally, covenants are added by lenders to protect their investment and minimise the risk of defaulting on payments by the company. Covenants are usually described in terms of financial ratios that must be maintained within a specific range of value. These ratios are covered in Chapters 7, 8 and 16, but could include:

- liquidity ratios
- leverage ratios
- efficiency ratios
- profitability ratios
- market value ratios

Covenants can cover everything from dividend payments to an asset holding that must be maintained. If a covenant is broken, the lender has the right to collect back the investment from the borrower. Covenants could be keeping or maintaining a certain level of financial measures (affirmative covenants) or not going beyond or below a certain measure (negative covenants).

Bank and institutional loans are covered more in detail in Chapter 9.

7 Leasing

A **leasing** agreement is formed between two parties: a lessor (who owns the asset but does not have use of it) and a lessee (who does not own the asset but does have the use of it). A financier (the lessor) purchases the asset and

leasing
An agreement between two parties whereby the lessor (who owns the asset) provides the lessee (who has use of the asset) with access to and use of the asset in exchange for payments.

provides it for use by the company (the lessee). The lessor is considered to be the legal owner and can claim capital allowances for the asset. The lessee makes payments to the lessor for the use of the asset.

The accounting and financial reporting issues this raises are covered in Chapter 5. In this section, we consider its usage as a form of long-term finance.

7.1 Advantages

- The biggest advantage of leasing is that cash outflow or payments related to leasing are spread out over several years, hence saving the burden of one-time significant cash payment to purchase an asset outright. This helps a business to maintain a steady cash flow profile.
- While leasing an asset, the ownership of the asset still lies with the lessor whereas the lessee just pays the rental expense. Given this agreement, it becomes plausible for a business to invest in good quality assets which might look unaffordable or expensive otherwise.
- Given that a company chooses to lease over investing in an asset by purchasing, it releases capital for the business to fund its other needs or to save money for a better capital investment decision.
- Leasing expense or lease payments are considered as operating expenses and are tax deductible.
- Lease expenses usually remain constant for over the asset's life or lease tenure, or grow in line with inflation. This helps in planning expense or cash outflow when undertaking a budgeting exercise.
- For businesses operating in sectors where there is a high risk of technology becoming obsolete, leasing yields great returns and saves the business from the risk of investing in a technology that might soon become outdated. For example, it is ideal for the technology business.
- At the end of the leasing period, the lessee holds the right to buy the property and terminate the leasing contract, thus providing flexibility to business.

7.2 Disadvantages

- At the end of the leasing period, the lessee does not become the owner of the asset despite paying a significant amount of money towards the asset over the years.
- The lessee remains responsible for the maintenance and proper operation of the asset being leased.
- Lease payments can become a burden in cases where the use of asset does not serve the requirement (usually after the passage of some years).
- If paying lease payments towards a land, the lessee cannot benefit from any appreciation in the value of the land. The long-term lease agreement also remains a burden on the business, as the agreement is locked and the expenses for several years are fixed.

- Although a lease does not appear on the statement of financial position of a company, investors still consider long-term lease as debt and adjust their valuation of a business to include leases.
- Given that investors treat long-term leases as debt, it might become difficult for a business to access capital markets and raise further loans or other forms of debt from the market.

7.3 Sale and leaseback

A **sale and leaseback arrangement** (sometimes only called leaseback) is a structured transaction in which the owner (a company raising finance) sells an asset to another party (the buyer or lessor), while maintaining the legal rights to use the asset ('lease back') from the buyer or lessor.

Sale and leaseback arrangements usually work in the following way. A company sells its asset (such as a building) to an investment company. The purchasing company (lessor) acts like the landlord of the property and the selling company becomes the lessee, renting the building which it previously owned. The rent is usually reviewed every few years. There is a risk that the lessor will have the right to rent the property to another company if the original lessee is unable to pay rent for the property. Properties that are rising in value, are well maintained and have a potential for increase in rental revenue are preferred in this type of arrangement.

The main advantage of this method of financing is that the company can raise more money than from a normal mortgage arrangement. A practical advantage is that, where a building is sold and leased back, the company's occupancy and use of the building does not change. The disadvantages are that fewer assets remain to support future borrowing and the market may view the company negatively if it has to sell its property. It may also turn out to be disadvantageous

sale and leaseback arrangement
A sale and leaseback (sometimes called leaseback) arrangement is a structured transaction in which the owner sells an asset to another party (the buyer-lessor), while maintaining the legal rights to use the asset or lease back from the buyer-lessor.

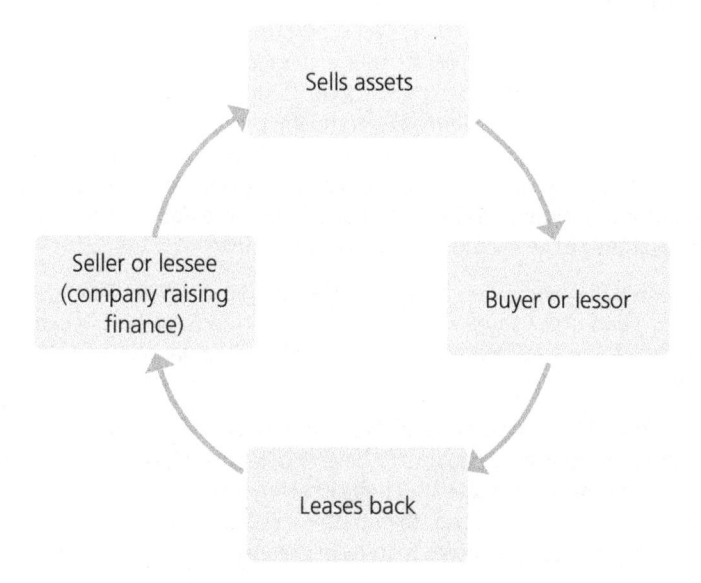

Figure 11.1 Sale and leaseback

if the market rent keeps increasing rapidly and the lessee has to pay an exorbitant rent as time goes by. The lessee also loses the opportunity to profit from capital gains of the property as it no longer owns it.

Test yourself 11.4

How can purchasing assets via leases assist in managing a company's cash levels?

8 Securitisation of assets

securitisation
The process of taking an illiquid asset, or group of assets and transforming it (or them) through financial engineering into a security that can be sold to raise more finance.

Securitisation is the financial practice of pooling together illiquid assets and repackaging them into an interest-bearing security that can be traded (just like stocks and bonds) to raise more finance. This is commonly practised by financial institutions (such as banks, mortgage companies and credit card companies) to reduce their risk on the illiquid assets (such as mortgages and credit card cards) by selling or removing them from its statement of financial position.

Through securitisation, various cash flow generating assets (such as mortgages, bonds and loans) are pooled together and their related cash flows are sold to investors as securities, which may be described as bonds, pass-through securities, or collateralised debt obligations (CDOs). The pooled assets are essentially debt obligations that serve as collateral. Securities backed by mortgage receivables are called mortgage-backed securities (MBS), while those backed by other types of receivables are asset-backed securities (ABS). Investors are repaid from the principal and interest cash flows collected from the underlying debt.

special purpose vehicle
A special purpose vehicle (SPV), also referred to as special purpose entity (SPE), is a legal entity created for a specific purpose. It provides a funding structure whereby pooled assets are transferred to a SPV, for legal and tax reasons. The SPV then issues interest-bearing securities, such as mortgage-backed securities, which are used to raise more finance.

A **special purpose vehicle** (SPV), also referred to as special purpose entity (SPE), is a legal entity created for a specific purpose. It provides a funding structure whereby the pooled assets are transferred to a SPV for legal and tax reasons. The SPV then issues interest-bearing securities such as MBS, which are used to raise more finance. Normally a company transfers assets to the SPV to finance a large project, thereby narrowing its goals without putting the entire firm at risk. SPVs are commonly used to securitise loans and other receivables. Special purpose vehicles may be owned by one or more entities and allow tax avoidance strategies unavailable in the home country.

The securitisation market is extremely large – running in the multiple millions of pounds – and allows large investors such as pension funds and hedge funds to buy these securities as a way of receiving a regular payment on their investments.

Securitisation offers investors a diversification of risks from a pool of assets. Special purpose vehicles (SPVs) usually have excellent credit ratings. Investors get the benefit of the payment structure closely monitored by an independent trustee and yields that are higher than those of similar debt instrument. Securitisation provides the flexibility to tailor the instrument to meet the investor's risk appetite.

However, there have been irregularities and misuse of SPVs in the recent past. Special purpose vehicles were misused to mask crucial financial information from investors. Enron's financial collapse in 2001 revealed that Enron used SPVs to hide assets and debt from the public and investors.

The 2006 US subprime housing market crisis revealed that banks converted pools of risky mortgages into marketable securities and sold too many of them to investors through the use of SPVs. The SPVs financed the purchase of the assets by issuing bonds secured by the underlying mortgages. When home prices fell, it triggered defaults that led to the collapse of the housing market in late 2006, followed by the banking crisis of 2007.

8.1 Advantages

- Securitisation is an efficient way of raising large amounts of funding.
- Special purpose vehicles (SPVs) are entirely separate from the originating company. They allow off-balance sheet treatment of assets that are wiped off from the originator's financial statements.
- Interest rates on securitised bonds are normally lower than those on corporate bonds.
- Private companies get access to wider capital markets – domestic and international.
- Shareholders can maintain undiluted ownership of the company.
- Intangible assets such as patents and copyrights can be used for security to raise cash.
- The assets in the SPV are protected, reducing the credit risk for investors and lowering the borrowing costs for issuers raising finance.
- An SPV usually has an excellent credit rating and low borrowing costs.

8.2 Disadvantages

- Securitisation can be a complicated and expensive way of raising long-term capital compared to traditional types of debt such as a bank loan.
- It may restrict the ability of the company to raise money in the future.
- There is a risk from loss of direct control of some of the company assets, potentially reducing the company's value in the event of flotation.
- Transactions may not always lead to off-balance sheet treatment
- The company may incur substantial costs to close the SPV and reclaim the underlying assets.

9 Private finance initiatives

Governments and public institutions require long-term finance to execute their projects. In order to share the risks and rewards of such projects, the **private finance initiative (PFI)** was introduced in 1992 in the UK as a means of obtaining private finance for public sector projects (such as the building of

private finance initiative (PFI)
An important (and controversial) policy designed to provide funds for major capital investments. It refers to private firms being contracted to handle the up-front costs, complete and manage public projects.

libraries, social housing, defence contracts, schools and hospitals). In 1997, the PFI was moved within the organisation of the Public-Private Partnership (PPP) initiative, which also has the objective of providing private sector funding for public projects.

A PFI is an important and controversial procurement method which uses private sector investment to provide funds for major public sector capital investment. Private firms are contracted to complete, manage and handle the upfront costs of public projects. Typically, a PFI contract is repaid by the government over a 30-year period. It places the risks of buying and maintaining the asset with the private sector, while allowing the public sector to procure high-quality and cost-effective public services while avoiding the need to raise taxes in the short term. The ultimate risk with a project, however, lies with the public sector (government).

National Health Service (NHS) trusts in the UK use PFI for construction projects and to fund projects supporting education and health services. These are funded out of future income that the projects help to generate. The Olympic Delivery Authority that delivered the 2012 London Olympic Games is a good example of a PFI project.

However, PFI schemes are controversial due to the wasteful spending built into the public sector procurement agreements that are part of PFI projects. There are many stories of flawed projects. Controversial projects include rising car parking charges at many local hospitals, the M25 widening scheme that cost £1 billion more than forecast and the kennels at the Defence Animal Centre, which cost more per night than rooms at the London Hilton. The cost of private sector finance in the 2000s increased the overall debt cost of the UK government, indirectly costing taxpayers.

9.1 Advantages

- The main advantage of PFI is that the public sector does not have to fund large capital outflows at the start of the project. It allows the public sector to procure high-quality and cost-effective public services whilst avoiding financing through higher borrowing and taxes.

- The public obtains valuable operational and management expertise and overall cost efficiencies from the private sector and vice versa. There is the opportunity for the development of new ideas and the transfer of skills in both sectors.

- The private sector takes on the risks of financing, constructing and then managing the project. It is expected that there would be higher value for money through PFI than through public sector financing. Extra investment can kickstart more projects, bringing economic and social benefits.

- PFI projects are nearly all fixed-price contracts in which the private sector is not paid until the asset has been delivered. PFI firms eventually pay tax, making the overall costs cheaper for the government.

- All PFI projects go through a bidding process, encouraging competition for design and quality of delivery.

9.2 Disadvantages

- The biggest disadvantage is the typically high annual costs charged to the public sector for the projects. The costs have been significantly larger than the annual costs of comparable projects. Many projects have run over budget.
- Since the asset ownership is transferred to the private sector, it may lead to a loss of control and accountability from the public sector.
- The ultimate risk of inflexibility and poor value for money with a project lies with the public sector. There have been many stories of flawed projects and wasteful spending.
- Repair or maintenance costs may be higher.
- The administration cost of spending on advisers and lawyers and the costs of the bidding process, could cost millions.

Test yourself 11.5

What are the limitations of PFI?

10 Government grants and assistance

Governments also provide financial support to companies in the form of grants, loans and government assistance. **Government grants** are financial grants provided by government bodies and trusts to normally support projects that are beneficial to the society and the public (such as projects with the aim to generate jobs and stimulate the economy).

Government grants are available in all forms, from cash awards or benefits to reductions in costs and free equipment. There is usually no obligation to repay the initial investment. However, they generally have fixed terms and conditions on how the money may be used.

Government loans are normally provided to companies that are not able to receive financial support from the normal commercial market and are provided at an interest rate that is much lower than any commercial market rate. However, government grants/loans and assistance come with a lot of red tape and conditions and may only be available to companies meeting the criteria set out by the government. The funds are also impacted by budget allocations in the financial year.

Some of the common schemes that the government have made available in the UK are the Enterprise Investment Scheme (EIS) and the Enterprise Finance Guarantee (EFG) scheme. The EIS provides added incentives for investors to invest in small or medium-sized enterprises (SMEs) by providing benefits in terms of tax relief on the investment amount and having greater control in the management of the company. As per many government financial assistance schemes, investors must adhere to EIS conditions. It is designed to encourage

government grants
Government grants are financial grants provided by government bodies and trusts to normally support projects that are beneficial to the society and the public (such as projects with the aim to generate jobs and stimulate the economy).

investment in ventures by providing exemption from capital gains tax and claim leases tax relief for capital losses.

The EFG scheme is a loan guarantee scheme intended to facilitate additional bank lending to viable SMEs that have been turned down for debt finance due to inadequate security or lack of a proven track record. The government will act as a guarantor for the loan, thus providing assurance to the lending financial institutions against loss due to defaults.

The Covid-19 pandemic also led to a plethora of government grants and assistance schemes. In the UK, this included:

- A Business Interruption Loan Scheme of up to £5 million per company, available to small companies whose finances had been affected by the pandemic. The government guaranteed 80% of the finance to the lender and paid interest and any fees for the first 12 months.
- A Business Bounce-Back Loan Scheme of up to £50,000 per company, aimed at helping smaller companies access financial support more quickly. The government guaranteed 100% of the loan and there were no fees or interest to pay for the first 12 months.
- A Job Retention Scheme, under which companies could furlough staff who were not actively deployed by the business instead of making them redundant. The government paid 100% of their salaries up to a maximum of £2,500 per employee per month.

10.1 Advantages

- Government assistance is a cheap form of financial support.
- Interest rates on government loans are much lower than market rates.
- Unlike loans, most government grants don't have to be repaid – they are essentially 'free' money.
- Information about grants is easily accessible through government websites and literature.
- Government-funded projects are normally beneficial to society and the public at large.

10.2 Disadvantages

- Applications can be time consuming.
- They may require outcomes that are beneficial to society, sometimes at the expense of financial profit.
- There may be a long waiting period between applying for the grant or loan and approval.
- There may be lot of competition from other companies applying for the same grant or loan.
- There may be detailed requirements for eligibility.
- There are usually strict rules and conditions on how the money can be used.

Chapter summary

- Finance is important for companies who require capital to finance long-term investments and overall working capital. A company can look at various sources to fulfil these long-term financial requirements. The choice is generally between equity finance (from shareholders) and debt finance (from lenders).
- Equity finance refers to the finance relating to the owners or equity shareholders of the company. Equity finance is represented by the issued equity share capital (raised through new issues, including rights issues) plus other components of equity such as retained earnings.
- Debt is the main alternative to equity. It involves the payment of interest. It can be used for both short-term and long-term purposes and may or may not be secured.
- Preference shares take the following forms:
    - Cumulative and non-cumulative
    - Redeemable and irredeemable
    - Participating and non-participating
    - Convertible and non-convertible
- Bonds and debentures (bonds and loan stocks) take the following forms:
    - Bonds with fixed interest (coupon payment)
    - Deep discount and zero-coupon bonds
    - Eurobonds
    - Share warrants (options)
- A leasing agreement is formed between two parties: a lessor (who owns the asset but does not have use of it) and a lessee (who does not own the asset but does have the use of it). The lessor is considered to be the legal owner and can claim capital allowances for the asset. The lessee makes payments to the lessor for the use of the asset.
- The biggest advantage of leasing is that cash outflow or payments related to leasing are spread out over several years, hence saving the burden of one-time significant cash payment to purchase an asset outright. This helps a business to maintain a steady cash flow profile.
- A sale and leaseback arrangement is a structured transaction in which an owner sells an asset to another party (the buyer-lessor), while maintaining the legal rights to use the asset or lease back from the buyer-lessor.
- Other forms of long-term finance include:
    - bank and institutional loans
    - securitisation of assets via the use of special purpose vehicles
    - private finance initiatives
    - government assistance

Part four

Chapter 12
The cost of capital and capital structure

Chapter 13
Project appraisal techniques

Chapter 14
Risk assessment in investment appraisal techniques

Chapter 15
Company analysis and company valuation methods

The cost of capital and capital structure

Overview

Part four covers two important concepts used in financial decision making: cost of capital and capital structure. It also looks at the various aspects of investment and project appraisal, including different methods of project appraisal, risk assessment, company analysis and company valuation.

Chapter 12 discusses the cost of capital and its influence on designing an optimal capital structure and evaluating investments. It covers key techniques in determining the cost of equity and the cost of debt, before looking at the calculation of weighted average cost of capital. It examines capital structure decision making from theoretical and practical perspectives, including the choice between equity and debt financing and discusses various theories around optimal capital structures, including gearing ratios.

Chapter 13 examines project or investment appraisal, including the key principles and methods of investment appraisal with and without discounting.

Chapter 14 considers the impact of risk and the uncertainty around returns on investment appraisal and portfolio management. It highlights the importance of non-probabilistic as well as probabilistic risk assessment models that aid decision making. It also discusses the role of portfolio management in reducing overall portfolio risk.

Chapter 15 discusses techniques used to evaluate the financial health and future prospects of a company. It discusses the principles of ratio analysis used by equity investors, as well as the valuation methods used to draw conclusions about the worth of a company. It also provides an overview of the objectives of shareholder wealth creation, shareholder value analysis and alternatives to shareholder value analysis.

At the end of this Part, students will be able to:

- discuss the importance of cost of capital in the world of financial management and demonstrate a clear conceptual understanding of the related financial theories;
- discuss how the costs of equity and debt and the overall cost of capital, are determined;
- explain what is meant by capital structure, critically analyse and evaluate various models related to capital structure decision making and explain why a company might choose one type of financing over another;
- calculate and interpret gearing ratios and explain how they can be used to evaluate the risks of failure associated with debt financing;
- discuss the nature and purpose of working capital and explain what is meant by optimal level of working capital;
- explain what is meant by project or investment appraisal and discuss the factors that should be considered;
- undertake investment appraisal using a range of different techniques;

- calculate, interpret and critically evaluate non-discounted and discounted appraisal methods;
- discuss the effects of inflation and tax on project appraisal and how their impacts are incorporated in the calculation of net cash flows;
- demonstrate how companies apply capital rationing strategies to prioritise limited funds on the most profitable projects;
- demonstrate an understanding of various risk assessment models that incorporate risk into decision making;
- explain and apply the use of non-probabilistic approaches in assessing the risk of a project or an investment and making financial decisions;
- explain, apply and evaluate investments using probabilistic approaches of risk assessment;
- describe the role of portfolio management in balancing risk and return;
- explain the role and value of the investment ratios related to dividends and earnings and critically interpret their results;
- demonstrate how different valuation methods can be used to determine the current value of an investment; and
- calculate and explain the concept of free cash flows and how it is applied in shareholder value analysis, as well as discuss alternatives to shareholder value analysis.

Chapter twelve
The cost of capital and capital structure

Contents

1. Introduction
2. The importance of the cost of capital
3. Cost of equity using the capital asset pricing model
4. Cost of equity using the dividend valuation model
5. Cost of debt
6. The weighted average cost of capital
7. Capital structure
8. Factors affecting capital structure
9. Financial gearing
10. Operating gearing
11. The traditional approach to capital structure
12. The Modigliani and Miller theory of capital structure
13. Real world approaches

1 Introduction

The cost of capital is an important concept in financial decision making. Financial managers use cost of capital to design an optimal **capital structure** and to evaluate investments using discounted cash flows (covered in detail in Chapter 13).

capital structure
The mix of debt and equity financing in a company. It shows how the company is financed.

Capital structure is the composition of the company's equity and liabilities in its financial statements that show how the company, or its overall operation, is financed. The key objective of a company is to maximise the value of the company and should be considered when designing its optimal capital structure.

This chapter will look at key techniques for determining the cost of equity (for example, the return required by shareholders) and the cost of debt, before looking at the calculation of weighted average cost of capital (WACC), commonly referred to as the company's cost of capital.

```
                          Cost of capital
                                |
         ┌──────────────────────┴──────────────────────┐
    Cost of equity:                               Cost of debt:
  • Capital asset pricing model (CAPM)          • Irredeemable debt:
    RADR = RFR + ß(RM − RFR)                      Kd = (I (1-t)) ÷ Sd
  • Dividend valuation model                    • Redeemable debt:
    ke = [Do (1+g) ÷ Po] + g                      IRR (Internal Rate of Return)
```

```
                    Capital structure decision
                              |
          ┌───────────────────┴───────────────────┐
   Capital structure theories              Factors in designing an
      Traditional approach                 optimal capital structure
   Modigliani–Miller (MM) approach                 |
         Pecking order                       Business risk
       Real world approach                   Operating gearing
                                             Financial gearing
                                             EBIT-EPS analysis
                                    Other factors (growth, tax, market conditions)
```

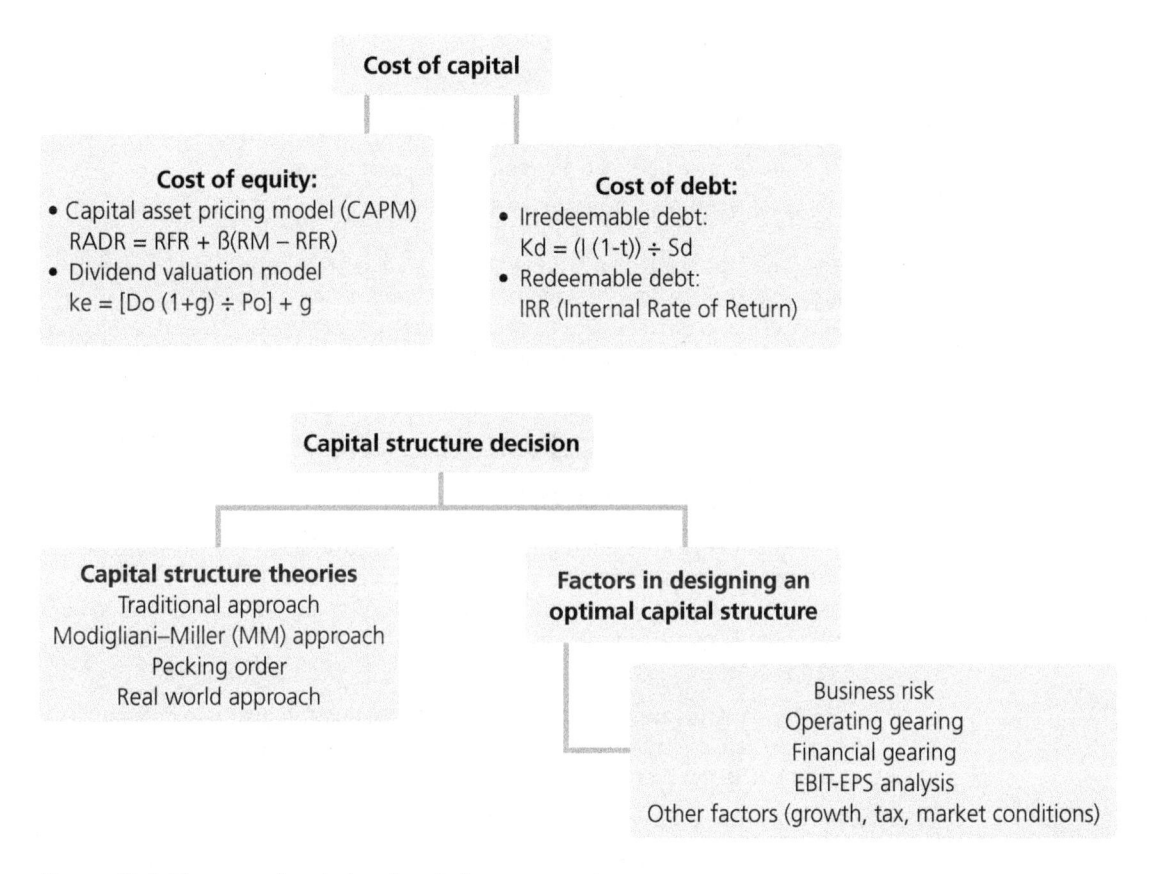

Figure 12.1 The cost of capital and capital structure

This chapter considers the choice between equity versus debt financing by looking at the overall risk that determines the rate of return an investor demands. The chapter will discuss different factors and theories relevant to deciding on the optimal capital structure. It will also look at one of the key ratios used in financial decision making – gearing – and how it is related to shareholders' risk.

2 The importance of the cost of capital

A company's cost of capital is the rate of return required by the providers of capital for making an investment in the company. While equity investors receive their returns in the form of dividends and capital growth from increases in the share price, debt providers (normally in the form of a bond) receive fixed interest payments and normally a date is set for when the debt will be redeemed or repaid.

The cost of capital is an important concept in financial decision making. It represents the investor's opportunity cost of taking on the risk by making a specific investment. In other words, it is the rate of return that could have been earned by putting the same money elsewhere.

The financial manager uses cost of capital when:

- designing a balanced and optimal capital structure
- evaluating new project or investment options

The use of discounted cash flows (DCF) is an important approach to investment appraisal. Companies calculate their weighted average cost of capital (WACC) and use it as a discount rate to determine the present value of future cash flows of its investment. Discounted cash flows are covered in Chapters 13 and 15.

3 Cost of equity using the capital asset pricing model

The cost of equity is the return investors expect to achieve on their shares in a company. The rate of return an investor requires is based on the level of risk associated with the investment. Equity shareholders are the last investors to be paid out of company profits, as well as the last to be paid on the winding up of a company.

Equity investors face the greatest risk of all investors and therefore demand a higher rate of return to justify the risk taken. There are two methods of determining the cost of equity:

- the capital asset pricing model
- the dividend valuation model

3.1 Capital asset pricing model

The capital asset pricing model (CAPM) was developed by Sharpe (1964) and Lintner (1965) as a means to measure the cost of equity. The model studies and establishes an equilibrium relationship between the expected returns from each security and its associated risks. It can be used to assess risk in individual company shares or a portfolio of securities.

risk-adjusted discount rate
The rate used to discount riskier assets or investments such as real estate. It represents the required periodical returns by investors to compensate for the higher risk.

The cost of equity capital obtained under CAPM is called the **risk-adjusted discount rate** (RADR). Once the market portfolio has been established, the required rate of return for any security can be calculated using this model provided the beta factor (explained in section 3.4) is known.

3.2 Risk-adjusted discount rate

The risk inherent in a project depends on the type of activity involved. Higher risk does not necessarily make a project unattractive.

The RADR is the rate used to discount a risky asset or investment such as real estate. It represents the required periodical returns by investors to compensate for the higher risk involved. The higher the risk involved in the project, the higher the discount rate. The cash flows from riskier assets will be discounted at a higher rate. This adjusted discount rate is typically referred to as expected rate of return. It forms the basis for CAPM.

The RADR is based on the risk-free rate (RFR) (such as a short-term interest rate from government securities or a fixed deposit rate) and a risk premium for the riskier assets.

RADR = RFR + risk premium

Where:
RADR = Risk-adjusted discount rate
RFR = Risk-free rate

Worked example 12.1

If a short-term government securities interest rate for 12 months is 2.8% and the risk premium associated with equity markets is 12% calculate the risk-adjusted discount rate.

Solution

The RADR can be calculated as the risk-free interest rate plus a risk premium required for the riskier assets.

RADR = RFR + risk premium

RADR = 2.8% + 12%

The risk-adjusted discount rate for the equity market investor will be 14.8%.

The formula for calculating RADR is simple and it incorporates risk in the expected rate of return. The real challenge occurs when measuring the risk premium. The quantification of risk involves good amount of subjectivity and detailed analysis of asset classes. The approach to dealing with higher risk projects is to use a higher rate, effectively adding a premium for the market risk.

3.3 Unsystematic and systematic risk

It is essential to diversify risk for an investor to earn adequate returns. There are two types of risk: unsystematic risk and systematic risk.

Unsystematic risks are risk factors specific to a particular company or industry which can be eliminated or diversified away in a large portfolio of shares. These risks are not impacted by political and economic factors. Examples include weak labour relations, adverse press reports and strikes. These are different for different companies; they might even cancel each other out in some circumstances. Studies have shown that if the portfolio consists of 15 to 20 shares, then most of the unsystematic risk tends to be diversified.

Systematic risk (or market risk) relates to the markets and the economy. It is largely caused by macroeconomic factors and affects all the shares in the market. It is unavoidable and cannot be diversified. An example may be an economic recession affecting both the markets and the economy of the country. The level to which each share will be affected will differ, although it is known that all shares will be affected.

It should be noted that, even in a severe recession like that caused by the Covid-19 pandemic, there might be a small number of companies doing well. This is usually for a specific reason that affcets a niche market. A good example relating to the Covid-19 pandemic would be companies providing remote working solutions, such as Zoom or Cisco, due to the large increase in people working from home.

The degree of systematic risk is different in different industries. For instance, the food retailing sector faces lower systematic risk in comparison to the hospitality sector, as food is a necessity. Irrespective of a recession, people will still require their daily essentials. It is possible for an investor to select shares with a low systematic risk. Thus, investors need to select shares that will provide returns over and above its risk-free rate of return.

The CAPM suggests that investors can eliminate the unsystematic risk and thus reduce the overall risk by choosing an optimal portfolio. It assumes that investors will behave rationally.

3.4 Measuring systematic risk and calculating RADR

The CAPM assumes that unsystematic risk can be diversified and eliminated, whereas systematic risk cannot be eliminated and diversified. Investors will expect a higher return from shares with a higher systematic risk. Therefore, it is important to measure systematic risk. The steps involved in CAPM are:

- measuring the systematic risk
- linking the systematic risk with the required rate of return

Measuring systematic risk
Sharpe and others used regression analysis to study the relationships between the excess returns (in excess of the RFR) earned on a share and the stock market portfolio. It is summarised in Figure 12.2.

The outcomes are summarised as follows.

- There is a direct correlation between the excess returns earned on a share and the stock market. In other words, in times of boom or recession, individual shares tend to perform in line with the market movements.
- The gradient of the regression line is termed beta (ß).
- The greater the ß, the greater the systematic risk and the expected return from the share.
- When ß is at 45 degrees, it indicates that the systematic risk of the share is equal to the systematic risk of the market. The ß of the share is 1 in this case and the movement on the vertical and horizontal axis is similar. The higher (or lower) return of the share is in line with the return on the stock market.

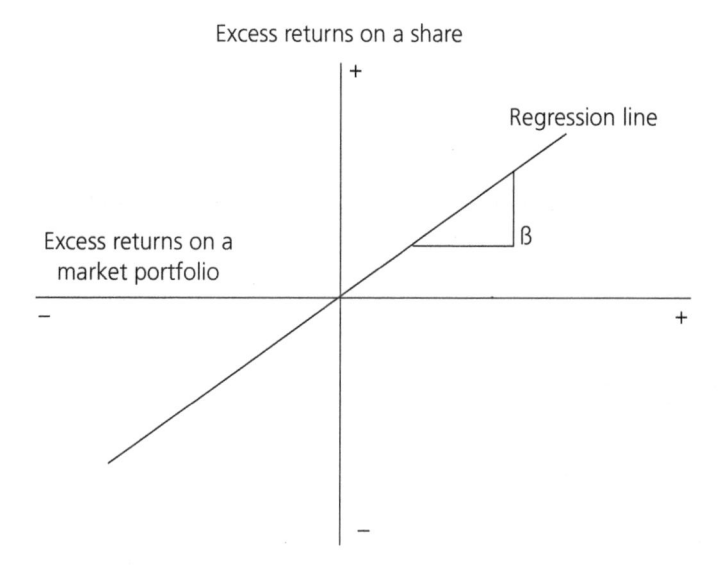

Figure 12.2 Measuring systematic risk

- When the gradient of the regression line is greater than 45 degrees, it indicates that the systematic risk of the share exceeds the systematic risk of the stock market; hence, the excess return on the share is greater than the excess return on the stock market. The ß is greater than 1 in this case.
- When the gradient of the regression line is less than 45 degrees, it indicates that the systematic risk of the share is lower than the systematic risk of the stock market; hence, the excess return on the share is less than the excess return on the stock market. The ß is less than 1 in this case.
- The vertical intercept point of the regression line is termed alpha (a). In a perfect world, the alpha coefficient should be zero, that is, the regression line should go through the graph's origin. If the alpha coefficient is greater than zero, this implies that the return on the share is generating an abnormal return due to an element of unsystematic risk. However, over time, such abnormal returns should cancel out and the alpha coefficient will become zero.

3.5 Linking ß with required returns: the security market line

The ß of any specific share can be estimated. If the market return is known, the cost of equity of any share is worked out using the security market line (SML). For any level of systematic risk, the risk-adjusted return is plotted graphically with the help of SML.

The ß of risk-free capital (such as government bonds) is zero and the ß for the stock market as a whole is 1. The cost of capital in this case is represented as the RADR. Any share which has a ß of more than zero will have a risk premium attached to it, which is the incentive or the extra return to be earned by the shareholder for holding the share.

RADR | SML
RFR
β

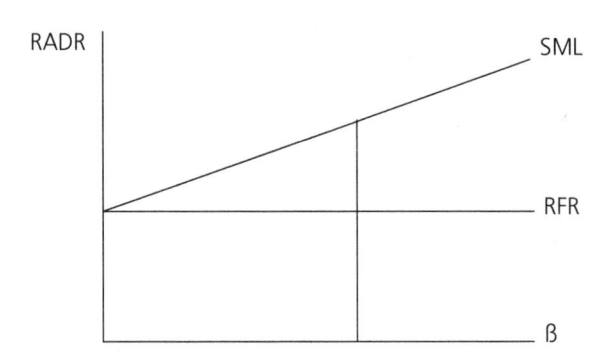

RADR = Risk-adjusted discount rate
SML = Security market line
RFR = Risk-free rate

Figure 12.3 Linking β with required returns

When the β is less than 1, the RADR will be lower than the return on the market and to the left of the SML. When the β is higher than 1, the RADR will be higher than the return on the market and to the right of the SML. The SML can thus be used to calculate the return for any level of systematic risk. The cost of equity can be determined by using the formula below:

RADR = RFR + β (RM − RFR)

Where:

RFR = Risk-free rate
RM = return on stock market portfolio
β = risk premium statistically derived
RM − RFR = market risk premium (the expected return on the market minus the risk-free rate).

Worked example 12.2

Nayu plc has a β of 1.40 and the market return is 14%. The RFR is 10%. Calculate the cost of equity based on the CAPM.

Solution

RADR = RFR + β (RM − RFR)

RADR = 10 + 1.4(14 − 10) = 10 + 5.6 = 15.6%

The cost of equity of Nayu plc is 15.6%

Test yourself 12.1

Calculate the cost of equity of three shares – A, B and C – given that the RFR is 4.25% and the market return is 12%. The ßs of the three securities are 1.35, 2.10 and 0.78 respectively.

3.6 Assumptions and criticisms of CAPM

Assumptions
- Investors are rational and possess full knowledge about the market.
- Investors expect greater returns for taking greater risks.
- It is possible for an investor to diversify the unsystematic risk by actively managing the portfolio.
- Borrowing and lending rates are equal.
- There are no transaction costs.
- Markets are perfect and market imperfections tend to correct themselves in the long run.
- The RFR is the same as the returns on the government bonds.
- There is no taxation and no inflation.

Criticisms
- Research has shown that the linearity of the SML has been lost with changes of gradient at different levels of ß during some periods.
- Apart from changes in ß, there are also other reasons (such as company size or market value) for the shares to give excess returns. These are not considered by CAPM.
- There are practical difficulties in deriving the systematic risk and the ß of any company as trading on the stock market is subject to numerous factors.
- Companies with more than one division and company channel might have different systematic risks for each division – yet ß is derived on the basis of a single share price.
- The CAPM is a one-year model and is relevant for a year only.

4 Cost of equity using the dividend valuation model

The dividend valuation model (or dividend growth model) states that the value of the company/share is the present value of the expected future dividends discounted at the shareholders' required rate of return.

Assuming a constant growth rate in dividends:

$$P = D_0(1 + g) \div (K_e - g)$$

Where:
P = current share price
D_0 = current level of dividend
g = estimated growth rate in dividends

If we need to derive Ke, the formula can be rearranged to:

$$K_e = [D_0 (1 + g) \div P_0] + g$$

$D_0 (1 + g)$ is the dividend at the end of the year (D_1).

The dividend valuation model is covered in detail in Chapter 15, where it is used for the purposes of investment appraisal.

Worked example 12.3

Nehi plc has £1 equity shares in issue with a market value of £1.20 per share. A dividend of 15p per share has just been paid. Estimate the cost of equity required by the equity shareholders if the rate of growth in dividends is 6%.

Solution

$$K_e = [D_0 (1+g) \div P] + g$$

$$K_e = [15(1 + 0.06) \div 120] + 0.06 = (15.9 \div 120) + 0.06 = 0.1925 = 19.25\%$$

The cost of equity of Nehi plc is 19.25%

5 Cost of debt

Raising debt to finance a company's operations comes at a cost. Conceptually, the cost of debt refers to the effective interest rate a company pays on its debt (such as bonds, mortgages or debentures). The cost of debt is usually expressed as an after-tax rate, = (1 − t), because interest is a tax-deductible expense.

5.1 Irredeemable debt

irredeemable debt
Debt, which is never repaid, also referred to perpetual debt. It is rare in practice.

Irredeemable debt is a perpetual debt which is never repaid. The cost of debt after tax is calculated using the following equation.

$$K_d = \frac{I(1-t)}{S_d}$$

Where:
K_d = Cost of debt capital
I = Annual interest
t = Corporate tax rate
S_d = Market price of the debt

The higher the rate of corporate tax payable by the company, the lower the after-tax cost of debt capital.

While calculating the cost of debt, we assume that the interest payable on debt instruments attracts the tax deduction. The cost of preference shares with the same coupon rate and market value will be higher than the cost of debt capital as there is no tax relief on a preference share dividend. The cost of any debt with no tax relief and the cost of preference shares is calculated using the following equation.

$$K_d = I \div S_d$$

Worked example 12.4

Sanepa Ltd has issued 10% irredeemable debentures with a face value of £100. The current market price is £95. The corporate tax rate is 20%. Calculate the cost of debt for the company before and after tax.

Solution

Cost of debt before tax:

$$K_d = I \div S_d$$

$$K_d = \frac{10}{95} = 10.5\%$$

Cost of debt before tax is 10.5%.

Cost of debt after tax:

$$K_d = \frac{I(1-t)}{S_d}$$

$$\frac{10(1-0.20)}{95} = 8.4\%$$

Cost of debt after tax is 8.4%

The cost of debt before tax with the same coupon rate and market value will be higher than the cost of debt after tax.

Test yourself 12.2

Guava Ltd issued 10% irredeemable debentures with a market price of £105 per £100 par value. The corporate tax rate is 20%. Calculate the cost of debt after tax.

5.2 Redeemable debt

redeemable debt
Redeemable debt is usually repaid at its nominal value (at par) but may be issued as repayable at a premium on nominal value. It is repayable at a fixed date (or during a fixed period) in the future.

internal rate of return (IRR)
A method used for investment appraisal that calculates the rate of return at which the net present value of all cash flows from a project or investment is equal to zero. It evaluates the profitability and the attractiveness of potential investments.

net present value
The net value of a capital investment or project is obtained by discounting all cash outflows and inflows to their present value by using an appropriate discount rate of return.

weighted average cost of capital
The minimum return that a company must earn on its existing assets. It reflects the weighted average rate of return a company is expected to pay to all the providers of long-term finance.

Redeemable debt is usually repaid at its nominal value (at par) but may be issued as repayable at a premium on nominal value. It is repayable at a fixed date (or during a fixed period) in the future.

A company raises redeemable debt to pay back at a fixed future date. The cost of debt on redeemable debt can be calculated by the **internal rate of return (IRR)**. The internal rate of return is a method used for investment appraisal that calculates the rate of return at which the **net present value** of all the cash flows (both positive and negative) from a project or investment is equal to zero. It evaluates the profitability and the attractiveness of potential investments. Calculation of IRR is covered in Chapter 13.

The cost of debt helps to understand the company's risk level compared to others. Companies carrying higher risk will have a higher cost of debt.

6 Weighted average cost of capital

The **weighted average cost of capital** (WACC), commonly referred to as the company's cost of capital, represents the minimum return that a company must earn on its existing assets. It reflects the weighted average rate of return a company is expected to pay to all the providers of long-term finance. The weights are the fraction of each financing source in the company's total capital. WACC is influenced by the external market.

The WACC is derived by averaging a company's cost of equity and cost of debt according to the market value of each source of finance. The appropriate weights are the target capital structure weights expressed in market value terms.

$$WACC = K_e \times \frac{E}{E + D} + K_d (1-t) \times \frac{D}{E + D}$$

Where:

WACC = Weighted average cost of capital

E = Total market value of equity

D = Total market value of debt

t = Corporate tax rate

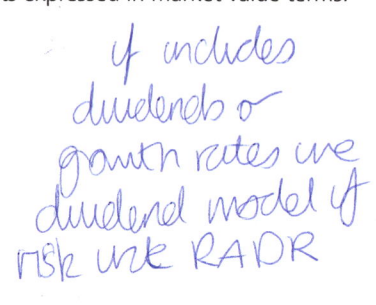

Worked example 12.5

Below is an extract from the financial statements of Jamica Ltd.

	£'000
Equity share capital (25p shares)	250
Other components of equity	750
10% irredeemable debentures	400

The company has issued £1 million equity shares with a current market price at £4.50 (ex-dividend). The company will pay a final dividend of 30p. Historically, the dividend has a growth rate of 7%. The company has also issued irredeemable debentures trading at £105 per £100. The corporate tax rate is 20%.

Calculate the WACC for Jamica Ltd.

Solution

$$WACC = K_e \times \frac{E}{E + D} + K_d (1-t) \times \frac{D}{E + D}$$

Cost of equity

$K_e = [d_0 (1 + g) \div P_0] + g$

$= [0.30 (1+0.07) \div 4.50] + 0.07$

$= 0.07130 + 0.07$

$= 0.1413$

$K_e = 14.13\%$

Cost of debt

$$K_d = \frac{I(1 - t)}{S_d}$$

$$= \frac{10(1 - 0.20)}{105}$$

$= 0.0762$

$K_d = 7.62\%$

As we have the information on dividend and growth rate, we have used the dividend growth model to calculate the cost of equity.

Market values

		£'000
Equity	1,000,000 shares × £4.50	4,500
Debt	400,000 × (105 ÷ 100)	420
Equity + debt		4,920

WACC

	Market value £'000	Weight	K (%)	K (W)
Equity	4,500	(4,500/4,920) 0.9146	14.13%	12.92%
Debt	420	0.0854	7.62%	0.65%
Equity + debt	4,920	1.0000		13.57%

The weighted average cost of capital for Jamica Ltd is 13.57%

Test yourself 12.3

On formation, Apindra Ltd issued 4 million equity shares with a nominal value of 50p each.

The current market price of a share is 140p (ex-dividend). The company is growing and it has just paid a dividend of 17p per share. Historically, dividends are growing at a rate of 6% p.a.

Apindra Ltd has also issued irredeemable debentures of £3.5 million. The current market price of the debentures is £90.01 per £100. The debentures have been issued with a coupon rate of 13%. The corporate tax rate is 20%.

Calculate the WACC for Apindra & Co.

7 Capital structure

After determining the finance required for an investment or project, a company must consider the use of various sources of finance. Capital structure refers to the mix of equity and debt financing that shows how the company, or its overall operation, is financed. It is concerned with the balance between equity (shares and retained earnings) and non-current liabilities (loans, debentures or fixed-return capital). The sources and the mix of capital are decided on the basis of need of the company and the cost of capital.

The key objective of a company is to maximise the value of the company. This should be considered when deciding upon the optimal capital structure. Decisions need to be made about:

- the sources (form of capital)
- their quantity (amount to be funded)
- the use of their relative proportions in total capitalisation

The value of the company can be measured using the following two formulae.

EBIT ÷ overall cost of capital or (WACC)

Market value (MV) = future cash flows ÷ WACC

For example, if a project generates future cash flows of £100,000 at 10% WACC:

MV = £100 ÷ 10% = £1,000

Capital investment refers to funds invested by a company for furthering its objectives such as replacement of a non-current asset, expansion of its production capacity or diversification to a new product line. Capital structure decisions are involved whenever funds are to be raised for financing a capital investment. Raising funds generates a new capital structure in terms of its quantity, mix and forms of capital: the different sources of long-term finance and how they are raised are discussed in Chapter 11.

```
                    Capital investment decision
                    For replacement, expansion,
                         diversification
                              │
                              ▼
                        Raising of funds
                    Internal vs external source;
                         equity vs debt
                              │
                              ▼
                   Capital structure decisions
                              │
        ┌─────────────────────┼─────────────────────┐
        ▼                     ▼                     ▼
   Existing capital    Desired debt/ equity mix   Other factors
     structure         (Analysis of risk and      such as:
                            returns)              growth, market
                                                  and tax
                                                  exposure.
                         ┌────┴────┐
                         ▼         ▼
                  Effect of return   Effect of risk
                                    (Financing, business
                                    and operating risks)
                              │
                              ▼
                   Consider the impact on cost of
                         capital (WACC)
                              │
                              ▼                Optimum
                                            capital structure
                                            (Decision making)
                   Goal: Minimize WACC and (decision
                   making) maximise company's value
```

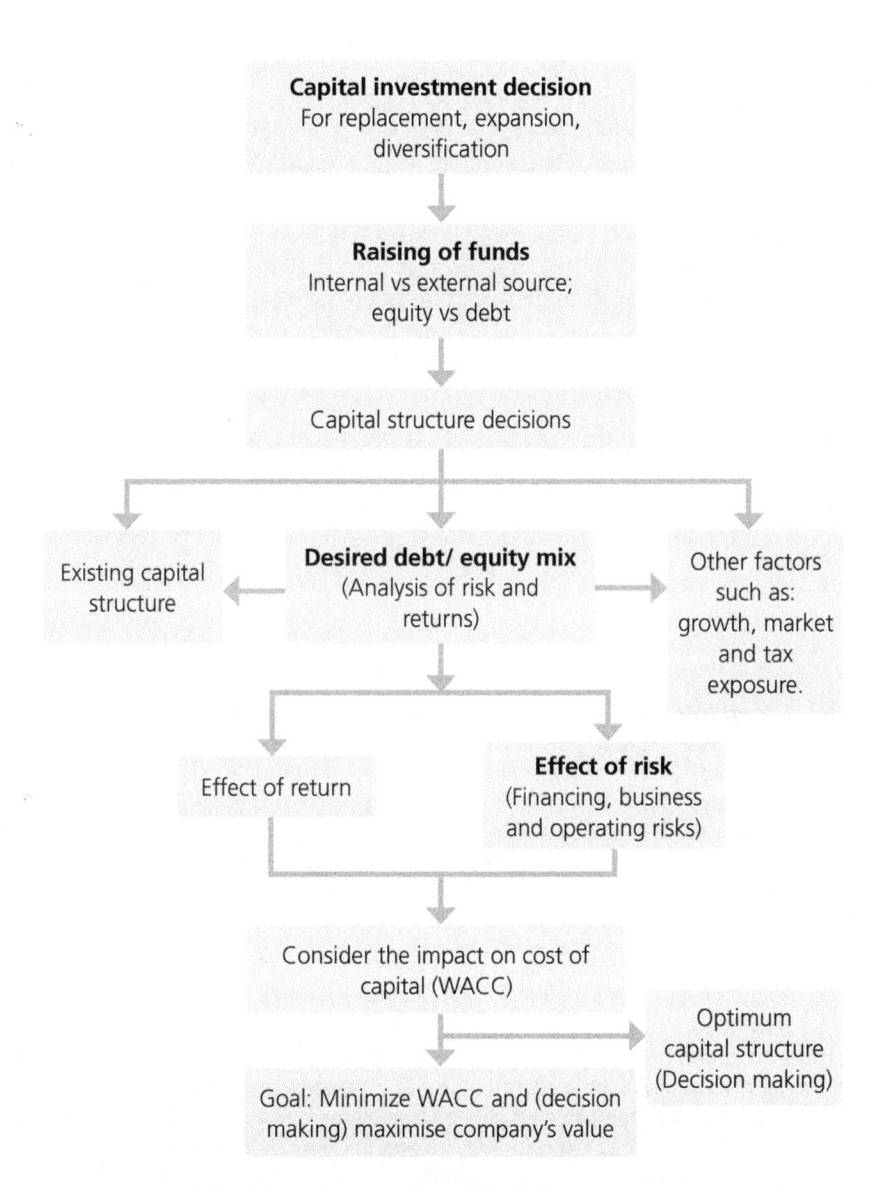

Figure 12.4 Capital structure decision-making process

8 Factors affecting capital structure

Companies need to consider certain factors when deciding on a sound and optimum capital structure,.

8.1 Financial leverage or gearing

Debt is normally cheaper than equity. Earnings per share (EPS) will increase with use of long-term debt and preference share capital if the company yields a return higher than cost of debt.

However, increasing the use of a high level of long-term debt or gearing also increases risks for the shareholder because fixed interest must be paid each year before the company is able to pay dividends. It reduces the earnings of shareholders if the rate of interest is more than the expected rate of earnings of the company.

8.2 Growth

Equity financing is popular in start-ups and high growth industries, such as the technology sector. The high cost of servicing the debt restricts growth.

8.3 Cost principle

Debt capital is cheaper than equity capital because debt is considered to be a less risky investment compared to investing in shares. The interest on debt is deductible for corporate tax purposes, making debt capital even cheaper. No such deduction is allowed for dividends. Based on the cost principle, debt financing should minimise the cost of capital and maximise the EPS.

8.4 Risk principle

There are three risks associated with this principle.

company risk
The possibility a company will have inadequate profit or even result in losses due to uncertainties in the company.

operating risk
The risk of disruption of the core operations of a company resulting from breakdowns in internal procedures, people and systems. It measures risk from fixed operating costs.

operating gearing
Operating gearing measures the proportion of fixed costs a company has relative to its variable costs.

financial risk
Risk associated with financing, including risk of default from investing in a company that has debt.

financial gearing
The proportion of debt a company has relative to its equity. Also known as capital gearing.

- **Company risk** is the risk of variability of earnings resulting in an inadequate profit, or even a loss, due to uncertainties in the company. Company risk can be internal as well as external. Internal risk is caused by poor product mix, inadequate resources, absence of strategic management and so on. External risk is influenced by numerous factors, including competition, the overall economic climate and government regulations. In reality, there is little that a financial manager can do to alter the company risk due to external factors.

- **Operating risk** is the risk of disruption of the core operations of a company resulting from breakdowns in internal procedures, people and systems. It may be caused by inadequate policies, system failures, criminal activity and loss faced by litigations against the company. It measures the risk from operating costs that are fixed. **Operating gearing** is the proportion of fixed costs a company has relative to its variable costs. There may only be limited opportunities for altering operating gearing.

- **Financial risk** refers to the risk from financing. It is the risk of default when the company may not be able to cover its fixed financial costs. The extent of financial risk depends on the leverage of the company's capital structure. A company with debt financing has higher financial risk. A company should be in a position to meet its obligations in paying the loan and interest charges as and when these fall due. The risk associated with how the company is financed can be most easily controlled by changing the level of **financial gearing**.

```
                    Business risk
                (internal and external
                factors associated with
                 being in the business)
                    ↙           ↘
    Operating gearing    ←→   Financial gearing
    (risk from operating      (risk from financing
     costs that are fixed)    associated with debt)
```

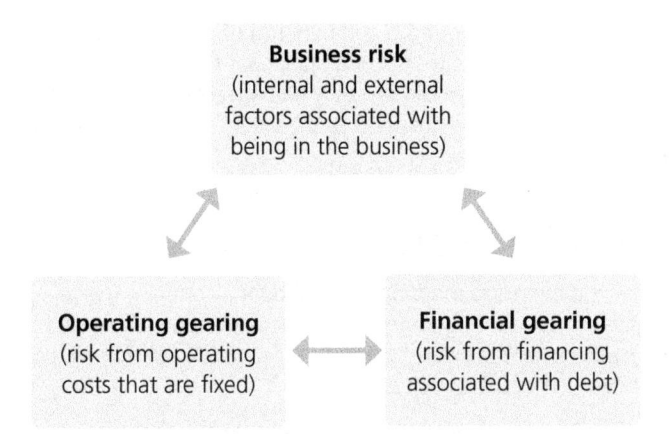

Figure 12.5 Risk factors affecting capital structure

It is a financial manager's role to consider the volatility that cannot be avoided and balance these risks faced by investors to an acceptable degree. The level of overall risk determines the rate of return equity investors demand.

8.5 Control principle

When funds are raised through equity capital, excepting a rights issue to existing shareholders, the control of the existing shareholders (owners) over the company's affairs is diluted or adversely affected. The number of the company's shareholders will increase when funds are raised by issuing equity shares. Conversely, when funds are raised through debt capital, there is no effect on the control of the company because the debenture holders have no control over the affairs of the company. Debt may be preferred over equity to minimise possible risk of loss of control.

8.6 Market conditions

A company's capital structure can be affected by the market and economic conditions. For example, the interest rate to borrow may be higher in a struggling market due to economic uncertainties when compared to the market under a 'normal' state.

8.7 Tax exposure

The tax deductibility of the debt interest payments can make debt financing attractive.

8.8 Other factors

Other factors that influence capital structure decision making may include:

- government regulations (such as tax rates)
- trends in capital markets
- the capital structure of other companies
- flotation costs

When making a decision about the optimum mix of debt and equity, the capital structure should be conservative (for example, debt financing should not be used at excessive levels). It should be easily manageable and easily understood by investors. Debt should only be used to the extent that it does not threaten the solvency of the company.

9 Financial gearing

Financial gearing measures the proportion of debt a company has relative to its equity. It is a measure of a company's financial leverage (also called 'trading on equity') and shows the extent to which its operations are funded by interest bearing lenders versus shareholders.

Debt is normally cheaper than equity. Lenders are likely to require a lower return than shareholders because debt is considered to be a less risky investment compared to investing in shares. Interest payable to debt lenders is normally tax deductible, which makes the net cost of debt even lower. Debt financing should minimise the cost of capital and maximise the EPS. A company with significantly more debt than equity is regarded as highly geared (or leveraged).

However, increasing the amount of debt or gearing in a company also increases risks for the shareholder because fixed interest must be paid each year before the company is able to pay dividends.

Financial gearing can be calculated using one of the following two formulae:

$$\text{Equity gearing} = \frac{\text{Debt borrowing} + \text{preference share capital}}{\text{Ordinary share capital} + \text{equity}}$$

$$\text{Total or capital gearing} = \frac{\text{Debt borrowing} + \text{preference share capital}}{\text{Total long-term capital}}$$

Debt is the book or market value of interest-bearing financial liabilities. It could be in the form of a secured or unsecured loan such as debentures, loans, redeemable preference shares, bank overdrafts or lease obligations. If available, market values should be used for debt and for equity to get the best measure of gearing. An investor looks for the market required rate of return on the market value of the capital, not the book value of the capital. When not available, values from financial statements can be used.

With both methods, gearing will increase with higher proportions of debt.

9.1 Interest gearing

Interest gearing shows the percentage of profit absorbed by interest payments on borrowings. It measures the impact of gearing on profits. It is calculated as:

$$\text{Interest gearing} = \frac{\text{Debt interest} + \text{preference dividends}}{\text{Operating profit}}$$

9.2 Effect on EPS

The impact of changes to operating profit on EPS can be examined using the ratio below:

% change in EPS ÷ % change in EBIT

Reviewing the gearing ratio is key to the funding decisions made by financial managers and investors. It affects the risk, returns and controls associated with equity capital. According to the control principle, debt may be preferred over equity to minimise possible risk of loss of control.

Other stakeholders who have an interest in the profitability and stability of the company – such as employees, customers and creditors – will also be interested in the level of gearing.

9.3 Problems around high levels of gearing

A high level of gearing implies a higher obligation for a company to pay interest when using debt financing. It has a higher risk of insolvency than equity financing. While dividends on equity shares need only be paid when there are sufficient distributable profits, the interest on debt is payable regardless of the operating profit of a company. Other problems associated with high gearing include:

- bankruptcy risk increases with increased gearing;
- agency cost and restrictive conditions imposed in the loan agreements constrain management's freedom of action, such as restrictions on dividend levels or on the company's ability to borrow;
- after a certain level of gearing, companies will have no tax liability left against which to offset interest charges (tax exhaustion);
- companies may run out of suitable assets to offer as security against loans with high gearing;
- gearing increases the cost of borrowing; and
- directors have a natural tendency to be cautious about borrowing and the related solvency issues.

Worked example 12.6

Kyrat plc has the following summarised statement of financial position as at 31 December 20X1.

	£'000
Non-current assets	13,000
Current assets	4,000
Total assets	17,000
Equity	
Equity shares (£1 shares)	5,000

Retained earnings	6,500
Total equity	**11,500**
Non-current liabilities	
Debentures	3,000
Preference shares	2,000
Current liabilities	500
Total equity and liabilities	**17,000**

The market values at the date of the statement of Kyrat plc are:

Equity shares:	£2.10 per share
Preference shares:	£1.50 per share
Debentures:	95% of book value

The nominal value of the preference shares was £1.00. Calculate the total or capital gearing ratio of Kyrat plc using:

1. book values
2. market values

Advise which method is preferred.

Solution

(All monetary amounts shown as £'000 unless otherwise stated).

$$\text{Gearing} = \frac{\text{Debt borrowing} + \text{preference share capital}}{\text{Ordinary share capital} + \text{reserves}}$$

1. **Book values**

   Total gearing = (3,000 + 2,000) ÷ (3,000 + 2,000 + 11,500) = 30%

2. **Market values**

   The market value of equity = 5,000 × £2.10 = £10,500

   The market value of the debt = (3,000 × 0.95) + (2,000 × £1.50) = £5,850

   Total gearing = 5,850 ÷ (5,850 + 10,500) = 36%

If available, market values should be used for debt and for equity to get the best measure of gearing. Investors demand the market required rate of return on the market value of the capital, not the book value of the capital.

Test yourself 12.4

1. What is meant by a highly geared company?
2. When might investors and other stakeholders prefer gearing and why?
3. What are the problems around high gearing?

10 Operating gearing

Operating gearing measures the proportion of fixed costs a company has relative to its variable costs. As with financial gearing, fixed operating costs increase the risk for the shareholders in the same way as fixed interest payments. For example, the costs of staff employed on annual contracts are fixed, whereas those employed on a day-to-day basis are variable.

In times of growth, a high proportion of fixed costs and a low proportion of variable costs can be advantageous. There is a cost advantage for producing a higher level of output, also referred to as economies of scale. Higher fixed costs mean greater operational gearing that makes a company's profits sensitive to a change in sales revenue – a small percentage change in sales will lead to a large percentage in operating profit. With each pound in sales revenue earned beyond the break-even point, the company makes a profit. The opposite is true in times of recession.

The common method of measuring operating gearing is to consider the level of contribution earned in relation to sales – known as the contribution-to-sales ratio (C/S ratio). The contribution margin is the excess of total sales over total variable costs. The margin will be positive if sales exceed variable costs and vice versa. Operating gearing can be calculated using any one of the three ratios below:

$$\text{Contribution-to-sales ratio} = \frac{(\text{sales revenue} - \text{cost of sales})}{\text{sales revenue}} \times 100$$

The higher the operational gearing, the higher the sensitivity of profit to a change in sales.

$$\frac{\%\ \text{change in earnings before interest and tax}}{\%\ \text{change in sales}}$$

The higher the operational gearing, the higher the sensitivity of EBIT to a change in sales.

$$\frac{\text{fixed costs}}{\text{variable costs}}$$

The higher the fixed costs, the higher the operating gearing.

Worked example 12.7

Nagaland Ltd and Manipur Ltd have the following cost structures. They have the same revenue and operating profit, but different fixed and variable cost.

	Nagaland Nagaland	Manipur Ltd
	£m	£m
Sales revenue	30	30
Variable costs	(15)	(5)
Fixed costs	(10)	(20)
Operating profit	5	5

1. Calculate the level of operating gearing for each company.
2. What would be the impact on each of a 20% increase in sales revenue?

Solution

1. Operating gearing can be calculated as follows.

Fixed costs ÷ variable costs	Nagaland Ltd	Manipur Ltd
	10 ÷ 15 = 0.66 or 66%	20 ÷ 5 = 4 or 400%

As Manipur Ltd has higher fixed costs than Nagaland Ltd (as a proportion of its total costs), it has a higher operating gearing.

2. A 20% increase in sales revenue would have the following impact.

	Nagaland Nagaland	Manipur Ltd
	£m	£m
Sales revenue	36	36
Variable costs	(18)	(6)
Fixed costs	(10)	(20)
Operating profit	8	10
Increase in operating profit	60%	100%

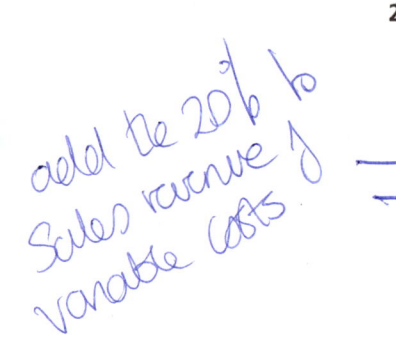

A higher proportion of fixed costs mean greater operational gearing, which makes profits more sensitive to a change in sales revenue. Manipur Ltd would enjoy an increase in operating profit of 100%, whereas Nagaland's operating profit would only increase by 60%.

In the same way, a decrease in sales would have a greater fall in the operating profit of Manipur Ltd than in Nagaland Ltd.

Test yourself 12.5

A summarised statement of profit or loss and OCI for Ealing Ltd is shown below.

	Ealing Ltd £m	
Sales revenue	20	16
Variable costs	(5)	(4)
Fixed costs	(8)	
Operating profit	7	
Interest expense	(2)	
Profit before tax	5	9

How would a 20% fall in sales affect operating profit and shareholder return?

11 The traditional approach to capital structure

Capital structure theories attempt to discover:

- whether an optimal capital structure exists;
- the optimal mix between debt and equity finance; and
- the relationship between WACC, the market value of the company and the level of gearing in the capital structure.

The traditional approach suggests an optimal capital structure is obtained by a blend of equity and debt financing that minimises WACC while maximising its market value.

The WACC changes with the level of gearing because equity is more expensive than debt. Higher levels of gearing, however, increase the risk to shareholders and therefore result in higher equity costs.

A company's value initially increases alongside debt financing, as debt is cheaper than equity. After a certain point, it begins to plateau and eventually decreases as levels of gearing increase. This decrease in value is caused by excessive borrowings, also referred to as over-leveraging. Lenders will require higher rates of interest in order to compensate for increased risk.

Under the traditional view, the only way of finding the optimal mix is by trial and error, as WACC will change with the level of gearing. The optimal level of gearing is achieved when the WACC is at a minimum. This is illustrated in Figure 12.6.

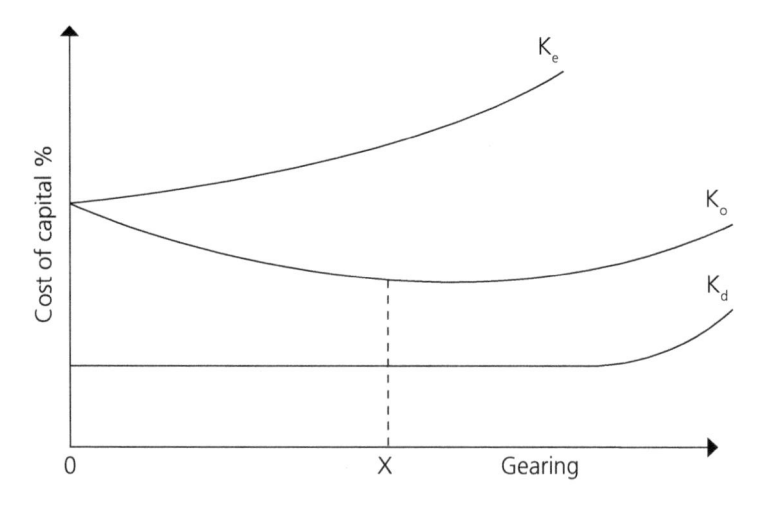

Notes:

K_e is the cost of equity
K_d is the cost of debt
K_o is the overall or weighted average cost of capital.
X = Position of optimum gearing

Figure 12.6 Traditional theory of optimum gearing

11.1 Gearing and the cost of equity (Ke)

An investor return (Ke) equals the risk-free rate (RFR) plus an additional return for financial risk (related to the gearing of the company). At higher levels of gearing, the risk of investors increases with increased gearing due to the added financial risk of borrowing.

11.2 Gearing and the cost of debt (Kd)

The cost of debt remains constant until a point at which the increasing gearing increases the risk of lenders. The lender will also require higher rates of interest in order to compensate for increased risk to interest payments and principal.

11.3 Gearing and the cost of debt (Kd) and WACC

The overall cost of capital initially falls due to the introduction of debt, which is cheaper than equity. The low cost of debt immediately reduces WACC until a point at which the increase in gearing causes both the cost of equity (Ke) and the cost of debt (Kd) to increase. This causes WACC to increase. Point X is the optimal level of gearing, after which the cost of capital carries on increasing as debt and gearing increase.

In the traditional approach, the financial manager should raise debt finance until it achieves the optimal level of gearing – that which gives the cheapest overall cost of capital. Once achieved, the optimum level of gearing must be maintained by keeping the same ratio of gearing (part equity/part debt) in future financing.

11.4 Limitations of the traditional view

- The traditional theory illustrates the importance of gearing and the optimal balance between equity and debt, but does not quantify the effect of changes in gearing. It locates the optimal point by trial and error.
- The traditional theory of capital structure ignores other real-world factors such as corporate tax rates and the investment habits of investors.
- It is based on the following assumptions:
   - the company distributes all of its earnings as a dividend
   - the company's total assets and revenue are fixed
   - only debt and equity financing is available
   - investment habits remain rational
   - there are no taxes

12 The Modigliani and Miller theory of capital structure

12.1 The Modigliani and Miller (1958) approach: without taxes

Modigliani and Miller (1958) argued that the relationship between the cost of capital, capital structure and the valuation of the company should be explained by the net operating income approach. Under this approach, the levels of operating income influence market value. This is known as the capital structure irrelevancy theory. It suggests that the valuation of a company and the weighted average cost of capital are irrelevant to the capital structure of a company.

The basic concept of Modigliani and Miller's (MM) approach is that the value of a company is independent of its capital structure. Market value is determined solely by investment decisions. When the gearing increases, the increase in the cost of equity (associated with the higher financial risk) exactly offsets the benefit of the cheaper debt finance. As WACC remains unchanged, the value of a leveraged company is the same as the value of an unleveraged company if they operate in the same type of company and have similar operating risks. The value of a company depends upon the future operating income generated by its assets.

The MM hypothesis can be explained through two propositions.

MM proposition I
With the assumption of no taxes, capital structure or leveraging does not influence the market value of the company. It assumes that debt holders and

equity shareholders have the same priority in the earnings of a company and that the earnings are split equally,

> Value of the geared company = Value of the ungeared company (net operating income (NOI) ÷ WACC).

MM proposition II

The cost of equity is a linear function of the company's debt equity ratio. With an increase in gearing, the equity investors perceive a higher risk and expect a higher return, increasing the cost of equity. The rate of return required by shareholders (Ke) increases in direct proportion to the debt/equity ratio.

> The cost of equity in geared company K_g = the cost of ungeared company K_u + a premium for financial risk.

As the gearing increases, the cost of equity rises just enough to offset any benefits conferred by the use of apparently cheap debt (Kd). This means that WACC remains constant at all levels of gearing. This is illustrated in Figure 12.7.

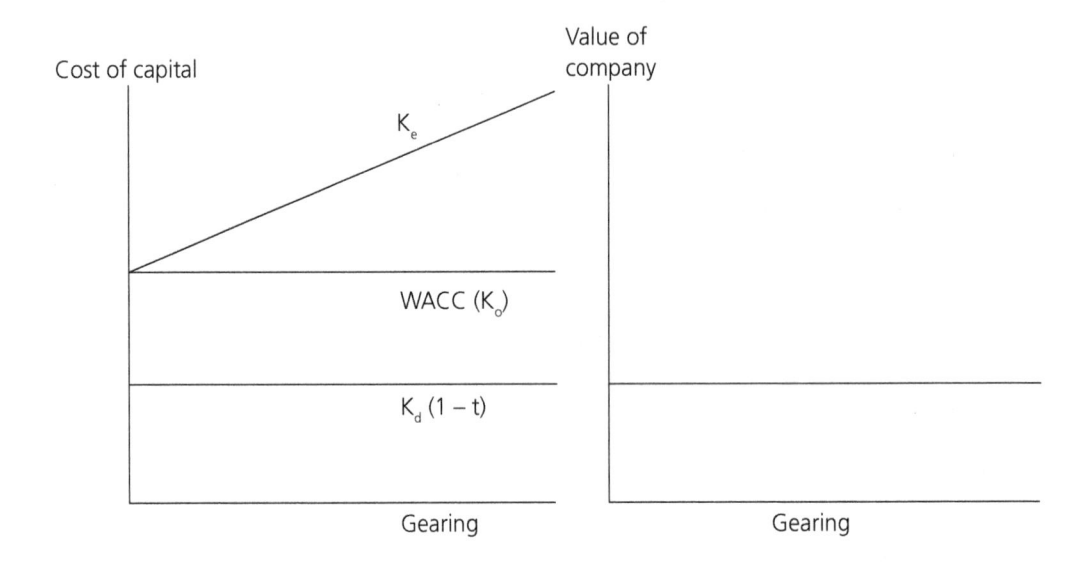

Figure 12.7 The Modigliani and Miller theory without taxes

Under the MM theory, the company value depends upon future operating profits. The essential point made by M&M is that the company's cost of capital is independent of the way in which investment is financed. Arbitrage (market pressures) will ensure that two identical companies, with same company risk and identical provisions before interest and tax (PBIT), will have the same overall market value and cost of capital irrespective of their gearing level.

12.2 Assumptions of the MM approach without taxes

- No corporate taxation.
- No transaction costs relating to buying and selling securities or bankruptcy costs.
- Perfect capital markets with a symmetry of information. An investor will have access to same information that a company would and they react rationally.
- The cost of borrowing is the same for investors and companies.
- Debt is risk free.

12.3 The Modigliani and Miller (1963) approach with taxes: the trade-off theory

The impact of tax cannot be ignored in the real world, since debt interest is tax deductible. Modigliani and Miller revised their theory in 1963 to recognise tax relief on interest payments.

The actual cost of debt is less than the nominal cost of debt because of tax benefits. However, the same is not the case with dividends paid on equity. The trade-off theory advocates that a company can use debt as long as the cost of distress or bankruptcy does not exceed the value of tax benefits. This is illustrated in Figure 12.8.

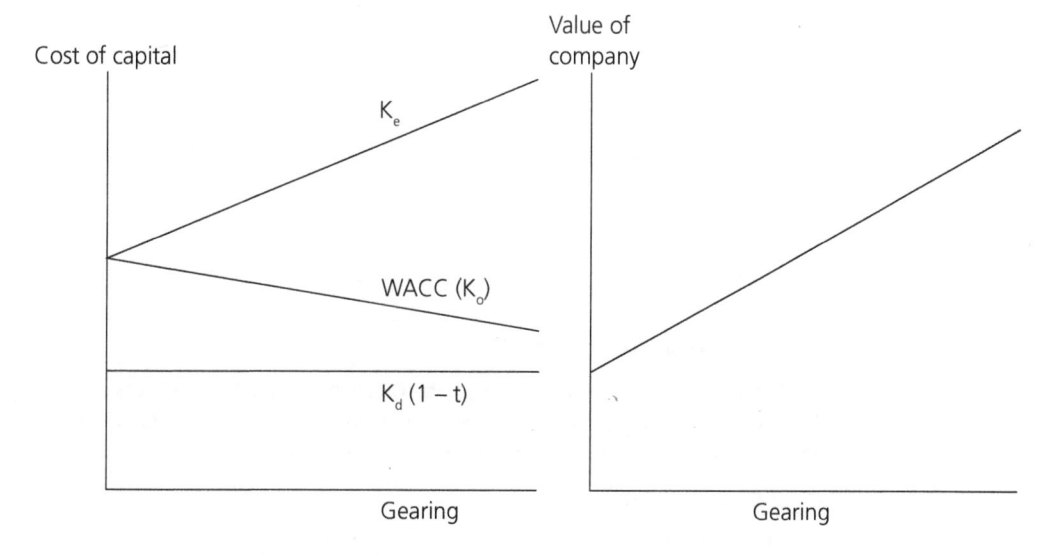

Figure 12.8 The Modigliani and Miller theory with taxes

As gearing increases, the cost of equity (Ke) increases in direct proportion with gearing. However, as the overall cost of debt after tax relief (Kd(1-t)) is lower than the nominal cost of debt (Kd), investor returns are less volatile. This leads to lower increases in Ke, causing the WACC to fall as gearing increases.

Therefore, gearing up reduces the WACC and increases the market value of the company. The optimal capital structure is 99.9% gearing. This means the higher the debt, the lower the WACC and the higher the market value. The company should use as much debt as possible.

12.4 Criticisms of the MM trade-off theory

- It ignores bankruptcy risk. In practice, companies never gear up to 99.9%. As gearing increases, so does the possibility of bankruptcy. If the company is considered to be risky, the share price will go down, increasing the company's WACC.
- Restrictive conditions in the loan agreements associated with debt finance can constrain a company's flexibility to make decisions (such as paying dividends, raising additional debt or disposing of any major fixed assets).
- After a certain level of gearing, companies may no longer have any tax liability left against which to offset interest charges. $Kd(1-t)$ simply becomes Kd due to tax exhaustion.
- High levels of gearing may not be possible with companies exhausting assets to offer as security against loans.
- Different risk tolerance levels between shareholders and directors may impact the gearing level.
- It can be argued that directors have a tendency to be cautious about borrowing.

Test yourself 12.6

Outline the Modigliani and Miller theory of capital structure.

13 Real world approaches

13.1 Pecking order theory

The 'pecking order' theory popularised by Myers and Majluf (1984) was developed as an alternative theory on capital structure. It states that companies have the following order of preference for financing decisions:

- retained earnings
- straight debt
- convertible debt
- preference shares
- equity shares

The reasoning is that as companies are risk averse and will prefer retained earnings to any other source of finance, they will choose debt and equity last of all. They invariably prefer internal finance over external finance. The costs of borrowing also follow the same order, equity shares being the most expensive.

The value of a project depends on how it is financed. If a company follows the pecking order approach, only projects funded with internal funds or with relatively safe debt will be accepted. Risky projects funded by risky debts or equity will be rejected.

13.2 Real world factors

Companies take a balanced approach in the real world, whereby the different theories can be reconciled to make the correct financing decisions. Capital structures can also be affected by other factors such as growth, market conditions and tax exposure.

Companies consider the signalling effect of raising new finance by assessing the impact of the new finance on a company's statement of profit or loss and OCI and statement of financial position.

Profitable companies will tend to drift away from their optimal gearing position over time – known as 'gearing drift', whereby the level of the debt-equity ratio gradually decreases as accumulated retained earnings help to increase the value of equity. Companies tend to increase their gearing positions by occasionally issuing debt, paying a large dividend or buying back shares.

Stop and think 12.1

If a company has adopted a pecking order approach to capital structure, which form of finance is it likely to select after it has exhausted the retained earnings?

Chapter summary

- The cost of capital is an important concept in financial decision making. It represents the investor's opportunity cost of taking on risk by making a specific investment. Financial managers use cost of capital as a discount rate when designing an optimal capital structure and evaluating new investment options.
- Cost of equity is the return investors expect to achieve on their shares in a company. Equity investors face the greatest risk of all investors and therefore demand a higher rate of return to justify the risk taken. There are two methods of determining the cost of equity:
    - the capital asset pricing model (CAPM)
    - the dividend valuation model
- The CAPM states that the expected return on an asset is related to its risk as measured by beta (ß).

- The dividend valuation model states that the value of the company share is the present value of the expected future dividends, discounted at the shareholders' required rate of return.
- The cost of debt refers to the effective interest rate a company pays on its debt. The cost of irredeemable debt, cost of debt with no tax relief and the cost of redeemable debt are all calculated differently.
- Weighted average cost of capital (WACC), commonly referred to as the company's cost of capital, reflects the weighted average rate of return a company is expected to pay to all the providers of long-term finance.
- Capital structure refers to the mix of debt and equity financing in a company that shows how the company, or its overall operation, is financed. The key objective of a company is to maximise the value of the company and should be considered when deciding upon the optimal capital structure.
- Factors to be considered on deciding on a sound and optimum capital structure include financial leverage or gearing, growth, the cost principle and the risk principle. Three types of risk should be taken into account under the risk principle:
  - company risk (internal and external factors associated with being in the company)
  - operating risk (risk from operating costs that are fixed)
  - financial risk (risk from financing associated with debt)
- Financial gearing measures the proportion of debt a company has relative to its equity. Debt is normally cheaper than equity. However, increasing the amount of debt or gearing in a company also increases risks for the shareholder due to the fixed interest payments.
- Operating gearing measures the proportion of fixed costs a company has relative to its variable costs. Fixed operating costs increase the risk for the shareholders in exactly the same way as fixed interest payments. The higher the operational gearing, the higher the sensitivity of profit to a change in sales revenue.
- According to the traditional approach to capital structure, the overall cost of capital initially falls due to the infusion of debt, until a point at which the increase in gearing causes both the cost of equity and the cost of debt to increase. This causes WACC to increase. An optimal capital structure is obtained by a blend of equity and debt financing that minimises WACC while maximising market value.
- The Modigliani and Miller approach (without taxes) argues that the value of a company is independent of its capital structure: market value is determined solely by investment decisions. When the gearing increases, the increase in the cost of equity (associated with the higher financial risk) exactly offsets the benefit of the cheaper debt finance. The WACC remains unchanged.

- The MM theory (with taxes) recognises tax relief on interest payments. It advocates that a company can use debts as long as the cost of distress or bankruptcy does not exceed the value of tax benefits. The optimal capital structure is 99.9% gearing.
- Pecking order theory states that companies have a following order of preference for financing decisions:
    - retained earnings
    - straight debt
    - convertible debt
    - preference shares
    - equity shares
- In real-world scenarios, companies take a balanced approach and take a number of factors into consideration – such as growth, market conditions and tax exposure.

Chapter thirteen
Project appraisal techniques

Contents

1. Introduction
2. Identification and analysis of projects
3. Factors affecting project appraisal
4. Project appraisal techniques
5. Non-discounted methods: payback period
6. Non-discounted methods: accounting rate of return
7. Discounted cash flow techniques based on the time value of money
8. Discounted cash flow methods: net present value
9. Discounting annuities
10. Discounted cash flow methods: internal rate of return
11. Discounted cash flow methods: discounted payback
12. Impact of inflation and tax on project appraisal
13. Capital rationing situations and the use of the profitability index

1 Introduction

Project (or investment) appraisal, is the financial and economic appraisal of a project or investment to assess its viability and the value it may generate. Companies normally undertake investment appraisal to identify the attractiveness of an investment before committing to high levels of capital expenditure, such as investing in a new factory, buying new machinery or making investment portfolio decisions.

This chapter will look at the basic principles of investment appraisal. It will also discuss a number of project appraisal techniques used by financial managers to evaluate possible investment opportunities and to determine which of these opportunities will generate the best return for shareholders. There are two types of project appraisal techniques: those using non-discounted cash flows and those using discounted cash flows. Both types will be covered in this chapter.

This chapter also looks at important project appraisal concepts and factors, such as:

- cash flows and the time value of money
- relevant factors such as cash flow, financing costs, timing of returns, incremental costs, working capital, taxation and inflation
- non-relevant factors such as sunk costs, overhead costs and depreciation

2 Identification and analysis of projects

A project can be defined as a work plan that is carefully designed to achieve a specific objective, within a specified time limit, while consuming a planned amount of resources.

2.1 Costs, benefits and risks

The costs and benefits of a proposed capital project should be estimated and evaluated over its expected useful life, along with any risks from the projects. Investment appraisal assesses:

- costs and benefits over the project's life
- the level of expected returns from the project or invested expenditure
- the risks involved, including uncertainty about the timing and volume of returns

Costs are likely to include expenditure on a non-current asset and running costs for the asset over its expected project life. These costs could provide benefits through increased sales revenue or through savings in operating costs. Additionally, the asset might have a 'residual value' at the end of its useful life. For example, it might be sold in a second-hand market or scrapped.

When analysing a project, the following questions need to be asked to ascertain if the project is viable.

- **What for?** The objectives of the project – such as launching a new product.
- **How?** The process and the internal and external resource requirements.
- **Who?** For whom, by whom – project partners, stakeholders.
- **When?** The time factor.
- **Where?** The location.

These questions above are in addition to the core financial questions around how much needs to be invested and what amount of return investors need. These financial objectives of a project are considered in a formal project appraisal methodology.

3 Factors affecting project appraisal

Most project approval decisions are made by company directors who have a duty to act in the interests of their shareholders. The most common investment appraisal objective is to maximise shareholder value. This is linked to:

- **cash**: cash flow is more closely linked to shareholder wealth than profit;
- **return on the cost of capital**: a company or a project is in profit when the returns from the investment exceed the cost of capital; and
- **long-term value:** the stock market places a value on the company's future potential, not just its current profit levels.

Future cash flows are more relevant than accounting profits in capital investment appraisal because:

- profits are subjective and cannot be spent
- cash is required to pay dividends

Long-term cash flow forecasting of revenues, savings and costs is an essential part of project appraisal. It is extremely difficult to produce reliable forecasts but every effort should be made to make them as reliable as possible. This often involves making assumptions during the decision-making process, taking relevant factors into consideration.

3.1 Relevant versus non-relevant factors

Relevant factors

Relevant factors are those vital for making investment decisions based on future net incremental cash flows. In the case of project appraisals, these include the following.

- **Future costs:** an estimated quantification of the amount of a prospective expenditure.
- **Incremental costs:** additional costs incurred from undertaking an additional activity or increasing the level of production.
- **Cash flows or cash-based costs**: any expenses or costs that are predicted to be paid in cash. Non-cash items such as depreciation should be ignored.
- **Financing costs:** opportunity costs. For example, a company bears an opportunity cost in the interest foregone on cash by investing it in £50,000 of new machinery.
- **The timing of returns**: early returns are preferred to later ones. Returns can be reinvested to generate a higher value at the later date.
- **Working capital:** new projects require additional working capital such as inventory and trade receivables in running the project, which must be taken into consideration.
- **Taxation:** the profits subject to taxation and tax relief from the capital cost of the project must be considered.

- **Future inflation:** future revenues and costs will be impacted by inflation to different degrees. For example, the cost of oil, gas and electricity is likely to be impacted more quickly than wages and salaries.

Non-relevant factors

Non-relevant factors are those that are irrelevant for project appraisal decision making. They include the following.

- **Sunk costs**: past expenditure that cannot be recovered and hence cannot be influenced by the current decision.
- **Committed costs:** obligations that cannot be revoked.
- **Noncash items**: items such as depreciation which are just accounting entries with no impact on cash flows.
- **Allocated costs**: costs that are clearly assigned to specific projects, processes or departments, such as the apportionment of overheads that would be incurred in any event.

Stop and think 13.1

Why are future cash flows more relevant than accounting profits in capital investment appraisal?

4 Project appraisal techniques

Project appraisal methodologies are used to assess a proposed project's potential success.

These methods evaluate a project's viability, considering factors such as available funds and the economic climate. A good project will service debt and maximise shareholder wealth.

Companies normally undertake investment appraisal before committing to capital investment. Appraisal of capital projects typically involves the estimation of future costs and benefits over the project life, particularly the forecasting of revenues, costs and savings. Forecasting should be as reliable as possible. The assumptions on which the forecasts are based should be stated clearly, so they can be assessed and approved by the senior management working on behalf of the shareholders. There should also be an assessment of expected returns compared with the expenditure or investments made.

The initial capital cost of a project could include any of the following:

- the purchase cost of a non-current asset
- realisable value of existing assets to be used in the project
- investment in additional working capital
- capitalised research and development expenditure

Investment in capital expenditure is usually made with the intention of generating returns by increasing sales revenue or by making savings in operating costs over the life of the assets. At the end of the asset's useful life, some assets such as computer equipment or machinery might be sold for scrap or in a second-hand market for their residual value.

There are two basic approaches to project appraisal: discounted and non-discounting cash flow methods. Discounted cash flow methods based on the time value of money are more sophisticated.

Some of the key project appraisal techniques include:

Non-discounting methods
- Payback method
- Accounting rate of return (ARR)

Discounted cash flow methods
- Net present value
- Internal rate of return
- Discounted payback

5 Non-discounting methods: payback period

The payback period is the time (number of years) it takes for a project to recover the original investment. It is based on expected cash flows rather than profits and provides a measure of liquidity. It ignores non-cash items such as depreciation. The payback period is based on cash flows. The formula for the payback period method is:

> Original cost of investment or initial cash outflows ÷ annual cash inflows

Where annual cash flows are uneven, the cumulative cash flows over the life of the project is used to calculate the payback period.

Decision rules
- A project is accepted when it pays back the original investment within the specified time period or a target period. The company must therefore set a target payback period.
- When choosing between mutually exclusive projects, the project with the shortest payback should be chosen. The project with the quicker or shorter payback period provides more certainty of making a surplus. The longer the payback period, the more uncertain the cash flows and the forecast are likely to be.

5.1 Advantages

- The payback period uses cash flows, not profits.
- It is simple to calculate.
- It is adaptable to changing needs.
- It encourages a quick return and faster growth.

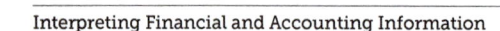

- It is useful in certain situations such as those involving rapidly changing technology.
- It maximises liquidity.

5.2 Disadvantages

- The payback period ignores cash flows after the project payback period.
- It is very subjective, as it gives no definitive investment answer to help managers decide whether or not to invest.
- It ignores the timings of the cash flows. This can be resolved using the discounted payback period which accounts for the time value of money.
- It only calculates the payback period and ignores profitability.

Worked example 13.1

Konyak Ltd is considering three investment projects, A, B and C, whose estimated cash flows are summarised below. All of the projects involve purchasing a different type of capital equipment.

This scenario will form the basis of most of the examples in this chapter.

Project A	£	£	£	£	£	£
Year	0	1	2	3	4	5
Cash outflow	(220,000)					
Cash inflows		55,000	55,000	55,000	55,000	55,000
Scrap value						10,000

Project B	£	£	£	£	£	£
Year	0	1	2	3	4	5
Cash outflow	(220,000)					
Cash inflows		53,000	55,000	57,000	59,000	61,000
Scrap value						10,000

Project C	£	£	£	£	£	£
Year	0	1	2	3	4	5
Cash outflow	(198,000)					
Cash inflows		46,000	52,000	52,000	58,000	58,000
Scrap value						18,000

Even annual cash flows

Konyak Ltd is looking to spend £220,000 on a new project (Project A) relating to the purchase of capital equipment. It is expected to generate net cash inflows of £55,000 each year for the next five years.

What is the payback period for the project?

Solution

Payback period is calculated as:

> Original cost of investment or initial cash outflows ÷ annual cash inflows
> = £220,000 ÷ £55,000
> = 4 years

It would take exactly four years to pay back the initial investment.

Uneven annual cash flows

In practice, there will be times when annual cash flows from project will not be constant. In such a situation, payback is calculated using cumulative cash flows over the project's life.

Konyak Ltd is also considering making an investment in new capital equipment (Project B) costing £220,000. It has set a target period of four years for it to recover the initial investment.

The useful life of the new equipment is expected to be five years with an anticipated scrap value of £10,000. The use of this equipment is expected to generate additional operating cash inflows in the company.

Calculate the payback period of project B and comment on whether Konyak Ltd should accept the project.

Solution

Year		£	Cumulative net cash flows £
0	Investment	(220,000)	(220,000)
1	Cash inflow	53,000	(167,000)
2	Cash inflow	55,000	(112,000)
3	Cash inflow	57,000	(55,000)
4	Cash inflow	59,000	4,000
5	Cash inflow	71,000	75,000

The payback period is between three and four years (actually 3.93 years or 3 years and 11 months), if cash is received evenly (during the fourth year) when it achieves a positive cash flow.

This project is just acceptable as it does pay back the initial investment within the target period of four years. Note the cash inflow for year 5 includes the scrap value of the asset.

Test yourself 13.1

A project is expected to have the following cash flows:

Year	Cash flows £'000
0	(1,500)
1	100
2	400
3	600
4	500
5	800

1. What is the expected payback period?
2. What are the basic decision-making factors to consider when making a choice between two or more projects using payback period?
3. How do depreciation and sunk costs affect the decision-making process in project appraisal?

6 Non-discounted methods: accounting rate of return

The accounting rate of return (ARR) method is also known as the return on capital employed (ROCE) method. It uses accounting profits to estimate the average rate of return that a project is expected to yield over the life of the investment.

The ARR is measured as:

Average annual profits ÷ average capital investment × 100%

Where:

Average capital cost = (initial investment + scrap value) ÷ 2

And:

Average annual profits = total accounting profit over the investment period ÷ years of investment

Decision rules
- The project is undertaken when ARR is equal to or greater than the target rate of return.

- Where projects are mutually exclusive, the project with highest ARR (that also meets the target rate) is selected.

6.1 Advantages

- ARR is widely accepted and simple to calculate.
- It uses profits which are readily recognised by most managers. Managers' performance may be evaluated using ROCE. As profit figures are audited, it can be relied on to some degree.
- It focuses on profitability for the entire project period.
- It is easy to compare with other projects as it is linked with other accounting measures.

6.2 Disadvantages

- ARR ignores factors such as project life (the longer the project, the greater the risk), working capital and other economic factors which may affect the profitability of the project.
- It is based on accounting profits that vary depending on accounting policies (such as depreciation policy).
- It does not take into account the time value of money.
- The return calculated via ARR can be calculated using different formulas. For example, the return can be calculated using profit after interest and tax, or profit before tax – thus leading to different outcomes. It is important to ensure that returns calculated via ARR are calculated on a consistent basis when comparing investments.
- It is not useful for evaluating projects where investment is made in stages at different times.
- It does not take into account any profits that are reinvested during the project period.

Worked example 13.2

Taking Worked example 13.1 further, Konyak Ltd makes an initial investment of £220,000 in project A, which is expected to generate annual cash inflows of £55,000 for five years.

Depreciation is allowed on a straight-line basis. It is estimated that the project will generate a scrap value of £10,000 at end of the fifth year.

Calculate the ARR, assuming that there are no other expenses on the project. Comment on whether the project should be undertaken if the target ARR is 5%.

Solution

Annual depreciation = (initial investment − scrap value) ÷ useful life in years
Annual depreciation = (£220,000 − £10,000) ÷ 5 = £42,000
Average accounting profit = £55,000 − £42,000 = £13,000

The ARR is measured as:

Average annual profits ÷ average capital cost × 100%

Where: average capital cost = (initial investment + scrap value) ÷ 2

And: average annual profits = Total accounting profit over the investment period ÷ years of investment

Using the average capital cost:

ARR = £13,000 ÷ (£220,000 + £10,000) ÷ 2 = 11.30%

The project should be undertaken as the ARR is greater than the 5% target rate of return.

Worked example 13.3

What if projects B and C that Konyak Ltd were considering are mutually exclusive projects?

On the basis of ARR, which project should be selected? Use the straight-line depreciation method.

Solution

Project B:

Step 1: Average capital cost = (220,000 + 10,000) ÷ 2 = 115,000
Step 2: Annual depreciation = (220,000 − 10,000) ÷ 5 = 42,000

Step 3:

	£'000	£'000	£'000	£'000	£'000	£'000
Year	1	2	3	4	5	Total
Cash inflow	53,000	55,000	57,000	59,000	61,000	
Depreciation	(42,000)	(42,000)	(42,000)	(42,000)	(42,000)	
Accounting profit	11,000	13,000	15,000	17,000	19,000	75,000

Step 4: Average accounting profit = (11,000 + 13,000 + 15,000 + 17,000 + 19,000) ÷ 5 = 15,000

Step 5: Accounting rate of return = 15,000 ÷ 115,000 = 13.04%

Project C:

Step 1: Average capital cost = = (198,000 + 18,000) ÷ 2 = 108,000
Step 2: Annual depreciation = (198,000 − 18,000) ÷ 5 = 36,000

Step 3:

Year	£'000 1	£'000 2	£'000 3	£'000 4	£'000 5	£'000 Total
Cash inflow	46,000	52,000	52,000	58,000	58,000	
Depreciation	(36,000)	(36,000)	(36,000)	(36,000)	(36,000)	
Accounting profit	10,000	16,000	16,000	22,000	22,000	86,000

Step 4: Average accounting profit = (10,000 + 16,000 + 16,000 + 22,000 + 22,000) ÷ 5 = 17,200

Step 5: Accounting rate of return = 17,200 ÷ 108,000 = 15.93%

The project with highest ARR is selected where projects are mutually exclusive. Project C's ARR is higher and it is therefore more favourable than project B.

Test yourself 13.2

A project involves the immediate purchase of an item of plant costing £150,000. It will generate annual cash flows of £29,000 for five years, starting in year one, with the convention that discounted cash flows are always received on the last day of the year. The plant will have a scrap value of £15,000 in five years when the project terminates. Depreciation is on a straight-line basis. Determine the project's ARR using average capital investment

What are the limitations of using ARR for evaluating projects?

7 Discounted cash flow techniques based on the time value of money

The use of discounted cash flows (DCF) is important for investment appraisal. It is based on the concept of the 'time value of money', as well as the discount rate (or cost of capital, introduced in Chapter 12). Three DCF methods are used to evaluate capital investments:

- Net present value (NPV)
- Internal rate of return (IRR)
- Discounted payback period

Discounted cash flow models take into account the timing of cash flows over a project's life. They look at the cash flows of a project, not accounting profits, because cash flows show the costs and benefits of the project when they actually occur and ignore notional costs such as depreciation.

7.1 The time value of money

The time value of money is the concept that money received today is worth more than the same sum received in the future. This occurs for three reasons.

- **The potential for earning interest and savings on the cost of finance:** if money is received today it can either be spent or reinvested to earn more in future. Hence, investors have a preference for having cash/liquidity today. Savings now can also be used to repay debts, saving on cost of finance.
- **Impact of inflation:** the value of future cash flows can be eroded by inflation.
- **Effect of risk:** Future cash receipts may be uncertain, unlike cash received today.

7.2 Compounding

Money invested today will earn interest in future. **Compounding** calculates the future value (FV) of a given sum invested today for a number of years.

For example, if £10,000 is invested to earn 10% interest on the base amount, we would expect the initial amount to be compounded in future years. In the next three years the base amount will be compounded as follows:

After one year: £10,000 × 1.10 = £11,000
After two years: £10,000 × (1.10)² = £12,100
After three years: £10,000 × (1.10)³ = £13,310.

compounding
Compounding is the process of determining the future value of present investment or cashflows by considering interest that can be earned on the amounts invested today.

Formula
The formula for compounding is as follows:

$$FV = PV(1 + r)^n$$

Where:
FV = future value
PV = present value
r = rate of compound interest
n = number of years

The compound interest rate for each year can either be calculated or found using compounding tables.

Worked example 13.4

Instead of pursuing Project A or Project B, Konyak Ltd could consider investing the £220,000 in another way.

If Konyak Ltd made an investment of £220,000 today, which provides a return (or interest) at the rate of 10% per annum, what is the value of the investment after two years? What would be its value in five years' time?

Solution

Value after one year: 220,000 × 1.1 = £ 242,000

Value after two years: 242,000 × 1.1 = £266,200

The £220,000 will be worth £266,200 in two years at an interest rate of 10%.

The value of the investment after five years can be calculated using the formula:

$FV = PV(1 + r)^n$

$= £220,000 \times (1 + 10\%)^5 = £354,312$

If Konyak Ltd could find a low-risk investment with a 10% return, this could provide a potential alternative to projects A and B.

7.3 Discounting

discounting
The process of determining the present value of future cash flows by using a discount rate that considers factors such as inflation, risk of an uncertain future and the ability to earn interest.

The timing of cash flows is taken into account by **discounting**. This is the opposite of compounding: it starts with a future value (FV) to reach a present value (PV).

This provides a 'discounted value' of a future sum of money or stream of cash flows using a specified rate of return. Present value means a current cash equivalent of a discounted sum of money receivable or payable at a future date.

discount rate
The rate of return used in discounted cash flow analysis to determine the present value of future cash flows. The discount rate will give the current worth of the future value.

A **discount rate** is the rate of return used in discounted cash flow analysis to determine the present value of future cash flows. The discount rate will give the current worth of the future value. For example, at any discount rate, £1 earned after one year will have a current worth or present value of less than £1.

In a discounted cash flow analysis, the sum of all cash flows at FV over the holding period (n), is discounted back to PV using a rate of return (r). The formula is:

$PV = FV \div (1 + r)^n$

Where:
FV = future value
PV = present value
r = rate of compound interest
n = number of years

present value factor
The current value today per £1 received at a future date. The future value can be calculated by multiplying the present value factor by the amount received at a future date.

The **present value factor** (PV factor) is calculated as:

$1 \div (1 + r)^n$

The PV factor is the current value today per £1 received at a future date. The future value can be calculated by multiplying the present value factor by the amount received at a future date.

Worked example 13.5

1. Konyak Ltd is forecasting its cash inflows from Project B. It expects the investment to generate cash inflows of £53,000, £55,000, £57,000 and £59,000 in years 1-4 and £71,000 in the fifth year (including scrap value). If Konyak Ltd had a cost of capital of 12% and used this as the discount factor in investment appraisal decisions, calculate the present value of future returns from its investment.
2. Briefly explain what the result means.

Solution

(1)

Year	Cash flows £	Discount rate or PV factor	Present value £
1	53,000	$1 \div 1.12 = 0.893$	47,329
2	55,000	$1 \div 1.12^2 = 0.797$	43,835
3	57,000	$1 \div 1.12^3 = 0.712$	40,584
4	59,000	$1 \div 1.12^4 = 0.636$	37,524
5	71,000	$1 \div 1.12^5 = 0.567$	40,257
		Present value	209,529

The present value of the future returns is £209,529, discounted at 12%. If Konyak Ltd invests £220,000, the present value of this investment would be £209,529 at a 12% discount rate. On this basis, Kanyak Ltd would not proceed with this project.

Test yourself 13.3

1. If you have £5,000 now to invest for six years at an interest rate of 5% pa, what will be the value of the investment after six years?
2. If a company expects to earn a compound rate of 10% interest on its investment, how much will it need to invest now to earn:
   a. £11,000 in the first year?
   b. £12,100 in the second year?
   c. £13,310 in the third year?

7.4 Negative interest rates

Discounting and compounding use the rate of compound interest, or r. Throughout this text and any examination, r is always assumed to be a positive figure. However, discounting and compounding work differently in a negative interest rate environment.

Negative interest rates are an unconventional and seemingly counterintuitive, monetary policy tool.

Central banks impose the drastic measure of negative interest rates when they fear their national economies are slipping into a deflationary spiral, in which there is no spending – which results in dropping prices, no profits and no growth.

With negative interest rates, cash deposited at a bank yields a storage charge, rather than the opportunity to earn interest income; the idea is to incentivise lending and spending, rather than saving and hoarding.

In recent years, several European and Asian central banks have imposed negative interest rates on commercial banks.

The time value of money says that money received today is worth more than the same sum received in the future. This is reversed if the interest rate is negative. Money received today is worth less than the same sum received in the future. This is calculated using the formula for compounding, as follows:

$$FV = PV(1 + r)^n$$

If r is negative then $1 + r$ will be less than 1. As we compound it by n, the value will get smaller, rather than larger.

8 Discounted cash flow methods: net present value (NPV)

The DCF method can be used to calculate the net present value (NPV) of a company or an investment.

Net present value is the net value of a capital investment or project, obtained by discounting all cash outflows and inflows to their present values by using an appropriate discounted rate of return.

8.1 Use of NPV for project appraisal

Net present value is a commonly used DCF method of project appraisal. It uses cash flows (that can be spent and have an opportunity cost) rather than accounting profits (that cannot be spent). It ignores non-cash items such as depreciation while including the initial cost of the project and any residual value in the calculation of net cash flows.

The timings of the cash flows are important. Initial investment occurs at the start of the year (T_0). By convention, other cash flows start at the end of the first year (T_1) and the end of each subsequent year. The NPV method compares the present values of cash inflows with the present value of cash outflows for an investment. It can be summarised as:

NPV = PV of cash inflows − PV of cash outflows

The project or investment could be undertaken if its NPV is positive.

Decision rules
- The project could be undertaken if its NPV is positive.
- When comparing mutually exclusive projects, the project with the highest positive NPV is selected.

When NPV is:	
Positive	Returns from investment or PV of net cash inflows exceeds the cost of capital. The project could be undertaken.
Negative	Returns from investment or PV of net cash inflows are less than the cost of capital. The project should not be undertaken.
Nil	Returns from investment or PV of net cash inflows is equal to the cost of capital.

Table 15.1 Net present value and investment appraisal

8.2 Advantages

- Theoretically, the NPV method of investment appraisal is superior to all other methods.
- It considers the time value of money through the discount rate.
- It is an absolute measure of return.
- It is based on cash flows, not profits (which vary depending on accounting policies).
- It takes into account all cash flows throughout the life of a project.
- It maximises shareholder wealth by only undertaking projects with positive NPVs that ensures a surplus over and above the costs of finance.

8.3 Disadvantages

- The NPV method can be difficult to explain to managers as it uses cash flows rather than accounting profits.
- The calculation of discount rates can be challenging and requires knowledge of the cost of capital.
- It is relatively complex compared to non-discounting methods such as the payback period and ARR.

Worked example 13.6

Konyak Ltd is looking to invest (Project B) by investing in capital equipment. The expected cash flows from this project are as follows:

Year	Cash flow £
0	(220,000)
1	53,000
2	55,000
3	57,000
4	59,000
5	71,000

The company's cost of capital is 6%. Calculate the NPV of the project and decide whether it should be undertaken.

The present value (or discount) factors can be calculated or found in the PV table. (A PV table would be provided as part of any examination question.)

Solution

Year	Cash flows £	Discount factors at 6%		Present value £
0	(220,000)	1	1.000	(220,000)
1	53,000	$1 \div 1.06 =$	0.943	49,979
2	55,000	$1 \div (1.06)^2 =$	0.890	48,950
3	57,000	$1 \div (1.06)^3 =$	0.840	47,880
4	59,000	$1 \div (1.06)^4 =$	0.792	46,728
5	71,000	$1 \div (1.06)^5 =$	0.747	53,037
			net present value (NPV)	26,574

The NPV is positive where the PV of cash inflows exceeds the PV of cash outflows. A positive NPV ensures that all costs are covered by the project and surplus (NPV) is generated over and above the costs of finance.

With a cost of capital of 6%, the above project could be undertaken by Konyak Ltd.

Test yourself 13.4

Dhimal Ltd is considering a capital investment in new equipment. The estimated cash flows are as follows:

Year	Cash flows
	£
0	(250,000)
1	100,000
2	120,000
3	70,000
4	40,000
5	20,000

The company's cost of capital is 9%. Calculate the NPV of the project to assess whether it should be undertaken? The discount factor you will need can be found using the present value table in the Appendix on page 411.

9 Discounting annuities

An **annuity** is a series of fixed payments made at regular intervals during a specified period of time. When a loan is repaid in annuity, each instalment is a fixed amount usually consisting of a repayment of part of the principal and the interest expense for the period. The principal repayment increases over time while the interest expense decreases.

annuity
A series of payments made at regular intervals during a specified period of time.

9.1 Annuity factors

An annuity factor (AF) is used to calculate the present value of an annuity. The PV of an annuity stream is the current value of future periodic payments, calculated by multiplying the fixed periodic payment by the annuity factor. Annuity factors are based on the number of years involved and an applicable rate of return or discount rate.

The AF is the sum of the individual discount factors. The PV of an annuity can be found using the formula:

$$PV = \text{annual cash flow} \times AF$$

Where:
$AF = [1 - (1 + r)^{-n}] \div r$
r = the discount rate
n = the number of periods in which payments will be made

The above formula is used to find the PV when the FV of the annuity is known. The higher the discount rate, the lower the PV of the annuity. Annuity factors can also be found using the annuity tables.

In this formula the discount rate, r, appears (see section 7.3). The formula shows how the discount rate is used in calculating the annuity factor. The annuity factor is the sum of the discount rates for maturities 1 to n inclusive.

Test yourself 13.5

Mizher Ltd is expected to make a payment of £5,000 every year for the next six years, with the first payment occurring in one year's time. The interest rate is 8%. What is the PV of the annuity?

9.2 Discounting a perpetuity

A perpetuity is a type of annuity or a constant stream of cash flow that continues indefinitely. Certain types of government bonds pay annual fixed coupons for as long as the bondholders hold the bonds. Discounting a perpetuity is used in valuation methodologies (such as shareholder value analysis or SVA) to find the present value of a company's cash flows when discounted at an applicable rate of return. The PV formula for a perpetuity is as follows:

PV = annuity per period (cash flow) ÷ discount rate

Worked example 13.7

Assume the cash inflow of £55,000 (per annum) for Konyak Ltd's Project A continues indefinitely, rather than just for five years. What is the PV of the annuity if the interest rate is 10%?

Solution

PV = annuity ÷ discount rate
PV = £55,000 ÷ 0.10
PV = £550,000

As the interest rate is 10%, the PV of the annuity that continues into perpetuity is £550,000.

10 Discounted cash flow methods: internal rate of return

The internal rate of return (IRR) calculates the rate of return at which the NPV of all the cash flows from a project or investment equals zero. In other words, IRR is the discount rate at which NPV is zero – the discount rate that allows the project to break even. IRR uses the same concepts as the NPV method.

Decision rules
- Projects should be accepted if the IRR is greater than the cost of capital.
- If IRR is less than the target rate (often WACC), the investment does not add value to the company.

- If the IRR exceeds the cost of capital or the discount rate, it is worth undertaking the project.
- If IRR is greater than the target rate (often WACC), the investment adds value to the company. In case of mutually exclusive projects, the project yielding the highest IRR should be selected.

10.1 Calculating IRR

Internal rate of return is the most complex of all the investment appraisal methods to calculate. Therefore, IRR is usually calculated by interpolation that requires its estimation by trial and error. The steps for calculating IRR by interpolation are as follows:

1. Find discount rates that give a positive NPV and a negative NPV. If the NPV is positive, use a higher discount rate to get a negative NPV. If the NPV is negative, use a lower discount rate to get a positive NPV.
2. Estimate a discount rate between these two rates that will produce zero NPV.
3. Calculate IRR using the following formula:
   $$IRR = L + [NPV_L \div (NPV_L - NPV_H)] \times (H - L)$$

   Where:
   L and NPV_L represent the lower discount rate and its NPV
   H and NPV_H represent the higher discount rate and its NPV

The estimation is made easier if one NPV used in the formula is positive and the other one is negative.

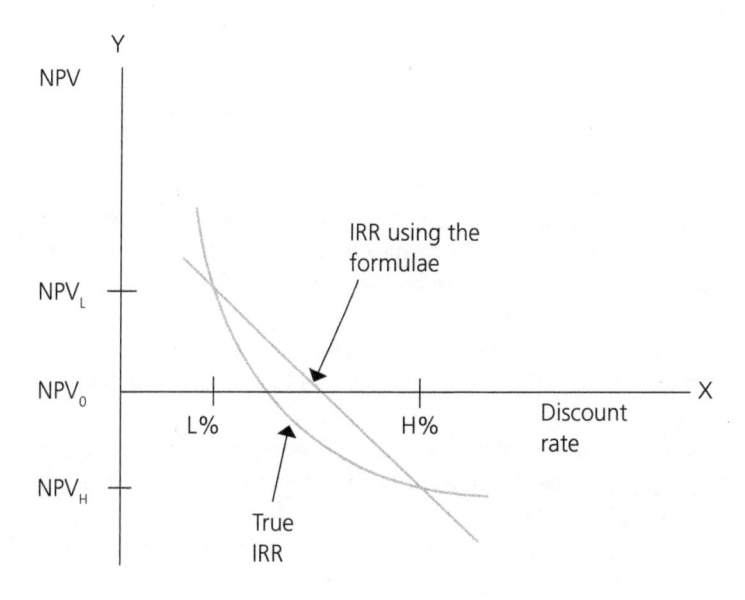

Figure 13.1 Calculation of IRR

The NPVs of the cash flows of the project, discounted using L% and H%, are represented by NPV$_L$ and NPV$_H$ in Figure 13.1. The line joining these two points should produce a curve. The point at which the curve crosses the X-axis is the true IRR, where NPV = 0. However, the formula above approximates the curve with a straight line: the point at which the straight line crosses the X-axis is therefore the IRR. This is the point at which the discount rate equals IRR and NPV equals zero.

The IRR method works well when cash flows have traditional patterns, such as a cash outflow at the beginning of a project followed by a series of cash inflows. When the cash flow pattern is non-traditional (with a mix of positive and negative future cash flows), it can result in the existence of multiple IRRs that could result in the wrong decision being taken. NPV should be used when making decisions in such cases.

10.2 Advantages

- The IRR method evaluates potential returns and the attractiveness of potential investments.
- It uses real cash flows rather than profits, which can be manipulated by the use of different accounting policies.
- It takes account of the time value of the money.
- It considers risk of future cash flows (through comparison with the cost of capital in the decision rule).
- Excess IRR over the cost of capital indicates the excess return for the risk contained in the project.
- It gives a percentage rate that can be compared to a target (cost of capital). This is easier for management to understand and interpret than the concept of NPV.

10.3 Disadvantages

- The IRR is a relative measure that gives a percentage rate that can be compared to a target cost of capital. It ignores other factors such as project duration, future costs and the relative size of the investments. A larger project with a lower IRR may generate a larger surplus than a smaller project with a higher IRR.
- It is not a measure of profitability in absolute terms (unlike the NPV method). The IRR method does not measure the absolute size of the investment or the return.
- It is the most complex of all the investment appraisal methods to calculate. Interpolation by trial and error only provides an estimate, thus requiring a spreadsheet for a more accurate estimate.
- It may not lead to value maximisation when used to compare mutually exclusive projects.
- It may not lead to value maximisation of projects when used to choose projects when there is capital rationing.

- The interpolation method cannot be used for non-conventional cash flows. A project that has large negative cash flows later in its life may give rise to multiple IRRs.
- It assumes that the positive future cash flows are reinvested to earn the same return as the IRR. This may not be possible in real life.

Worked example 13.8

Konyak Ltd is appraising a potential project – purchasing new capital equipment (Project B).

The predicted cash flows from the investment give a positive NPV of £26,574 at a discount rate of 6% (as already seen in Worked example 13.6). Using a discount rate of 12% would produce a negative NPV of £10,471 (£209,529 – £220,000, as seen in Worked example 13.5). Calculate the IRR.

Solution

IRR = L + [NPV_L ÷ (NPV_L – NPV_H)] × (H – L)

IRR = 6% + [26,574 ÷ (26,574 + 10,471)] × (12% – 6%)

IRR = 10.30%

IRR is the discount rate at which NPV is zero (when the project breaks even).

Note: The formula states – NPVH, yet in the answer you will see it is + 10,471. This is because the NPV is -£10,471 and mathematically two negatives are a positive.

Test yourself 13.6

Jollof Rice Ltd undertakes high-risk investments and requires a minimum expected rate of return of 18% pa on its investments. A proposed capital investment has the following expected cash flows:

Year	Cash flows
	£
0	(100,000)
1	46,000
2	35,000
3	40,000
4	20,000

Estimate the IRR of the project using the NPVs at 15% and 20% cost of capital. Make a recommendation on whether this project should be accepted.

11 Discounted cash flow methods: discounted payback

The discounted payback period method (or adjusted payback period) helps determine the time period required by a project to break even. It combines the techniques used in the payback period and DCF to calculate a discounted payback period. This involves discounting the cash flows and then calculating how many years it takes for the discounted cash flows to repay the initial investment.

Discounted payback was developed to overcome the limitations of the traditional payback period method, which ignores the time value of money. Discounted payback is calculated using the same formula as the straight payback method, but uses discounted cash flows to take into account the time value of money.

> Discounted payback period = original cost of investment or initial cash flows ÷ PV of annual cash flows

Worked example 13.9

Calculate the discounted payback period for Konyak Ltd Project B. Refer to Worked example 13.6 for the discounted cash flow and NPV figures.

Discounted payback period = original cost of investment or initial cash flows ÷ PV of annual cash flow

Year	Cash flows	Discount factors at 6%	Present value	Cumulative present value
	£		£	£
0	(220,000)	1.000	(220,000)	(220,000)
1	53,000	0.943	49,979	(170,021)
2	55,000	0.890	48,950	(121,071)
3	57,000	0.840	47,880	(73,191)
4	59,000	0.792	46,728	(26,463)
5	71,000	0.747	53,037	26,574

The discounted payback period is sometime during the fourth and fifth year – halfway through year five if cash is received evenly through the fifth year – when the project will achieve a positive present value.

In Worked example 13.1, we calculated that the undiscounted payback period was between the third and fourth year. Discounting the future cash flows has extended the payback period.

11.1 Advantages

- The discounted payback method considers the time value of money.
- It uses cash flows, not profit.
- It considers the riskiness of the project's cash flows (through the cost of capital).
- It determines whether the investments made are recoverable.

11.2 Disadvantages

- The discounted payback method is subjective as it gives no concrete decision criteria that indicates whether the investment increases the firm's value.
- It requires an estimate of the cost of capital in order to calculate the payback period.
- It ignores cash flows beyond the discounted payback period.
- Calculations can become complex if there are multiple negative cash flows during the project's life.

12 Impact of inflation and tax on project appraisal

Inflation affects project appraisals that use NPV techniques, particularly in terms of discount rates (or interest rates) and cash flows. Tax also has an impact on investment appraisal.

12.1 The impact of inflation on interest or discount rates

Inflation is a general increase in the money price of goods and services leading to a general decline in the real value or the purchasing power of money. In times of inflation, lenders will require a return made up of two elements:

- a real return to compensate for the use of their funds (the expected return with no inflation in the economy); and
- an additional return to compensate for their lost purchasing power from inflation.

The overall required return is called the money, nominal or market rate of return. The nominal rate of return and real rate of return are linked by the equation proposed by Irving Fisher in 1930:

real interest rate = nominal interest rate − inflation rate

If a loan has a 10% interest rate and the inflation rate is 3%, we subtract the inflation rate from the nominal interest rate to get the real return of 7%. The borrower and lender use their expectations of future inflation to determine the interest rate on a loan.

12.2 The impact of inflation on cash flows

Cash flows at current prices do not account for expected inflation. The expected cash flows that are increased to account for inflation are referred to as money (or nominal) cash flows. They represent expected flows of money and, unless otherwise stated, are normally assumed to be the money cash flows.

Inflation affects both the estimated cash flows and the discount rate. Inflation is incorporated into NPV calculations using one of the following two methods.

- Using nominal future cash flows that incorporate expected inflation by building in expected price increases and discounting using the nominal discount rate. This is the better method for taking into account price increases.
- Using real cash flows that are expressed at today's price level and discounting them using the real discount rate (the cost of capital after removing the rate of general inflation). It is assumed that the future price changes will be the same as the general rate of inflation.

12.3 Tax effects

Corporate tax is charged on taxable profits for most companies. Therefore, tax must be considered in any investment appraisal. The impact of taxation on cash flows is felt in different ways but the most common impacts for NPV purposes include:

- tax charges on profit figures;
- tax relief for an acquired asset in the form of capital allowance or writing down allowances; or
- tax on the sale or disposal of an asset at the end of the project.

Tax is normally payable one year in arrears. It is therefore included in NPV calculations with a one-year delay. The discount rate can be either pre or post-tax.

The tax effect is incorporated into the overall discount rate (WACC) by adjusting for the tax relief on interest paid on the cost of debt. When calculating WACC, the after-tax discount rate is used to calculate the cost of debt (see Chapter 12).

12.4 Writing down allowances

Companies can also benefit from writing down allowances (WDAs, also known as capital allowances). This tax relief is an alternative to depreciation deductions from accounting profit. It provides a tax benefit by reducing the amount of tax payable. Writing down allowances are calculated on the written-down value of the assets. They are claimed as early as possible in the asset's life and are claimed annually until the total allowances equate the cost less any scrap proceeds.

A further balancing allowance arises in the year of disposal or scrapping if the disposal proceeds are lower than the tax written-down value. A balancing charge can arise if the disposal proceeds are greater than the tax written-down value.

Tax implications will not be examined via calculation questions in the examination.

13 Capital rationing and use of the profitability index

Shareholder wealth is maximised if a company undertakes all possible positive NPV projects. However, when there are insufficient funds to do so, investment capital is rationed or limited. **Capital rationing** is a strategy implemented when a company has more acceptable projects than can be financed from existing funds. A choice will have to be made between acceptable projects. Capital rationing can apply to a single reporting period or to multiple periods.

capital rationing
A strategy that firms implement when there are insufficient funds. It places limitations or restrictions on the amount of new investments or projects undertaken by a company.

13.1 Types of capital rationing

There are two types of capital rationing.

- **Hard capital rationing**: when lending institutions impose an absolute limit on the amount of finance available. The reasons may include:
  - industry-wide factors limiting funds; or
  - company-specific factors like a poor track record, lack of asset security or poor management limiting funds.
- **Soft capital rationing**: when a company voluntarily imposes restrictions that limit the amount of funds available for investment in projects. This is contrary to the rational view of shareholder of wealth maximisation. The reasons may include:
  - internal company policies;
  - limited management skills for handling multiple financing options;
  - the desire to maximise return on a limited range of investments;
  - limiting exposure to external finance; and
  - focusing on existing substantial profitable businesses or divisions.

13.2 Dealing with single-period capital rationing using the profitability index

When there is a shortage of funds for one period, it is referred to as single-period capital rationing.

Divisible projects
Projects are considered to be divisible when any fraction of the project can be undertaken. The returns from the project should be generated in exact proportion to the amount of investment undertaken.

The profitability index (PI) or benefit–cost ratio can be used for dealing with divisible projects or comparing individual projects. The profitability index calculates the present value of cash flows generated by the project per a unit of capital outlay. It can provide a solution when the company cannot undertake all acceptable projects due to limited budgets. The PI formula is as follows:

PI = NPV ÷ original cost of investment or initial cash outflows

Decision rules
- When there are alternative projects, rank the projects according to PI and allocate funds according to the projects' rankings – for example, projects with the highest PI would be approved
- The aim when managing capital rationing is to maximise the NPV earned for each pound invested in a project.

Worked example 13.10

Projects B and C for Konyak Ltd require initial outlays of £220,000 and £198,000. At a 6% cost of capital, they have respective NPVs of £26,574 and (for information) £38,046.

How would you allocate available funds of £250,000? Please answer on the basis that the projects are not divisible.

Solution

One way of choosing projects is to compute the profitability index (PI).

PI = NPV ÷ initial investment
PI for project B = 26,574 ÷ 220,000 = 0.121
PI for project C = 38,046 ÷ 198,000 = 0.192

Project C has a higher PI and would make better use of scarce capital. It should be ranked first in the allocation of the available funds.

Chapter summary

- Project or investment appraisal is the financial and economic appraisal of projects or expenditure incurred now in order to determine its feasibility and return in the future. When a proposed capital project is identified, the costs and benefits of the project should be estimated and evaluated over its expected useful life; any risks from the project should be considered.
- The common objective in investment appraisal is to maximise shareholder value, which is linked to cash flows, the cost of capital and long-term value. A long-term cash flow forecasting of revenues, costs and savings is an essential part of project appraisal. This often involves making assumptions by taking into consideration the relevant factors such as cash flow, financing costs, timing of returns, incremental costs, additional working capital, inflation and tax. Non-relevant factors include sunk costs, overhead costs and depreciation.

- Two basic appraisal techniques are discounted and non-discounted cash flow methods.
- Non-discounted methods include the payback period and the accounting rate of return method.
- The payback period is the time (number of years) it takes a project to recover the original investment.
- The accounting rate of return (ARR) method is also known as the return on capital employed (ROCE) method. It uses accounting profits to estimate the average rate of return that the project is expected to yield over the life of the investment or project.
- Compounding is the process of determining the future value of present investment or cash flows, by considering interest that can be earned in the amounts invested today.
- Discounted cash flow (DCF) techniques are based on the concept of the 'time value of money'. Discounting is the process of determining the present value of future cash flows by using a discount rate that considers factors such as inflation, risk of an uncertain future and the ability to earn interest. There are three methods of using DCF to evaluate capital investments – the net present value method, internal rate of return and discounted payback.
- The net present value (NPV) method produces a positive, negative or neutral NPV. The project is undertaken when NPV is positive. When comparing mutually exclusive projects, the project with the higher positive NPV is selected.
- Internal rate of return (IRR) calculates the rate of return at which the NPV of all the cash flows (both positive and negative) from a project or investment equals zero. Projects should be accepted if IRR is greater than the cost of capital.
- The discounted payback period method (or adjusted payback period) helps to determine the time period required by a project to break even. It combines the techniques used in the payback period and DCF techniques to calculate a discounted payback period.
- Inflation affects both the cash flows to be estimated and the discount rate to be used. The nominal (money) returns and real returns are linked by the Fisher equation. The NPV calculation compares the present value of money today to the present value of money in the future, taking inflation and returns into consideration.
- Tax impacts must be considered in any investment appraisal. The tax effect is incorporated into the overall discount rate (WACC) by using the after-tax discount rate to calculate the cost of debt. The impact of tax on profits, capital allowances and tax on capital gains are incorporated in the calculation of the net cash flows.
- Capital rationing is a strategy that firms implement to place limitations on the amount of new investments or projects that can be undertaken by a company, prioritising limited funds for the most profitable projects.

Chapter fourteen
Risk assessment in investment appraisal techniques

Contents

1. Introduction
2. Risk and investment decisions
3. Risk assessment models
4. Sensitivity analysis
5. Scenario analysis
6. Simulation modelling
7. Expected net present value and standard deviation
8. Event tree diagrams
9. The role of portfolio management

1 Introduction

Investment decisions are largely influenced by risk and return. Because large sums of money are often tied up in an investment for a long period of time, there is an element of risk and uncertainty about returns not turning out as expected.

This chapter considers the impact of risk on investment appraisals and its impact on portfolio management. It looks at non-probabilistic approaches to project appraisal, such as sensitivity analysis, scenario analysis and simulations. It also looks at the use of probabilistic information to calculate expected NPV and discuss the use of event tree diagrams.

This chapter discusses the role of portfolio management in reducing overall portfolio risk. Whereas portfolio return is simply a weighted average of returns for elements in the portfolio, portfolio risk can be reduced when the returns from its component securities move in opposite ways in boom or slump conditions.

Chapter fourteen Risk assessment in investment appraisal techniques

```
                    Risk assessment in          Risk preferences of the
                    investment appraisal                investors
                         techniques              'risk return trade off'
                                                 • Risk-seeker
                                                 • Risk-averse
                                                 • Risk-neutral

              Risk assessment                    Role of portfolio
                  models                           management
                                              (Aims for optimum returns
                                               while minimising risk)

Non-probabilistic    Probabilistic    Risk-adjusted      • Asset allocation
   approach            approach       discount rate      • Diversification
• sensitivity      • Expected net      (covered in       • Rebalancing
  analysis           present value     Chapter 11)
• scenario           (ENPV) and
  analysis           standard
• simulation         deviation
  modelling        • Event tree
                     diagram
```

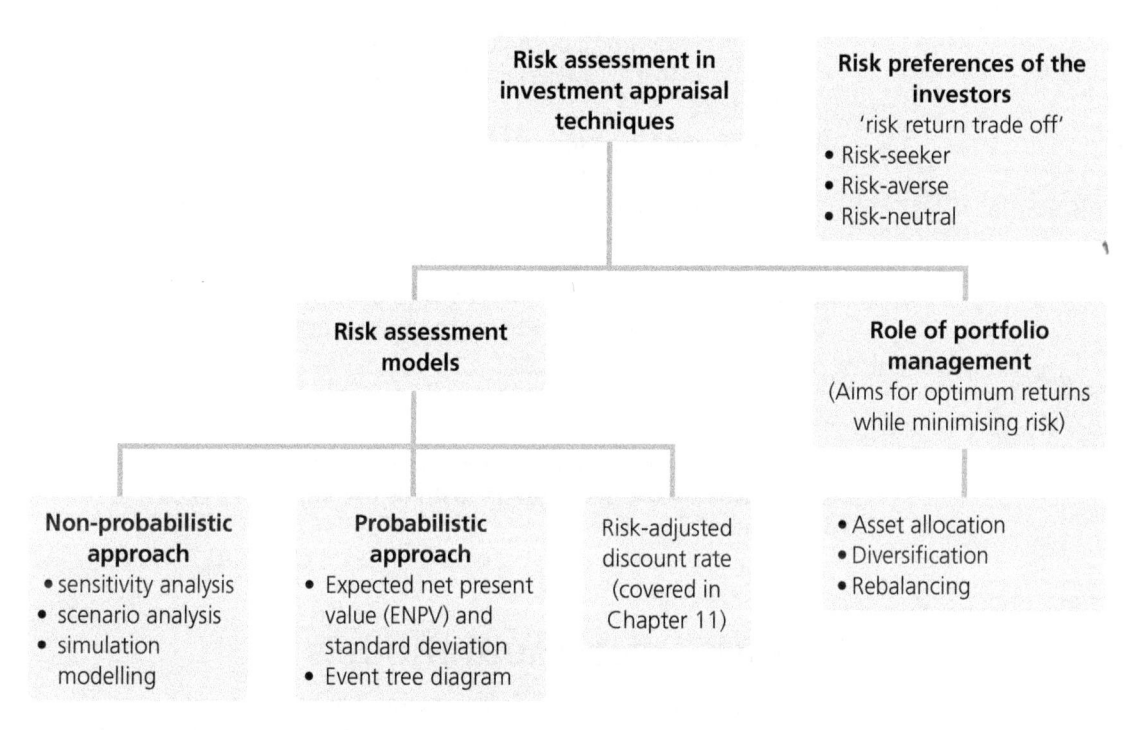

Figure 14.1 Risk assessment in investment appraisal techniques

2 Risk and investment decisions

In investment decisions, the risk relates to uncertainty around returns not turning out as expected. In financial management, risk is measured by the volatility of the returns. The more volatile the returns, the higher the risk. Returns that fluctuate and can be unpredictable are riskier than returns with no volatility.

2.1 Risk preferences of investors

The attitude of investors to risk plays a vital part in the investment appraisal process. Investors can be categorised as one of the following in terms of risk preference.

◆ **Risk-seeking investors**: these are investors who accept greater volatility and uncertainty in investments or trading in exchange for anticipated higher returns. Risk-seeking investors are more interested in capital gains from speculative assets than investments with lower risks with lower returns. For example, a risk seeker would prefer investing their money in stocks as they have the potential to give higher returns than fixed deposits.

◆ **Risk-averse investors**: these are investors who avoid risks and prefer lower returns with known risks rather than higher returns with unknown risks. Most investors and managers are risk-averse and require an additional return to compensate for any additional risk. For example, a risk-averse person would prefer investing in fixed deposits, government bonds and so on that involve less risk and provide a more certain return compared to stocks.

- **Risk-neutral investors:** these investors overlook risk when deciding between investments. They are only concerned with an investment's estimated return.

An investor faces a 'risk-return trade off' when considering investment decisions. Higher risk is linked with a greater probability of a higher return and lower risk with a greater probability of a smaller return.

Stop and think 14.1

Think of a risk-return trade off situation faced by a company of your choice. How would the attitude towards risk influence a choice of investment?

3 Risk assessment models

All companies face the risk of variable returns. The actual outcome could be better (from upside potential) or worse than expected (from downside risk exposure). For example, a company cannot predict future sales with certainty because they could be higher or lower than expected. An important aspect of risk assessment is to identify and assess potential sources of risk in terms of their potential impact on the company and how likely (probable) they are.

There are several risk assessment models that incorporate risk into decision making. These techniques involve both non-probabilistic as well as probabilistic approaches (that use a range of possible values) to project appraisal. They include:

- **Non-probabilistic approaches**
    - sensitivity analysis
    - scenario analysis
    - simulation modelling
- **Probabilistic approaches**
    - **expected net present value** (ENPV) and standard deviation
    - event tree diagrams
- **Risk-adjusted discount rate** (covered in Chapter 12)

4 Sensitivity analysis

Sensitivity analysis is a non-probabilistic approach used in investment appraisal that allows the analysis of changes in assumptions made in the forecast. It is a tool for quantitative risk assessment that predicts the outcome of a decision by ascertaining the most critical variables and their effect on the decision. It examines how sensitive the returns on a project are to changes made to each of the key variables, such as any increase or decrease in:

- capital costs
- projected sales volumes
- variable costs

The methodology follows the steps below.

1. Specify a base case situation and calculate the NPV of the project based on the best estimates and assumptions. Only projects that generate a positive NPV are accepted.
2. Calculate the percentage change (or sensitivity) of each of the variables that would result in the breakeven position (with a NPV of zero). Any further change resulting in negative NPV would change the decision.
For example, what impact would the projected sales have on NPV if they decreased or increased by 10%? What if demand fell by 10% compared to the original forecasts? Would the project still be viable? How much of a fall in demand can be accepted before the NPV falls below zero or below the breakeven?

Sensitivity margin = (NPV ÷ PV of flow under consideration) × 100%

The lower the sensitivity margin, the more sensitive the decision to the particular variable under consideration. A small change in the estimate could change the NPV from positive (accept) to negative (reject).

Worked example 14.1

Moringa Ltd is looking to invest £100,000 in equipment with a life of 10 years and a scrap value of £10,000. The cost of capital is 10%. The equipment will produce 10,000 units per annum (p.a.) generating a contribution of £2.20 per unit (p.u.). It is also expected to incur an additional fixed cost of £5,000 pa.

1. **Determine whether the project is worthwhile.**
2. **Calculate the sensitivity to change of the:**
   a. **initial investment**
   b. **sales volume p.a.**
   c. **contribution p.u.**
   d. **fixed costs p.a.**
   e. **scrap value**
   f. **cost of capital.**

Solution:

1

Year	Cash flow	£	10% DF	PV
0	Cost	(100,000)	1.000	(100,000)
1–10	Contribution	22,000	6.1446	135,181
1–10	Fixed costs	(5,000)	6.1446	(30,723)
10	Scrap	10,000	0.3855	3,855
	Accept Project		NPV	8,313

2 a Sensitivity to change of the initial investment

$$\frac{8,313}{100,000} \times 100\% \qquad 8.31\%$$

For the decision to change, the NPV must fall by £8,314 (which gives an NPV of zero). For this to occur, the initial investment must rise by £8,314. This is a rise of 8.31%.

b Sensitivity to change of the sales volume

$$\frac{8,313}{135,181} \times 100\% \qquad 6.15\%$$

If the NPV is to fall by £8,314 (giving an NPV of zero), sales must fall by 6.15%. Sensitivity of the sales volume can be calculated using sensitivity of contribution per unit, which is calculated as selling price pu – variable cost pu. Contribution changes directly in proportion to the level of sales volume.

c Sensitivity of contribution pu

$$\frac{8,313}{135,181} \times 100\% \qquad 6.15\%$$

If the NPV is to fall by £8,313 (giving an NPV of zero) contribution must fall by 6.15%

d Sensitivity of fixed costs

$$\frac{8,313}{30,723} \times 100\% \qquad 27.06\%$$

If the NPV is to fall by £8,313 (giving an NPV of zero), fixed costs must rise by 27.06%.

e Sensitivity of scrap value =

$$\frac{8{,}313}{3{,}855} \times 100\%$$ 215.64%

If the NPV is to fall to zero, scrap value must rise by 215.64%.

f Sensitivity of cost of capital

If NPV is to fall, cost of capital must rise. The figure which the cost of capital must rise to is the project's IRR. To find the IRR, which is probably not much above 10%, the NPV is calculated at 15%:

Year	Cash flow	£	15% DF	PV
0	Cost	(100,000)	1.000	(100,000)
1–10	Contribution	22,000	5.0188	110,414
1–10	Fixed costs	(5,000)	5.0188	(25,094)
10	Scrap	10,000	0.2472	2,472
			NPV	(12,208)

For the investment decision to change, the cost of capital would have to increase from 10% to:

$$IRR = R1 + \frac{NPV1}{(NPV1 - NPV2)} \times (R2 - R1)$$

R1 = Lower discount rate chosen

R2 = Higher discount rate chosen

$$IRR = 10\% + \frac{8{,}313}{(8{,}313 + 12{,}208)} \times 5\%$$ 12%

The cost of capital would have to increase from 10% to 12% before the investment decision changes.

Test yourself 14.1

John Dove Ltd is considering investing £200,000 in equipment to produce a new product line that will generate sales revenue of £200,000 for the next five years. The scrap value of the equipment at the end of five years is £70,000. It is also estimated to incur annual variable costs of £100,000 while annual fixed costs will increase by £55,000.

Assuming that all cash flows occur at annual intervals, calculate the NPV of the project using the 'best estimate' figures. Determine whether the project should be undertaken. John Dove Ltd has a cost of capital of 10%.

Prepare a sensitivity analysis and calculate the percentage changes required in the following estimates for the investment decision to change:

1. initial investment
2. sales volume
3. sales revenue
4. variable costs
5. fixed costs
6. scrap value
7. cost of capital

4.1 Advantages of sensitivity analysis

- The analysis is based on a simple theory, can be calculated on a spreadsheet and is easily understood.
- It identifies areas and estimates crucial to the success of the project. These critical areas are carefully monitored if the project is chosen.
- It provides information to allow management to make subjective judgements based on the likelihood of the various possible outcomes.
- The analysis is used by a range of organisations. For example, this technique is popular in the National Health Service (NHS) for capital appraisal.

4.2 Disadvantages

- The technique changes one variable at a time which is unlikely to happen in reality. For example, if the cost of materials goes up, the selling price is also likely to go up. However, simulation techniques (discussed later) take into consideration changes in more than one variable at a time.
- It also does not identify other possible scenarios.
- It considers the impact of all key areas (one at a time). The amount of information may overwhelm the decision maker.
- The probability of each of the assumptions is not tested.
- It only provides information to help managers make decisions. It is not a technique in itself for making a decision.

5 Scenario analysis

Scenario analysis provides information on possible outcomes for the proposed investment by creating various scenarios that may occur. It evaluates the expected value of a proposed investment in different scenarios expected in a certain situation.

As with sensitivity analysis, the method involves calculating NPV. Unlike sensitivity analysis, scenario analysis also calculates NPVs in other possible scenarios or 'states of the world'. The most used scenario analysis involves calculating NPVs in three possible states of the world: a most likely view, an optimistic view and a pessimistic view.

By changing a number of key variables simultaneously, decision makers can examine each possible outcome from the 'downside' risk and 'upside' potential of a project, as well as the most likely outcome. However, this technique has several key weaknesses:

- as the number of variables that are changed increases, the model can become increasingly difficult and time consuming;
- it does not consider the probability of each 'state of the world' occurring when evaluating the possible outcomes; and
- it does not consider other scenarios that may occur.

6 Simulation modelling

The Monte Carlo simulation method is an investment modelling technique that shows the effect of more than one variable changing at the same time. Complex structures of capital investment are investigated through simulation techniques, particularly modelling the impact of uncertainty. Simulation models are programmed on computers to deal with variable factors by use of random numbers.

The model identifies key variables that drive costs and revenues (such as market size, selling price, initial investment, changes in material prices, rates of use of labour and materials and inflation). It then assigns random numbers and probability statistics to each variable that might affect the success or failure of a proposed project. For example, if the most likely outcomes are thought to have a 50% probability, optimistic outcomes a 30% probability and pessimistic outcomes a 20% probability, then a random number representing those attributes can be assigned to costs and revenues in those proportions. These randomly selected values are used to calculate the project NPV.

Computer modelling repeats the decision many times, calculating a different NPV each time. This gives management a view of all possible outcomes. The resulting set of NPVs can be used to show how the NPV varies under the influence of all the variable factors. A more informed decision can then be taken depending on the management's attitude to risk. This approach can also be used to test the vulnerability of outcomes to possible variations in uncontrolled factors.

The key weaknesses of this technique are as follows.

- It is not a technique for decision making, rather providing information about the possible outcomes upon which management makes a decision.
- It is a complex method which is not simple to calculate.
- The time and costs involved may outweigh the benefits gained from the improved decision making.

7 Expected net present value

Unlike the previous approaches, this method makes use of probabilities. In a complex world, most investment appraisal decisions are based on forecasts which are subject to uncertainties, resulting in multiple outcomes. It is imperative that these uncertainties are reflected in the investment decision. These uncertainties can be captured by assigning a probability to each outcome. The project performance is evaluated based on its expected value derived on a probability-driven cash flow.

To understand the term 'probabilities' or 'probability of outcomes', some key points are illustrated below.

- The numerical value of probability ranges between 0 to 1 and the sum of probabilities must always be exactly 1. For example, the table below shows two scenarios of a new product being launched in the market. The result is distributed between the probability of it being profitable (which is 0.9) and the probability of it going into loss (which is 0.1).

Outcomes	Probability
Profit	0.9
Loss	0.1
Total	1.0

- Usually, the probability is estimated based on historical data or past performance trends. In the above example, the probabilities would have been derived by looking at company statistics, its past record and reputation, the trend of similar products in the market, their profitability and their success rate.
- In practice, probabilities can be subjective. Investment managers can assign different probabilities based on their experience and market research. These should be accepted if they are backed up by experience, understanding and good judgement.

Stop and think 14.2

Can you think of a scenario where one can apply probabilities to make a decision?

Probabilities in an investment decision are measured on return and risk metrics. These measures are:

- expected value and expected net present value (ENPV): these measure return
- **standard deviation**: this measures risk or volatility

standard deviation
A statistical tool that measures the amount of variation or dispersion of a set of data from its mean. It is a measure of risk or volatility.

7.1 Expected value

The expected value is the average value of the outcome, calculated on probability estimates. The methodology is as follows.

1. The probability of an outcome and value of that outcome is specified.
2. The expected value of each outcome is calculated.
3. All the expected values are added with each probability to arrive at the expected value.

The formula for calculating expected value is:

   Expected value = ΣPX

Where:
Σ = the sum of
P = the probability of outcome
X = the value of the outcome

Worked example 14.2

Swahili Investments Ltd invests in new projects and evaluates the sales with multiple forecast assumptions for the upcoming season. Probabilities are assigned for each of the three scenarios or economic conditions.

The following table indicates the probability of sales in the next season.

Economic conditions	Probability (P)	Sales (X) (£)	PX (£)
Boom	0.3	10,000	3,000
Normal	0.5	8,000	4,000
Recession	0.2	5,000	1,000
Expected value of sales			8,000

7.2 Expected net present value

Expected net present value (ENPV) is a capital budgeting and appraisal technique. It is a simple tool to evaluate the feasibility of a project. It is based on net present value under different scenarios, probability weighted to adjust for uncertainties in each of these scenarios. A project with a positive ENPV will be accepted, taking the much of guesswork out of decision making. Unlike traditional NPV, ENPV produces a more realistic picture by considering any uncertainties inherent in project scenarios.

7.3 Advantages

- ENPV provides a clear 'rule' to aid decision making.
- The expected value and ENPV tools are simple and easy to calculate.
- A positive ENPV increases shareholder wealth if a project proceeds and outcomes follow expectations.

7.4 Limitations

- Expected value and ENPV are measures of return. They do not take the volatility or the risk of a project into consideration. Variability (volatility) or dispersion is measured by standard deviation.
- While ENPV takes probabilities into account, they are subjective and may be difficult to estimate.

Worked example 14.3

Dodoma Co is considering an investment of £1 million in a coffee plantation project expected to generate substantial cash inflows over the next five years. The annual cash flows from this investment are uncertain due to unpredictable weather conditions. Management has derived the following probability distribution based on historical data and market trends. The cost of capital is 10%. Calculate the ENPV to help Dodoma Co decide whether to proceed with the project.

Annual cash flow (£)	Probability (P)
400,000	0.4
500,000	0.3
700,000	0.2
800,000	0.1

Year	Cash flow	P	Outcome (X)	PX	10% discount factor	
0	Project cost	1	1,000,000	1,000,000	1	(1,000,000)
0–10	Annual cash flow	0.4	400,000	160,000		
		0.3	500,000	150,000		
		0.2	700,000	140,000		
		0.1	800,000	80,000		
	Expected annual cash flow			530,000	6.145	3,256,850
	ENPV					2,256,850

As the expected net present value is positive, the company should go ahead with the project.

Chapter fourteen Risk assessment in investment appraisal techniques

Worked example 14.4

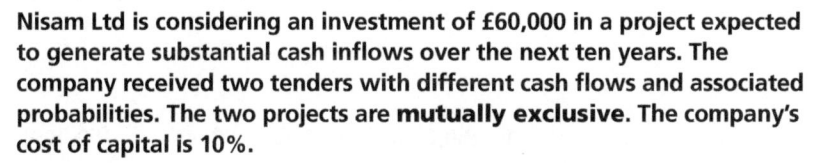

Nisam Ltd is considering an investment of £60,000 in a project expected to generate substantial cash inflows over the next ten years. The company received two tenders with different cash flows and associated probabilities. The two projects are **mutually exclusive**. The company's cost of capital is 10%.

Project Norik	
Annual cash flow (£)	Probability (P)
4,000	0.4
10,000	0.3
14,000	0.2
25,000	0.1

Project Nirzan	
Annual cash flow (£)	Probability (P)
7,000	0.3
9,500	0.3
12,000	0.25
14,200	0.15

Nirzan Co uses the ENPV approach to help decide which project should proceed.

ENPV calculation – Project Norik

Year		P	Outcome (X) £	PX £	10% discount factor	Discounted cash flows £
0	Project cost	1.0	(60,000)	(60,000)	1.000	(60,000)
0–10	Annual cash flow	0.4	4,000	1,600		
		0.3	10,000	3,000		
		0.2	14,000	2,800		
		0.1	25,000	2,500		
	Expected annual cash flow			9,900	6.145	60,836
	ENPV					836

ENPV calculation – Project Nirzan

Year		P	Outcome (X) £	PX £	10% discount factor	Discounted cash flows £
0	Project cost	1	(60,000)	(60,000)	1.000	(60,000)
0–10	Annual cash flow	0.3	7,000	2,100		
		0.3	9,500	2,850		
		0.25	12,000	3,000		
		0.15	14,200	2,130		
	Expected annual cash flow			10,080	6.145	61,942
	ENPV					1,942

Project Nirzan has a higher positive ENPV and should be selected over Project Norik. ENPV is simply a measure of return and does not take account of differences in variability. Variability (also referred to as volatility) will be measured using standard deviation.

7.5 Standard deviation and the coefficient of variation

Standard deviation is a statistical tool which measures the amount of variation or dispersion of a set of data from its mean. It is a measure of risk or volatility of returns. A project can be best evaluated by measuring the standard deviation, along with the expected value and ENPV. The higher the standard deviation, the larger the variance and the higher the risk of a project. Standard deviation is an absolute figure. It cannot be used to compare projects unless they have the same expected return.

Standard deviation is calculated as the square root of the variance. It measures how spread out numbers are from their mean. Variance is the average of the squared differences from the mean.

Standard deviation is calculated using the steps below:

1. Deviation (d) = NPV − expected value (EV)
2. The deviation is squared (d^2) to remove the negative number
3. The variance is calculated as pd^2 = probability × squared deviations
4. The standard deviation (Sd) is the square root of the variance

coefficient of variation
The ratio of standard deviation to the mean, applying in a single variable dataset. It measures extent of variability or the dispersion of data points in a dataset in relation to the mean of the population.

The **coefficient of variation** is the ratio of standard deviation to the mean (average). It measures the extent of variability or the dispersion of data points in a dataset in relation to the mean of the population.

The coefficient of variation allows comparison of different projects or investments. It can be used to compare standard deviations from projects of different sizes. While the standard deviation measures the volatility or dispersion of returns, the coefficient of variation is a better measure of the relative risk. It measures the relative dispersion of returns in relation to the expected return.

coefficient of variation = standard deviation ÷ expected value or ENPV

8 Event tree diagrams

Event tree diagrams are a commonly used tool for risk mapping when a project or task has multiple outcomes with different probabilities. Tree diagrams represent all possible outcomes of an event, allowing managers to calculate their probability. Each branch in a tree diagram represents one possible outcome of the project. If two events are independent, the outcome of one has no effect on the outcome of the other.

event tree diagrams
Event tree diagrams represent all possible outcomes of an event that allow users to calculate their probability.

This diagrammatic approach allows all possible outcomes to be accurately mapped. The construction of event tree diagram follows the steps below:

1. An initiating event or a project that leads to further sequential events is identified (such as a product launch).
2. The sequential events or outcomes associated with the specific scenarios are identified, building the event tree diagram.
3. Probabilities for the sequential events (rate of success and failure) are determined.
4. The expected value for each sequential event is calculated.
5. The sum of all expected values gives the expected value for the project.

8.1 Limitations

- It is not normally realistic to identify the various possible outcomes and then attach probabilities to each of them.
- Success or failure probabilities are difficult to find.
- Event tree diagrams require an analyst with practical training and experience.
- Event tree diagrams are not efficient where many events must occur in combination.
- All events are assumed to be independent, which may not be always the case.
- An initiating event is identified. The analysis is limited and dependent on one initiating event that leads to further sequential events.

A simple example of an event tree diagram for a company is shown in Figure 14.2.

A company is researching a new area of diversification and looking at three new products and will launch one in the new financial year. It has collected some

Project/initiating event	Probability	Event	Probability	Outcome	Expected Value
		Product A	35%	Large Revenue (5m)	50% × 35% × £5m = £875,000
	50%		65%	Small Revenue (2m)	50% × 65% × £2m = £650,000
Launch new product	30%	Product B	60%	Large Revenue (4m)	30% × 60% × £4m = £720,000
			40%	Small Revenue (1m)	30% × 40% × £1m = £480,000
	20%	Product B	65%	Large Revenue (3m)	20% × 65% × £3m = £390,000
			35%	Small Revenue (1m)	20% × 35% × £1m = £70,000
				Project total	£3,185,000

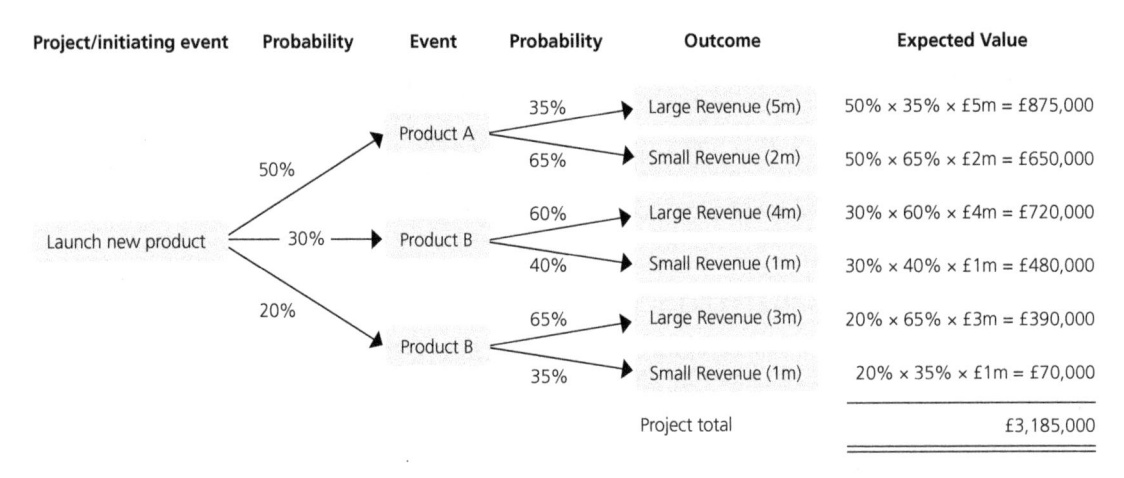

Figure 14.2 Event tree diagram

market research data and wants to look at what the expected outcome for the project might be.

9 The role of portfolio management

portfolio
A mix of investments in the form of group of assets such as banknotes, bonds, debentures and stocks. It can also refer to a portfolio of projects managed together to achieve an organisation's strategic objectives.

A **portfolio** is a mix of investments or projects in a company. It can refer to external or internal portfolios of investments or projects. When a company has surplus funds available, it may make external investments in a portfolio of assets such as banknotes, bonds, debentures and stocks. These external portfolios are also referred to as passive investments as they do not entail active management from the issuing company. An internal portfolio refers to a group of projects managed together to achieve an organisation's strategic objectives.

For instance, a company in the energy sector could include a portfolio of projects such as 'development of solar energy production' or 'improving efficiency by investing in new techniques'. All of these will help it meet its objective of 'reducing carbon emissions'.

9.1 Objectives and elements of portfolio management

The objective of portfolio management is to select the right investments in the right proportions to generate optimum returns while minimising risk. The key elements of a good portfolio are listed below.

- **Return:** the portfolio should yield steady returns that at least match the opportunity cost of the funds invested. In general, the better the growth prospects of the company, the better the expected returns.
- **Risk reduction**: minimisation of risks is the most important objective of portfolio management. A good portfolio tries to minimise the overall risk to an acceptable level in relation to the levels of return obtained.

- **Liquidity and marketability:** it is desirable to invest in assets which can be marketed without difficulty. A good portfolio ensures that there are enough funds available at short notice.
- **Tax shelter**: the portfolio should be developed considering the impact from taxes. A good portfolio enables companies to enjoy a favourable tax shelter from income tax, capital gains tax and gift tax.
- **Appreciation in the value of capital**: a balanced portfolio must consist of certain investments that appreciate in value, protecting investor from any erosion in purchasing power due to inflation.

9.2 Elements of portfolio management

The need for effective portfolio management arises once an entity builds a portfolio of investments. Effective portfolio management increases the probability of higher returns through risk reduction. Portfolio theory helps investment managers to construct portfolios that best meet the requirements of investors in terms of risk and return. Portfolio management reduces risk and uncertainties through a number of strategies.

9.3 Asset allocation

Asset allocation is an investment strategy that aims to balance risk and reward by adjusting the percentage of each asset in an investment portfolio according to the investor's risk tolerance, goals and investment horizon.

Investments are made in suitable mix of assets according to the risk appetite or risk preferences of investors. Risk-seeking investors can opt for more volatile assets with higher returns, while risk-averse investors look for 'safer' investments. For example, if an entity that manages savings of pensioners is risk averse, it will adopt a policy of investing the pension savings in government or treasury bonds to avoid the risk of losing the entire capital.

asset allocation
An investment strategy that aims to reduce uncertainties and balance risk and reward within a portfolio by using a mix of assets that have low correlation to each other.

9.4 Diversification

Spreading the risk across multiple investments within an asset class is known as **diversification**. This is based on the well-known rule of thumb 'don't put all your eggs in one basket'. Effective diversification includes investments across different asset classes, securities, sectors and geography. This will not only help to boost the returns but also lower the level of risk of a portfolio.

diversification
Spreading risk across multiple investments within an asset class.

For example, a portfolio that is comprised of only bonds carries less risk (and lower returns) than a portfolio of only equities. If the percentage of equities is increased to, say, 20%, the risk of the portfolio increases but it will also increase the potential returns. A unit trust typically spreads its funds among a large number of investments.

9.5 Rebalancing

Portfolio management is a continuous process of monitoring the performance of the portfolio, incorporating the latest market conditions and implementing the strategies in tune with investment objectives that maximises returns and minimises risk. Rebalancing is this continuous process of comparing portfolio weightings with planned asset allocation. Rebalancing is usually done on an annual basis. However, it can be done at any time if a significant need arises.

Asset allocation
Uses a mix of assets according to the investor's risk tolerance, goals and investment horizon

Diversification
Spreading risk across multiple investments

Rebalancing
Continuous process of monitoring portfolio performance

Figure 14.3 Elements of portfolio management

Stop and think 14.3

Can you think of reasons why spreading the risk across multiple investments would increase the return of a portfolio?

9.6 Portfolio risk and return

A well-diversified portfolio contains multiple investments. The relationship between the risk and return of the individual investments determines the overall risk and return of the portfolio. A company can measure the average return for the portfolio by calculating the correlation among the individual investments. **Correlation**, in terms of portfolio management, is a statistical tool that measures the degree to which two securities move in relation to each other. One reason for this might be that two securities have generally opposite reactions to the same external news or event. For instance, financial stocks such as banks or insurance companies tend to get a boost when interest rates rise, while the real estate and utilities sector get hit particularly hard when interest rates increase.

correlation
Correlation, in terms of portfolio management, is a statistical tool that measures the degree to which two securities move in relation to each other.

Correlation is computed by using the correlation coefficient, which has a value that ranges between minus 1 and plus 1. The correlation coefficient is a statistical measure of the strength of the relationship between the relative movements of two variables. The values range between minus 1.0 and 1.0. You will not need to know how to calculate a correlation coefficient, but you do need to understand the meaning of the results.

There are three possible results of a correlational study.

Positive correlation (Coefficient = 1)
The correlation of investments in a portfolio is positive (or +1) when their prices move in same direction or offer same kind of return in the specified period.

Usually, the investments in the same industries, or with same set of products that can substitute each other, demonstrate positive correlation.

For example, if the price of stock A increases by 5% and price of stock Z also increases by 5% in a month, stock A and stock Z are said to have a positive correlation of +1. When a company invests in Stock A and Z at the same time, the portfolio price will increase by 5% (assuming the same amount of investment in both stocks). The positive correlation also applies in case of falling prices. Holding both investments can dramatically increase returns but can also dramatically increase losses.

Negative correlation (Coefficient = minus 1)
The correlation of investments in a portfolio is negative (or minus 1) when their prices move in opposite directions. There is an inverse relationship between two variables. Usually, the investments in industries which are dependent on each other for raw materials or services offer negative correlation. When the price of oil rises, it is likely to result in the rise of the price of an oil company's shares (ignoring other factors), but the shares of companies such as airlines are likely to fall in value.

For example, if the price of stock A increases by 5% and the price of stock Z decreases by 5% in a month, stock A and stock Z are said to have negative correlation of minus 1. When a company invests in stock A and Z at the same time, the portfolio will be constant with no change in the price (assuming the same amount is invested in both the stocks). Essentially, gain from stock A is offset by the loss in stock Z.

Zero correlation (Coefficient = 0):
Zero correlation applies where underlying investments have no relationship that indicates any kind of correlation. Usually, investments in different asset classes or different geographic locations have zero correlation. With zero correlation, each investment performance holds the price and risk without any dependency on the performance of other investments.

9.7 The efficient frontier

The 'efficient frontier' is a modern portfolio theory tool that shows investors the best possible return they can expect from their portfolio for a defined level of risk. The efficient frontier aims for optimum correlation between risk and return. The portfolio manager scouts for the investment opportunities which offer optimum correlation to maximise return for the portfolio. The efficient frontier is curved (see Figure 14.4), representing a diminishing marginal return to risk.

Portfolios that do not provide enough return for the level of risk are considered as suboptimal (they lie below the efficient frontier). Each point on the efficient frontier line represents optimal portfolio.

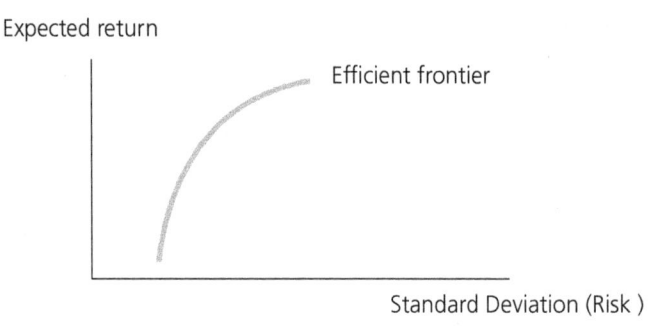

Figure 14.4 The efficient frontier

9.8 The application and limitations of portfolio theory

The core principles of portfolio theory are based on asset allocation, diversification and rebalancing – diversifying away the risk with carefully selected investments or optimum portfolios. It can be applied to a selection of projects and company ventures as well as securities. Companies can reduce risk and stabilise profits by investing in negatively correlated companies.

Limitations of portfolio theory
- It is a single-period framework.
- Probabilities are only estimates.
- It is based on several assumptions, including:
  - investors are risk-averse and behave rationally
  - the risk of bankruptcy, legal and administrative constraints are ignored
- Portfolio theory assumes that the correlation between assets is constant. This may not be applicable in the real world as every variable is constantly changing.
- Correlation analysis requires computation of the coefficient of each underlying security. It is very complex in terms of gathering historical numbers, model selection and calculating with accuracy.
- The theory does not assume any tax payouts or legal and administrative costs. These are essential factors in determining investment decisions.
- The theory ignores the timeframes (short term, medium term or long term) of the investments. Return expectations may change depending on these timeframes. Some randomly selected portfolios may have performed better than optimally selected portfolios, at least for a short time.
- Despite the availability of software programs to perform the calculations, the portfolio model is still not widespread as portfolio managers are sceptical about the accuracy of the forecast data. They may prefer to use their own judgement in selecting investments.

Chapter summary

- Risk assessment models are important for investment decision making and its impact on investment or project management.
- In investment decisions, the risk relates to uncertainty around returns not turning out as expected. The more volatile the return, the higher the risk. The attitude of investors to risk plays a vital part in the investment appraisal process. Based on the risk preference, investors can be categorised as:
    - risk seeking
    - risk averse
    - risk neutral
- An important aspect of risk assessment is identifying and assessing potential sources of risk in terms of potential impact on the company and how likely (probable) they are. Various risk assessment models incorporate risk into decision making. These techniques involve both non-probabilistic as well as probabilistic approaches to project appraisal. While non-probabilistic approaches use sensitivity analysis, scenario analysis and simulation modelling, probabilistic approaches use techniques such as expected net present value (ENPV), standard deviation and event tree diagrams.
- Sensitivity analysis is a tool for quantitative risk assessment that predicts the outcome of a decision by ascertaining the most critical variables and their effect on decision making.
- Scenario analysis evaluates the expected value of a proposed investment in different scenarios – a most likely view, an optimistic view and a pessimistic view. The method involves calculating net present value (NPV) but, unlike sensitivity analysis, scenario analysis also calculates NPVs in other possible scenarios.
- Simulation modelling provides information about possible outcomes (using random numbers) to assist decision making.
- Expected net present value (ENPV) is a capital budgeting and appraisal technique based on NPV under different scenarios, probability weighted to adjust for uncertainties.
- Standard deviation is a measure of risk or volatility. Standard deviation must be measured when evaluating a project, along with the expected value and ENPV. The higher the standard deviation, the higher the risk of a project.
- Event tree diagrams are commonly used for risk mapping when a project or task has multiple outcomes with different probabilities. Tree diagrams represent all possible outcomes of an event, allowing decision makers to calculate their probability. A portfolio can refer to both external or internal portfolios of investments or projects. The three aspects of portfolio management are asset allocation, diversification and rebalancing.

- The relationship or the correlation between the risks and returns of the individual investments determines the overall risk and return of the portfolio. The correlation can be positive, negative or zero.
- Securities with negative correlation act best in reducing risk. Whereas portfolio return is simply a weighted average of returns for elements in the portfolio, portfolio risk can be reduced when the returns from its individual investments move in opposite directions.

Chapter fifteen
Company analysis and company valuation methods

Contents

1. Introduction
2. Investment valuation ratios
3. Earnings per share
4. Price/earnings ratio
5. Relative value measures
6. Valuation using the dividend valuation model
7. Valuation using discounted cash flows
8. Appraisal using the capital asset pricing model
9. The application of the efficient market hypothesis in company valuation
10. Shareholder value analysis
11. Economic value added
12. Measuring value creation

1 Introduction

Analysis of published financial statements is carried out to evaluate the financial health, risks and future prospects of a company. This chapter outlines some common methods and techniques used by investors for company analysis and company valuation.

While lenders are interested in the repayment ability of the company, equity investors are interested in long-term dividend growth and share price appreciation. Any potential investor or purchaser will review the financial ratios of a company before deciding whether to invest. They will use investment ratios such as earnings per share and the price/earnings ratio, along with other valuation methods such as relative value measures, the dividend discount model, the discounted cash flow model and the capital asset pricing model to draw conclusions about the worth of the company.

The implications of the efficient market hypothesis for company shares and company valuation in general will also be considered. The chapter also examines shareholder value analysis (SVA) and the objective of shareholder wealth creation. Shareholders invest in companies with an anticipation of returns. Hence, the concept of shareholder value creation has evolved. The chapter concludes by examining economic value added and market value added as an alternative to shareholder value analysis and assessing the features of different aspects of value creation for shareholders.

2 Investment valuation ratios

There is a wide array of ratios that can be used by investors and shareholders to evaluate the performance of a company's shares and assess its valuation. Investment valuation ratios compare relevant data that will estimate the attractiveness of a potential or existing investment. Investors assess the performance of a company's shares by looking at how ratios compare from one company to another.

In all of these ratios, we are referring to equity (ordinary) shares, as we have already excluded any preference dividends. In doing this we are guided by the IAS 32 (Financial Instruments: Representation) requirement that preference dividends are an expense and that preference shares are a liability (not part of equity).

From an equity shareholder's point of view, the relevant information will be contained in the following ratios.

Dividends
- dividend payout ratio (DPR)
- dividend yield

Earnings
- earnings per share (EPS)
- price/earnings ratio (P/E)

2.1 Dividend payout ratio

This ratio measures the earnings attributable to equity shareholders that are paid out in the form of dividends. A higher payout ratio indicates that the company is sharing more of its earnings with its equity shareholders. A lower payout ratio indicates that the company is using more of its earnings to retain in the company to reinvest and grow further.

The payout ratio depends on company policy and the industry in which it operates. For example, fast-growing companies have a lower DPR as earnings are retained for expanding market share.

$$DPR = \text{Equity dividend(s) paid in the year} \div \text{Profit for the year} \times 100$$

2.2 Dividend yield

Dividend yield indicates how much a company pays out in dividends each year relative to the equity share price. Normally, only profitable companies pay out dividends. A stable dividend yield can be a sign of a stable and safer company. It allows investors to compare the annual cash return with other investments. Of course, the return from equity is a combination of the annual dividend and capital growth. This refers to dividends paid in the year, which are normally last year's final dividend payment and the current year's interim dividend payment.

Dividend yield = Dividend(s) per share ÷ market price per equity share × 100

Worked example 15.2 on page 361 shows how these ratios are applied in practice.

3 Earnings per share

Earnings per share (EPS) can be defined as the residual profit (or earnings) attributable to each equity shareholder. Residual profit means the profit for the period after charging interest and other finance charges, corporate tax, preference dividends and any transfers to other component of equity. The balance is the profit available for equity shareholders (usually reported as profit after tax or profit for the period/year).

This is the basic measure of a company's performance from an equity shareholder's point of view, calculated as profit attributable to each equity share.

EPS = profit attributable to equity shareholders for the period ÷ weighted average number of outstanding equity shares during the period.

International Accounting Standard 33 (Earnings per Share) prescribes how quoted companies should calculate their EPS figures. These figures should be published at the base of a statement of profit or loss and OCI by all quoted companies. The very detailed level of prescription on IAS 33 is to ensure consistent calculation of EPS so investors can rely on consistent P/E ratios.

Worked example 15.2 on page 361 shows how EPS is applied in practice.

3.1 Interpretation

Analysis of published financial statements reviews an organisation's financial situation using ratios and metrics such as revenue, gross margin and operating cash flow. If revenue indicates how much money is flowing into the company, EPS indicates how much money is ultimately attributable to the equity shareholders. It serves as an indicator of the profitability of the company that tells us how much money the company is making on every individual outstanding equity share.

- The higher the EPS, the more attractive the shares will be to potential investors and higher the stock market value. An appreciating EPS trend indicates the growth of a company. Investors can also look at the estimates of future EPS to get an idea of the profits they will earn in future years.

- A high EPS indicates a company in good health, with enough profits available to pay dividends to the equity shareholders or to plough back into the company for future prospects and long-term growth. A company with a reported loss gives a negative EPS which is usually reported as 'not applicable'.
- EPS is a measure of the management performance. It shows how effectively the available capital and opportunities have been fully utilised in the reporting period.
- It sets an upper limit for dividends, which some consider to be an important determinant of share price – although users should be aware that dividends are sometimes financed from distributable profits from previous years.

basic EPS
Basic earnings per share is profit attributable to equity shareholders for a period divided into the weighted average number of outstanding equity shares for that same period.

diluted EPS
Diluted EPS is the adjusted profit attributable to equity shareholders for a period divided into the weighted average number of outstanding equity shares assuming all conversion rights are exercised. Diluted EPS is normally less than basic EPS.

Earnings per share changes when the level of profit increases or decreases. In addition, EPS will be altered or diluted when there is a new share issue, giving rise to the calculation of **basic EPS** and **diluted EPS**. Basic EPS is profit attributable to equity shareholders for a period, divided into the weighted average number of outstanding equity shares for that same period. Diluted EPS is the adjusted attributable profit for a period, divided into the outstanding equity shares and adjusted to include all potential dilution. A diluted EPS assumes that all the convertible securities such as convertible preferred shares, convertible debt, equity options and warrants will be exercised. Diluted EPS is generally less than basic EPS.

Diluted EPS = adjusted profit attributable to equity shareholders for a period ÷ weighted average number of outstanding equity shares + diluted shares

For example, a company with a profit for the year of £6 million and 2 million equity shares also has convertible debt that could be converted to 1 million equity shares.

Basic EPS = £6,000,000 ÷ 2,000,000 = 300p/share.
Diluted EPS = £6,000,000 ÷ (2,000,000 + 1,000,000) = 200p/share

Notice this excludes any savings in interest payments from the convertible debt.

3.2 Limitations

- Earnings per share does not represent actual income to the shareholder. It uses earnings, which are not directly linked to the objective of maximising shareholder wealth.
- Companies have the option to buy back their shares. In this case, the number of shares outstanding decreases, increasing the EPS without an actual increase in the profit. Companies can make EPS look better without profit actually improving.

- EPS does not consider the debt element of the company. It may not be an ideal comparison of two companies where one company has debt and the other company does not.
- EPS trend analysis shows the growth of a company in recent years. However, it may not be meaningful to compare EPS of different companies. The figures are dependent on the number of shares and their nominal value, that each company has in issue. Different companies are also likely to have different accounting policies.

4 Price/earnings ratio

The price/earnings (P/E) ratio, also referred to as the 'earnings multiple' of a company, measures the current market price of the share relative to its EPS. The current market price is driven by the forces of supply and demand along with overall stock market performance.

P/E ratio = Market price per share ÷ EPS

This ratio indicates the relationship between the market value of equity share capital and the profit for the year. The P/E ratio valuation method is a simple and commonly used method of valuation. This approach uses the price earnings ratio of a similar quoted company to value shares in unquoted companies.

Value of a share = EPS × suitable industry P/E ratio

The P/E ratio applied should be from the same industry, with similar:

- company risk (in the same industry)
- finance risk (a similar level of gearing)
- growth rate

This may be difficult to achieve in practice. The P/E ratio used is often negotiated between parties involved in the acquisition. If using a quoted company's P/E to value an unquoted company, a substantial discount (around 25%) is often applied to reflect the lower marketability of unquoted shares.

4.1 Interpretation

- The P/E ratio gives a stock market view of the quality of the underlying earnings. Generally, a high P/E ratio indicates that investors anticipate higher earnings and higher growth in the future. The average market P/E ratio has often been stated at 20–25 times earnings. In reality, different markets at different times may have averages well above or well below this range. A P/E ratio is most useful when compared with a benchmark: for example, the average P/E ratio for a specific sector of a market.
- A loss-making company does not have a P/E ratio.
- A company with a high P/E ratio can indicate that the equity shares are being overvalued. If a company has a high P/E, investors are paying a higher price for shares compared to its earnings.

- A company with a low P/E may indicate undervalued shares. This can make a company with a low P/E a good value investment with potential opportunity to be profitable, but it can also simply indicate that investors are not confident about the company's future prospects.
- The P/E ratio shows the number of years it would take for the company to pay back the amount an investor paid for the share. In other words, the number of multiples over one year's earnings an investor is willing to pay for a share.

4.2 Limitations

- The P/E ratio is applied to earnings based on accounting policies, which are more subjective than cash flows. A company can inflate their earnings to make them look better.
- The P/E ratio simply assumes that the market is valuing earnings and ignores many important variables in an equity share's worth: dividends, earnings growth, risk and so on.
- The P/E ratio assumes that the market accurately values equity shares.
- The P/E ratio is actually a backward-looking indicator, providing little help where economic conditions have changed significantly.
- It does not consider debt. Companies with high debt levels are higher risk investments and the market price of an equity share is not always a good indicator of fair value.
- The P/E ratio is a useful valuation method used by investors, but it should never be used as the sole reason for investing in a company.

Worked example 15.1

1. The shares of Good plc are currently trading at £42. Its EPS for the most recent 12-month period is £3. Calculate the P/E ratio.

    P/E ratio = £42 ÷ £3 = 14 times

    For every £1 of earnings from the company's profits, the investor has to invest £14 in the company's shares. Put another way, the payback period is 14 years, based on the current share price and current earnings.

2. From the latest set of financial statements of ABC Ltd (a small printing company) it can be calculated that its basic EPS is 50p and the average P/E ratio of similar quoted printing companies is currently 20. What is the price per share for ABC Ltd?

    Value of a share = EPS × suitable industry P/E ratio
    Price per share = £0.50 × 20 = £10

Worked example 15.2

Calculate the investment ratios (for each of the two years) of Ina plc based on the financial information below.

Statements of financial position as at 31 December

	20X2	20X1
	£'000	£'000
Non-current assets	200,000	215,000
Current assets	55,000	50,000
Total assets	255,000	265,000
Equity share capital (10p shares)	40,000	40,000
Retained earnings	101,000	93,000
Total equity	141,000	133,000
Non-current liabilities		
Total non-current liabilities	94,000	94,000
Current liabilities	20,000	38,000
Total equity and liabilities	255,000	265,000

Extracts from statements of profit or loss (and retained earnings) for the year ended 31 December

	20X2	20X1
	£'000	£'000
Revenue	340,000	320,000
Operating profit	35,000	33,000
Interest/finance charges	(4,000)	(4,000)
Profit before tax	31,000	29,000
Tax expense	(8,000)	(7,000)
Profit for the year	23,000	22,000
Dividends paid:		
Equity shares	(15,000)	(12,000)
Retained profit for the year	8,000	10,000

Market values at 31 December:

	20X2	20X1
	£	£
Equity shares	0.88	0.78

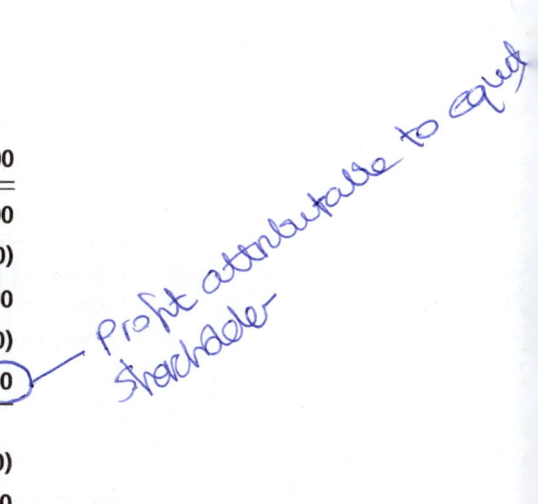

For 20X2:

EPS = Profit attributable to equity shareholders for the period ÷ weighted average number of outstanding equity shares during the period (in pence)	23,000 ÷ 400,000 × 100	58p
P/E ratio = Market price per share ÷ EPS	0.88 ÷ 0.058	15.2
DPR = equity dividends paid in the year ÷ Profit for the year	15,000 ÷ 23,000 × 100	65.2%
Dividend yield = (dividends ÷ number of equity shares) ÷ market price per share	(15,000 ÷ 400,000)/0.88	4.3%

*[handwritten: 40,000 × 10p = 400,000 shares in total *]*

For 20X1:

EPS =	22,000 ÷ 400,000 × 100	55p
P/E Ratio =	0.78 ÷ 0.055	14.2
DPR =	10,000 ÷ 22,000 × 100	45.5% *[handwritten: 54.5]*
Dividend yield =	(12,000/400,000)/0.78	3.8%

EPS shows residual profits attributable to each equity shareholder. This has improved marginally in 20X2.

The P/E ratio is the measure of the current market price of the share relative to its EPS. In 20X2, the P/E ratio of 15.2 means that, the investor has to invest £15.20 in the company's shares for every £1 of earnings from the company's profits. The ratio has improved by 7.0% in 20X2. Generally, a high P/E ratio indicates that investors anticipate higher earnings and higher growth in the future. However, a company with a high P/E ratio can also indicate that the share is being overvalued.

The dividend payout ratio measures the earnings attributable to equity shareholders that are distributed in the form of dividends. The pay-out ratio was higher in 20X2, meaning that the company is sharing a greater proportion of its earnings with its equity shareholders and retaining a lesser proportion for reinvestment than in 20X1.

Test yourself 15.1

The shares of Sira plc are trading at £30 and the company has an EPS of £2 over the last year.

1. Calculate the P/E ratio.
2. How is the P/E ratio used and interpreted by investors?

5 Relative value measures

Relative value is a method of determining an asset's value that takes into account the value of similar assets of competing companies in the same industry. This is in contrast with other valuation methods, which look only at an asset's intrinsic value and do not compare it to other assets. It is based on the approach that the investors are not just interested in the absolute figures on the financial statements, but also in the valuation of the asset in relation to its peers. The investor measures share value (or the attractiveness measured in terms of risk, liquidity and return) in relation to a comparable share of another company.

5.1 Steps in relative value analysis

1. Identify comparable companies. Revenue and market capitalisation are the widely used parameters.
2. Calculate price multiples such as P/E ratio, equity share price to sales revenue and equity share price to operating cash flow.
3. Compare these ratios with those of peers and the industry average. This will help in understanding whether the security is overvalued or undervalued.

Worked example 15.3

Equity shares in Sumnima plc, a hospitality company, are trading at £40 in the market. The company has an EPS of £2. The average P/E ratio of the hospitality industry is 15 times.

Calculate the relative value of Sumnima plc's shares.

Solution

Share price ÷ EPS = P/E ratio

40 ÷ 2 = 20 times

This is higher than the industry average of 15 times, which implies that the equity shares of Sumnima plc are overvalued. If Sumnima plc equity shares had been trading at the industry average of 15 times, then their current market value would have been £30 (the relative value of the share). Since the current market price is £40 it represents an opportunity to sell.

Since the analysis is based on comparison with peers and the industry average, only companies with a similar market capitalisation should be compared in order to arrive at the relative values.

Market capitalisation = equity share price x number of equity shares outstanding

6 Valuation using the dividend valuation model

The dividend valuation model (DVM) – also known as the dividend discount model (DDM) – is based on the principle that the current value of an equity share is the discounted value of all expected dividend payments that the share is expected to yield in the future years. The NPV is calculated using an appropriate risk-adjusted rate that discounts the value of future cash flows to today's date. This discount rate (see Chapter 12) is also referred to as the cost of capital for equity and the cost of capitalisation. It is the rate of return expected by the equity shareholders as compensation for the risk of owning and holding the shares.

Future cash flows would include dividends and the selling price of the share when sold. For shares that do not pay dividends, the future cash flows would be equal to the intrinsic value of the selling price of the share.

> Current intrinsic value of an equity share = sum of present value of all future cash flows
>
> Sum of present value of all future cash flows = sum of present value of future dividends + present value of the share price

6.1 Assumptions

- The future income stream is the dividends paid out by the company.
- Dividends will be paid in perpetuity.
- Dividends will be constant or growing at a fixed rate.

6.2 Variable growth model

In a real-life scenario, dividends paid by companies do not remain constant over a number of years. The variable growth model – also known as the dividend growth model – divides the dividend growth into three phases:

- an initial phase of fast growth;
- a slower transition phase; and
- a sustainable 'long run' lower growth rate.

This model is a refinement of the DVM, but the basic principles remain the same. The capitalisation factor (the required rate of return) and the dividend growth rate might vary in these three phases. The intrinsic value of the share is the PV of each of these stages added together.

Different investors and analysts might have different predictions about the company's future dividends, which might lead to different growth rates and required rates of returns. The exact intrinsic value of the share is indeterminable in most cases.

Growth rate (g) = r × b

Where:
r = annual rate of return from investing
b = the proportion of annual earnings retained

7 Valuation using discounted cash flows

A discounted cash flow (DCF) calculation is used to estimate the value of potential investments. It determines the current value of an investment using future cash flows adjusted for the time value of money (TVM).

Net present value of a capital investment discounts all cash outflows and inflows to its present value by using an appropriate discount rate of return. Positive NPVs or current discounted values that are higher than the initial investment typically indicate that an investment may be worthwhile.

The concept of TVM and the DCF model are discussed in detail in Chapter 13.

8 Valuation using the capital asset pricing model

The capital asset pricing model (CAPM) describes the relationship between systematic risk and expected return for assets, particularly shares. Capital asset pricing is widely used for the pricing of risky securities, generating expected returns for assets given the risk of those assets and calculating the cost of equity. Chapter 12 covers CAPM in more detail, including how the cost of equity can be determined using this model. This chapter provides a quick recap of how CAPM can be used to appraise an investment and to determine whether it is worthwhile.

The cost of equity under the capital asset pricing model is calculated as follows.

K_e = Risk-free rate + (beta coefficient × market risk premium)

Where the market risk premium (also called equity risk premium) = market return − risk free rate of return, or:

RADR = RFR + ß (RM − RFR)

Where:
RADR = risk-adjusted discount rate
RFR = Risk-free rate of return
RM = return on stock market portfolio
ß = a measure of a stock's risk (volatility) in relation to its market, where 1.0 is the market level

The risk-free rate (RFR) is the rate of return of an investment with zero risk. The RFR may not exist in practice. Investors often use the return from government securities, such as 10-year UK treasury bonds, as the RFR.

The beta coefficient (ß) is a statistic that measures the systematic risk of a company's shares. Most investors use a beta calculated by a third party (an analyst or broker) who compares price changes of an asset to the price changes of the broader market. It reflects the volatility of its returns compared to those of the market on average. The ß of risk-free capital (for example government bonds) is zero and the ß for a stock market as a whole is 1.

The market rate of return (RM) is the overall rate of return on the market. The return on some relevant benchmark index such as the S&P500 is a good estimate for market rate of return. RADR represents the cost of capital in this case.

The capital asset pricing model provides a rate of return that is proportional to an asset's systematic risk and the expected excess return to the market. The rate calculated using CAPM can be used to discount an investment's future cash flows to their present value, which helps to determine the fair price of an investment. The calculated fair value of an asset can be compared to its market price.

Assuming that CAPM is correct, an investment is considered to be correctly priced when its market price is the same as the present value of its future cash flows, discounted at the rate suggested by CAPM.

If the market price is lower than the fair value arrived using CAPM valuation, the investment is considered to be undervalued (a bargain). If the market price is above the price calculated using CAPM rate, it is considered to be overvalued. The calculation of present value using the discount rate is covered in Chapter 13.

Worked example 15.4

The shares of Calmen plc are currently paying a return of 9%. Assume the following for Calmen plc's shares:

- ß: 1.3
- RFR: 12%
- RM: 18%

Using CAPM, calculate the minimum required return from the shares. Explain how you calculate the price you would pay for these shares.

Solution

The minimum required return is calculated using the formula.

RADR = RFR + ß(RM − RFR)

Where
RFR = Risk-free rate
RM = return on stock market portfolio
ß = measure of a stock's risk (volatility)

12% + 1.3(18% − 12%) = 19.8%

The minimum return required from the share is 19.8%. Note that the share is actually paying a return of 9%, well below the minimum return required calculated by CAPM.

The rate calculated using CAPM can be used to discount an investment's or a share's future cash flows to their present value to determine the fair price of an investment or a share. Assuming that the CAPM is correct, an investment or share is correctly priced when its market price is the same as the present value of its future cash flows, discounted at the rate suggested by CAPM.

If the market price is lower, the share is considered to be undervalued. If the market price is higher than the price calculated using CAPM rate, it is considered to be overvalued.

9 The application of efficient market hypothesis in company valuation

Chapter 10 discussed the efficient market hypothesis (EMH), which suggests that share prices always reflect the underlying value of the company. An efficient market ensures that the market price of all securities traded on it reflects all the available relevant information. Based on this hypothesis, it would not be possible for investors or valuation experts to identify any overpriced or underpriced securities. This provides an equal opportunity to everyone in the stock markets.

If the market is fully efficient, the share price is fair and the company can raise funds at a fair value.

Given the fact that most stock markets are 'semi-strong' in terms of market efficiency, the share price reflects not just the historical data but all information which is currently publicly available. Any new information is rapidly reflected in the share price. There is the potential for share prices to be inaccurate or outdated because of unpublished information. In such cases, share price can be predicted only if private information is known through insider dealing. The market value of the company will only be as good as the quality of public information available. Thus, managers can achieve the overall objective of maximising shareholder wealth by communicating the relevant public information to the market.

Investors and analysts therefore study the fundamental factors that underpin the share price, such as sales revenues, costs and risks associated with the company and other factors such as macroeconomic and industry conditions, key personnel, technological changes and so on. They use this information with a share valuation model (such as P/E ratio or dividend valuation model (DVM)) to estimate the intrinsic value of the shares. This value is then compared to see if the current market share price is overvalued or undervalued.

10 Shareholder value analysis

10.1 Value creation

Shareholder value analysis (SVA) was developed in the 1980s. It is a management strategy that focuses on the creation of economic value or wealth for shareholders. Wealth creation is a dominant company objective and occupies a central place in planning and analysis. The basic assumption of SVA is that a company is worth its ability to create value for shareholders, which is measured as the net present value of its future cash flows, discounted at the appropriate cost of capital.

The value of a share is typically the amount the shareholders are willing to pay, dependent on two factors:

- the expected dividends to be earned
- the expected returns from the share

Net present value and IRR are the most common standardised approaches for estimating a company's future cash flows and finding its present value. They are also the most popular techniques in capital investment appraisal that measure wealth creation for shareholders. Net present value is the difference between the present value of cash inflows and cash outflows over a period of time. It indicates whether the cash inflows are sufficient to cover the outflows. It also estimates the number of years it will take to break even (when NPV equals 0). A high NPV indicates that a company is able to generate sufficient cash flows to cover all costs incurred in a project and pay higher dividends with its surplus. The market price of a share increases with the expectation of higher dividends. Net present value and IRR are covered more in detail in Chapter 13.

10.2 Value drivers

Value drivers are factors that drive a company, which in turn creates value in a company. These factors impact a company's future cash flow and its NPV. Managers use these value drivers to make approximate estimates of future cash flows that could have an impact on the calculation of the NPV. Key financial value drivers include:

- growth in sales revenue
- improvement of profit margins
- investment in non-current assets and other capital expenditure
- investment in working capital
- cost of capital
- corporate tax rate(s)

Managers are required to pay attention to decisions influencing the value drivers and their ultimate impact on value creation. Disney and Pepsi use this approach.

10.3 Free cash flow

Free cash flow (FCF) is central to SVA. Projects undertaken by the company can either have a positive NPV or a negative NPV. A positive NPV indicates that the cost of the project would be completely recovered. Free cash flow is the surplus cash available after recovering all the costs needed to fund all projects that have positive NPVs. It also indicates the amounts free to be distributed to equity shareholders. Companies do not always distribute all the remaining surplus cash: some is retained for the following reasons:

- to make new investments
- to retain flexibility in decision making and such other powers within the company
- to absorb losses in times of economic downturn, thus avoiding administration or liquidation

Calculation of free cash flow:
Free cash flow is calculated as follows from the figures available in financial statements.

Sales revenue less operating costs = operating profit

Less: corporate tax, incremental investment in working capital and incremental investment in non-current assets = free cash flow from operations.

Investment in non-current assets includes:

- investment in new projects (incremental investment that allows the company to grow); and
- cost of replacement of existing non-current assets, which is assumed to be equal to the annual depreciation in order to simplify the calculation of free cash flow. This assumption avoids adding back depreciation (a non-cash expense) and also deducting replacement capital investment.

Worked example 15.5

Extracts from the financial statements of Takura plc are below.

Statements of profit or loss (and retained earnings) for the year ended 31 May	20X7 £m	20X6 £m
Revenue	265	220
Cost of sales	(80)	(60)
Gross profit	185	160
Operating costs	(95)	(88)
Operating profit	90	72
Corporate tax	(18)	(14)
Profit for the year	72	58
Equity dividends	(12)	(10)
Retained profit for the year	60	48

Statements of financial position at the year ended 31 May	20X7	20X6
	£m	£m
Non-current assets	1,373	1,386
Current assets		
Inventory	520	480
Trade receivables	385	410
Cash and cash equivalents	45	62
Total current assets	950	952
Total assets	2,323	2,338
Equity		
Equity shares (£1 each)	225	225
Retained earnings	1,153	1,093
Total equity	1,378	1,318
Non-current liabilities	650	695
Current liabilities: trade payables	295	325
Total equity and liabilities	2,323	2,338

Additional investment in non-current assets for the year ended 31 May 20X7 amounted to £95 million.

Calculate the company's free cash flow for the year ended 31 May 20X7 and comment on the results.

Solution

	£m	£m
Revenue		265
Operating costs (80 + 95)		(175)
Operating profit		90
Corporate tax		(18)
		72
Less: Incremental investment in working capital		
Inventory (increase) (520 – 480)	40	
Trade receivables (decrease) (385 – 410)	(25)	
Trade payables (decrease) (295 – 325)	30	45
		117
Less: Incremental investment in non-current assets		(95)
Free cash flow (FCF) from operations		22

Based on the calculation above, the company has a positive free cash flow (FCF) for the year ended 31 May 20X7. FCF measures the level of cash available to a company's investors, net of all required investments in working capital and capital expenditure (on non-current assets). The statement of financial position strengthens as positive FCF increases. It enhances shareholder value through opportunities to expand production, develop new products, reduce the cost of debt and pay higher dividends.

Negative FCF indicates an inability to generate enough cash after meeting its expenses. A negative FCF could indicate ineffective credit management, shortage of funds, or an actual loss and mismatch of income and expenditure. However, it is not always a bad sign. It can also indicate that a company is making significant investments which could potentially add value in the long term.

Test yourself 15.2

ABC plc generated sales revenue of £200 million during the year with an operating profit margin of 15%. The company pays corporate tax at a rate of 20%. The incremental investment in working capital was £13 million and the incremental investment in non-current assets was £6 million.

1. Calculate the free cash flow for the year.
2. What is the significance of identifying value drivers in SVA?

Stop and think 15.1

Think of the practical relevance and applicability of wealth creation for a company of your choice.

10.3 Calculation of shareholder value in SVA

Shareholder value analysis involves carrying out the following calculations.

- Calculating the free cash flow by using the value drivers as the base. This FCF is calculated for the period of the planning horizon.
- Calculating the NPV of the FCF.
- Estimating the value attributable for the period beyond the planning horizon. This is also known as the terminal period or residual period. Its value is worked out by calculating the value of **perpetuity** over the last year of the planning period. The present value of a perpetuity is calculated using the discounting method (covered in Chapter 13).

perpetuity
A perpetuity is an annuity or a series of fixed payments that lasts indefinitely.

As it is assumed that the company will generate cash flows indefinitely, the sales revenue and operating profit of the last year are taken as a base. The application of all the above steps leads to the 'corporate value'. The total shareholder value is worked out by deducting the market value of total long-term borrowings.

	£
NPV of FCF for the planning period	xxx
Add: present value over the terminal period or value of perpetuity	xxx
Less: market value of total long-term borrowings	xxx
Shareholder value	**xxx**

10.4 Strengths of SVA

- Shareholder value analysis uses accounting values and is easy to understand, apply and interpret. It does not involve any complex calculations.
- The reliability of the valuation is established by the use of universally accepted techniques such as NPV and DCF measures.
- Shareholder value analysis allows management to focus on the value drivers to make useful managerial decisions.
- Value drivers can also be used to benchmark the company against its competition.

10.5 Weaknesses of SVA

- The DCF flow technique uses a fixed rate for all future years, whereas companies go through ups and downs and generate different rates of returns.
- Value drivers are also assumed to grow at a constant rate which might not be the case in reality.
- Calculations depend on accounting figures including sales revenue and profits. In reality, it is almost impossible to predict the share value, irrespective of the approaches and accuracy levels, beyond a certain period of time.

11 Economic value added

Stern Stewart and Co developed the concept of economic value added (EVA) as an alternative to SVA. It is a measure of profitability and wealth created for shareholders over and above the cost of invested capital. It is calculated as follows:

EVA = operating profit after tax (OPAT) − (WACC × capital invested)

Capital invested comprises equity plus long-term debt at the beginning of the period.

The weighted average cost of capital (covered in Chapter 12) is the average rate of return a company expects to pay its investors; the weights are derived from a company's capital structure.

WACC = (proportion of equity × cost of equity) + (proportion of debt × post-tax cost of debt)

If a company is financed by 70% equity with a cost of 10% and 30% debt with after-tax costs of 8%:

WACC = (0.70 × 0.10) + (0.30 × 0.08) = 0.094 = 9.4%

The rationale behind multiplying the capital invested by WACC is to assess the cost of using the capital invested by the shareholders. It determines whether the company is adding more wealth to shareholder value by earning a higher rate of return on the funds invested than the cost of the funds.

A positive EVA indicates that a project has recouped its cost of capital, while a negative EVA indicates that the company has not made sufficient profits to recover its cost of running the company.

Worked example 15.6

The details of Mimang plc are below. Mimang plc is a services company: its profit is high given the amount of capital invested. Calculate the EVA of the company.

	£'000
Operating profit after tax (OPAT)	3,380
Capital invested	10,300
WACC	5.6%

OPAT − (WACC × capital invested) = EVA

3,380,000 − (5.6% × 10,300,000) = 2,803,200

A positive EVA indicates that the company or project has recovered its cost of capital. The value of the profitability or wealth created for shareholders over and above their cost of capital is £2,803,200.

Test yourself 15.3

Mirak Ltd invested £15 million at the start of the year and has generated operating profit after tax of £3 million. The company's weighted average cost of capital is 12%.

1. Calculate Mirak Ltd's EVA.
2. Explain the concept of EVA to a layperson using the above illustration.

11.1 Strengths of EVA

- It uses accounting concepts that are familiar to managers, such as profit and the cost of capital.
- It looks at economic value and presents a better picture of the company based on the idea that a company must cover both the operating costs as well as the capital costs.
- There are no requirements to produce any additional reports or data collection procedures.
- It is best used for asset-rich companies that are stable or mature.

11.2 Weaknesses of EVA

- EVA is restricted to specific or short-term projects as it does not take into account the present value of future cash flows.
- Its reliance on accounting profit makes it subjective in nature.
- Assets such as brand and reputation, that enhance the value of the company but are not recorded in the statement of financial position, are not considered in EVA. This limits its scope for companies with intangible assets, such as technology companies.

12 Measuring value creation

12.1 Total shareholder return

Total shareholder return (TSR) is the total amount returned to an investor, equal to the capital gain or loss on a share plus all dividends received. It is calculated as:

TSR = ((selling price + all dividends received) − purchase price) ÷ purchase price

It measures the performance of different companies' shares between buying and selling a block of shares.

Despite the ease of calculation, this method is subject to limitations as it uses market prices as the base. These are subject to market volatility. Therefore, it would only be meaningful if the performance is compared between companies in the same sector with same level of risk.

12.2 Market value added

The concept of market value added (MVA) was also developed by Stern Stewart and Co. It measures the value of the company as a result of its existence and operation in the market. It is calculated as follows:

MVA = market value − total amount invested

Market value represents the current value of the company, whereas capital represents the funds invested by the shareholders and long-term debt holders. It represents the increase in the value above the level of capital invested. However, it does not consider any loans raised by the company.

12.3 The effects of dividend payments on shareholder wealth

When a company pays a dividend, market value and equity are reduced by the same amount. The calculation of MVA remains unaffected. The following changes do happen on payment of an equity dividend:

- the market value of the share reduces by the amount of dividend paid; and
- the total equity balance on the statement of financial position, included in the MVA, is also reduced by the amount of dividend.

It can be assumed that dividend payments do not have an impact on MVA or shareholder wealth.

12.4 Stock market influences

Stock markets are influenced by a variety of factors. For any public issue or rights issue to be successful, it is essential that the shareholders are kept informed about how funds are used and the (positive) NPV of any new projects. The amount of value increase is not essential, but shareholders should be kept informed about the success of the project. Communications to shareholders and the stock exchange are an important part of the process of maintaining confidence in a company and, therefore, access to capital funds at fair prices.

The concepts of market efficiency and competitive advantage are relevant here. Market efficiency is measured by how quickly the markets respond to the news or information that is reflected by an increase or decrease in the share price. Competitive advantage is attained by the value created as a result of undertaking the new project or venture.

Worked example 15.7

Fortune plc has been trading for 10 years. It has 6 million £1 equity shares which have a market value of £1.65 each. It is also has £4 million in 5% debentures with a current market value of £98 (per £100). The company has retained earnings of £2 million. Calculate the MVA.

Solution

	£m	£m
Market value:		
Equity shares (6 million × £1.65)	9.9	
5% debentures (4 million × 0.98)	3.92	13.82
Total amount invested:		
Equity shares	(6.0)	
5% debentures	(4.0)	
Retained earnings	(2.0)	(12.0)
Market value added		1.82

Chapter summary

- There is a wide array of investment value ratios that can be used by investors and shareholders to assess the performance of a company's shares and get an idea of its valuation. Investment valuation ratios attempt to simplify this evaluation process by comparing relevant data that will estimate the attractiveness of a potential or existing investment.

- Earnings per share (EPS) is the residual profit (or earnings) attributable to each equity shareholder, divided into the weighted average number of equity share outstanding. It is the basic measure of a company's performance from an equity shareholder's point of view, calculated as profit attributable to each equity share outstanding.

- The price/earnings (P/E) ratio, also referred to as the 'earnings multiple' of the company, is the measure of the current market price of the share relative to its EPS. The current market price is driven by the forces of supply and demand and overall stock market performance.

- Relative value is a method of determining an asset's value that takes into account the value of similar assets of competing companies in the industry. It is based on the approach that the investors are interested in the valuation of a share in relation to its peers, not just in the absolute figures on the financial statements. The investor measures a share as a relative value or the attractiveness measured in terms of risk, liquidity and return in relation to a comparable share of another company.

- Valuation using the dividend valuation model (DVM), the dividend discount model (DDM) and the dividend growth model are based on the principle that the current value of the share is the discounted value of all expected dividend payments that the share is going to yield in the future years. The dividends paid by any company can be either fixed or variable. Based on this, there are three scenarios: zero growth rate, constant growth rate and variable growth.

- Valuation using discounted cash flows (DCF) is a method for determining the current value of an investment using future cash flows adjusted for the time value of money. Net present value is the net value of a capital investment or project obtained by discounting all cash outflows and inflows to its present value by using an appropriate discount rate of return.

- The capital asset pricing model (CAPM) describes the relationship between systematic risk and expected return for assets. The rate calculated using CAPM can be used to discount an investment's future cash flows to their present value, which helps to determine the fair price of an investment. The calculated fair value of an asset/investment using CAPM can be compared to its market price. Assuming that CAPM is correct, an investment or share is correctly priced when its market price is the same as its present value of future cash flows, discounted at the rate suggested by CAPM.

- The efficient market hypothesis (EMH) can also be applied together with a share valuation model (such as P/E ratio or DVM), to estimate the intrinsic value of the shares. The market value of the company will only be as good an estimate of intrinsic value as the quality of public information available.
- Shareholder value analysis (SVA) is a management strategy that focuses on the creation of economic value or wealth for shareholders. The basic assumption of SVA is that a company is worth its ability to create value for shareholders, which is measured as the NPV of its future cash flows, discounted at the appropriate cost of capital. Value drivers are identified to understand the drivers of the company that creates value in a company. Free cash flow, a concept central to the idea of SVA, is the surplus cash available after recovering all the costs and incremental investment in non-current assets and working capital.
- Economic value added (EVA) is a measure of profitability and wealth created for shareholders over and above the cost of invested capital.
- Market value added (MVA) measures the value of the company as a result of its existence and operation in the market. It represents the market value added over and above the funds invested by the shareholders and long-term debt holders.

Part five

Chapter 16
Interpretation and evaluation of accounting and financial information

Interpretation and evaluation of accounting and financial information

Overview

This Part consists of a single chapter intended to help draw together several different areas you have learnt about in this book. It will help you to analyse the types of financial information which were introduced in previous chapters, with the purpose of providing practical demonstrations of the interpretation and evaluation of accounting and financial information.

Chapter sixteen
Interpretation and evaluation of accounting and financial information

Contents

1. Introduction
2. Accounting and financial ratios
3. Interpretation and evaluation
4. Limitations of ratios
5. Introduction to the case studies
6. Company A: a FTSE 100 manufacturing company
7. Company B: a retail bakery company
8. Company C: an early stage IT company

1 Introduction

This study text has covered the need to regulate financial reporting and how to prepare and interpret financial statements and the information in a company's annual report. It expanded on these topics to cover sources of finance, the cost of capital and financial decision making. This chapter pulls together key strands from all these areas and focuses on the interpretation and evaluation of accounting and financial information.

This chapter looks at the analysis, interpretation and evaluation of accounting and financial information in a practical and applied way. It applies the knowledge gained elsewhere in this module through three in-depth case studies featuring very different companies.

The case studies show the key financial statements taken from the companies' published annual reports. They show the ratios that are identified in various sections of the study text. The accompanying commentaries shows elements of trend and segment analysis for each company, supporting analysis of the financial performance and position of each company.

The commentaries interpret this information and what it tells us about the companies, as well as evaluate what may be taking place in the companies. To interpret, we often need to bring in other information. This might be further analysis, but equally it can be sector or competitor information, economic indicators, or information contained elsewhere in the financial statements or annual report of a company. Analysis of financial statements is discussed in Chapter 7.

This section should be core preparation for any question requiring:

- the calculation of ratios;
- trend analysis; and
- any questions that require the interpretation or evaluation of accounting and financial information.

This specifically includes the compulsory Section B question. Therefore, this chapter includes investment valuation ratios, which are calculated from publicly available information. It does not include some of the working capital cycle ratios, because these rely on detailed internal information – such as the amount of credit sales, credit purchases and so on – which are not usually available in published financial statements. Ratios such as trade receivables collection, trade payables payments and the cash operating cycle would not be included in a Part B question.

2 Accounting and financial ratios

Financial ratios can be divided into five categories, summarised below and in Table 16.1.

- **Profitability ratios** (covered in Chapter 7): Profitability ratios measure the capability of the company to generate profit compared to revenue, expenses, assets and shareholders' equity. They indicate the effectiveness of the capital and adequacy of profit earned.
- **Asset efficiency or turnover ratios** (covered in Chapter 8): efficiency ratios measure how efficiently a company uses its assets to generate revenue and manages its liabilities.
- **Liquidity or solvency ratios** (covered in Chapter 8): financial managers use liquidity or working capital ratios to control and monitor investment in working capital and monitor long-term solvency.
- **Gearing or debt ratios** (covered in Chapter 12): financial gearing measures the proportion of debt a company has relative to its equity. It is a measure of a company's financial leverage (also called 'trading on equity') and shows the extent to which its operations are funded by interest-bearing lenders versus shareholders. A firm with significantly more debt than equity is regarded as highly geared (or leveraged).
- **Investment or market value ratios** (covered in Chapter 15): investment valuation ratios compare relevant data that will estimate the attractiveness of a potential or existing investment. Investors assess the performance of a company's shares by looking at how ratios compare from one company to another, as well as the ratios above

Profitability (Chapter 7)

Return on capital employed (ROCE) (%) Or accounting rate of return (ARR) (see Chapter 13, section 6)	$\dfrac{\text{Operating profit}}{\text{Equity + non-current liabilities (debt)}} \times 100$ [= capital employed]
Or: return on total assets (ROA) (%)	$\dfrac{\text{Operating profit}}{\text{Total assets}} \times 100$
Return on shareholders' equity (ROE) (%)	$\dfrac{\text{Net profit (profit for the period)}}{\text{Equity}} \times 100$
Operating profit margin (%)	$\dfrac{\text{Operating profit}}{\text{Revenue}} \times 100$
Gross profit margin (%)	$\dfrac{\text{Gross profit}}{\text{Revenue}} \times 100$
Net profit margin (%)	$\dfrac{\text{Net profit (profit for the period)}}{\text{Revenue}} \times 100$

Efficiency (Chapter 8) – asset efficiency and liquidity

Asset turnover (times)	$\dfrac{\text{Revenue}}{\text{Capital employed}}$
Or: total asset turnover (times)	$\dfrac{\text{Revenue}}{\text{Total assets}}$
Non-current asset turnover (times)	$\dfrac{\text{Revenue}}{\text{Non-current assets}}$
Inventories turnover (times)	$\dfrac{\text{Cost of goods sold}}{\text{Inventory}}$
Or: inventory holding period (days)	$\dfrac{\text{Inventory}}{\text{Cost of goods sold}} \times 365$
Rate of collection of trade receivables (days)	$\dfrac{\text{Trade receivables}}{\text{Credit sales (or revenue)}} \times 365$
Rate of payment of trade payables (days)	$\dfrac{\text{Trade payables}}{\text{Credit purchases (or cost of goods sold)}} \times 365$
Working capital cycle (days)	Inventory holding period + Trade receivables collection period – trade payables payment period

liquidity ratios

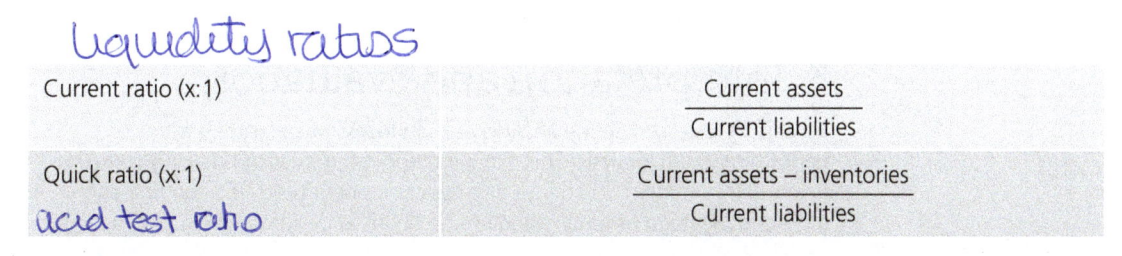

Current ratio (x:1)	$\dfrac{\text{Current assets}}{\text{Current liabilities}}$
Quick ratio (x:1) *acid test ratio*	$\dfrac{\text{Current assets} - \text{inventories}}{\text{Current liabilities}}$

Financial gearing (Chapter 12)

Equity gearing (%)	$\dfrac{\text{Borrowings (debt)} + \text{preference share capital}}{\text{Equity}} \times 100$
Or: Total or capital gearing (%)	$\dfrac{\text{Borrowings (debt)} + \text{preference share capital}}{\text{Capital employed}} \times 100$ [Note: capital employed = equity + debt + preference share capital]
Interest gearing (%)	$\dfrac{\text{Debt interest} + \text{preference share dividends}}{\text{Operating profit} + \text{investment income}} \times 100$
Or: Interest cover (times)	$\dfrac{\text{Operating profit} + \text{investment income}}{\text{Debt interest} + \text{preference share dividends}}$

operating gearing $\dfrac{\text{Fixed costs}}{\text{Variable cost}}$ *(times)*

Investment valuation (Chapter 15)

Dividend payout ratio (DPR) (%)	$\dfrac{\text{Equity share dividend(s) paid in the year}}{\text{Profit for the year}} \times 100$
Or: dividend cover (times)	$\dfrac{\text{Profit for the year}}{\text{Equity share dividend(s) paid in the year}}$
Dividend yield (%)	$\dfrac{\text{Equity share dividend(s) per share}}{\text{Market price of an equity share}} \times 100$
Earnings per share (EPS) (pence or £)	$\dfrac{\text{Profit attributable to equity shareholders for the year}}{\text{Weighted average number of outstanding equity shares during the year}}$
Diluted EPS (pence or £)	$\dfrac{\text{Adjusted profit attributable to equity shareholders for the year}}{\text{Weighted average number of outstanding equity shares during the year} + \text{diluted equity shares}}$
P/E ratio (times)	$\dfrac{\text{Market price of an equity share}}{\text{Earnings per share (EPS)}}$

Table 16.1 Financial ratios

3 Interpretation and evaluation

For this module, we define analysis as the process of calculating ratios or performing trend analysis. This is the methodical process of breaking complex financial information down into discrete component parts. It is the first and most critical, stage of understanding the financial performance of a company.

Interpret and evaluate this information and what it tells users about the company's financial performance and position, can be undertaken by comparing the financial performance of a company year on year, or through a trend analysis of its performance over a number of years. Identifying changes in performance between years is a key aspect of interpreting and evaluating financial statements.

Most published financial statements are consolidated statements for a group of companies, which tend to be companies of a significant size or scale. They are highly likely to be listed companies, or companies seeking a listing. You will encounter case studies of similar companies in the examination.

Other information is often required to effectively interpret information, providing essential context for financial information. This might be:

- further analysis of financial information;
- sector or competitor information;
- general economic indicators; or
- information contained elsewhere in the published financial statements or annual report of a company.

Additional information might provide insight into the following issues.

- **Competitive advantages or disadvantages:** comparing a company's ratios to those of competitors or sector averages often reveals specific financial strengths or weaknesses. It might demonstrate whether the company is more efficient in certain areas of performance, or that it has a higher debt-to-equity ratio and may be particularly vulnerable to a downturn in the industry.
- **Performance trends:** if the gross margin is decreasing, then the company leaders will focus on the direct costs of sales and how they may be managed differently or reduced.
- **Company, financial or economic factors:** any of these might be affecting and contributing to financial performance.
- **Further activities** that the company could consider or undertake to better understand its financial performance and underpin a deeper understanding of where it might improve performance.

4 Limitations of ratios

Ratio analysis provides company owners with trend or time-series analysis and trends within their industry, called industry or cross-sectional analysis. While ratio analysis is useful, it does have its limitations.

- Ratio analysis is only the first step towards financial statement analysis. Final conclusions cannot be drawn based on mere percentages shown by the ratios, as they may not reflect the holistic picture about a company's situation. One needs to be vigilant while conducting research on the company.
- Mathematical calculation does not work when a base figure is zero or negative, as it may not reflect the true picture. For example, if bad debts for the base period and the current period are zero and £500, respectively, one cannot calculate the change as a percentage.
- Company projections based on trend and ratio analysis are inadequate as trends will reflect historical actions which may or may not be applicable in the future. Moreover, ratios are purely based on accounting data. An accurate company forecast depends on economic and industry performance, management plans, supply and demand situations, competitor analysis and so on.
- Benchmarking focuses on company-to-company comparisons of how products and services perform against their toughest competitors, or those companies recognised as leaders in their industry. The benchmark used for financial ratios may not always be the most appropriate.
- The time-series analysis which makes use of historical financial information may be distorted by inflation or seasonal factors.
- Ratios are meaningless without a comparison against trend or industry data and without looking at the causation factors.
- There may be window dressing intended to manipulate financial statements – namely transactions made at the end of a company's year-end or quarter-end to improve the appearance of its financial statements.

5 Introduction to the case studies

In choosing the case studies, consideration has been given to choosing three different industry sectors and three different financial performance and position scenarios. This is intended to show how a strong and methodical approach to the analysis, interpretation and evaluation of financial statements can be applied to companies from different industry sectors and in very different financial situations.

Following a thorough and sound methodological approach to analysis and interpretation is important. However, it is necessary to recognise that it is *how* this is applied to the company in question that gives the approach validity. What does it tell you about the financial performance of this company? What context or other information can you bring in to help with the interpretation? What questions or areas for further analysis does it flag?

The companies selected are as follows.

1. A large manufacturing sector company, which is a FTSE 100-listed public limited company. The company wins and delivers major manufacturing projects on a global basis. It is growing and performing strongly financially.

2. A retail bakery company, which makes ands sell baked products in retail outlets. It is clearly not performing well financially. Indeed, it shows the signs of a company which is getting into financial difficulties.
3. An early stage company, which is a leading company in the area of cyber security and is undertaking market-leading research in that area. However, it is making large deficits and is currently fundraising to generate cash. Its financial position is difficult to interpret.

6 Company A: a FTSE 100 manufacturing company

6.1 The financial and accounting information

A: FTSE 100 manufacturing company

Statements of profit or loss and OCI for the year ended 31 December

	20X5 £m	20X4 £m
Revenue	5,630	5,077
Cost of goods sold	(3,493)	(3,107)
Gross profit	2,137	1,970
Distribution costs	(986)	(972)
Administrative expenses	(674)	(622)
Loss on asset disposals	(23)	(25)
Operating profit	454	351
Finance costs	(64)	(54)
Profit before tax	390	297
Tax expense	(107)	(37)
Profit for the year (net profit)	283	260

Statements of financial position

	20X5 £m	20X4 £m
ASSETS		
Non-current assets		
Goodwill	150	187
Property, plant and equipment	8,201	7,609
Long-term contract receivables	1,210	818
Total non-current assets	9,561	8,614

Current assets		
Inventories	269	285
Trade and other receivables	5,750	5,378
Cash and cash equivalents	468	311
Total current assets	6,487	5,974
Total assets	16,048	14,588
EQUITY AND LIABILITIES		
Share capital	1,008	1,008
Retained earnings	1,045	918
Total equity	2,053	1,926
Non-current liabilities		
Long-term borrowings	6,528	5,937
Deferred revenue	1,070	778
Total non-current liabilities	7,598	6,715
Current liabilities		
Trade and other payables	6,214	5,809
Tax and related payments	183	138
Total current liabilities	6,397	5,947
Total liabilities	13,995	12,662
Total equity and liabilities	16,048	14,588
Share information		
Shares at £0.02 nominal value	50,400,000	50,400,000
Share price (market)	£141.20	£114.80
Dividend (per share)	£3.10	£3.00

Notes

- Retained earnings for 20X5 of £1.045m are calculated from £918m + £283m – £156m dividends paid.
- Company A signed contracts for £11.4 billion worth of future work in 20X4. This was a record for the company and much greater than its regular £4 to £5 billion of orders p.a. and included two very large long-term contracts.
- The share price of Company A was boosted by the news of these very large long-term contracts.
- Company A invested over £900 million in 20X5 on new property, plant and equipment needed to fulfil these very large long-term contracts which was partly funded by an increase in long-term borrowings.
- Company A operates on an international market and is exposed to volatility in exchange rates, especially in relation to US dollars and the Euro.

6.2 The ratios

	Class	Ratio	Formula	20X5	20X4
1	Profitability ratios	Return on capital employed	(Operating profit ÷ (debt + equity)) × 100	5.3%	4.5%
2		Return on shareholders' equity	Net profit ÷ equity × 100	13.8%	13.5%
3		Gross profit margin	Gross profit ÷ revenue × 100	38.0%	38.8%
4		Operating profit margin	Operating profit (PBIT) ÷ revenue × 100	8.1%	6.9%
5		Net profit margin	Net profit ÷ revenue × 100	5.0%	5.1%
6	Efficiency ratios	Asset turnover	Revenue ÷ (debt + equity)	0.7 times	0.6 times
7		Non-current assets turnover	Revenue ÷ non-current assets	0.6 times	0.6 times
8		Inventory holding period	Inventory ÷ cost of goods sold × 365	28.1 days	33.5 days
9	Liquidity ratios	Current ratio	Current assets ÷ current liabilities	1.0	1.0
10		Quick ratio	(Current assets – inventories) ÷ Current liabilities	1.0	1.0
11	Gearing ratios	Capital gearing	(Debt ÷ (debt + equity)) × 100	76.1%	75.5%
12		Equity gearing	Debt ÷ equity × 100	318.0%	308.3%
13		Interest cover	(PBIT ÷ interest expense)	7.1 times	6.5 times
14	Investment ratios	Earnings per share (EPS)	Net profit ÷ average outstanding shares	£5.62	£5.16
15		Price/earnings ratio (P/E)	Market price per share ÷ EPS	25.1	22.2
16		Dividend yield	Dividends per share ÷ market price per share × 100	2.2%	2.6%

6.3 Interpretation and evaluation

Profitability

Both return ratios improved in 20X5 compared with 20X4. In 20X5, Company A had a higher capability to generate profit compared with either of these bases. The higher these ratios, the more favourable it is for the company, as they indicate increased effectiveness of capital and asset utilisation.

To interpret the profitability of Company A, there are a few additional steps or pieces of information we might require. If we knew the ROCE for other manufacturing companies in the same area of work was 10%, this would assist our interpretation. Assuming this is the case, we would be able to interpret the ROCE for Company A in 20X5 as strong compared with its market sector. We could conclude that Company A was efficient at generating profit from the capital it utilised.

Margin ratios might assist our assessment further. The gross margin for Company A dropped between 20X4 and 20X5 from 38.8% to 38.0%. Gross profit refers to the margin that company charges above cost of goods sold. It indicates how much the company is earning, considering the required costs to produce its goods and services.

The underlying drivers behind this ratio are selling prices, product mix, purchase costs, production costs and inventory valuations. We would need further information or analyses to interpret which of these might be the main drivers for Company A. For example, we can see that revenue for Company A rose from £5.077 million to £5.63 million: an increase of £553 million or 10.9%. This is a significant increase for a company of this size and maturity, likely to be well above any underlying inflationary pressure and, therefore, represents a substantial increase in the volume of sales. The notes to the financial statements tell us that Company A has won large new contracts (or clients, or markets). These could be at a lower gross margin. If not, this would still be a reasonable interpretation of the analysis we have.

The operating profit margin for Company A increased between 20X4 and 20X5 from 6.9% to 8.1%. This is essentially the percentage of revenue remaining after accounting for operating expenses. Companies with higher operating profit margins can comfortably pay for costs and interest.

Several factors such as employment policy, depreciation methods, write-offs of bad debts and selling and marketing (distribution) expenses may impact on the ratio. Some trend analysis might help us analyse and interpret this.

The distribution costs in 20X5 are £986 million and 17.5% of revenue; in 20X4 they were £972 million and 19.1% of revenue. If they had remained at 19.1% in 20X5, they would have been at £1,075 million and the operating profit margin would have decreased. Analysis tells us something significant has happened to make distribution costs more efficient in 20X5 and this has increased the operating margin. Here we can see how some further analysis assists with interpreting the change in the operating margin. It is possible this is due to winning the two large new contracts, but with relatively low direct selling or distribution costs. There could be other interpretations, but this is a reasonable one.

The net profit margin for Company A reduced marginally between 20X4 and 20X5, down from 5.1% to 5.0%. We are most likely to interpret this as a well-managed and stable company, producing a good level of net profit. We might be able to evaluate this further if we knew that Company A's main competitor produced a net margin of, say, 3% in these two years.

Some segment reporting analysis could also be useful in interpreting the changes in profitability in Company A. It could clearly indicate if this was a general improvement or if it was specific to one segment of the company. It might be that one product line or market is performing less well and this would clearly help us to understand what was happening and why.

Efficiency

Company A is profitable and is investing in more long-term assets. Its non-current assets have both increased significantly in 20X5, up from £8.614 million to £9.561 million: a £947,000 or 11% increase. There are also increases in current assets and shareholders' equity. We can see a significant growth in assets: efficiency ratios measure how efficiently a company uses its assets to generate revenue and manage its liabilities. Is Company A doing this efficiently?

In terms of net asset turnover, Company A has increased this from 0.7 times from 0.6 times. The increase in net assets has been exceeded by the level of increase in revenue. Company A has increased its overall ability to generate revenue from its assets. Given the material increase in total assets, this is good performance and suggests that the company is increasing its assets in an appropriate manner. Shareholders might take particular notice of this.

The non-current asset turnover ratio is stable at 0.6 times. Given the 11% increase in non-current assets, it is good to see this ratio has not moved. There could be expected to be a time delay between this increase and additional revenue being generated, which would lead to this ratio dropping. This has not happened for Company A and the strong revenue growth has occurred at the same speed, which is good news.

From the financial statements, we can calculate another type of efficiency ratio: the inventory days for Company A. This decreased from 33.5 days to 28.1 days in 20X5.

Any downward trend in the inventory days ratio means that inventory levels are being kept under control in relation to the level of sales. However, care must be taken not to let the inventory days ratio fall too low, as this may eventually result in inventory shortages when demand fluctuates. To interpret this further we would need to note the following.

- The days of inventory on hand will vary from industry to industry. To make comparisons you need to use a comparable company operating in your sector.
- The days in inventory should be a low as possible without causing inventory shortages. It is generally accepted that money tied up in inventory earns very little or nothing for the company.

Liquidity

Companies need cash. The primary motive of holding cash is to maintain a financial position in situations of certainty and uncertainty. Therefore, every analysis of a company's financial statements will look at liquidity – the ability of a company to turn its assets into cash.

The current ratio for Company A in 20X4 was 1:1 and this remained at 1:1 in 20X5. A current ratio of less than one could indicate liquidity problems:

Company A is above this level, but only just. While there is a general target current ratio of 2:1, the acceptability of the ratio will depend on the nature of the company and how it compares with those of a similar company.

However, the fact that the current ratio has stayed at 1:1 despite the 11% growth in revenue and large profits, would suggest that further analysis of the reasons for this would be helpful. We have seen that Company A is profitable, so it is not due to an inability to generate profits. This could be due to Company A using some of its current assets to invest in an investment opportunity, with the intention of increasing profitability and cash generation in the future. This would be looked upon favourably by shareholders or other investors and looks likely to be the situation in Company A.

This indicates how analysis can reveal what has happened in the performance of a company, but it alone cannot tell us whether this is a good thing for the company or a cause for concern. This requires additional information and comparators so that we can interpret the analysis. Sometimes this is provided in the notes to the financial statements.

It is worth noting that the quick ratio for Company A has also remained flat at 1:1 to 1:1. The quick ratio excludes inventory which cannot easily and quickly be converted into cash. It would not appear that inventory levels are a material factor for Company A. This is interesting, given it is a manufacturing company. One possibility is that that Company A utilises a just in time inventory approach.

Gearing

Ratio analysis shows us that the capital and equity gearing for Company A both increased materially between 20X4 and 20X5. The capital gearing increased from 75.5% to 76.1%. The equity gearing increased from 308.3% to 318.0%. Company A is taking on materially more debt to finance the company in relation to its equity funding.

In absolute terms, we can see that long-term borrowings increased from £5,937 million to £6,528 million while retained earnings and therefore equity levels reduced. When using ratios to analyse a company's performance, it can be useful to refer to the actual numbers in the financial statements. This is an increase in long-term borrowings of £591 million or 10%.

Gearing measures the proportion of debt a company has relative to its equity. It is a measure of a company's financial leverage (also called 'trading on equity') and shows the extent to which its operations are funded by interest-bearing lenders versus shareholders. A firm with significantly more debt than equity is regarded as highly geared (or leveraged). With comparators, we would be able to see if Company A was highly geared or not and this would help us interpret the analysis.

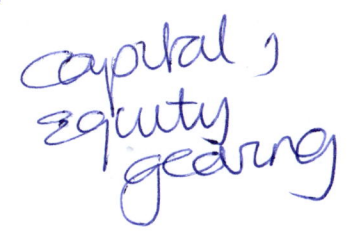

We can interpret that Company A has significantly increased its long-term borrowings and as it is a profitable company it is reasonable to assume that has been for some form of investment. The significant increase in non-current assets would support that. Assuming the company is well managed, this investment will be in a project or assets intended to increase the long-term profitability and cash generation of the company. This would be viewed very differently by shareholders and other investors than an increase in gearing to support the short-term cash flow needs of the company. We might ascertain this without reading the notes to the financial statements, but they confirm that Company A has invested in new property, plant and equipment to deliver the large new contracts.

We can also see that this level of investment would seem to be affordable to Company A. The interest cover ratio indicates how many times greater profit before interest and tax (PBIT) is than annual interest payments. The higher this is, the less risk is involved. This increased for Company A from 6.5 to 7.1 times. Even though Company A would be considered to be increasing its gearing, it does not appear to be taking on a level of borrowing that is likely to cause the company financial distress.

Investment

There is a wide array of ratios that can be used by investors and shareholders to evaluate the performance of a company's shares and assess its valuation. Investment valuation ratios compare relevant data that will estimate the attractiveness of a potential or existing investment. Investors assess the performance of a company's shares by looking at how ratios compare from one company to another.

From an equity shareholder's point of view, the relevant information will be included in the following ratios:

- earnings per share (EPS): increased from £5.16 to £5.62
- price/earnings (P/E): increased from 22.2 to 25.1

As EPS shows the proportion of profits available for equity shareholders, this is the basic measure of a company's performance from an equity shareholder's point of view. This has increased materially (by 8.9%) in 20X5, so we would expect the equity shareholders to be pleased with this.

The P/E ratio indicates the relationship between the market value of shares and the profit for the year. The P/E ratio valuation method is a simple and commonly used method of valuation. This approach uses the price/earnings ratio of a similar quoted company to value shares in unquoted companies. Company A's P/E ratio has increased, but to know whether it's at a good level we really need to have comparator information. However, we can say that Company A's P/E ratio has improved.

We can also look at the dividend yield for Company A. Dividend yield indicates how much a company pays out in dividends each year, relative to its share price. Normally, only profitable companies pay out dividends. A stable dividend yield can be a sign of a stable and safer company.

The dividend yield has decreased from 2.6% to 2.2%. This is because the dividend increased in 20X5, but the market price of the shares increased more significantly. As the dividend increased, this is not indicative of a problem but could be a factor for investors valuing the company.

Conclusion

Company A is a high-performing and well-managed company. We can support this interpretation because:

- Company A is profitable and its profitability is increasing. Its revenue is increasing significantly and overall it appears to be managing its costs well.
- Company A is increasing its long-term borrowings and gearing. It appears to be investing in some projects or assets intended to improve the long-term profitability and cash generation of the company. It appears to be doing this in an affordable way.
- Company A has a reasonable level of liquidity. It has not increased in line with profits in 20X5 and we are assuming this is part of funding some investment.
- Company A appears to be maintaining its overall level of efficiency, although we may want to investigate further or monitor the non-current assets turnover ratio.
- Company A's EPS and P/E ratios improved.

This shows us how analysis and interpretation can identify a company which is performing well financially. However, it can be equally adept at helping us to identify a company which is not.

7 Company B: a retail baking company

7.1 Financial and accounting information

Statements of profit or loss and OCI for the year ended 31 December

	20X5 £'000	20X4 £'000
Revenue	37,955	39,528
Cost of goods sold	(32,700)	(33,163)
Gross profit	5,255	6,365
Distribution costs	(375)	(340)
Administrative expenses	(5,246)	(4,440)
Operating profit/(loss)	(366)	1,585
Finance costs	(331)	(245)
Profit/(loss) before tax	(697)	1,340
Tax expense	(15)	(128)
Profit/(loss) for the year (net profit/(loss))	(712)	1,212

Statements of financial position as at 31 December

	20X5 £'000	20X4 £'000
ASSETS		
Non-current assets		
Goodwill	89	103
Property, plant and equipment	11,242	12,604
Total non-current assets	11,331	12,707
Current assets		
Inventories	410	440
Trade and other receivables	2,207	2,931
Cash and cash equivalents	748	730
Total current assets	3,365	4,101
Total assets	14,696	16,808
EQUITY AND LIABILITIES		
Share capital	5,148	5,148
Retained earnings	396	1,108
Total equity	5,544	6,256
Non-current liabilities		
Long-term borrowings	1,142	658
Others	2,366	5,394
Total non-current liabilities	3,508	6,052
Current liabilities		
Trade and other payables	4,807	3,521
Others	837	979
Total current liabilities	5,644	4,500
Total liabilities	9,152	10,552
Total equity and liabilities	14,696	16,808
Share Information		
Shares of £1 nominal value	5,148,000	5,148,000
Share Price (market)	£21.72	£47.50
Dividend (per share)	0.0p	12.8p

Notes
- Retained earnings for 20X5 of £396,000 are calculated from £1.108m − £712,000.

- The year 20X5 was a challenging year for Company B. The company faced continuing challenging trading conditions in its country of operations, due to high street retail outlets experiencing reduced footfall and increasing cost pressures.
- The notes to the financial statements show that there was an exceptional item in 20X4: the waiver of an inter-company loan. This reduced administrative expenses by £1.295 million.
- In the independent auditor's report for 20X5, they had **nothing to report** in respect of the following matters:
    - the director's use of the going-concern basis of accounting in preparation of the financial statements is not appropriate; or
    - that may cast significant doubt about the company's ability to continue to adopt the going concern basis of accounting for a period of at least 12 months from the date when the financial statements are authorised for issue.
- The directors have not disclosed in the financial statements any identified material uncertainties.

7.2 The ratios

	Class	Ratio	Formula	20X5	20X4
1	Profitability ratios	Return on capital employed	(Operating profit ÷ (debt + equity)) × 100	minus 5.5%	22.9%
2		Return on shareholders' equity	Net profit ÷ equity × 100	minus 12.8%	19.4%
3		Gross profit margin	Gross profit ÷ revenue × 100	13.8%	16.1%
4		Operating profit margin	Operating profit (PBIT) ÷ revenue × 100	minus 1.0%	4.0%
5		Net profit margin	Net profit ÷ revenue × 100	minus 1.9%	3.1%
6	Efficiency ratios	Asset turnover	Revenue ÷ (debt + equity)	5.7 times	5.7 times
7		Non-current assets turnover	Revenue ÷ non-current assets	3.3 times	3.1 times
8		Inventory holding period	Inventory ÷ cost of goods sold × 365	4.6 days	4.8 days
9	Liquidity ratios	Current ratio	Current assets ÷ current liabilities	0.6	0.9
10		Quick ratio	(Current assets − inventory) ÷ Current liabilities	0.5	0.8

	Class	Ratio	Formula	20X5	20X4
11	Gearing ratios	Capital gearing	(Debt ÷ (debt + equity)) × 100	17.1%	9.5%
12		Equity gearing	Debt ÷ equity × 100	20.6%	10.5%
13		Interest cover	(PBIT ÷ interest expense)	minus 1.1 times	6.5 times
14	Investment ratios	Earnings per share (EPS)	Net profit ÷ average outstanding shares	£0.00	£0.24
15		Price/earnings ratio (P/E)	Market price per share ÷ EPS	0.0	237.5
16		Dividend yield	Dividends per share ÷ market price per share × 100	0.0	0.269%

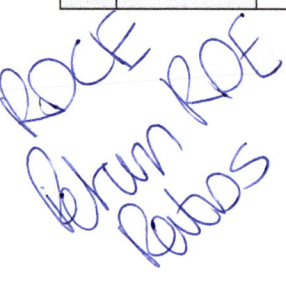

7.3 Analysis and interpretation

Profitability

It is notable that both the return ratios worsened in 20X5 compared with 20X4. This means that Company A has had a lower capability to generate profit in 20X5 compared with any of these bases.

Indeed, in 20X5, both of these return ratios are negative because Company B made an operating and a net loss in 20X5. Given the level of loss made by Company B and the level of decline in profitability from 20X4, we already have enough analysis to be concerned about the financial performance of Company B. Some event or combination of events has taken place in 20X5 that have materially affected the financial performance of the company, quickly turning it from a profitable company to a loss-making one.

The margin ratios might assist our interpretation further. At gross margin level, the gross margin for Company B dropped between 20X4 and 20X5, from 16.1% to 13.8%. Gross profit refers to the margin that company charges above cost of goods sold. It indicates how much the company is earning, considering the required costs to produce its goods and services.

The underlying drivers behind this ratio are selling prices, product mix, purchase costs, production costs and inventory valuations. Something within the core company for this retail bakery company has materially changed in 20X5. We can see that overall gross profit dropped from £6.365 million to £5.255 million – a drop of £1.108 million. This represents a major part of the drop in both operating and net profit.

Information on the marketplace and the competitors for Company B – which might be included in its annual report – would likely give us the context we require to interpret this significant drop. Were there specific market or economic factors that affected the entire sector, or more specific issues for Company B?

The operating profit margin for Company B decreased between 20X4 and 20X5 from a positive 4.0% to −1.0%. Essentially, this is the percentage of revenue remaining after accounting for operating expenses. A negative operating profit margin is a clear indication of performance problems, as it shows the company is not making any profit even before it even considers any financing or tax costs.

From the financial statements, we can see that this is due to a significant increase in distribution costs and administrative expenses, from £4.78 million in 20X4 to £5.62 million in 20X5. You would see this trend with a vertical trend analysis of Company B's statements of profit or loss and OCI. An extract of that would be as follows, showing costs as a percentage of revenue:

Line item	20X5	20X4	Trend
Cost of goods sold	86.2%	83.9%	Uptrend
Distribution costs	1.0%	0.9%	Uptrend
Administrative costs	13.8%	12.1%	Uptrend
Finance costs	0.87%	0.62%	Uptrend

Table 16.2: Vertical trend analysis, Company B

Vertical trend analysis is clearly designed to show this sort of trend. The analysis in Table 16.2 shows that administrative costs increased from 12.1% of revenue in 20X4 to 13.8% of revenue in 20X5. You use trend analysis to identify this type of material change and then investigate further.

This increase in administrative expenses is despite the decrease in revenue and gross margin. Normally, you would expect the company management to be seeking to control and reduce these costs to protect the operating profit. This is a further indication that something of concern is taking place at Company B.

The notes to the financial statements do state that in 20X4 there was an exceptional item, this being the waiver of an inter-company loan which reduced the administration costs by £1.295 million. If this had not been included, then Company B would have had administration costs in 20X4 of £6.075 million and would have made a net loss of £84,000. The analysis led us to look for this and the notes to the financial statements gave us material further information to assist us with interpreting the figures.

The net profit margin for Company B also decreased between 20X4 and 20X5 from a positive 3.1% to minus 1.9%. This net loss and level of decline would allow us to identify that Company B has some significant financial performance concerns.

Efficiency

Company B is not profitable and its long-term assets base is reducing. Its non-current assets and total assets both decreased significantly in 20X5. Efficiency ratios measure how efficiently a company uses its assets to generate revenue and manage its liabilities. Is Company B doing this efficiently?

For Company B we have the following two efficiency ratios:

- The net asset turnover ratio has remained at 5.7 times.
- The non-current asset turnover ratio has increased from 3.1 to 3.3 times

Overall, these asset turnover ratios do not seem to show any serious concerns about Company B. This is where interpretation needs to take a holistic approach, rather than simply concluding all is well when it comes to efficiency at Company B by looking at these ratios in isolation. We already know that Company B has negative trends in terms of profitability, gearing and liquidity. We also know that the net, non-current and total assets of Company B are declining materially.

The total assets of Company B have reduced from £16.808 million in 20X4 down to £14.696 million in 20X4. This is a reduction of £2.112 million (12.5%) and is a more significant cause of concern than the fact the total assets turnover has increased marginally. Efficiency of use of the assets may appear to have been increased, but what is really happening is a material reduction in the total assets of the company because of the significant net loss.

It is more likely that there may be some timing factors at play. For example, revenue for Company B may have dropped more strongly at the end of 20X5 when compared with 20X4 and the revenue projections for 20X6 may show much lower revenue numbers. Revenue is the numerator in all of these asset efficiency calculations. We would be very interested to see the monthly figures for 20X5 and the forward projections for 20X6 before making any conclusions on the efficiency of Company B.

From the financial statements we can calculate another type of efficiency ratio: inventory days for Company B. This decreased from 4.8 days to 4.6 days in 20X5. This is a retail bakery company, producing a perishable product, so one would expect inventory levels and days to be low.

Any downward trend in the inventory days ratio normally means that inventory levels are being kept under control in relation to the level of revenue. However, care must be taken not to let the inventory days ratio fall too low as this may eventually result in inventory shortages as demand fluctuates. It is possible the tough trading conditions are affecting this and fewer baked products are being made. In order to interpret this further we would need to note:

- The days of inventory on hand will vary from industry to industry. To make comparisons you need to use a comparable company operating in your sector. These numbers are much lower than Company A, as that is a manufacturing company.
- The days in inventory should be a low as possible without causing inventory shortages. It is generally accepted that money tied up in inventory earns very little or nothing for the company and in the case of a bakery company could lead to wasted products.

Liquidity

The current ratio for Company B in 20X4 was 0.9:1; this dropped to 0.6:1 in 20X5. A current ratio of less than one could indicate liquidity problems and Company B is below this level. This would appear to be a major cause of concern. Not only is the current ratio below 1, it has also decreased materially. This has the makings of a company heading for a cash crisis, with concerns about the ongoing viability of the company.

Our concern about Company B based on the current ratio is increased by the fact that we have seen this despite an increase in gearing (see below). If the increase in long-term borrowing has been made to support the cash flow needs of the company, then it is only partially succeeding in doing that.

The quick ratio for Company B has a very similar trend to the current ratio, dropping from 0.8:1 to 0.5:1. The quick ratio excludes inventory which cannot quickly and easily be converted into cash. For a retail bakery, inventory might be considered as a quick or liquid asset (as a perishable product with a very short shelf life) and not excluded and this would be a valid approach in this case.

However, it would not appear that a material change in inventory levels is what has caused the reduction in the current ratio. We can be clear that it is the fact that Company B is making a net loss, affecting its liquidity.

Gearing

Ratio analysis shows us that the capital and equity gearing for Company B both increased materially between 20X4 and 20X5. The capital gearing increased from 9.5% to 17.1%. The equity gearing increased from 10.5% to 20.6%. Company B is taking on materially more debt to finance the company in relation to its equity funding.

These do not seem like high gearing levels. The gearing levels for Company A – which we concluded was a solvent, profitable and well-managed company – were at four or five times this level. However, Company A was from a very different sector and was performing well in terms of profitability. Company B clearly has a profitability problem: that, combined with the increase in gearing, is something worth taking note of.

With direct comparators, we would be able to see if Company B was highly geared or not. This would help us interpret the analysis. All we can interpret from these numbers is that Company B has significantly increased its long-term borrowings and as it is not a profitable company it is reasonable to be concerned about this. As it is not a profitable company, it would be reasonable for shareholders and other investors to be concerned if this increase in gearing is to support the short-term cash flow of the company.

The interest cover ratio indicates how many times greater PBIT is than annual interest costs. The higher this is, the less risk is involved. This increased for Company B from (positive) 6.5 times to −1.1 times. Company B is increasing its gearing and is potentially taking on a level of borrowing that is likely to cause the company financial distress. The very fact that Company B has a negative interest cover ratio is a further indication of the serious trouble the company has got itself into is in.

Investment

From an equity shareholder's point of view, the relevant information about Company B will be contained in the following ratios:

- earnings per share: decreased from 0.24p to 0.0p
- price/earnings: decreased from 237.5 to 0.0

As EPS shows the proportion of profits available for equity shareholders, this is the basic measure of a company's performance from an equity shareholder's point of view. This has decreased materially in 20X5, so we would expect equity shareholders to be unhappy with this. An EPS of 0 means the company has traded at a net loss.

The P/E ratio indicates the relationship between the market value of shares and the profit for the year. The P/E ratio valuation method is a simple and commonly used method of valuation. This approach uses the price/earnings ratio of a similar quoted company to value shares in unquoted companies. The P/E ratio has increased, but in order to know whether it is at a good level we need to have comparator information. However, we can say that Company B also has a P/E ratio of 0, as it made a net loss.

We can also look at the dividend yield for Company B. Dividend yield indicates how much a company pays out in dividends each year relative to its share price. Normally, only profitable companies pay out dividends. A stable dividend yield can be a sign of a stable and safer company. This has decreased for Company B from 0.269% to 0.0% because no dividend was paid in 20X5.

The investment valuation ratios make it very clear that Company B does not look like a company ripe for investment. All of the key ratios that a potential investor would use have declined materially and are actually at zero in 20X5.

Conclusion

Company B is performing poorly financially and does not appear to be a well-managed company. We can support this interpretation because:

- Company B is making a loss and that loss-making is increasing. Its revenue is decreasing significantly and it does not appear to be managing its costs well overall.
- Company B is increasing its long-term borrowings and gearing; it appears to be doing this to support its current cash flow needs to a level that is neither affordable nor sustainable.
- Company B has a poor level of liquidity, which has reduced materially in 20X5 and is likely to be approaching a critical level.
- Company B appears to be maintaining its overall level of efficiency. We may want to investigate further as we suspect that revenue may be on a rapidly declining trend and we are more concerned by its material drop in total assets.
- Company B had a decrease in EPS and P/E ratio and indeed both were at zero in 20X5.

It is no surprise that Company B became insolvent in 20X6 and went into administration some six months into the next trading year. The sharp decline and material financial issues are evident in the analysis and interpretation. Indeed, one suspects we would likely have already had cause for concern if we had analysed the 20X2 and 20X3 financial statements.

However, it is not always easy to interpret the financial performance of a company from financial statements alone.

8 Company C: an early stage IT company

8.1 The financial and accounting information

Statements of profit or loss and OCI for the year ended 31 December

	20X5	20X4
	£'000	£'000
Revenue	106,798	59,717
Cost of goods sold	(11,516)	(5,428)
Gross profit	95,282	54,289
Distribution costs	(78,535)	(51,198)
Administrative expenses	(13,963)	(6,537)
Research and development costs	(24,830)	(22,764)
Operating loss	(22,046)	(26,210)
Finance costs	0	0
Loss before tax	(22,046)	(26,210)
Tax expense	1,167	(1,284)
Loss for the year (Net loss)	(20,879)	(27,494)

Statements of financial position

	20X5	20X4
	£'000	£'000
ASSETS		
Non-current assets		
Goodwill	7,233	5,762
Property, plant and equipment	3,942	1,963
Right-of-use assets	22,240	11,877
Other	24,927	16,048
Total non-current assets	58,342	35,650

Current assets

Inventories	16,403	10,835
Trade and other receivables	47,263	38,022
Cash and cash equivalents	57,213	24,362
Total current assets	120,879	73,219
Total assets	179,221	108,869

EQUITY AND LIABILITIES

Share capital	134,165	96,616
Retained earnings	(91,208)	(70,329)
Total equity	42,957	26,287

Non-current liabilities

Long-term borrowing	0	0
Deferred income	18,136	16,713
Lease liabilities	21,115	11,346
Total non-current liabilities	39,251	28,059

Current liabilities

Trade and other payables	34,884	19,602
Deferred income	62,129	34,921
Total current liabilities	97,013	54,523
Total liabilities	136,264	82,582
Total equity and liabilities	179,221	108,869

Share information

Shares with nominal value of £1	134,165,000	96,616,000
Share price (market)	£2.76	£2.40
Dividend (per share)	0	0

Notes

- Retained earnings for 20X5 of minus £91.208m are calculated from minus £70.239m less the £20.879m net loss.
- Company C is a world-leading cyber security and artificial intelligence company.
- Founded In 20X1, the company has grown rapidly and employs over 1,200 people in its offices in the UK and USA.
- Company C has significant levels of deferred income due to receiving subscriptions (for use of specialised software) in advance which are then

released over the life of the contracts. This was £76.4 million at year end 20X5 and £49.7 million at year end 20X4. This is included in 'current liabilities – others'.
- The right-of-use assets are long-term leases relating to the main software sold by the company. These are capitalised under IFRS 16, hence the large non-current lease liabilities.
- In October 20X5, the company raised £50 million of fundraising, led by a venture capital firm, all included in equity shares.
- The inventories are hardware appliances for the deployment of the company's software.
- Company C identifies Its key financial risk as securing enough investment to meet foreseeable cash needs. Cash flow is forecast and closely monitored, as are working capital requirements.
- Company C had a net cash outflow of £12.914 million from operations in 20X5.

8.2 The ratios

	Class	Ratio	Formula	20X5	20X4
1	Profitability ratios	Return on capital employed	(Operating profit ÷ (debt + equity)) × 100	minus 51.3%	minus 99.7%
2		Return on shareholders' equity	Net profit ÷ equity × 100	minus 48.6%	minus 104.6%
3		Gross profit margin	Gross profit ÷ revenue × 100	89.2%	90.9%
4		Operating profit margin	Operating profit (PBIT) ÷ revenue × 100	minus 20.6%	minus 43.9%
5		Net profit margin	Net profit ÷ revenue × 100	minus 19.5%	minus 46.0%
6	Efficiency ratios	Asset turnover	Revenue ÷ (debt + equity)	2.5 times	2.3 times
7		Non-current assets turnover	Revenue ÷ non-current assets	1.8 times	1.7 times
8		Inventory holding period	Inventory ÷ cost of goods sold × 365	519.9 days	728.6 days
9	Liquidity ratios	Current ratio	Current assets ÷ current liabilities	1.2	1.3
10		Quick ratio	(Current assets – inventories) ÷ Current liabilities	1.1	1.1
11	Gearing ratios	Capital gearing	(Debt ÷ (debt + equity)) × 100	0.0%	0.0%
12		Equity gearing	Debt ÷ equity × 100	0.0%	0.0%
13		Interest cover	(PBIT ÷ interest expense)	0.0	0.0

	Class	Ratio	Formula	20X5	20X4
14		Earnings per share (EPS)	Net profit ÷ average outstanding shares	0.0	0.0
15	Investment ratios	Price/earnings ratio (P/E)	Market price per share ÷ EPS	0.0	0.0
16		Dividend yield	Dividends per share ÷ market price per share x 100	0.0	0.0

8.3 Analysis and interpretation

Profitability

It is notable that both of the return ratios – return on capital employed (ROCE) and shareholders' equity (ROE) – improved in 20X5 compared with 20X4. In 20X5, Company C has had a higher capability to generate profit (i.e. a smaller loss) compared with either of these bases.

Both of these return ratios are negative in 20X5 because Company C made an operating and a net loss in 20X5. Although they all improved materially, a ROCE of minus 51.3% is clearly still a matter of note. We know this is an early stage company, albeit a world-leading one, but we still need to note these negative return ratios. If we were simply looking at these profitability return ratios, we might be very concerned about the financial performance of Company C.

The margin ratios might assist our interpretation further. Starting at gross margin level, the gross margin for Company C dropped slightly between 20X4 and 20X5, from 90.9% to 89.2%. Gross profit refers to the margin that company charges above cost of goods sold. It indicates how much the company is earning considering the required costs to produce its goods and services. Clearly, Company C is providing services that require a low level of direct cost and a high level of gross margin.

Company C saw very strong revenue growth between 20X4 and 20X5. Revenue grew from £59.717 million to £106.798 million. This is growth of £47.081 million or 79%, which is a remarkable level of growth in one year. To have achieved that and in doing so to have maintained a gross margin at around 90%, is a good indicator for the future of Company C. We can see that overall gross profit increased from £54.289 million to £95.282 million because of this revenue growth. Company C certainly appears to be growing a profitable core business.

When the numbers are changing materially like this, a horizontal trend analysis helps us interpret this further. See Table 16.3 for an extract.

Line item	20X5	20X4	Change	Change
	£	£	£	%
Revenue	106,798	59,717	+ 47,081	+ 78.8%
Distribution costs	78,535	51,198	+ 27,337	+ 53.4%
Administrative expenses	13,963	6,537	+ 7,426	+ 113.6%
Research and development costs	24,830	22,764	+ 2,066	+ 9.1%

Table 16.3 Horizontal trend analysis, Company C

A significant growth in distribution costs and a larger percentage growth in administrative expenses, mean that the improvements in revenue and gross margin did not lead to material improvements in the operating loss or net loss. Company C is growing very rapidly, with a revenue growth of 78.8%. It appears to be scaling up its operations at an equally rapid speed. If the rapid growth in revenue continues, we might expect some economies of scale to come into play on the operating costs of the company. At that stage, operating and net profits might begin to appear.

A negative operating and net margin would normally be clear indicators of serious financial performance problems. However, when we take the context into account for Company C, as well as the revenue and profit increases, it is not as simple or clear as that. Simple analysis could be misleading in this case.

We know that Company C is a world-leading cyber security and artificial intelligence company and that its revenue and gross profits are growing very rapidly. Further analysis is required to understand Company C: the liquidity and gearing ratios will be critical to evaluating this company.

Efficiency

Efficiency ratios measure how efficiently a company uses its assets to generate revenue and manage its liabilities. Is Company C doing this efficiently?

Company C has had some material moves in equity and non-current asset levels. It should be noted that Company C has no long-term borrowings, although it does have the right-of-use assets accounted for as leases. The efficiency ratios are as follows:

- The net asset turnover ratio has increased from 2.3 to 2.5 times.
- The non-current asset turnover ratio has increased from 1.7 to 1.8 times.

It would appear that, in spite of some material changes in its asset base, Company C is performing well in generating revenue from this base. If anything, it is showing an improving trend in its ability to do this. We could only tell whether these are strong performing numbers overall by benchmarking with similar companies. Care would need to be taken to select close competitors or comparators against which to assess the performance of Company C.

From the financial statements, we can calculate another type of efficiency ratio: the inventory days for Company A. This decreased from 728.6 days to 519.9 days in 20X5. We can see that in 20X4 and 20X5 that inventory levels are valued at two years of the cost of sales number.

Any downward trend in the inventory days ratio means that inventory levels are being kept under control in relation to the level of sales. These do appear to be very high figures. We would want to understand more about the nature of Company C's inventory and how it uses it to deliver its service. It is an IT services company, so the inventory days ratio may not be a meaningful ratio at all. The notes tell us that the inventories are hardware appliances for the deployment of the company's software. This could be a secondary business line for Company C. Alternatively, if the hardware is specialised it could be a part of their core business. We might look at this quite differently depending on which of those is true.

Liquidity

The current ratio for Company C in 20X4 and 20X5 decreased from 1.3:1 to 1.2:1. A current ratio of greater than one is a general minimum indicator for reasonable solvency. As an early stage company and one still making losses, maintaining solvency has been identified by Company C as their key financial risk. It would appear from these ratios that they are managing this effectively at this point.

The quick ratio for Company C has a very similar trend to the current ratio and has been maintained at 1.1:1. The quick ratio excludes inventory which cannot easily and quickly be converted into cash. For Company C, this means hardware appliances for the deployment of their software. Even on this indicator, Company C is managing to stay above 1:1.

As Company C is taking on more equity shareholders and therefore diluting ownership in order to secure its working capital, it would be prudent not to have excessive amounts of cash within the company. Current and quick ratios just above 1:1 would seem to be appropriate.

We do not have a statement of cash flows for Company C, but it is reasonable to assume that the £20.879 million net loss would have resulted in a significant net outflow from operating activities. This has probably been the way Company C has been performing financially since it was founded. Indeed, we can see from the notes that Company C had a net cash outflow of £12.914 million from operations in 20X5. Therefore, liquidity is the key financial risk for the company.

Company C is clearly funding the cash flow needs of the company by raising equity finance from venture capitalists at a point when it knows it requires another cash injection. This is a different operating model than most companies, but not unusual for start-up or early stage companies. They can continue to operate in this way until they start generating profits (and cash): this can be over many years if the market and investors have the appetite to invest in the company.

All we can see in the historic liquidity ratios is that Company C is managing its liquidity effectively at this point. We would need wider contextual information to be confident in this going forwards, which we will discuss more in the next section.

Gearing
Company C has no long-term borrowings. Therefore, the equity and capital gearing ratios for Company C are both nil. In terms of financial risk this is clearly a zero-risk position. However, we need to consider this a bit more carefully for Company C.

Clearly, Company C is fully funded by equity. This is the operating model it has adopted at this stage of its development and growth. It would be reasonable to note:

- Debt is generally considered to be cheaper than equity financing, the major reason for this being that it is tax free.
- Equity finance dilutes the ownership and control of the company.

The generalisation about debt being cheaper than equity might not be true for Company C. As an early stage company – and a company making net losses and with limited physical assets – it is possible it might find it difficult to obtain significant levels of debt financing. Furthermore, if it did obtain finance, it would be at high interest rates. Company C might well be in one of those situations where debt financing is materially more expensive than equity financing.

Although Company C has no long-term borrowings, it does have right-of-use assets with a book value of £22.24 million in 20X5. We know from the notes that these are rights to use specialised software. Although there is no interest payment in the accounts relating to these, there is likely to be a cost associated with these assets. We would need more information to evaluate what that might be: for example, share options.

Investment
There are some very clear challenges with Company C. It has made significant operating and net losses in both years. Therefore, there are no earnings to calculate an EPS value and no EPS to calculate the P/E ratio. These are the normal calculations with which shareholders or investors would begin an evaluation exercise.

The EPS shows the proportion of profits available for equity shareholders, this is the basic measure of a company's performance from an equity shareholder's point of view. The P/E ratio indicates the relationship between the market value of share capital and the profit for the year. The P/E ratio valuation method is a simple and commonly used method of valuation. Clearly, neither of these are any use in seeking to try and value Company C.

Furthermore, we cannot look at the dividend yield for Company C. Dividend yield indicates how much a company pays out in dividends each year relative to its share price. Company C has made net losses and paid no dividends.

However, we do have some strong indicators that Company C is valued by the market and seen to be performing well:

- The share price at the end of 20X4 was £2.40. This increased to £2.76 per share at the end of 20X5. This is a £0.36 (15%) increase in the share price.
- If the market and investors are acting rationally, then the market believes that the value of Company C is increasing rapidly.
- Company C was able to raise £50 million of funding in 20X5 from venture capitalists, who will be looking for a long-term return on their investment.

Clearly, the market is not simply looking at investment ratios when valuing Company C. What is it looking at?

This is a clear reminder that context is important in looking at that value of a company. We are told that Company C is a world-leading cyber security and artificial intelligence company. These areas are seen by many analysts and company investors as the critical growth sectors in the world economy over the coming decades. Companies that become the leading players in this marketplace could rationally be expected to be the most successful companies of future decades. Indeed, amongst them we might see the next giant technology companies to join the likes of Microsoft, Google, Apple, etc.

Therefore, a company such as Company C might be better valued based on discounted cash flow (DCF) or future cash flow projections. It would:

- run cash flow forecast scenarios for the company;
- ask investors what their required return is or what cost of capital they would assume;
- map the resulting value range; and
- check their long-term growth with a compound growth analysis.

Company C is therefore putting its emphasis on the future potential of the company to generate significant cash flows, rather than the historic performance of the company in generating profits.

This form of future projection method can be further refined by a return on investment-based valuation. In a loss-making company, you would look at expected future cash flows (and profits) mapped to invested capital to produce future ROCE projections. Consider incremental return If the company is reinvesting all surplus cash back into the company and factor in future dividends and share buyback options if you are not reinvesting it all.

It is also important to get into an 'investor mindset' when looking at the value of a company. The £50 million raised in 20X5 by Company C was from venture capitalists. Venture capitalists will be much more likely, willing and able to take investment risks than most potential investors. They will gamble on a portfolio of start-ups or early stage companies, with the hope that one gets them a double-digit (or even treble-digit) multiple on their investment.

Conclusion

Company C's financial performance is difficult to assess based simply on traditional ratios and analysis. We can support this interpretation because:

- Company C is making losses, although its loss-making is decreasing. Its revenue is increasing significantly and it appears, overall, to be managing its costs well.
- Company C has no long-term borrowings or gearing and appears to be fully funding the company via equity issues.
- Company C has a reasonable level of liquidity which it maintained in 20X5. It appears to be managing this key risk effectively.
- Company C appears to be slightly increasing its overall level of efficiency.
- Company C had zero EPS and P/E ratio in 20X4 and 20X5.

We do have some strong indicators that Company C is valued by the market and seen to be performing well:

- The share price at the end of 20X4 was £2.40; this increased to £2.76 per share at the end of 20X5. This is a £0.36 (15%) increase in the share price.
- If the market and investors are acting rationally, then the market believes that the value of Company C is increasing rapidly.
- Company C was able to raise £50 million of funding in 20X5 from venture capitalists, who will have been looking for a long-term return on their investment.

Chapter summary

- The analysis, interpretation and evaluation of accounting and financial information should be carried out in a practical and applied way, as demonstrated in this chapter.
- There are several key documents and tools that can be used for analysis, which have been discussed throughout this study text. These include:
    - the key financial statements extracted from published annual reports;
    - the various ratios that are identified throughout this study text; and
    - elements of trend and segment analysis.
- Interpreting this information can tell a user a lot about a company and can be taken further to attempt to evaluate what is going on in the companies.
- Very different types of companies can be analysed using the same tools, as shown by the three case studies here.

- To interpret financial information properly, we often need to bring in other information. This might be further analysis, but equally it can be:
    - sector or competitor information;
    - economic indicators; or
    - information contained elsewhere in the financial statements or the annual report of a company.
- This chapter should be core preparation for any questions requiring calculation of ratios or trend analysis and any questions that require the interpretation or evaluation of accounting and financial information. This specifically includes the compulsory Section B question.

Appendix

The below present value table can serve as a template for calculating NPV, such as in Test yourself 13.4.

Present value table

Present value (in £) of a single payment of £1, n years from now, discounted at a rate of r% per annum

Discount rate (r)

Years (n)	1%	2%	3%	4%	5%	6%	7%	8%	9%	10%
1	0.990	0.980	0.971	0.962	0.952	0.943	0.935	0.926	0.917	0.909
2	0.980	0.961	0.943	0.925	0.907	0.890	0.873	0.857	0.842	0.826
3	0.971	0.942	0.915	0.889	0.864	0.840	0.816	0.794	0.772	0.751
4	0.961	0.924	0.888	0.855	0.823	0.792	0.763	0.735	0.708	0.683
5	0.951	0.906	0.863	0.822	0.784	0.747	0.713	0.681	0.650	0.621
6	0.942	0.888	0.837	0.790	0.746	0.705	0.666	0.630	0.596	0.564
7	0.933	0.871	0.813	0.760	0.711	0.665	0.623	0.583	0.547	0.513
8	0.923	0.853	0.789	0.731	0.677	0.627	0.582	0.540	0.502	0.467
9	0.914	0.837	0.766	0.703	0.645	0.592	0.544	0.500	0.460	0.424
10	0.905	0.820	0.744	0.676	0.614	0.558	0.508	0.463	0.422	0.386
11	0.896	0.804	0.722	0.650	0.585	0.527	0.475	0.429	0.388	0.350
12	0.887	0.788	0.701	0.625	0.557	0.497	0.444	0.397	0.356	0.319
13	0.879	0.773	0.681	0.601	0.530	0.469	0.415	0.368	0.326	0.290
14	0.870	0.758	0.661	0.577	0.505	0.442	0.388	0.340	0.299	0.263
15	0.861	0.743	0.642	0.555	0.481	0.417	0.362	0.315	0.275	0.239

	11%	12%	13%	14%	15%	16%	17%	18%	19%	20%
1	0.901	0.893	0.885	0.877	0.870	0.862	0.855	0.847	0.840	0.833
2	0.812	0.797	0.783	0.769	0.756	0.743	0.731	0.718	0.706	0.694
3	0.731	0.712	0.693	0.675	0.658	0.641	0.624	0.609	0.593	0.579
4	0.659	0.636	0.613	0.592	0.572	0.552	0.534	0.516	0.499	0.482
5	0.593	0.567	0.543	0.519	0.497	0.476	0.456	0.437	0.419	0.402
6	0.535	0.507	0.480	0.456	0.432	0.410	0.390	0.370	0.352	0.335
7	0.482	0.452	0.425	0.400	0.376	0.354	0.333	0.314	0.296	0.279
8	0.434	0.404	0.376	0.351	0.327	0.305	0.285	0.266	0.249	0.233
9	0.391	0.361	0.333	0.308	0.284	0.263	0.243	0.225	0.209	0.194
10	0.352	0.322	0.295	0.270	0.247	0.227	0.208	0.191	0.176	0.162
11	0.317	0.287	0.261	0.237	0.215	0.195	0.178	0.162	0.148	0.135
12	0.286	0.257	0.231	0.208	0.187	0.168	0.152	0.137	0.124	0.112
13	0.258	0.229	0.204	0.182	0.163	0.145	0.130	0.116	0.104	0.093
14	0.232	0.205	0.181	0.160	0.141	0.125	0.111	0.099	0.088	0.078
15	0.209	0.183	0.160	0.140	0.123	0.108	0.095	0.084	0.074	0.065

Test yourself answers

Chapter 1

Test yourself 1.1

What is the role of a regulatory framework in the preparation of financial statements?

The role of regulatory frameworks for the preparation of financial statements is:

- to ensure financial reporting is regulated through financial reporting standards such as UK and US GAAP and IFRS;
- to ensure financial information is reported objectively to provide relevant, reliable and faithfully represented information that enable users to make financial decisions;
- to provide an adequate minimum level of information for users of financial statements;
- to ensure financial information is comparable and consistent in the relevant economic arena (this is especially important with the growth in multinational companies and global investment);
- to ensure and improve transparency and credibility of financial reports, promoting users' confidence in the financial reporting process;
- to regulate the behaviour of companies and directors through the corporate governance framework; and
- to achieve desired social goals through environmental and CSR reporting.

Test yourself 1.2

List the key objectives of accounting standards.

The key objectives of financial accounting standards are to:

- improve the transparency of financial reporting and make financial information reliable, relevant and easier to understand;
- reduce the risk of creative accounting;
- make the financial statements of different period or of different entities comparable;

Interpreting Financial and Accounting Information

- increase the credibility of financial statements by improving the uniformity of accounting treatment between companies; and
- provide quality financial reports and accounting information which can be relied upon for consistency, commonality and overall transparency.

Test yourself 1.3

- What are the key arguments for adopting harmonisation of accounting standards across the world?
- Financial statements presented under IFRS make global comparisons easier.
- Cross-border listing is facilitated, making it easier to raise funds and make investments abroad.
- Multinational companies with subsidiaries in foreign countries have a common, company-wide accounting language.
- Foreign companies can be more easily appraised for mergers and acquisitions.
- Multinational companies benefit for the following reasons:
    1. preparation of group financial statements may be easier;
    2. a reduction in audit costs might be achieved;
    3. management control would be improved; and
    4. transfer of accounting knowledge and expertise across national borders would be easier.

Test yourself 1.4

Why is there an ever-growing need for businesses to account for and report on environmental issues?

Environmental reporting allows organisations to account for and report on the environmental effects of an organisation's economic actions. It has economic implications, some of which are listed below.

1. **Risk management:** financial, legal and reputation implications.
2. **Marketing advantages:** public image and brand enhancement by demonstrating its environmental responsibilities. Businesses that are considered environmentally irresponsible are likely to lose market share.
3. **Legal needs:** a business may be legally required to provide environmental reports. It is a legal requirement for quoted companies and those that carry on insurance market activity.
4. **Competitive advantage:** it can improve relationships with key stakeholders such as investors, suppliers and the wider community. Improved environmental performance should lead to cost savings.
5. **Ethics:** showing a commitment to accountability and transparency.
6. **Compliance and accounting requirements:** the annual review is expected to include environmental matters, including the company's impact on the environment.

7. **Green (ethical) investors:** companies with environmental disclosures are in a better position to be considered in investment decisions by trustees. For example, UK pension fund trustees must disclose how they have considered social, economic and environmental matters.
8. **Employee interests:** applicants increasingly look at the environmental performance of a business.
9. **Value-added reporting:** environmental key performance indicators are now used to report on environmental matters to add value to corporate reports and communicate to a wider range of stakeholders.
10. **Integrated reporting:** a move towards integrated reporting on CSR and environmental issues that allows interactivity on web-based publication of such reports. Standalone environmental reporting is primarily web-based disclosure that is usually separate from a company's annual report.

Chapter 2

Test yourself 2.1

What is the purpose of the IASB's Conceptual Framework?

The purpose of the Conceptual Framework is:

a) to assist the IASB in the development of future IFRS and in its review of existing IFRS;
b) to provide a basis for reducing the number of alternative accounting treatments permitted by IFRS and thus assist the harmonisation of regulations, accounting standards and procedures relating to financial reporting;
c) to assist national standard setting bodies in developing national standards;
d) to assist preparers of financial statements in applying IFRS and in dealing with topics that are not covered by a standard or where there is choice of accounting policy;
e) to assist auditors in forming an opinion as to whether financial statements comply with IFRS;
f) to assist users of financial statements in interpreting the financial statements prepared in compliance with IFRS;
g) to provide those who are interested in the work of the IASB with information about its approach to the formulation of IFRS.

Test yourself 2.2

Why is there a need for businesses to prepare financial statements for their users?

The key benefits of preparing financial statements for their users are listed below.

- **Investors:** financial statements help investors to decide about buying or selling shares by providing information about the level of dividend and any changes in share price. It also helps investors to see the company's prospects, present liquidity position and how the company's shares compare with those of its competitors.
- **Employees and management:** company performance is related to the security of employment and future prospects for jobs in the company. The financial position and performance help management in managing the business.
- **Lenders:** the information in the financial statements help lenders decide whether to lend to a company. This information is checked for adequacy of the value of security, ability to make interest and capital repayments and to ensure financial covenants have not been breached.
- **Suppliers:** are interested in information to assess whether the company will be a good customer and pay its debts.
- **Customers:** the company should be in a good financial position to be able to continue producing and supplying goods or services.
- **Government:** is specifically concerned with compliance with tax and company law, ability to pay tax and its general contribution to the economy.
- **The public:** All of the reasons stated above could be useful to the general public.

Test yourself 2.3

Briefly explain the meaning of faithful representation.

Faithful representation means that financial information must meet three criteria: completeness, neutrality and be free from error.

- **Completeness:** all information that users need to understand the item is given.
- **Neutral or unbiased:** there is no bias in the selection or presentation of information.
- **Free from error:** there are no omissions, errors or inaccuracies in the process to produce the information.

The idea of 'substance over form' is key for the faithful representation of financial information. It may be necessary to override the legal form of a transaction to portray a true economic position.

Test yourself 2.4

Management commits to purchase assets in the future. Does this give rise to a liability?

An essential characteristic of a liability is that the entity has a present obligation. A liability is present obligation of the entity to transfer economic benefit as a result of past transactions or events. For example, a trade payable is a liability.

It is important to distinguish between a present obligation and a future commitment. A management decision to purchase assets in the future does not, in itself, give rise to a present obligation. It is rather a future commitment.

Test yourself 2.5

Explain how you would report a transaction that fails to satisfy the recognition criteria.

Where an essential element is not recorded as an asset, liability, income or expense because it is unable to meet the criteria for recognition, it can be disclosed in the form of explanatory notes if the knowledge would be relevant to the users of the financial report in making and evaluating their decisions. The revised recognition criteria refer explicitly to the qualitative characteristics of useful information.

For example, an entity may be engaged in litigation in defence of a claim for a certain amount of damages. Although the claim may not meet the recognition criteria of a liability, such information may be considered to be relevant to the users of the financial report in making and evaluating their decisions. Accordingly, it may warrant disclosure in the notes in the financial report.

Test yourself 2.6

Explain the most commonly used measurement in financial statements.

Historical cost is the measurement basis most commonly used today. It is usually combined with other measurement bases. Examples of this include:

- assets on finance leases are to be carried at the lower of:
  - fair value at the date of its acquisition; or
  - discounted value of the minimum lease payments at that date
- construction contracts shall be carried at historical cost plus a proportion of the expected profit;
- inventories are also measured as per IAS 2 at the lower of cost and net realisable value.

Consideration of different factors is likely to result in different measurement bases for different assets, liabilities, income and expenses. The factors to be considered when selecting a measurement basis are relevance and faithful representation, because the aim is to provide information that is useful to investors, lenders and other creditors.

Chapter 3

Test yourself 3.1

1. *What is the key objective of financial statements?*

According to the IASB Conceptual Framework for the preparation and presentation of financial statements, the objective of general purpose financial statements is to provide useful information about the financial position, financial performance and cash flows of an entity to a wide range of users who are making economic decisions.

The objective of IAS 1 is to ensure comparability of financial statements with the entity's financial statements of previous periods and with the financial statements of other entities. Under IAS 1 an entity must present a complete set of financial statements (including prior period comparative information) on at least an annual basis.

2. *What are the components of a complete set of financial statements as required by IAS 1?*

A complete set of financial statements comprises:

- a statement of financial position (also called a balance sheet)
- a statement of profit or loss and other comprehensive income
- a statement of changes in equity
- a statement of cash flows
- notes to the financial statements (comprising a summary of significant accounting policies and other explanatory notes).

Test yourself 3.2

1. *What is meant by a current asset, a non-current asset, a current liability and a non-current liability?*

Current assets are assets (such as inventories and trade receivables) that are sold, consumed or realised as part of the normal operating cycle even when they are not expected to be realised within 12 months after the reporting period. They also include assets held primarily for the purpose of trading and the current portion of non-current financial assets. The normal operating cycle is the cash conversion cycle an entity takes to realise its purchases into cash or cash equivalents from customers. It is normally assumed to be 12 months when it is not clearly identifiable.

All other assets should be classified as non-current assets. Non-current assets include tangible, intangible and financial assets of a long-term nature.

A liability is classified as current by IAS 1 when it is:

- expected to be settled in the entity's normal operating cycle;
- held primarily for the purpose of trading;

- due to be settled within 12 months after the reporting period; or
- it does not have an unconditional right to defer settlement of the liability.

Liabilities not falling within the definitions of 'current' are classified as non-current.

2. *How does having an agreement to refinance and an unconditional right to defer settlement of the liability impact on an entity's current/non-current classification.*

Debt under an existing loan facility which is due to expire within 12 months of the year end is treated as current. However, the debt becomes non-current if there is an agreement to refinance and if the lender has agreed, on or before the balance sheet date, to provide a period of grace lasting 12 months or more from the end of the reporting period, during which the lender is unable to enforce repayment of the loan.

Test yourself 3.3

What is the key difference between the statement of profit or loss and other comprehensive income?

The statement of profit or loss includes all items of income or expense (including reclassification adjustments) except those items of income or expense that are recognised in OCI as required by IFRS. IAS 1 lists the following as the minimum items to be presented in the profit or loss section:

1. revenue
2. finance costs
3. share of profits and losses of associates and joint ventures accounted for using the equity method
4. a single amount for the total of discontinued operations
5. tax expense
6. a total for profit and loss
7. gains and losses from the de-recognition of financial assets measured at amortised cost

Other comprehensive income includes all of the items that cannot be included in the statement of profit and loss. These include the change in a company's net assets from non-owner sources, including all income and expenses that bypass the income statement because they have not yet been realised. Examples of the types of changes captured by other comprehensive income include:

1. changes in the revaluation surplus on long-term assets
2. actuarial gains and losses on re-measurement of defined benefit plans
3. exchange differences (gains and losses) arising from the translation of the financial statements of a foreign operation
4. certain gains and losses relating to financial instruments, including on certain instruments used for hedging

5. correction of prior period errors and the effect of changes in accounting policies

Test yourself 3.4

What is the primary purpose of the statement of cash flows?

The primary purpose of the statement of cash flows is to provide information about a company's gross receipts and gross payments for a specified period of time. As per IAS 7, cash flows are classified under operating, investing and financing activities. The statement of cash flows shows movement of money into or out of a business. It highlights the activities that directly and indirectly affect a company's overall cash balance.

Chapter 4

Test yourself 4.1

What are the primary uses of published accounts?

Published accounts provide information about the company's activities and financial performance throughout the preceding year. To some extent, they indicate the future prospects of the business.

Published accounts are a key element of communication with shareholders, the market and other interested parties such as bank lenders or suppliers. The published accounts are used by investors and other parties to examine:

- **profitability:** investors and shareholders will be interested in the profitability ratios and financial numbers such as dividends and retained profits;
- **sources or nature of profit:** for example, whether the profit generated is from the sales of assets or normal trading;
- **balance sheet strength:** by looking at liquidity, insolvency and gearing positions; and
- **trends:** for example, looking for revenue and profit trends to identify strengths or any potential risks.

Test yourself 4.2

What are the objectives of the strategic report?

The strategic report is a detailed report within the annual report and accounts, written in non-financial language. It provides clear and coherent information about the company's activities (such as what it does and why), performance, position, the strategic position of the business and probable risks attached with the business. It ensures information is accessible by a broad range of users, not just analysts and accountants who have sophisticated knowledge.

The purpose of the strategic report is to provide information to the members of the company and help them assess how the directors have performed their duties and functions. The strategic report must contain and provide the following information:

- a fair review of the company's business
- a description of the principal risks and uncertainties the company faces
- any change in the going concern assessment
- references to the annual accounts

The strategic report of a quoted company must also include information on the company's strategy, business model and disclosures about environmental, employee and social issues (including human rights and gender diversity).

Test yourself 4.3

Briefly discuss the purpose of notes to the accounts in a published annual report.

The notes to the accounts in an annual report provide information not presented elsewhere in the report. This includes:

- more detailed analysis of figures in the statements
- narrative information explaining figures in the statements
- additional information, such as contingent liabilities and commitments

IAS 1 requires the notes to the accounts in the annual report to disclose the following key information:

- the basis for the preparation of the financial statements that includes specific accounting policies chosen and applied to significant transactions/ events;
- information which is required by IFRS but not presented elsewhere in the annual report; and
- any additional information that is relevant to understanding which is not shown elsewhere in the annual report.

Test yourself 4.4

A plc sold a property to B plc on terms that the property will be leased back to A plc under a lease agreement and A plc continues to occupy the property. How will this transaction be recorded in the financial statements of A plc?

The substance over form concept will be applied. The company must first determine whether the transfer qualifies as a sale based on the requirements for satisfying a performance obligation in IFRS 15 'Revenue from Contracts with Customers'. Under IFRS 15, the transfer of goods and services is based upon the transfer of control – the ability to direct the use of and obtain substantially all of the remaining benefits from, the asset. In view of this, the transaction will not be recorded as a sale transaction in the books of A; instead it will be treated as a lease and accounted for as per IAS 17.

IAS 17 provides a single lessee accounting model, requiring lessees to recognise assets (representing its right to use the assets) and liabilities (representing its obligation to make lease payments). The asset will remain in the books of A and the money received from B by A will be recorded as a secured loan.

Test yourself 4.5

Outline the reasons why managers may engage in earnings management or creative accounting.

Creative accounting arises when managers use their knowledge of accounting choices available to them to manipulate the figures reported in the accounts of a business. They may resort to such practices due any of the following reasons:

- managers may be attempting to secure performance bonuses;
- to minimise tax liability;
- to increase share values, especially if the directors are shareholders;
- to disguise the fact that the business is close to insolvency; or
- to use as a bargaining tool in negotiations with suppliers, customers and employees.

Test yourself 4.6

What are the key limitations of historical cost as a basis for the measurement of assets?

Historical cost is the most widely used basis of measurement of assets. Use of historical cost presents various problems for the users of published accounts as it fails to account for the change in price levels of assets over a period of time. This not only reduces the relevance of accounting information by presenting assets at amounts that may be far less than their realisable value but also fails to account for the opportunity cost of using those assets. The published accounts neither represent the value for which fixed assets can be sold nor the amount which will be required to replace these assets.

Chapter 5

Test yourself 5.1

How are changes in new accounting policy, the correction of material prior year errors and changes in accounting estimates applied in the financial statements in order to comply with IAS 8?

The application of a new accounting policy or the correction for a material prior period error requires retrospective application. It requires the restatement of the comparative financial statements for each prior accounting period that is being presented to account for the new accounting policy and/or the material error. The details of the changes must be disclosed in the notes to the financial statements for completeness.

- An example of a change in accounting policy would be a change in the depreciation method from straight line to reducing balance.
- Examples of a material prior period error include a material over/understatement of sales or inventory or other expenses due to mathematical mistakes, mistakes in applying accounting policies, oversights or misinterpretations of facts and fraud.

IAS 8 only allows for the prospective application of both a change in accounting policy and material prior period errors if it is impracticable to perform the retrospective adjustment. A material change in an accounting estimate requires the prospective application. The change would also be disclosed in the notes to the financial statements. Examples of changes in accounting estimates include a change in the estimated lifespan of a fixed asset or a change in the estimate used in the calculation of the provision of doubtful debtors.

Test yourself 5.2

Konyak Plc imports goods from Nepal and sells them in the local market. It uses the FIFO method to value its inventory. The following are the purchases and sales made by the company during the current year.

Purchases

- January: 10,000 units @ £15 each
- March: 15,000 units @ £20 each
- July: 10,000 units @ £45 each

Sales

- May: 15,000 units
- November: 15,000 units

Based on the FIFO method, calculate the value of inventory at the end of May, September and December.

January purchases	10,000 × 15	150,000
March purchases	15,000 × 20	300,000
	Total	450,000
May sales	10,000 × 15	(150,000)
Nov	5,000 × 20	(100,000)
	Total	(200,000)
Inventory valued on FIFO basis at 31 May:	10,000 × 20	200,000
July purchases	10,000 × 45	450,000
Inventory valued on FIFO basis at 30 September:		650,000

November sales	10,000 × 20	(200,000)
	5,000 × 45	(225,000)
	Total	225,000
Inventory valued on FIFO basis at 31 December:	5,000 × 45	225,000

Test yourself 5.3

Cuba Ltd acquired a new plant in exchange for land with a book value of £10 million (fair value amounted to £15 million), plus cash paid upfront of £5 million.

1. *What will be the cost of the acquired plant in the financial statements of Cuba Ltd?*

As per IAS 16, the cost of the acquired asset will be:

[fair value of asset transferred ± cash]

Therefore, the cost of the acquired plant will be:

£15 million + £5 million = £20 million

2. *What are the criteria set out by IAS 2 for the recognition of the cost of an item of property, plant and equipment as an asset?*

The cost of an item of property, plant and equipment should be recognised as an asset only if:

- it is probable that future economic benefits associated with the item will flow to the entity; and
- the cost of the item can be measured reliably.

Items such as spare parts, standby equipment and servicing equipment are also accounted for under IAS 16 when they meet the definition of property, plant and equipment. Otherwise, they are recognised as inventories. Costs of ongoing servicing of assets are not added to the carrying amount but are recorded as an expense as they are incurred.

Test yourself 5.4

1. *Precipe Ltd recorded inventories at their cost of £500,000 in the statement of financial position as at 31 December 20X8. The entity sold 70% of these for £300,000 on 15 January 20X9. It also incurred a commission expense of 10% of the selling price of the inventory.*

The NRV of 70% inventory = £300,000 less commission expense of £30,000 = £270,000 and it has a cost of £350,000 (£500,000 × 70%).

A sale of inventory after the reporting date reflects that the NRV of its inventory is less than its cost value. The reduction in the value will be treated as an adjusting event, as it reflects the condition of the inventories at the balance sheet date. Therefore, the entity will need to adjust down the inventory value to its NRV in the statement of financial position for the year ended 31 December 20X8.

2. *The financial statements for the year ended 31 December 20X8 were authorised for issue on 10 January 20X9. The government introduced tax changes on 31 March 20X9. As a result, the tax liability recorded by the entity at 31 December 20X8 increased by £400,000.*

   How will these events be reported in the books of Precipe Ltd for the year ended 31 Dec 20X8?

The change in the tax rate occurred after the date when the financial statements were authorised for issue. Therefore, this will be treated as outside the scope of IAS 10. It would have been treated as a non-adjusting event if it had occurred after the reporting date but before the date of authorisation of financial statements, as the tax change arose after the reporting period.

Test yourself 5.5

Peter Telecom Ltd signs a mobile contract for two years with a customer. It provides a free handset as part of the contract. It also provides an option to insure the phone at an extra monthly cost. How are the performance obligations assessed, revenue allocated and at what point in time is revenue recognised as per IFRS 15?

An entity should recognise revenue to the extent that a performance obligation in a contract with a customer has been satisfied. The transaction price is the amount of consideration an entity expects from the customer in exchange for transferring goods or services.

The handset sale revenue will be recognised when the phone is delivered to the customer.

The revenue relating to the mobile monthly calls will be recognised when the customer uses the phone over the life of the contract.

Any revenue relating to the sale of mobile insurance will be treated as a separate performance obligation and recognised on a monthly basis. For services that are performed over time, an entity transfers control of a good or service over time. It satisfies a performance obligation and recognises revenue over time.

Test yourself 5.6

A court case was filed against Goldwyns Ltd by its major customer for compensation for a loss caused by the supply of poor-quality products in the last consignment of goods.

At the reporting year end of 31 December 20X7, the case was still pending with the value of the claim being disputed. The probability for the settlement of the loss was unlikely.

However, based on new developments in the case, the lawyer signalled that the entity's liability to compensate for the loss was probable at the year end of 31 December 20X8.

Discuss, as per the requirements of IAS 37, how the events will be accounted for in the financial statements of Goldwyns Ltd for the year to 31 December 20X7 and 31 December 20X8.

At 31 December 20X7

The past obligating event was the supply of poor-quality products under the contract which gives rise to a legal obligation. No present obligation was established, as the probability for the settlement of the loss was unlikely.

Therefore, provision will not be recognised. Rather it will be disclosed in the notes to the accounts as a contingent liability unless the probability for future liability is considered as remote.

At 31 December 2018

It was probable that Goldywns will be found liable to the loss settlement. As a result, it was probable that an outflow of economic resources will be required to settle the obligation Therefore, a provision will be recognised if the amount of obligation can be estimated reliably.

Chapter 6

Test yourself 6.1

Tea Limited is a new company which formed on 1 January 20X4. At the date of its formation the issued share capital of Tea Ltd consists of 100,000 equity shares of £1 each with equal voting rights. The directors of Tea Ltd retained 49,000 equity shares and Tea Ltd sold 51,000 equity shares to Ilam Ltd on 1 January 20X4 for the par value of the shares.

Does Ilam Ltd meet the criteria of a parent company?

Ilam Ltd becomes the parent company of Tea Ltd from 1 January 20X4 because it meets all the three elements of control as defined by IFRS 10.

Power over the investee, through most of voting rights (owning more than 50% of the equity shares).

Exposure or rights to variable returns (a dividend).

It can control the composition of the board of directors and affect the amount of investor returns.

Test yourself 6.2

Why are the subsidiary's identifiable assets and liabilities included at their fair values in the consolidated financial statements?

Consolidated accounts are prepared from the perspective of the group and must reflect their cost to the group (to the parent), not the original cost to the subsidiary. The book values of the subsidiary's assets and liabilities are largely irrelevant in the consolidated financial statements. The cost to the group is the fair value of the acquired assets and liabilities at the date of acquisition. Fair values are therefore used to calculate the value of goodwill.

Test yourself 6.3

1. Sandra plc purchased 100% of the equity shares of Hayden plc for consideration of £500,000 cash and 100,000 shares in Sandra plc. The market value of Sandra plc's equity shares was £5 per share on the date of acquisition. The total fair value of Hayden plc's assets and liabilities at the date of acquisition was £700,000. Calculate the goodwill that Sandra plc will include in its consolidated financial statements at the time of acquisition.

1. Fair value of consideration given	£	£
Cash	500,000	
Shares: £5 × 100,000	500,000	
		1,000,000
Fair value of assets and liabilities acquired		(700,000)
Goodwill		300,000

2. Explain why it is necessary to use the fair values of a subsidiary's identifiable assets and liabilities when preparing consolidated financial statements.

It is necessary to use the fair values of a subsidiary's identifiable assets and liabilities in the consolidated accounts for the following reasons.

a) As consolidated accounts are prepared from the perspective of the group, they must reflect the cost to the group, not the book values of the subsidiary's assets and liabilities. The cost to the group is their fair value at the date of acquisition.

b) The value of the purchased goodwill is meaningless without the use of fair values. Purchased goodwill is measured as the difference between the cost of an acquisition (the value of an acquired entity) and the aggregate of the fair values of that entity's identifiable assets and liabilities (the value of the subsidiary's net assets acquired).

Test yourself 6.4

1. **Why are pre-acquisition profits of a subsidiary not included in the group accounts?**

Pre-acquisition profits are the retained earnings of the subsidiary which exist at the date when it is acquired. They are excluded from group retained earnings as they belong to the previous shareholders and were earned under their ownership.

2. **Gorkha plc acquired Ye Ltd on 1 January 20X9. The retained earnings at 1 January 20X9 amounted to £500,000 and £800,000 respectively. Explain how the retained earnings of Ye ltd at 1 January 20X1 would be treated in the consolidated financial statements.**

The retained earnings of Ye Ltd have accrued during the period prior to acquisition and were earned under the ownership of the previous shareholders. They form a part of the shareholders' equity at acquisition in the subsidiary for the purpose of computing goodwill arising on consolidation.

3. **What are non-controlling interests? How are they accounted for in consolidated financial statements?**

In a situation where a parent has control but less than 100% of a shareholding, the portion of equity ownership in a subsidiary not attributable to the parent company is known as a non-controlling interest. This is also called a minority interest. A non-controlling interest should be presented separately in the consolidated statement of financial position within equity. Any share of a subsidiary's results that belongs to the non-controlling interest or minority interest is disclosed at the foot of the balance sheet and income statement and in the statement of changes in equity.

4. **How is an investment of the parent in a subsidiary accounted for in the parent's separate financial statements? How is it accounted for in the consolidated financial statements?**

Parent company financial statements include 'investments in subsidiary undertakings' as an asset in the statement of financial position, as well as income from subsidiaries (dividends) in the statement of profit or loss. The parent entity's investment in the subsidiaries, carried as an investment in its balance sheet, is also eliminated through the process of consolidation.

Test yourself 6.5

During the year ended 31 December 20X1, the parent company (P Plc) sells goods to its subsidiary (S Ltd) at cost plus a mark-up of 15%. Explain the accounting treatment of the intra-group trading and the profit arising from the intercompany sales.

Intra-group items including all transactions, balances and profits and losses must be eliminated to avoid double counting. The consolidated totals should consist of only transactions, balances and profits and losses created through transactions with parties outside the group. For consolidated financial statements, it is therefore necessary to eliminate intra-group balances and transactions.

Company P will make the following accounting adjustments for unrealised profits:

- Intra-group sales and purchases are eliminated. Reduce the retained earnings of Company P by 15% (the mark-up) or 15 ÷ 115 (13% of the selling price).
- Any unrealised profit relating to intercompany trading is eliminated. Reduce the inventory of Company B by 15% (the mark-up) or 13% of the price. The above adjustments only apply to unsold inventory.

Test yourself 6.6

How does the difference between the equity method and the full consolidation method affect the decisions of investing entities if the investee were a highly geared entity?

There are substantial differences between consolidation and equity accounting, thus influencing the behaviour of investing entities to structure transactions to achieve their desired accounting outcome. If an investee is highly geared with a lot of debt, the investor would bring 100% of the gross debt of the investee onto its consolidated balance sheet through consolidation. It increases the gearing for the group as a whole. This is avoided if the investee is treated as a joint venture and accounted using the equity method.

A controlling interest in the investee is not desirable in this scenario. However, if the investee were very profitable, the consolidated accounts would consolidate 100% of the investee's profits in its accounts with any portion relating to NCI disclosed at the foot of the balance sheet.

Test yourself 6.7

1. *When is a parent exempted from preparing consolidated financial statements?*

A parent is exempted from preparing consolidated financial statements when:

- the parent is itself a wholly owned subsidiary, or a partially owned subsidiary and the non-controlling interests do not object;
- its securities are not publicly traded or in the process of being traded; or
- its ultimate or intermediate parent publishes IFRS-compliant financial statements.

2. *When does IFRS allow subsidiary undertakings to be excluded from consolidation? Can they be excluded on the grounds of dissimilar activities?*

Very rarely. The rules on exclusion of subsidiaries from consolidation are strict because entities use them to manipulate their results. An exclusion originally allowed by IAS 27 (where control is intended to be temporary or where the subsidiary operates under severe long-term restrictions) has been removed. Instead, subsidiaries held for sale are accounted for in accordance with IFRS 5 (Non-Current Assets Held for Sale and Discontinued Operations) and the control must actually be lost for exclusion to occur.

IFRS 10 also rejects the argument for exclusion on the grounds of dissimilar activities. More relevant information must be provided about such subsidiaries by consolidating their results and providing additional information about the different business activities of the subsidiary.

Chapter 7

Test yourself 7.1

1. **What is meant by stewardship accounting?**

Stewardship refers to the traditional approach of accounting under which the owners of a business (the shareholders) entrust the management in managing business. Shareholders entrust the board of directors with the responsibility for managing the resources entrusted to them by giving it direction and providing both control and strategy. The board employs managers to implement their strategic vision and to and maximise the returns of the wealth of the shareholders. An obligation of stewards or agents, such as directors, is to provide relevant and reliable financial information relating to resources over which they have control, but which are owned by others.

2. **Who are the interested parties and how do they benefit from the analysis of financial statements?**

Different parties are interested in financial statements and their analysis for various reasons. These parties include investors, management, employees, lenders, suppliers, trade creditors, tax authorities, government and their agencies, researchers and stock exchanges.

Financial statements are prepared for decision-making purposes, which is driven by effective analysis and interpretation of financial statements. Financial analysis indicates the profitability and financial soundness of a business entity for a given period. It determines its financial strengths and weaknesses by assessing the efficiency and performance of an entity. Key measures include:

- evaluation of profitability
- financial trends of achievements
- growth potential
- comparative position in relation to similar businesses
- assessment of overall financial strength
- assessment of solvency

Test yourself 7.2

What are the key objectives of fundamental analysis and its components?

Fundamental analysis is a systematic approach to evaluating company performance based on historical data. The end goal of this analysis is to generate an insight about the company's future performance and business forecast. It is also used:

- to derive the valuation of the company
- to evaluate the performance of the company management and conduct internal audit of its business decisions
- to determine the intrinsic value of the share or the company's intrinsic value and its growth prospects

The components of fundamental analysis are:
- economic analysis, including analysis of:
  - GDP
  - interest rates
  - employment
  - foreign exchange
  - manufacturing
- industry analysis, including analysis of:
  - competitors
  - industry lifecycle
  - Porter's five forces
- company analysis, including analysis of:
  - business assets
  - liabilities
  - earnings

Test yourself 7.3

Ray Plc and Kevin Plc prepared their statements of profit or loss for the year ended 31 December 20X8 that include the comparative figures relating to the year ended 31 December 20X7. Both companies are in the same industry but operate in two different countries, namely France and Italy. What is your opinion on the performance of both companies?

Ray Plc – France			Kevin Plc – Italy		
	20X8	20X7		20X8	20X7
	£m	£m		£m	£m
Revenue	130	120	Revenue	350	230
Cost of goods sold	(60)	(50)	Cost of goods sold	(240)	(150)
Gross profit	**70**	**70**	**Gross profit**	**110**	**80**
Sales and administrative expenses	(20)	(10)	Sales and administrative expenses	(60)	(20)
Marketing expenses	(10)	(20)	Marketing expenses	(10)	(10)
Other operating expenses	(10)	(10)	Other operating expenses	(10)	(10)
Operating profit	**30**	**30**	**Operating profit**	**30**	**40**
Finance costs	(10)	NIL	Finance costs	(10)	(10)
Profit before tax	**20**	**30**	**Profit before tax**	**20**	**30**
Income tax	NIL	(10)	Income tax	NIL	(20)
Profit for the year (Net profit)	**20**	**20**	**Profit for the year (Net profit)**	**20**	**10**

Answer 7.3

First, calculate the profitability ratios and perform trend analysis based on two years' historical numbers.

Ray Plc			Kevin Plc		
	20X8	20X7		20X8	20X7
Sales growth rate	8%		Sales growth rate	52%	
Gross profit growth rate	0%		Gross profit growth rate	38%	
Operating income growth rate	0%		Operating income growth rate	−25%	
Net income growth rate	0%		Net income growth rate	100%	
Gross profit margin	54%	58%	Gross profit margin	31%	35%

Operating profit margin	23%	25%
Net income margin	15%	17%

Operating profit margin	9%	17%
Net income margin	6%	4%

Performance commentary

- In terms of sales, Kevin Plc made a tremendous improvement with 52% growth in 2018 sales while Ray Plc made an increase of 8% in sales. In absolute terms, gross profit and net income has grown for Kevin Plc whereas it is static for Ray Plc.
- In terms of margins, Ray Plc is a clear winner with 54% gross margin and 15% net income margin. The margins for Kevin Plc are nearly half of Ray Plc's margins. Profit margins and performances are influenced by various factors. For example, the higher margin in Ray Plc could be the result of a profit-driven strategy, focusing on products with high margins or via cost-saving initiatives.
- The net income margin for Kevin Plc has improved in 2018 by 2%, backed by efficient tax planning. This adjustment can be considered as a one-off item and analysts need to be aware of the change. Otherwise, both the gross margin and the operating margin have declined.
- Margins are declining for Ray Plc. There is a need to identify the underlying reasons.

Test yourself 7.4

The financial statements of Ray Plc and Kevin Plc are below (continuing from Test yourself 7.3). Calculate the profitability return ratios.

Statements of profit or loss for the years end 31 December

Ray Plc (France)	20X8	20X7
	£m	£m
Operating profit	3	3
Non-operating expense	(1)	NIL
Profit before tax	2	3
Income tax	NIL	(1)
Profit for the year (Net profit)	2	2

Kevin Plc (Italy)	20X8	20X7
	£m	£m
Operating profit	3	4
Non-operating expense	(1)	(1)
Profit before tax	2	3
Income tax	NIL	(2)
Profit for the year (Net profit)	2	1

Statements of financial position as at 31 December

Ray Plc (France)	20X8 £m	20X7 £m
Assets		
Non-current assets		
Property, plant and equipment	1	2
Long-term investments	6	3
Total non-current assets	**7**	**5**
Current assets		
Receivables	8	11
Cash and cash equivalents	6	2
Total current assets	14	13
Total Assets	**21**	**18**
Equity and liabilities		
Share capital	8	8
Retained earnings	8	7
Total shareholders' equity	**16**	**15**
Non-current liabilities	1	NIL
Current liabilities (payables)	4	3
Total liabilities	5	3
Total equity and liabilities	**21**	**18**

Kevin Plc (Italy)	20X8 £m	20X7 £m
Assets		
Non-current assets		
Property, plant and equipment	25	18
Long-term investments	2	1
Total non-current assets	**27**	**19**
Current assets		
Receivables	8	5
Cash and cash equivalents	12	5
Total current assets	20	10
Total Assets	**47**	**29**
Equity and liabilities		
Share capital	10	7
Retained earnings	14	9
Total shareholders' equity	**24**	**16**
Non-current liabilities	8	4
Current liabilities (payables)	15	9
Total liabilities	23	13
Total equity and liabilities	**47**	**29**

Here are the profitability return ratios based on historical numbers.

Ray Plc

	2017	2018
ROA = net income ÷ total assets	11%	10%
ROE = net income ÷ total equity	13%	13%
ROCE = EBIT × (1− tax rate) ÷ (total equity + debt)	13%	18%

Kevin Plc

	2017	2018
ROA	3%	4%
ROE	6%	8%
ROCE	10%	9%

Return on assets
The assets of the company are being used more effectively in comparison to the income earned by Ray Plc. Economies of scale help in improving this ratio.

Return on equity
Return on equity ratio measures the company's ability to provide returns to its equity holders. The return provided by Ray Plc is better at 10%, compared to Kevin Plc at 8%.

Return on capital employed
The ROCE is a measure of pre-tax income available to all investors and not just to shareholders. The profit figure used is the operating profit before any deductions for loan interest or dividends. The return provided by Ray Plc is better at 18% compared to Kevin Plc at 9%.

Ray Plc is a clear winner with better returns on total assets, equity and capital employed. The key drivers are the net income and profit available to investors in relation to its total assets, equity and the capital employed. The higher returns in Ray Plc could be the result of a profit-driven strategy, focusing on products with high margins or through cost-saving initiatives.

Chapter 8

Test yourself 8.1

What factors determine working capital requirements?

Working capital requirements change from time to time as per the size and nature of industries as well as other internal and external factors. In general, the following factors affect requirement or working capital.

Nature of business
The investment in working capital depends on the nature of the business, product type and production techniques. For example, retail companies have a low cash cycle with few credit customers, high supplies on credit terms and a large inventory to cater to the demands of customers. Manufacturing companies have a long cycle with significant current assets. The service sector does not hold any finished goods and has an insignificant amount of liabilities.

Size of business
The larger the size of business, the greater the working capital requirements to support its scale of operation. However, a small business may also need a large amount of working capital due to high overhead charges, inefficient use of available resources and other economic disadvantages of a smaller business.

Production policy
Some companies manufacture their products when orders are received while others manufacture products in anticipation of future demands.

Seasonal fluctuations
If the demand for the product is seasonal, the working capital required in that season will be higher. For example, there is greater demand for air conditioners in summer.

Credit policies
A liberal sales credit policy demands a higher level of working capital as it prolongs the debtors' collection period and vice versa. However, a liberal credit policy without consideration of the creditworthiness of the customers will land the business in trouble and the requirements of working capital will also unnecessarily increase. Similarly, a tight credit policy from suppliers shortens the creditors' settlement period and lengthens the WCC, requiring the need for alternative finance.

Changing technology
A firm using labour-oriented technology will require more working capital to pay labour wages.

Growth and expansion
Working capital requirements increase with the size of a firm to support larger scales of operation.

Taxation policies
Government taxation policy affects the quantum of working capital requirements. A high tax rate demands more working capital.

Test yourself 8.2

Why is working capital needed in a business? What is the optimal level of working capital?

Working capital is the total amount of cash tied up in current assets and current liabilities which normally includes inventories, receivables, cash and cash equivalents, less payables. All of these are available for day-to-day operating activities. Businesses need working capital in order to keep the business running. It enables businesses:

- to allow customers/trade receivables to buy on credit – offering credit provides a competitive advantage in the market;
- to carry inventories of finished goods to meet customer demand; and
- to have cash to pay the bills. A company needs working capital to pay salaries, wages and other day-to-day obligations.

The optimum level of working capital is the amount that results in no idle cash or unused inventory, but that does not put a strain on liquid resources needed for the daily running of the business. The company faces a trade-off between profitability and liquidity. Management decides on the optimal level of working capital to ensure that it is managed properly. Holding high levels of working capital implies holding idle funds with unnecessary cost implications, a phenomenon known as 'overcapitalisation'. Low working capital can result in a situation where the firm is not able to meet its demands.

Test yourself 8.3

The following are extracts from the financial statements of Kenya Ltd for the year ended 31 March 20X8.

Statement of financial position as at 31 March 20X8

£'000

Non-current assets	800
Current asserts	
Inventories	600
Trade receivables	950
Cash and cash equivalents	50
Total assets	2,400
Equity shares	700
Retained earnings	400
Total equity	1,100
Non-current liabilities	
11% preference shares	300
12% debentures	700
Total non-current liabilities	1,000
Trade payables	300
Total equity and liabilities	2,400

Statement of profit or loss for the year ended 31 March 20X8

£'000

Revenue (credit sales = 3,500)	3,527
Cost of goods sold (credit purchases 2,537)	(2,500)
Gross profit	1,027
Administrative expenses	(300)
Rent	(75)
Selling expenses	(100)
Depreciation	(80)
Operating profit	472
Interest charges	(72)
Profit before tax	400

Calculate:

1. Inventory holding period (days)
2. Rate of collection of trade receivables (days)
3. Rate of payment of trade payables (days)
4. Asset turnover ratio

How would you interpret the results?

Inventory holding period (days) = (Inventory x 365) / cost of goods sold

= (600 x 365) / 2,500 = 87.6 days

Inventory holding period (days) measures how well inventory is managed. It indicates how many days inventory is held before it is sold.

Rate of collection of trade receivables (days) = (Trade receivables x 365) / cost of goods sold

= (950 x 365) / 2,500 = 138.7 days

This indicates how quickly (the average number of days) debts are being collected.

Rate of payment of trade payables (days) = (Trade payables x 365) / credit purchases

= (300 x 365) / 2,537 = 43.2 days

This measure is used to quantify the rate at which a company pays off its suppliers. It indicates how quickly (the average number of days) payables are being paid.

Asset turnover = revenue ÷ capital employed

= 3,500,000 ÷ 2,400,000

= 1.46 times

This measures the ability of a company to generate sales or revenues from its assets.

Efficiency ratios measure how efficiently a company uses its assets to generate revenues and manage its liabilities.

Test yourself 8.4

1. How is working capital estimated from the working capital cycle?

The needs of working capital are estimated based on an understanding of the business's working capital cycle. WCC is directly proportionate to the amount of working capital invested. Assuming there are 365 days in a year, WCC is the sum of:

1	Receivables days	[Trade receivables ÷ credit sales] × 365
2	Inventory days	
	a) FG	[Finished goods ÷ cost of sales] × 365
	b) WIP	[WIP ÷ cost of production] × 365
	c) RM	[Raw material ÷ raw material purchases] × 365
3	Less: payables days	[Trade payables ÷ credit purchases] × 365

Estimation of inventory: The amount to be invested in inventory is estimated based on production budget, average holding period and cost per unit of inventory.

RM = Production units per day × RM cost per unit (p.u.) × average RM storage period.

WIP = production units per day × WIP cost p.u. × average WIP holding period.

FG = production units per day × cost of production p.u. × average FG storage period.

Estimation of receivables: Accounts receivables are estimated by the average number of days it takes to collect an account.

Receivables = credit sales units per day × average collection period

Estimation of payables: Accounts payables are estimated by the average number of days taken to make the payment from the date of invoice.

Payables = credit purchases per day × average payment period

Overheads and expenses are also estimated on the above basis.

2. Calculate the working capital requirement for Global Ltd from the following information:

Particulars	Cost per unit £
Raw materials	250
Direct labour	60
Overheads	140
Total cost	450
Profit	100
Selling price	550

- Raw materials are held in stock for one month on average.
- Materials are in process for 20 days on average.
- Finished goods are in stock for one month on average.
- Credit allowed by suppliers is 30 days and credit allowed to debtors is 45 days.
- Credit sales are 50% of total sales.
- Cash in hand and at the bank is expected to be £120,000. The expected level of production will be 126,000 units for a year of 360 days.

Using the above formulas, we can estimate the current assets and current liabilities based on the assumption that production is even throughout the year.

RM = (126,000 ÷ 360) × 250 × 30 = 2,625,000

Work in Process

= RM amount for 20 days + labour and OH for 10 days

= (126,000 ÷ 360) × 250 × 20 + (126,000 ÷ 360) × 200 × 10 = 2,450,000

FG = (126,000 ÷ 360) × 450 × 30 = 4,725,000

Accounts receivables = (126,000 ÷ 360) × 50% × 550 × 45 = 4,331,250

Cash and bank = 120,000

Account payables = (126,000 ÷ 360) × 250 × 30 = 2,625,000

Outstanding labour expenses = (126,000 ÷ 360) × 60 × 10 = 210,000

Outstanding overheads = (126,000 ÷ 360) × 140 × 30 = 1,470,000

Test yourself 8.5

1. How does the JIT system help a company to improve its relationships with customers and suppliers?

The key objective of the JIT system is to reduce flow times within production systems as well as response times from suppliers and to customers. It is defined by Monden Yasuhiro as a methodology used in 'producing the necessary items, in the necessary quantity at the necessary time'.

Reducing the level of inventory does not just reduce carrying costs. By using this technique, manufacturers also get more control over their manufacturing process, making it easier to respond quickly when the needs of customers change. This also reduces the amount of storage and labour costs a business needs.

The relationship with suppliers is an important aspect of the JIT system. If the supplier doesn't deliver the raw materials in time, it could become very expensive for the business. A JIT manufacturer prefers a reliable, local supplier to meet the small but frequent orders at shorter notice, in return for a long-term business relationship.

2. *What are the key features of ABC inventory control?*

ABC inventory control classifies inventory items based on the items' consumption values. In this method of inventory management, the materials are divided into three categories: A being the items requiring the highest investment, B being the medium level and C being the remaining items of stock with relatively low value of consumption.

This method of inventory control helps companies to maintain tighter controls over costly items. Better control over high-value inventory improves efficiency and improves overall profitability. For example, stock management resources can be dedicated to higher valued categories to save time and money. However, since this method focuses only on monetary values, it could ignore other factors which may be important to the business. It also requires keeping track of all inventory items and will be successful only if there is proper standardisation of inventories.

Test yourself 8.6

What are the objectives of trade receivables management?

The management of receivables is a key aspect of working capital management as a substantial amount of cash is tied up in receivables. The ultimate goal of receivables management is to maintain an optimum level of receivables by achieving a trade-off between:

- profitability from credit sales and
- liquidity (reducing the cost of allowed credit)

The objectives of receivables management are:

1. to control the costs associated with the collection and management of receivables: administration costs associated with receivables include maintenance of records, collection costs, default costs and writing off bad debts;
2. to achieve and maintain an optimum level of receivables in accordance with the company's credit policies; and
3. to achieve an optimum level of sales.

Test yourself 8.7

What are the risks of delaying payment to suppliers?

Companies may encounter the following problems by delaying payment to suppliers:

- suppliers may refuse to supply in future
- suppliers may only supply on a cash basis
- a company could exceed its credit period which could risk its credit status with the supplier and could result in supplies being stopped
- a company could also lose the benefit of any settlement discount offered by the supplier for early payment
- there may be loss of reputation suppliers may increase prices in future

Chapter 9

Test yourself 9.1

What are internal sources of short-term finance? How can increasing working capital management efficiency be a good source of short-term internal finance?

Internal sources of short-term finance are funds generated internally by the business in its normal course of operations. For example, the business can raise short-term finance through cash improvements gained by reducing or controlling working capital. Similarly, it can sell assets that are no longer really needed to free up cash or use its internally generated retained earnings.

Internal sources of short-term finance mainly include:

- reducing or controlling working capital
- reducing inventories
- tighter credit control
- delaying payments to suppliers
- sale of redundant assets
- retained profits

A higher level of working capital represents a large commitment of finance and a significant opportunity cost in interest. Efficiency savings generated through efficient management of trade receivables, inventory, cash and trade payables can reduce a bank overdraft and interest charges as well as increase cash reserves that be re-invested elsewhere in the business.

Test yourself 9.2

Kathmandu Ltd is a retail store that sells Himalayan trekking equipment.

Figures from its latest annual financial statements are as follows:

Statement of profit or loss

£'000

Revenue	2,700
Cost of goods sold	(900)
Gross profit	1,800
Administrative expenses	(400)
Marketing expenses	(640)
Operating profit	760

Statement of financial position

Raw materials: £100,000

Finished goods: £350,000

The annual raw materials consumed were £200,000 and the annual cost of goods sold was £900,000. The company introduces a JIT process as a measure to control inventory. As a result, Kathmandu Ltd will be able to reduce its raw materials to 40 days' consumption and Its finished goods inventory to 45 days' cost of goods sold.

The rate of interest charged on its overdraft is 10%. Calculate the reduction in raw materials and finished goods and the overall financial impact.

The reduction in inventory levels released cash that can be used to reduce the company's overdraft. The saving in interest charges at 10% per annum by reducing the overdraft is £31,700.

Inventory reductions also help the business to be more profitable by lowering its cost of goods sold the related administration expenses.

Test yourself 9.3

If a company is risk-averse, why might it be more likely to choose a higher level of working capital? What are the factors to consider in choosing the right balance of working capital?

If a company is risk-averse, it will choose to have a higher level of working capital so that it has more than enough current assets to meet all of its short-term financial obligations. A high level of working capital is considered a sign of a company with the potential for growth. Higher working capital indicates liquidity and that it will be easily able to convert its assets into liquid assets or cash to fulfil its obligations.

Working capital has the following components:

- current assets: inventory, accounts receivables and cash
- current liabilities: accounts payables and bank overdraft

The main objective of working capital management is to get the balance of current assets and current liabilities right. This can also be seen a trade-off between cash flow versus profits. A reduction in working capital and the efficiency savings generated through efficient management of trade receivables, inventory, cash and trade payables can reduce bank overdraft and interest charges as well as increasing cash reserves that can be re-invested elsewhere in the business.

However, too low a level of working capital can result in the inability of a company to meet obligations as they fall due, with the risk of default and insolvency. Similarly, too high a level of working capital represents a large commitment of finance and a significant opportunity cost in interest.

The optimum level of working capital is a trade-off between liquidity and profitability. A company should have current assets sufficiently liquid to reduce the risk of insolvency but also considering profitability by reducing the cost of overtrading and overstocking.

Chapter 10

Test yourself 10.1

Port Louis Ltd provides you with the following details.

				Amounts in £
Month/Year	Sales	Materials	Wages	Overheads
Apr 17	42,000	20,000	16,000	4,500
May 17	45,000	21,000	16,000	4,000
Jun 17	50,000	26,000	16,500	3,800
Jul 17	49,000	28,200	16,500	3,750
Aug 17	54,000	28,000	16,500	6,080
Sep 17	61,000	31,000	17,000	5,200

Other information

1. Sales are 20% on cash. Fifty per cent of credit sales are collected next month and 50% balance in the following month.
2. Credit allowed by suppliers is two months.
3. Wages and overheads are paid a month in arrears.
4. Dividends on investments amounting to £25,000 are expected to be received in the month of June 2017.
5. New machinery costing £400,000 is to be installed in June 2017. This is payable in 20 instalments starting from July 2017.

6. *The cash balance on 1 April 2017 is £45,000.*

Prepare a monthly cash budget statement for the six-month period April to September on the basis of the above information.

Cash budget for the period April 2017 to September 2017

	Apr 17	May 17	Jun 17	Jul 17	Aug 17	Sep 17
Opening balance of cash	45,000	53,400	58,700	88,500	75,000	59,150
Inflows						
Cash sales	8,400	9,000	10,000	9,800	10,800	12,200
Collection from debtors	–	16,800	34,800	38,000	39,600	41,200
Dividends	–	–	25,000	–	–	–
Total inflow	8,400	25,800	69,800	47,800	50,400	53,400
Outflows						
Materials	–	–	20,000	21,000	26,000	28,200
Wages	–	16,000	16,000	16,500	16,500	16,500
Overheads	–	4,500	4,000	3,800	3,750	6,080
Instalment of machinery	–	–	–	20,000	20,000	20,000
Total outflow	–	20,500	40,000	61,300	66,250	70,780
Cash balance to be carried forward to next month	53,400	58,700	88,500	75,000	59,150	41,770

Workings:
Calculation of receipts from sales

Cash sales	Amount	Apr 17	May 17	Jun 17	Jul 17	Aug 17	Sep 17
Apr 17	42,000	8,400					
May 17	45,000		9,000				
Jun 17	50,000			10,000			
Jul 17	49,000				9,800		
Aug 17	54,000					10,080	
Sep 17	61,000						12,200
		8,400	9,000	10,000	9,800	10,080	12,200

Credit sales	Amount	Apr 17	May 17	Jun 17	Jul 17	Aug 17	Sep 17
Apr 17	33,600		16,800	16,800			
May 17	36,000			18,000	18,000		
Jun 17	40,000				20,000	20,000	
Jul 17	39,200					19,600	19,600
Aug 17	43,200						21,600
Sep 17	48,800						
			16,800	34,800	38,000	39,600	41,200

Test yourself 10.2

How does a primary market differ from a secondary market?

A primary market is a 'new issues market' where companies can raise 'new' funds by issuing shares or loan stock. A secondary market permits the primary market to operate more efficiently by facilitating deals in existing securities.

Test yourself 10.3

What are the key advantages of a public market over a private market?

Public markets are markets where the general public can participate in such as stock market. A person can participate in such a market with as little as £10. Public markets also offer greater liquidity, thereby enabling a smooth purchase or sale. The risk profile of public markets is relatively small because of regulations, transparency and monitoring by seasoned investors and regulators.

Key advantages of public markets over private markets include:

- no qualification or net worth criteria is required to be fulfilled to enter the market;
- highly regulated and transparent markets, thereby reducing risk; and
- highly liquid investments.

Test yourself 10.4

1. *Why do companies list their shares on a stock exchange?*

Companies issue shares in the stock market to:

- raise funds for business requirements;
- to comply with the requirement of a stock exchange flotation where a minimum proportion of shares must be made available to the public;
- to provide an exit to investors who have invested in the company by providing liquidity to the stocks of the company;
- to increase the brand image of the company; and
- for many other reasons.

2. **What are the key functions of a stock exchange?**

Key functions of a stock exchange include:

- providing the value of stock of a company;
- acting as a barometer for the economic performance of the country;
- ensuring fair dealing between investors;
- regulating intermediaries and companies; and
- promoting economic growth.

Test yourself 10.5

1. **What are the three forms of market efficiency?**

There are three levels of market efficiency as per the EMH:

- **Weak form:** the market prices are reflective of all historical information contained in the record of past prices. Share prices will follow a 'random walk' and move up or down depending on the next piece of information about the company that reaches the market. The weak form implies that it is impossible to predict future prices by reference to past share price movements.
- **Semi-strong form:** the market prices reflect not just the past and historical data but all information which is currently publicly available. Investors are unable to gain abnormal returns by analysing publicly available information after it has been released. The price will alter only when new information is published. With this level of efficiency, share prices can be predicted only if unpublished information were known. This would be known as insider dealing.
- **Strong form:** share prices reflect all available relevant information, published and unpublished including- insider information. This implies that even insiders are unable to make abnormal returns as the market price already reflects all information.

2. **In what form of market efficiency can money be made by insider dealing?**

Evidence suggests that stock markets are semistrong market efficient at best. Any new information is rapidly reflected in the share price. In semi-strong efficiency, all public information is already reflected in the share price. With this level of efficiency, share price can be predicted only if unpublished information is known through insider dealing.

3. **Provide an example of exceptions when a sudden price change is not triggered by new information about the company reaching the market.**

There are times when sudden large price changes do not appear to be triggered by new information reaching the market. There are also instances when prices change quickly, but not instantaneously, over short periods before price-sensitive information is released by companies. For example, in October 1987 the value of shares on the London Stock Exchange fell by one-quarter during the course of the month with no specific new information identified as the cause of the fall. In contrast, the steep fall in share prices in 2008 could be associated with the accumulated impact of the global credit crisis that started with sub-prime lending failures in the US.

Test yourself 10.6

How can companies raise finance from the following institutional investors?

1. *Private equity*

Private equity finance is not publicly traded but raised through private investors that are typically large institutional investors, university endowments, or wealthy individuals. It is organised through the mediation of a venture capital company or private equity business. Raising private equity finance does not expose the company to the similar scrutiny and regulation of a stock market.

It is perceived to be an investment with relatively high risk for investors. Investors provide finance through placing as they yield higher returns than they would from a stock market listed company. Placing is a way of raising equity capital by selling shares directly to third party investors (usually a merchant bank). Business angels are a source of private equity finance to start-up and early-stage businesses in return for a share of the company's equity.

2. *Pension funds*

A pension fund, also known as a superannuation fund in some countries, is a fund from which pensions are paid.

Pension funds typically have large amounts of money to invest in both listed and private companies. Pension funds, along with insurance companies, make up a large proportion of the institutional investors that dominate stock markets. In most pension funds, there is a surplus of incoming funds from contributions over outgoings as pension payments. This surplus is invested to maximise the best possible return, while maintaining the security of the funds.

Chapter 11

Test yourself 11.1

1. *What are the advantages of issuing equity shares from a company perspective?*

The advantages of issuing equity shares are as follows.

- Equity shares are permanent capital and a long-term source of finance.
- Normally, the capital raised is not required to be paid back during the lifetime of the company, other than in the event of liquidation.

- The dividend on equity shares is not a liability for the company. To protect the interests of creditors, a company may declare a dividend only if it has sufficient profit available for the purpose.

A company that raises capital with equity shares gives a positive outlook of the company, providing greater confidence to investors and creditors.

2. How can companies raise finance from a rights issue?

Companies can raise finance by making a rights issue that offers existing shareholders the right to buy new shares in proportion to their existing shareholdings. Rights issues enables shareholders to retain their existing share of voting rights.

Test yourself 11.2

What factors should you consider when choosing between sources of finance?

The main factors to consider when choosing between sources of finance are summarised below.

1. **Access to finance:** the ability of a company to raise equity finance is dependent on its access to the investors. Quoted companies can issue both new shares and make rights issues. However, unquoted companies can only raise finance by rights issues and private placings due to its restricted access to public. There are also statutory restrictions: in the UK, only public limited companies may offer shares to the general public.
2. **Control**: Raising funds through internally-generated funds and rights issues results in no change to shareholder control. However, if diversification of control is desired, then an issue to the public will be preferred.
3. **Amount of finance:** the amount of finance that can be raised by a rights issue is limited and dependent on the amounts that can be raised from the existing shareholders. There is more flexibly for quoted companies for the amounts that can raised from the general public that opens up the full financial resources of the market.
4. **Cost of raising finance**: flotations incur significant costs in management and administrative time and may not be a viable option for smaller companies. Use of internally generated funds is the cheapest and simplest method. For shares, public offers are the most expensive, following by placings and then by rights issues.
5. **Pricing the issue:** setting the price correctly is the most difficult area for all shares. For public issues, there is a danger of undersubscription if it is set too high, unlike a placing which is pre-agreed and negotiated to be attractive enough to the subscribing institutions. A rights issue bypasses the price problem since the shares are offered to existing shareholders. For unquoted companies, pricing is more complex as they cannot refer to no existing market prices.

Test yourself 11.3

Why would investors be interested in preference shares with warrants attached?

Warrants attached to a preference share are attractive to investors because they offering the potential to earn a profit in the future. Warrants are rights given to lenders allowing them to buy new shares in a company at a future date at a fixed price (the exercise price). If the current share price is higher than the exercise price, then the warrant holder has a potential to make a profit by getting the shares at a cheaper exercise price in the future.

Test yourself 11.4

How can purchasing assets via leases assist in managing a company's cash levels?

The biggest advantage of leasing is that cash outflow or payments related to leasing are spread out over several years, hence saving the burden of one-time significant cash payment to purchase an asset outright. This helps a business to maintain a steady cash-flow profile.

Test yourself 11.5

What are the limitations of PFI?

PFI schemes are controversial due to the wasteful spending built into the public sector procurement agreements that are part of PFI projects. There are many stories of flawed projects.

The biggest disadvantage is the high annual cost charged to the public sector for the project. The costs have been significantly larger than the annual cost of comparable projects. Many of the projects have run over budget. For example, the cost of private sector finance in the 2000s increased the overall debt cost of the UK government, indirectly costing taxpayers.

Since the asset ownership is transferred to the private sector it may lead to a loss of control and accountability by the public sector. The ultimate risk of inflexibility and poor value for money with a project lies with the public sector. Repair or maintenance costs could also be higher. The administration cost spending on advisers and lawyers and the costs of the bidding process could cost millions.

Chapter 12

Test yourself 12.1

Calculate the cost of equity of three shares, A, B and C, given that the risk-free rate is 4.25% and the market return is 12%. The ßs of the three securities are 1.35, 2.10 and 0.78 respectively.

RADR = RFR + β (RM − RFR)

Share A
RADR = 4.25 + 1.35 × (12 − 4.25) = **14.71%**

Share B
RADR = 4.25 + 2.10 × (12 − 4.25) = **20.53%**

Share C
RADR = 4.25 + 0.78 × (12 − 4.25) = **10.3%**

Test yourself 12.2

Guava Ltd issued 10% irredeemable debentures with a market price of £105 per £100 par value. The corporate tax rate is 35%. Calculate the cost of debt after tax.

$$K_d = \frac{(I(1-t))}{S_d}$$

K_d = (10 × (1 − 0.20)) ÷ 105 = 7.62%

Cost of debt after tax for Guava Ltd is 7.62%.

Test yourself 12.3

On formation Apindra Ltd issued 4 million equity shares with a nominal value of 50p each. The current market price of a share is 140p (ex-dividend). The company is growing and it has just paid a dividend of 17p per share. Historically, dividends are growing at a rate of 6% p.a.

Apindra Ltd has also issued irredeemable debentures of £3.5 million. The current market price of the debentures is £90.01 per £100. The debentures have been issued with a coupon rate of 13%. The corporate tax rate is 20%.

Calculate the WACC for Apindra & Co.

The company is growing and it has just paid a dividend of 17p per share. Historically, dividends are growing at a rate of 6% p.a.

Apindra & Co has also issued irredeemable debentures of £3.5 million. The current market price of the debentures is £90.01 per £100. The debentures have been issued with a coupon rate of 13%. The corporation tax rate is 30%.

Calculate the WACC for Apindra & Co.

$$WACC = K_e [\frac{E}{E+D}] + K_d (1-t) [\frac{D}{E+D}]$$

Interpreting Financial and Accounting Information

Cost of equity

As we have the information on dividend and growth rate, we will use the dividend growth model to calculate the cost of equity.

$K_e = [d_0 (1 + g) \div P_0] + g$

$= [17 \times (1 + 0.06) \div 140] + 0.06$

$= 0.1287 + 0.06$

$= 0.1887$

$K_e = 18.87\%$

Cost of debt

$K_d = \dfrac{I(1 - t)}{S_d}$ ← coupon

$= \dfrac{13 \times (1 - 0.20)}{90.01}$

$= 0.1155$

$K_d = 11.55$

Market value

Equity	4,000,000 × 1.4 = 5,600,000	£5,600,000
Debt	3,500,000 × (90.01 ÷ 100) = 3,150,350	£3,150,350
Equity + debt		£8,750,350

WACC

	Market Value £	Weight	K (%)	K (W)
Equity	5,600,000	0.6400	18.87%	12.08%
Debt	3,150,350	0.3600	11.35%	4.16%
Equity + debt	8,750,350	1.000		16.24%

The weighted average cost of capital for Apindra & Co is 16.24%.

Typically, a high WACC is a sign of higher risk associated with a company. A WACC of 16.24% means the company has to pay its investors an average of £0.1624 in return for every £1 of extra funding.

Test yourself 12.4

1. What is meant by a highly geared company?

A highly geared company has a high ratio of long-term debt to shareholders' funds. A high level of gearing implies a higher obligation for the business in paying interest when using debt financing. It has a higher risk of insolvency than equity financing. While dividends on ordinary share capital need only be paid when there are sufficient distributable profits, the interest on debt is payable regardless of the operating profit of a company.

A review of the gearing ratio is key in the funding decisions made by financial managers and investors. It affects risk, returns and controls associated with equity capital. Investors may require a higher return to compensate for the higher risk associated with the higher gearing. According to the control principle, debt may also be preferred over equity to minimise possible risk of loss of control.

2. **When might investors and other stakeholders prefer gearing and why?**

Other stakeholders who have an interest in the profitability and stability of the company, including employees, customers and particularly creditors, will also be interested in the level of gearing. Since debt capital is cheaper than equity capital, debt financing should minimise the cost of capital and maximise the earnings per share. The interest on debt is deductible for income tax purposes, making debt capital cheaper, whereas no such deductions are allowed for dividends. Debt should be used to the extent that it does not threaten the solvency of the firm.

3. **What are the problems around high gearing?**

The problems of high gearing include:

- bankruptcy risk increases with increased gearing;
- agency costs and restrictive conditions imposed in the loan agreements constrain management's freedom of action, such as restrictions on dividend levels or on the company's ability to borrow;
- after a certain level of gearing, companies will have no tax liability left against which to offset interest charges (tax exhaustion);
- companies may run out of suitable assets to offer as security against loans with high gearing;
- gearing increases the cost of borrowing; and
- directors have a natural tendency to be cautious about borrowing and related solvency issues.

Test yourself 12.5

A summarised statement of profit and loss of Ealing Ltd is shown below.

	Ealing Ltd
	£'000
Sales	20
Variable costs	−5
Fixed costs	−8
Operating profit	7
Interest	−2
Profit before taxation	5

How would a 20% fall in sales affect EBIT and shareholder return?

	Ealing Ltd £000	Ealing Ltd £000 After fall in sales
Sales	20	16
Variable costs	−5	−4
Fixed costs	−8	−8
Operating profit	7	4
Interest	−2	−2
Profit before tax	5	2

The 20% decrease in sales reduces EBIT by:

$$\frac{7-4}{7} = 43\%$$

The increased volatility can be explained by the high operating gearing. Higher operational gearing makes EBIT more sensitive to a change in sales. The 20% drop in sales has caused the overall profit/shareholders' return to fall by 60% as per the following equation.

$(5 - 2) \div 5 = 60\%$

Test yourself 12.6

Outline the Modigliani and Miller theory of capital structure.

The Modigliani–Miller theory states that capital structure is irrelevant and efforts to reduce the cost of capital using gearing will not succeed.

The first proposition states that the value of the geared firm equals the value of the ungeared firm (earnings before interest ÷ WACC). The value of WACC is constant at all levels of gearing.

The second proposition states that savings from debt being cheaper than equity are equal to the increase in the cost of equity due to increased risk arising from gearing. The cost of equity in geared company K_g equals the cost of ungeared company K_u, plus a premium for financial risk.

Later developments in the theory with the introduction of tax state that debt interest is tax-deductible, whereas ordinary share dividends are not. The conclusions are that debt is, in fact, cheaper than equity. Tax relief on debt interest reduces the WACC. Therefore, gearing up reduces the WACC and increases the market value of the company. The optimal capital structure is 99.9% gearing. This means higher the debt, the lower the WACC and the higher the market value. The company should use as much debt as possible.

Chapter 13

Test yourself 13.1

A project is expected to have the following cash flows:

Year	Cash flow £
0	(1,500)
1	100
2	400
3	600
4	500
5	800

1. What is the expected payback period?

Year	Cash flow	Cumulative cash flow
0	(1,500)	(1,500)
1	100	(1,400)
2	400	(1,000)
3	600	(400)
4	500	100
5	800	900

Payback period = three years and nine months

[(400 ÷ 500) × 12 months = 9.6 months]

2. What are the basic decision-making factors to consider when making a choice between two or more projects using payback period?

A few factors need to be considered in deciding whether to accept this project:

- a project is acceptable if it pays back within the target period when choosing between two or more projects, the project(s) with the fastest payback is chosen.

3. How do depreciation and sunk costs affect the decision-making process in project appraisal?

Sunk costs and depreciation are non-relevant factors for project appraisal. Sunk costs are past expenditure that cannot be recovered and hence cannot influence the current decision. Depreciation is a non-cash item and does not affect future cash flows.

Test yourself 13.2

A project involves the immediate purchase of an item of plant costing £150,000. It will generate annual cash flows of £29,000 for five years, starting in year one. The plant will have a scrap value of £15,000 in five years when the project terminates. Depreciation is on a straight-line basis.

1. Determine the project's ARR using:
   average capital investment.

Annual depreciation = (initial investment − scrap value) ÷ useful life in years

Average annual depreciation = (£150,000 − £15,000) ÷ 5 = £27,000

Average annual profits = Annual cash flow less depreciation

£29,000 − £27,000 = £2,000

Using average capital investment:

Average annual profits = £2,000

Average book value of assets = (initial cost + final scrap value) ÷ 2

= (£150,000 + £15,000) ÷ 2

= £82,500

ARR = (Average annual profit ÷ average capital investment) × 100%

= (£2,000 ÷ £82,500) × 100%

= 2.42%

2. What are the limitations of using ARR for evaluating projects?

The key limitations of using ARR are listed below.

- It ignores factors such as project life (the longer the project, the greater the risk), working capital and other economic factors which may affect the profitability of the project.
- Accounting rate of return is based on accounting profits that vary depending on accounting policies (such as depreciation policy).
- Accounting rate of return does not take into account the time value of money.
- Accounting rate of return can be calculated using different formulas. For example, ARR can be calculated using profit after tax and interest, or profit before tax, thus leading to different outcomes. It is important to ensure that ARRs are calculated on a consistent basis when comparing investments.

- It is not useful for evaluating projects where investment is made in parts at different times.
- It does not take into account any profits that are reinvested during the project period.

Test yourself 13.3

1. *If you have £5,000 now to invest for six years at an interest rate of 5% pa, what will be the value of the investment after six years?*

The value of the investment is found by applying the compounding formula:

$FV = PV(1 + r)^n$

Where:

FV = future value of investment
PV = present value of investment
r = rate of compound interest
n = number of years

$FV = £5,000 (1 + 0.05)^6$

$= £5,000 \times 1.3401$

$= £6,700$

The value of the investment after six years would be £6,700.

2. *If a company expects to earn a compound rate of 10% interest on its investment, how much will it need to invest now to earn:*
   - *£11,000 in the first year*
   - *£12,100 in the second year*
   - *£13,310 in the third year?*

The amount of the investment is found by applying the discounting formula:

$PV = FV \div (1 + r)^n$

a. After one year = £11,000 × 1 ÷ 1.10 = £10,000

b. After two years = £12,100 × 1 ÷ $(1.10)^2$ = £10,000

c. After three years = £13,310 × 1 ÷ $(1.10)^3$ = £10,000

Discounting can be applied to both cash receivable and payable at a future date. The company would have to invest £10,000 now to generate the above returns.

Test yourself 13.4

Dhimal Ltd is considering a capital investment in new equipment. The estimated cash flows are as follows.

Year	Cash flows
0	(250,000)
1	100,000
2	120,000
3	70,000
4	40,000
5	20,000

The company's cost of capital is 9%. Calculate the NPV of the project to assess whether it should be undertaken? The discount factor you will need can be found using a present value table.

Year	Cash flow	DF @ 9%	PV
0	(250,000)	1	(250,000)
1	100,000	0.917	91,700
2	120,000	0.842	101,040
3	70,000	0.772	54,040
4	40,000	0.708	28,320
5	20,000	0.650	13,000
			38,100

The PV of cash inflows exceeds the PV of cash outflows by £38,100. This means that the project will earn a DCF return in excess of 9% and will earn a surplus of £38,100 after paying the cost of financing. It should be undertaken.

Test yourself 13.5

Mizher Ltd is expected to make a payment of £5,000 every year for the next six years, the first payment occurring in one year's time. The interest rate is 8%. What is the PV of the annuity?

The PV of an annuity can be found by adding together the PVs of each separate payment.

Year	Payment	DF (8%)	PV
1	5,000	0.926	4,630
2	5,000	0.857	4,285
3	5,000	0.794	3,970
4	5,000	0.735	3,675
5	5,000	0.681	3,405
6	5,000	0.630	3,150
		4.623	23,115

Sum of all DF is 4.623

Therefore,

PV = £5,000 × 4.623 = 23,115

Alternatively, $AF = [(1 - (1 + r)^{-n}] \div r$

$AF = [1 - (1.08)^{-6}] \div 0.08 = 4.623$

= £5,000 × 4.623 = £23,115

Test yourself 13.6

Jollof Rice Ltd undertakes high risk investments and requires a minimum expected rate of return of 18% p.a. on its investments. A proposed capital investment has the following expected cash flows:

Year	£
0	(100,000)
1	46,000
2	35,000
3	40,000
4	20,000

Estimate the IRR of the project using the NPVs at 15% and 20% cost of capital. Make a recommendation on whether this project should be accepted.

Year	Cash flow	DF 15%	PV15%	DF 20%	PV20%
0	(100,000)	1	(100,000)	1	(100,000)
1	46,000	0.87	40,020	0.833	38,318
2	35,000	0.756	26,460	0.694	24,290
3	40,000	0.658	26,320	0.579	23,160
4	20,000	0.572	11,440	0.482	9,640
NPV			4,240		(4,592)

Using the interpolation method:

the NPV1 is 4,240 at 15%

the NPV2 is −4,592 at 20%

The estimated IRR (between these two rates) is therefore:

IRR = 15% + (4,240 ÷ (4,240 − (−4,592))) × (20 − 15)%

IRR = 15% + 2.4%

IRR = 17.4%

The project is expected to earn an IRR of 17.4%, which is lower than the target rate of 18%. It is therefore not a worthwhile investment on financial grounds. However, this approach to appraising the investment ignores other risks and factors such as project duration, future costs and relative size of the investments.

Chapter 14

Test yourself 14.1

John Dove Ltd is considering investing £200,000 in equipment to produce a new product line that will generate sales revenue of £200,000 for the next five years. The scrap value of the equipment at the end of five years is £70,000. It is also estimated to incur annual variable costs of £100,000 while annual fixed costs will increase by £55,000.

Assuming that all cash flows occur at annual intervals, calculate the NPV of the project using the 'best estimate' figures. Determine whether the project should be undertaken. John Dove Ltd has a cost of capital of 10%.

Prepare a sensitivity analysis and calculate the percentage changes required in the following estimates for the investment decision to change:

1. *initial investment*
2. *sales volume*
3. *sales revenue*
4. *variable costs*
5. *fixed costs*
6. *scrap value*
7. *cost of capital*

NPV calculation

Year		Cash flow £'000	10% DF	PV £'000
0	Equipment	(200)	1.00	(200)
1–5	Revenue	200	3.7908	758
1–5	Variable costs	(100)	3.7908	(379)
1–5	Fixed costs	(55)	3.7908	(208)
5	Scrap value	70	0.6209	43
			NPV	14

On the basis of these estimates, the project should be accepted.

2. **Sensitivity analysis**

   (i) sensitivity to change of the initial investment

   14 ÷ 200 × 100% = 7%

   For the decision to change, the NPV must fall by £14,000 and the cost of the equipment must rise by £14,000.

   This is a rise of: 7.00%

   (ii) Sensitivity of scrap value

   For the NPV to fall by £14,000 (giving an NPV of zero), the PV of scrap proceeds must fall by £14,000. This is a fall of:

   14 ÷ 43 × 100% = 32.56%

   (iii) Selling price

   For the NPV of the project to fall by £14,000, the selling price (or the sales revenue) must fall by:

   14 ÷ 758 × 100% = 1.85%

   (iv) Variable cost

   Since the PV of variable costs is £379,000, a rise of £14,000 is an increase of:

   14 ÷ 379 × 100% = 3.69%

   (v) Annual fixed costs

   For the decision to change, the fixed cost must rise by £14,000.

   14 ÷ 208 × 100% = 6.74%

   (vi) Sales volume

   If sales volume falls, contribution (revenue less variable costs) also falls in direct proportion to sales volume.

If the NPV is to fall by £14,000, volume must fall by:

14 ÷ 379 × 100% = 3.69%

(vii) Cost of capital

If NPV is to fall to zero, the cost of capital must rise. The figure which the cost of capital must rise to, that gives an NPV of zero, is the project's IRR.

To find the IRR, which is probably not much above 10%, the NPV is calculated at 15%:

Year		Cash flow	15% DF	PV
		£'000		£'000
0	Equipment	(200)	1.00	(200)
1–5	Revenue	200	3.352	670
1–5	Variable costs	(100)	3.352	(335)
1–5	Fixed costs	(55)	3.352	(184)
5	Scrap value	70	0.497	35
			NPV	(14)

For the investment decision to change, the cost of capital would have to increase from 10% to:

IRR = R1 + NPV1 ÷ (NPV1 − NPV2) × (R2 − R1)

R1   Lower discount rate chosen
R2   Higher discount rate chosen

IRR = 10% + 14 ÷ (14 + 14) × (15 − 10) % = 13%

Chapter 15

Test yourself 15.1

The shares of Sira plc are trading at £30 and the company has an EPS of £2 over the last year.

1. Calculate the P/E ratio.

P/E ratio = Market price per share ÷ EPS

£30 ÷ £2 = 15 times

2. How is the P/E ratio used and interpreted by investors?

The P/E ratio is a widely used tool for stock analysis and investment decisions. Investors use this ratio for their own perceptions about the market and make decisions to buy or sell accordingly. The P/E ratio is compared with those of its competitors and with the industry average.

The P/E ratio gives a stock market view of the quality of the underlying earnings. Generally, a high P/E ratio indicates that investors anticipate higher earnings and higher growth in the future. The average market P/E ratio is 20–25 times earnings. A loss-making company does not have a P/E ratio. However, a company with a high P/E ratio can also indicate that the share is being overvalued. If a company has a high P/E, investors are paying a higher price for the share compared to its earnings.

A company with a low P/E may indicate undervalued shares. This makes a company with a low P/E a good value investment with potential opportunity to be profitable, but it can also simply indicate that investors aren't very confident about the company's future prospects.

The P/E ratio shows the number of years it would take for the company to pay back the amount paid for the share.

Test yourself 15.2

ABC plc generated sales revenue of £200 million during the year with an operating profit margin of 15%. The company pays tax at a rate of 20%. The incremental investment in working capital was £13 million and the incremental investment in non-current assets was £6 million.

1. Calculate the free cash flow for the year.

	£ million
Sales	200
Less: operating costs	170
Net operating profit	30
Less: tax	6
Less: incremental investment in working capital	13
Less: incremental investment in non-current assets	6
= Free cash flow from operations	5

A positive FCF indicates the surplus cash available to shareholders, net of all required investments in working capital and fixed capital (capital expenditure). It enhances shareholder value through opportunities to expand production, develop new products, reduce the cost of debt and pay higher dividends.

2. What is the significance of identifying value drivers in SVA?

Value drivers are factors that drive a business, which in return creates value in a company. These factors impact a company's future cash flow and the value of its NPV. Shareholder value analysis helps the management to focus on factors which create value to the shareholders, rather than on short-term profitability. Key value drivers include:

- growth in sales
- improvement of profit margin
- investment in fixed assets or fixed capital
- investment in working capital
- cost of capital
- tax rate

Managers are required to pay attention to decisions influencing the value drivers and its ultimate impact on value creation.

Test yourself 15.3

Mirak Ltd invested £15 million at the start of the year and has generated after-tax operating profits of £3 million. The weighted average cost of capital is 12%.

1. Calculate the EVA of the firm.

	£ million
NOPAT	3
Capital invested	15
WACC	12%
EVA	1.2

EVA = NOPAT − (WACC × capital invested)

= 3 − (12% × 15) = £1.2 million

A positive EVA indicates that Mirak Ltd has recovered its cost of capital. The value of the profitability or wealth created for shareholders over and above their cost of capital is £1.2 million.

2. *Explain the concept of EVA to a layperson using the above illustration.*

Economic value added (EVA) is a measure of a company's financial performance based on the residual wealth calculated by deducting its cost of capital from its operating profit. It attempts to capture the true economic profit of a company.

In the illustration above, the economic value of the profitability or wealth created for shareholders over and above their cost of capital is £1.2 million.

Directory of web resources

Accounting Web
https://www.accountingweb.co.uk

British Standards Institution
https://www.bsigroup.com/en-GB/

European Financial Reporting Advisory Group
https://www.efrag.org

Financial Conduct Authority
https://www.handbook.fca.org.uk/handbook

Financial Reporting Council
https://www.frc.org.uk

Global Reporting Initiative
https://www.globalreporting.org

International Auditing and Assurance Standards Board
https://www.iaasb.org

International Financial Reporting Standards Foundation
https://www.ifrs.org

National Bureau of Economic Research
https://www.nber.org

Pensions and Lifetime Savings Association
https://www.plsa.co.uk/

Public Company Accounting Oversight Board
https://pcaobus.org

Glossary

Agency cost – Agency costs are direct and indirect costs arising from the inefficiency of a relationship between shareholders and business managers. Examples of the direct agency costs include the monitoring costs such as fees payable to external auditors to assess the accuracy of the company's financial statements.

AIM – AIM (formerly the Alternative Investment Market) is a sub-market of the London Stock Exchange designed to provide a platform for smaller companies to raise capital from the general public without going through the rigors of compliance requirements which must be satisfied to raise capital from the main platform.

Amortised cost – Amortised cost is an accounting method which requires financial assets or financial liabilities to be measured at initial cost less principal repayment, adjusted for amortisation of discount/premium (if any) and foreign exchange differences (if any) less any reduction for impairment or uncollectability.

Annuity – A series of payments made at regular intervals during a specified period of time.

Asset allocation – An investment strategy that aims to reduce uncertainties and balance risk and reward within a portfolio by using a mix of assets that have low correlation to each other.

Associate – IAS 28 defines an associate as 'an entity over which the investor has significant influence and that is neither a subsidiary nor an interest in a joint venture'.

Authorised share capital – The maximum amount of share capital that a company may issue (as detailed in the company's Memorandum of Association).

Basic EPS – Basic earnings per share are residual profits for a period attributable to the shares outstanding for that same period.

Bond – A fixed income investment in which an investor loans money to an entity (private or government) for a defined period of time at a fixed interest rate. It is a general term for the various types of long-term loans to companies, including loan stock and debentures.

Bonus issue of shares – A bonus issue of shares, also known as a scrip issue, is additional free shares given to the current shareholders without any additional cost, based upon their existing number of shares, by transfer from other components of equity.

Breakup value method – Breakup value is based on net realisable value. It is calculated by taking the current market value of all assets of the business, then deducting the liabilities and reasonable liquidation fees. This method is used by entity reporting on non-going-concern basis that is based on cost/fair value (as per IFRS requirements).

Brexit – A term for the withdrawal of the United Kingdom from the European Union.

Budgeting – Budgeting is an outline of a company's financial plans, normally drawn for the next three to five years. It is the process of creating a plan, also referred to as a financial budget, to project incomes and outflows for the long term as well as the short term.

Business angels – Wealthy, private investors who provide their personal wealth to start-up and early-stage businesses in return for a share of the company's equity. While venture capitalists use pooled money, business angels usually invest their own funds.

Business risk – The possibility a company will have inadequate profit or even result in losses due to uncertainties in the business.

Capital market – A capital market is where long-term finance products with maturities of more than one year are traded. These include long-term debt or bond (over a year) or equity-backed securities.

Capital rationing – A strategy that firms implement when there are insufficient funds. It places limitations or restrictions on the amount of new investments or projects undertaken by a company.

Capital structure – The mix of debt and equity financing in a business. It shows how the business is financed.

Carrying amount – The recorded cost of an asset or a liability net of any accumulated depreciation or accumulated impairment losses. Also referred to as book value.

Cash budget – A cash budget sets out the cash inflows and outflows for a business over a specific period of time. It ensures there is enough cash within the business to operate.

Cash forecast – A cash forecast is an estimate of cash receipts and payments for a future period, including all the projected income and expenses under existing conditions.

Coefficient of variation – The ratio of standard deviation to the mean, applying in a single variable dataset. It measures extent of variability or the dispersion of data points in a dataset in relation to the mean of the population.

Commercial paper – Commercial paper is an unsecured, short-term debt instrument issued and backed by an issuing bank or company. It is essentially money lent to the issuing company or bank. They are sold at a discount but pay the full face amount on the maturity date of no more than 270 days from the date they were issued.

Compounding – Compounding is the process of determining the future value of present investment or cashflows by considering interests that can be earned in the amounts invested today.

Contingent liabilities – Possible liabilities that may occur depending on the outcome of an uncertain future event and present obligations, the settlement of which is not probable or the amount cannot be measured reliably.

Corporate governance – The set of internal rules, policies and processes that determine how a company is directed.

Correlation – Correlation, in terms of portfolio management, is a statistical tool that measures the degree to which two securities move in relation to each other.

Crowdfunding – A practice of raising money, most commonly via the internet, to support a business venture, project, or local initiative. The investors will sometime receive shares in the business. More often, they will receive a reward such as early receipt of the product being produced and/or a discount on the price of the product.

Cumulative preference share – A cumulative preference share accrues or accumulates its annual fixed-rate dividend in the following year, if it cannot be paid in any year.

De facto control – Control in fact, or 'de facto control', is a broader concept that focuses on influence rather than legal control. One party can have a substantial holding of voting rights and the remainder, while a majority, are held by a wide range of unconnected parties.

Debenture – A written acknowledgement of a debt used by large companies to borrow money, at a fixed rate of interest.

Debt factoring – A financial arrangement whereby a business sells all or selected accounts receivables at a price lower than the realisable value to a third party, known as the factor, who takes responsibility for collecting money from the customers. Also known as invoice factoring.

Debt finance – Borrowed money to be paid back at a future date with interest. It could be in the form of a secured as well as an unsecured loan.

Depreciation – The systematic spread of the cost of an asset over its useful life (period it will be used to generate benefit).

Diluted EPS – Residual profits for a period attributable to the outstanding shares adjusted to include all potential dilution. A diluted EPS assumes that all the convertible securities will be exercised.

Discount rate – The rate of return used in a discounted cash flow analysis to determine the current worth or present value of future cash flows.

Discounting – The process of determining the present value of future cash flows by using discounted rate that considers factors such as inflation, risk of uncertain future and the ability to earn interest.

Diversification – Spreading risk across multiple investments within an asset class.

Draft – A non-interest-bearing binding agreement by one party (the drawer) to another (the drawee) to pay a fixed amount of money for payment of goods and/or services as of a predetermined date or on demand.

Effective interest method – The method for amortising a financial instrument to its net present value by discounting the expected future cash flow using a market rate of interest.

Efficient frontier – A modern portfolio theory tool that shows investors the best possible return they can expect from their portfolio for a defined level of risk.

Environmental audit – An assessment of the extent to which an organisation meets the set criteria or standards that help to minimise harm to the environment.

Environmental reporting – The process of externally communicating the environmental effects of an organisation's economic actions through the corporate annual report or a separate stand-alone publicly available environmental report.

Equity finance – The finance relating to the owners or equity shareholders of the business who jointly exercise ultimate control through their voting rights. Equity finance is represented by the issued ordinary share capital plus reserves or retained earnings.

Equity method – A method of accounting investment when the investor holds significant influence over the investee (often referred to as an associate), but does not exercise full control over it, as in its subsidiary. An equity investment is initially recorded at cost and is subsequently adjusted to reflect the investor's share of the net profit or loss of the associate.

Event tree diagrams – Event tree diagrams represent all possible outcomes of an event that allow users to calculate their probability.

Expected net present value – A capital budgeting and appraisal technique based on net present value under different scenarios, after probability-weighting them to adjust for uncertainties on each scenarios.

External audit – An independent audit opinion on whether the financial statements give a 'true and fair' view of the company's state of affairs and operations for the period. The auditors ensure that the board receives accurate and reliable information and assesses the appropriateness of the accounting principles used by a company.

Extraordinary items – Extraordinary items are prohibited under IFRS. These were defined as items that were both unusual in nature and infrequent in occurrence.

Fair value – Fair value is the sale price agreed upon by knowledgeable and willing parties in an arm's length transaction.

First in, first out (FIFO) – A method used to account for inventory costs where the oldest inventory items are assumed and recorded as sold first.

Financial forecasting – The estimation of a company's future financial outcomes by examining its historical and current financial data.

Financial gearing – The proportion of debt a company has relative to its equity. Also known as capital gearing.

Financial instrument – A legally enforceable (binding) agreement, between two or more parties, that can be created, traded, modified and settled. International Accounting Standards define a financial instrument as 'any contract that gives rise to a financial asset of one entity and a financial liability or equity instrument of another entity'.

Financial market – A marketplace where financial wealth or assets (such as equities, bonds, currencies and derivatives) of individuals, institutions, government and so on are traded.

Financial regulator – An institution that supervises and controls a financial system to protect the interest of investors and to guarantee fair and efficient markets and financial stability.

Financial risk – Risk associated with financing, including risk of default from investing in a company that has debt.

Generally Accepted Accounting Principles – The Generally Accepted Accounting Principles (GAAP) are rules and regulations influenced by local issues that have given rise to particular accounting procedure.

Government grants – Government grants are financial grants provided by government bodies and trusts to normally support projects that are beneficial to the society and the public (such as projects with the aim to generate jobs and stimulate the economy).

Group accounts – Group accounts or consolidated accounts are a set of accounts which combine the results of a parent and all its subsidiary undertakings. They eliminate all trading and balances between group members, thus presenting accounts that show transactions and balances only with those outside the group.

Initial public offering (IPO) – An IPO or stock market launch is the very first sale of stock issued by a company to the public, in which shares of a company are sold to institutional investors and retail (individual) investors.

Insider dealing – Trading on the stock exchange to one's own advantage through having access to confidential information. In various countries, some kinds of trading based on insider information is illegal.

Integrated reporting – An integrated report is a holistic form of reporting about how an organisation's strategy, governance, performance and prospects lead to the creation of value over the short, medium and long term.

Intermediaries – Intermediaries are service providers in the market who establish a link between the investors and the users of funds. They include investment bankers or investment managers, registrars, brokers, mutual funds, leasing and finance companies.

Internal rate of return (IRR) – A method used for investment appraisal that calculates the rate of return at which the net present value of all cash flows (both positive and negative) from a project or investment equal zero. It evaluates the profitability and the attractiveness of potential investments.

International Financial Reporting Standard – IFRS (International Financial Reporting Standards) is the universal business language followed by companies across the globe. It is a set of accounting standards developed and issued by the International Accounting Standard Board (IASB).

Intrinsic value – Intrinsic value refers to the inherent or perceived worth of a share which may deviate from its market value. It is also referred to as fundamental value, which is determined through fundamental analysis without taking its market value into consideration.

Invoice discounting – Invoice discounting, also referred as 'bills discounting' or 'purchase of bills', is a short-term borrowing arrangement whereby a company can borrow cash from financial institutions against the invoices raised.

Irredeemable debts – Debts which are never repaid, also referred to perpetual debts. They do not exist in practice.

Issued share capital – The nominal or face value of share capital issued to shareholders. The rights and voting powers of shares and the differentials between the different classes of shares are listed in the Articles of Association.

Joint ventures – A business arrangement whereby the parties that have joint control of the arrangement agree to pool their resources for the purpose of accomplishing a specific task.

Just in time (JIT) – JIT is a series of manufacturing and supply chain techniques that aim to reduce inventory to an absolute minimum or eliminate it altogether. It aims to do this by manufacturing not only at the exact time customers require but also in the exact quantities they need and at competitive prices.

Leasing – An agreement between two parties whereby the lessor (who owns the asset) provides the lessee (who has use of the asset) with access to and use of the asset in exchange for payments.

Loan covenant – A clause in a loan agreement that places certain constraints on the borrower, such as forbidding the borrower from undertaking certain activities, restricting its ability to take on more debt without prior consent of the lender or requiring working capital to be maintained at a minimum level.

Loan stock – Shares of common or preferred stock that are used as collateral to secure a loan from another party. The loan is provided at a fixed interest rate.

Master budget – The master budget shows how all the budgets (such as purchases budget, sales budget and cash budget) work together to project combined incomes and outflows for the business.

Matching principle – An accounting concept in accrual basis accounting that requires expenses and the corresponding revenue to be recorded in the same period (whenever it is logical and feasible to do so).

Materiality – As per the IASB Conceptual Framework, items (or transactions) are material if their omission or misstatement could influence the economic decisions of users taken on the basis of the financial statements.

Mutually exclusive – A set of projects that are independent and separate of each other, out of which only one project can be selected for investment.

Net present value – The net value of a capital investment or project obtained by discounting all cash outflows and inflows to its present value by using an appropriate discount rate of return.

Nominal share value – The book or face value of a share. In the UK, it is generally of £1, 50p, 25p, 10p or 5p. The shares are said to be at par value if the market value and the nominal value are the same.

Non-controlling interest – Other equity interests in a subsidiary company in a situation where a parent company has control but less than 100% of the shareholding. Also called minority interests.

Off-balance sheet financing – A form of financing in which large capital expenditures and the associated liability (such as operating leases and partnerships) are kept off a company's balance sheet. It impacts a company's level of debt and liability and has serious implications.

Operating gearing – Operating gearing measures the proportion of fixed costs a company has relative to its variable costs.

Operating risk – The risk of disruption of the core operations of a business resulting from breakdowns in internal procedures, people and systems. It measures risk from fixed operating costs.

Over the counter (OTC) – A decentralised market where assets are traded through private securities dealers rather than through a formal exchange.

Overcapitalisation – Overcapitalisation is where the overall level of working capital is too high. Holding a high level of working capital means the firm is holding idle funds with unnecessary cost implications.

Overtrading – Overtrading (or under-capitalisation) is where the level of working capital is too low. It is associated with a rapid increase in turnover and current assets that is not supported by sufficient working capital.

Parent company – An entity that controls one or more entities. A company is a parent company of another company, its subsidiary, if it controls it through owning a majority of the voting shares, through having the power to appoint the board, through a control contract, by a power in the subsidiary's governing document or through other mechanisms specified in the Companies Act 2006 or accounting standards.

Permanent working capital – The permanent or fixed working capital is the minimum level of working capital required to continue uninterrupted day-to-day business activities.

Perpetuity – A perpetuity is an annuity or a series of fixed payments that lasts indefinitely.

Placing – A way of raising equity capital by selling shares directly to third-party investors (usually a merchant bank).

Portfolio – A mix of investments in the form of group of assets such banknotes, bonds, debentures and stocks. It can refer to a portfolio of projects managed together to achieve an organisation's strategic objectives.

Primary market – A new issues market where companies can raise 'new' funds by issuing shares or loan stock.

Private equity – Capital raised through private investors that are typically large institutional investors, university endowments or wealthy individuals. It is not publicly traded in a public exchange.

Private finance initiative (PFI) – An important (and controversial) policy designed to provide funds for major capital investments. It refers to private firms being contracted to handle the up-front costs, complete amd manage public projects.

Project appraisal – Project appraisal is the financial and economic appraisal of projects or expenditures incurred now in order to determine its feasibility and return in the future. Appraisals identify the attractiveness of an investment by assessing the viability of project, programme or portfolio decisions and the value it will generate. Also referred to as investment appraisal.

Public company – A company whose certificate of incorporation states it are a public company, or which has converted to public company status since incorporation and whose shares are traded freely on a stock exchange.

PV factor – The current value today per £1 received at a future date. The future value can be calculated by multiplying the present value factor by the amount received at a future date.

Quoted company – A company whose equity share capital is listed on a stock exchange such as the London Stock Exchange main market, the New York Stock Exchange or Nasdaq. AIM companies are not quoted.

Ratio analysis – Ratio analysis provides businesses owners with trend or time-series analysis and trends within their industry. It is one of the most powerful tools to gauge the performance of the company. Ratios are mathematical indicators and are calculated by dividing one variable by another, such as sales divided by number of stores or sales divided by operating profit.

Receivables – Receivables are debts owed to a company by its customers for goods or services sold on credit.

Redeemable debts – Redeemable debts are usually repaid at their nominal value (at par) but may be issued as repayable at a premium on nominal value. They are repayable at a fixed date (or during a fixed period) in the future.

Retail method – A technique used used by retailers to estimate the value of ending inventory using the cost to retail price ratio.

Retained earnings – Earnings not paid out as dividends but retained by the company to be reinvested in its core business or to pay debt. It is recorded under shareholders' equity on the balance sheet.

Rights issue – An offer to existing shareholders to buy new shares in proportion to their existing shareholdings.

Risk self-adjusted discount rate – The rate used to discount riskier assets or investments such as real estate. It represents the required periodical returns by investors to compensate for the higher risk.

Sale and leaseback – A sale and leaseback (sometimes called leaseback) is a structured transaction in which an owner sells an asset to another party (the buyer-lessor), while maintaining the legal rights to use the asset or lease back from the buyer-lessor.

Secondary market – A secondary market facilitates the dealing and trading of issued securities. It allows the primary market to operate more efficiently.

Securities – Tradable financial assets traded on a secondary market. Examples include debt securities (banknotes, bonds and debentures) equity securities (common stocks) and derivatives (forwards, futures, options and swaps).

Securitisation – The process of taking an illiquid asset, or group of assets and transforming it (or them) through financial engineering into a security that can be sold to raise more finance.

Segment reporting – Segment reporting provides financial information regarding the financial performance and position of the key operating units of a company to users of the financial statements.

Special purpose vehicle – A special purpose vehicle (SPV), also referred to as special purpose entity (SPE), is a legal entity created for a specific purpose. It provides a funding structure whereby pooled assets are transferred to a SPV, for legal and tax reasons. The SPV then issues interest-bearing securities, such as mortgage-backed securities, which are used to raise more finance.

Standard costing – The practice, usually associated with a manufacturing company, of assigning an expected or standard cost for an actual cost in the accounting records and periodically analysing variances between the expected and actual costs into various components (direct labour, direct material and overhead) to maintain productivity.

Standard deviation – A statistical tool that measures the amount of variation or dispersion of a set of data from its mean. It is a measure of risk or volatility.

Stock exchange – Public markets in which securities (shares and loan stocks) are bought and sold.

Stocks – Stocks refers to the overall ownership in one or more companies. The similar term 'shares' refers to the ownership certificates of a particular company.

Strategic report – A strategic report, also known as a business review, is a detailed report written in non-financial language to provide clear and coherent information about the company's activities, performance and position. It includes the strategic position of the business and probable risks attached with the business.

Subsidiary company – An entity controlled by another entity (parent company).

Temporary working capital – Additional financial requirements that arise out of events such as seasonal demand of the product or a higher level of business activity.

Tighter credit control – A strategy employed by businesses, particularly in manufacturing and retailing to ensure sales are promptly realised as cash or liquid resources.

Traded company – A company with securities traded on a regulated market, such as the London Stock Exchange's main market.

Treasury bills – Treasury Bills (or T-Bills) are short-term debt instruments issued and backed by government (such as US Treasury Department). It is essentially money lent to the government and hence considered safe. They have maturity of less than one year with no interest payable. They are sold at a discount to their face value but paid the full-face value at maturity.

Unit trust – A unit trust is a form of collective investment which is bought in units to allow small investors to hold a diversified portfolio of investments.

Weighted average cost – The weighted average cost is a method used to account for inventory costs that uses the average of the costs of the goods.

Weighted average cost of capital – The minimum return that a company must earn on its existing assets. It reflects the weighted average rate of return a company is expected to pay to all the providers of long-term finance. The weights are the fraction of each financing source in the company's total capital.

Window dressing – Transactions made at the end of a company's year end or quarter-end to improve the appearance of its financial statements.

Index

A
Accounting estimates 109–110
Accounting irregularities 180–183
Accounting policies 105–113
   application 108
   changes in 109
   changes in accounting estimates 109–110
   consistency 1098
   IAS 8 108
   objective 108
   prior period errors 110, 111
   selection 108
Accounting regulation 10
Accruals basis of accounting 58
Agency costs
   meaning 8
Agency theory 7–8
Alternative finance 220–223
Alternative Investment Market (AIM) 10, 247
Amortised cost 41
Analysis of published financial statements 157–185
   interested parties 158–159
   key financial indicators 159
   key measures 158
   need for 158–159
   ratio analysis 158
   stewardship of managers 158–159
Annual report and accounts 87–88
Annuity
   meaning 323
Asset allocation 349
Associate
   meaning 135

Authorised share capital 253

B
Bank and institutional loans 215–217, 263
   advantages 216
   disadvantages 217
   loan covenant 216
   secured versus unsecured 215–216
Banks 249–250
Barriers to global harmonisation 16–17
Basic EPS 358
Bills of exchange 189
Bonds 258–262
   advantages 260–261
   deep discount 261–262
   disadvantages 261
   fixed interest 261
   meaning 76
   types 259–260
   zero-coupon 261–262
Bonus share
   meaning 255
Bonus issue of shares
   meaning 74
Breakup value method
   meaning 74
Brexit 220
Budgetary control 235
Budgeting
   meaning 233
Business risk 277, 291

C
Capital
   concept of 43–44

Capital asset pricing model 278–283, 365–360
   assumptions 283
   criticisms 283
Capital maintenance 43–44
   financial concept 44
   physical concept 44
Capital market
   meaning 241
Capital rationing 331–332
   types 331
Capital structure 288–305
   control principle 291
   decision making process 289
   factors affecting 289–292
   meaning 288
   pecking order theory 302–303
   real world approaches 302–303
   risk factors affecting 291
   risk principle 290–291
   traditional approach 297–299
Carroll's CSR pyramid 23
Carrying amount
   meaning 42
Cash budget 233, 234, 235
Cash deficit 240
Cash forecast 235
Cash, need for 239
Cash surplus 239
Central banks 250
Coefficient of variation
   meaning 346
Commercial banks 250
Commercial paper
   meaning 242
Common-sized analysis 170
Company analysis 165, 355–410
Company angels 248

Company risk
  meaning 290
Conceptual framework of
    financial reporting
  IASB's 28, 30–31
  limitations 29
  need for 29–31
  objectives of general purpose
    financial reporting 31–32
  purpose 29
  scope 29
  users of general purpose
    financial reporting 31–32
Contingent assets 130–131
Contingent consideration
  meaning 143
Contingent liability 130
  meaning 94, 130
Controlling working capital
  224–225
Corporate governance
  meaning 4
Correlation 350
Cost of capital 275–303
  capital asset pricing model
    278–283
  dividend valuation model
    283–284
  importance 277–278
Cost of debt 284–285
Cost of equity
  capital asset pricing model 278
Creative accounting 182–183
  forms 182–183
  regulations to prevent 183
Crowdfunding 221–222

D
Debentures 258–262
  advantages 260–261
  disadvantages 261
  meaning 76
  types 259–260
Debt factoring 218–219
Debt finance 252–253
De facto control
  definition 137
Deferred consideration
  meaning 143
Delaying payments to trade
    payables 229–230

Depreciation
  meaning 40, 119
Diluted EPS 358
Directors' report
  contents 91–92
  purpose 91–92
Discount rate
  meaning 130
Discounted cash flow techniques
  compounding 317–318
  discounted payback 328–329
  discounting 318–319
  internal rate of return 325–328
    calculating 325–327
  negative interest rates 320
  net present value 320–323
  time value of money 316–317
Discounted cash flows 365
Discounting 318–319
Discounting annuities 323
  annuity factors 323–324
  discounting a perpetuity 324
Diversification 349
Dividend valuation model
  364–365
  valuation using 364–365

E
Earnings per share 357–359
  interpretation 357–358
  limitations 358–359
Economic analysis 161–163
Economic cycles and their impact
    161–163
Economic value added 372–374
Efficiency ratios 197
Efficient frontier 351
Efficient market hypothesis
    245–246
  application in company
    valuation 367
  levels of market efficiency
    245–246
EMH market efficiency 246
Enterprise Investment Scheme
    249
Environmental management
    systems 21
Environmental audit
  meaning 20
Environmental reporting 19–22

  economic implications 20
Equity finance 252–253
Equity shares 253–255
  advantages 254
  bonus shares or scrip issue 255
  disadvantages 254
  raising 254–255
  rights issues 255
Errors 181
EU Eco-Management and Audit
    Scheme 21–22
Eurobonds 262
European Commission
  role of 15
Event tree diagrams 347–348
Events after reporting period,
    accounting for 121–124
  adjusting events 122
  non-adjusting events 122
  scope and objective IAS10
    121
Expected net present value
    342–347
  standard deviation 346–347
External audit
  meaning 8
Extraordinary items
  meaning 71

F
FIFO
  meaning 116
Finance lease 132
Financial forecasting 233
Financial gearing 292
  effect on EPS 293
  high levels 293
  meaning 290
Financial instrument
  meaning 94
Financial markets
  banks 249
  budgetary control 235
  central banks 250
  commercial banks 250
  flexible versus static budgets
    234–235
  institutional investors 247
  investment banks 250
  meaning 240
  participants 240–241

planning, budgeting and
    forecasting 233–234
  retail banks 249
  types 241–242
Financial ratios 381–383
  categories 381–383
Financial regulator
  meaning 241
Financial reporting and
    accounting standards
  role of 9
Financial risk
  meaning 290
Financial statements
  accruals basis of accounting
    58
  aggregation 59
  amortised cost 41
  assets 37, 38–39
  categorisation of assets and
    liabilities 37
  compliance with IFRS 57
  components 54
  content 60–61
  derecognition 40
  disclosure 42
  disclosure of items 60
  elements 36–37
  equity 37, 39
  expenses 37, 39–40
  fair presentation 57
  going concern 36, 57–58
  how items are disclosed 60
  identification 61
  income 37, 39
  liabilities 37
  liability 39
  materiality 59
  measuring elements of 41–42
    carrying amount 42
    current cost 42
    current value basis 41–42
    fair value 42
    fulfilment value for liabilities
      42
    historical cost 41
    value in use for assets 42
  objective 35, 55
  offsetting 60
  overriding concepts 57–60
  presentation 42, 56
  comparative information 56
  consistency 56
  recognition of elements 38–40
  recycling 43
  reporting entity 36
  reporting period 36, 59–60
  scope 35
  single entity 54
  statement of financial position
    61–67
  statement of profit or loss 43
    other comprehensive income
      43
    recycling 43
  structure 60–61
Forecast
  meaning 234
Fraudulent financial reporting
    181–182
Free cash flow 368–369
Fundamental analysis 160–161

G

Generally Accepted Accounting
    Principles (GAAP) 5
Glossary 466–475
Government grants 269–270
  advantages 270
  disadvantages 270
Group financial statements
  meaning 10
Groups of companies 134–156
  associates 151
  business combinations 140
  consolidated financial
    statements 135–140
    laws 136
    regulations 136
  consolidated statement of
    financial position 147–149
    dividends paid by subsidiary
      148
    group retained earnings 148
    intra-group items 147
    investment 147
    non-controlling interests 148
    profits 147
    steps 149
  consolidated statement of
    profit or loss and OCI 150
  exclusion of subsidiary from
    consolidation 154–155
  exemptions from preparing
    consolidated financial
    statements 154–155
  fair value measurement in
    consolidated financial
    statements 142
    contingent consideration
      143
    deferred consideration 143
    net assets 144
    purchase consideration
      142–143
  financial reporting by 134–156
  goodwill 140–142
    impairment 141–142
    negative 141
  IAS 28 Equity method 152–153
    basic principles 152–153
    investments in associates and
      joint ventures 151
    joint ventures 151
  parent company's separate
    financial statements
    153–154
  principles for consolidation
    of financial statements
    136–140
    basic method of
      consolidation 138–139
    content 139–140
    control concept 136–137
    group structure 137–138

I

Identification and analysis of
    projects 307
Industry analysis 163–164
  attractiveness of industry 164
  decay stage 163
  expansion stage 163
  pioneer stage 163
  stagnation stage 163
  success factors required for
    company's survival 164
  underlying forces that drive
    industry 163–164
Insider dealing
  meaning 245
Interest gearing 292
Integrated reporting 7

Intermediaries
  meaning 241
Internal rate of return 286
International Accounting
    Standards 106–107
International Financial Reporting
    Standards (IFRS) 12–16
  advantages 13
  convergence 14–15
  disadvantages 13–14
  framework 12–13
  GAAP distinguished 17–19
  harmonisation 14–15
  meaning 5
Interpretation and evaluation
    of financial information
    380–410
  case studies 385–410
  company, financial or
      economic factors 384
  competitive advantages or
      disadvantages 384
  further activities 384
  limitations of ratios 384–385
  performance trends 384
Inventories, accounting for
    114–117
  disclosure 116
  expense recognition 116
  matching principle 116
  measurement and cost of
      inventories 115
  methods of costing 115–116
  scope and objective of IAS2
      114
  write-down to net realisable
      value 116
Investment banks 250
Investment valuation ratios
    356–357
  dividend payout ratio 356
  dividend yield 357
Investments in associates and
    joint ventures 151
Invoice discounting 219–220
Invoice factoring 218–219
Invoice trading third party
    payment 222–223
Irredeemable debt 284–285
Issued share capital
  meaning 65

J
Joint ventures
  meaning 151

K
Key financial indicators 159
  comparative position in
      relation to similar business
      159
  growth potential of company
      159
  overall financial strength and
      solvency of entity 159
  profitability 159
  trend of achievements 159

L
Leases 131–132
Leasing 263–265
  advantages 264
  disadvantages 264–265
Limitations of published
    financial statements
    100–102
  creative accounting 100–101
  earnings management
      100–101
  historical cost 100
  ignoring non-financial matters
      101
  intra-group transactions 101
  not always comparable
      101–102
  not forward looking 101
  only covers specific time period
      102
  seasonality of training 101
Liquidity ratios 196–197
Loan stock
  meaning 259
Long-term finance 252–271
  sources 252–271

M
Management of inventories
    202–208
  ABC inventory control 207
  determining inventory levels
      204–205
  economic order quantity
      203–204
  just in time systems 205–207
  re-order level 202–203
  techniques 203
  VED analysis 207–208
Management of trade payables
    210
Management of trade receivables
    208–210
  credit policy 209–210
  factors affecting size 209
Master budget 234
Materiality
  meaning 33
Matching principle
  meaning 58
Measuring value creation
    374–375
  effects of dividend payments
      on shareholder wealth 375
  market value added 374
  stock market influences 375
  total shareholder return 374
Misappropriation 181–182
Modigliani and Miller theory of
    capital structure 299–302
Money market 241–242

N
National and company law 10–12
Net present value 286
Nominal share value 253
  meaning 65
Notes to the financial statements
    93–95
  contents 93–94
  contingent liabilities 94
  financial instruments 94
  structure 93–94

O
Online innovations 220–223
Operating gearing 295–297
  meaning 290
Overcapitalisation 437
Operating lease 131
Operating risk
  meaning 290
Overdrafts 217–218
Over the counter
  meaning 251
Overtrading 212

P

Parent company
   meaning 134
Peer-to-peer lending 222
Pension funds 249
Permanent working capital 192
Placing
   meaning 248
Plant, property and equipment, accounting for 117–121
   additional disclosures 121
   depreciation 119
   derecognition 120
   disclosure 120
   initial measurement 118
   initial recognition 118
   recoverability of carrying amount 120
   revalued 121
   scope and objective of IAS 16 117–118
   subsequent measurement 119
   subsequent recognition 118–119
Pledge funds 248–249
Portfolio
   meaning 348
Portfolio management 348–352
   efficient frontier 351–352
   elements 348–349
   limitations of portfolio theory 352
   objectives 348–349
   rebalancing 349–350
   risk and return 350–351
Preference shares 257–258
Present value factor
   meaning 318
Present value table 411–412
Price/earnings ratio 359–362
   interpretation 359–360
   limitations 360
Private equity
   meaning 247
Private finance initiatives 267–269
   advantages 268
   disadvantages 269
Private markets 242–243
   advantages 243
   disadvantages 243

Primary market
   meaning 241
Profitability ratios 172–180
   gross profit margin ratio 173
   net profit margin ratio 173–176
   operating profit margin ratio 173
   return on assets ratio 176
   return on capital employed ratio 176
   return on equity ratio 176
Project appraisal
   factors affecting 308–309
   inflation, impact of 329–330
   tax effects 330
Project appraisal techniques
   non-discounted methods 313–316
   non-discounting methods 310–313
   payback period 313–316
Provisions 129–130
   definition 129
   measurement 129
   objective and scope of IAS 37 128–129
   recognition 129
   remeasurement 130
Public company
   meaning 11
Public markets 243
   advantages 243
   disadvantages 243

Q

Qualitative characteristics of financial information 33–35
   comparability 34
   enhancing 34–35
   faithful representation 33–34
   fundamental characteristics 33–34
   materiality 33
   relevance 33
   timeliness 35
   understandability 35
   verifiability 35
Quoted company
   meaning 11

R

Ratio analysis 171–172
   limitations 180
   meaning 180
Redeemable debt 286
Reducing inventory levels 225–227
Regulatory frameworks 4–26
   corporate governance frameworks 7
   environmental and sustainability reporting 7
   European Commission 15
   financial reporting standards body 6
   industry-specific and securities exchange rules 7
   legal requirements 6–7
   market regulation 6
   national or company law 6
   need for 5–7
   principles-based versus rules-based systems 6
Relative value measures 363
   steps in relative value analysis 363
Reporting substance of transactions 98–100
   consignment stock 99
   debt factoring 99
   invoice discounting 99
   sale and leaseback arrangements 99
   sale and repurchase arrangements 99
Retail banks 249
Retail method
   meaning 115
Retained earnings 231, 256–257
   advantages 256
   disadvantages 256–257
   meaning 72
Retained profits 231
Revenue from contracts with customers 124–128
   disclosure 128
   objective and scope of IFRS 15 125
   presentation 128
   recognition and measurement 125–128

Rights issue
　meaning 74
Risk-adjusted discount rate 278–279
Risk and investment decisions 335–336
　preference of investors 335–336
Risk assessment 334–354
Risk assessment models 336

S
Sale and leaseback 265–266
Sale of redundant assets 230
Scenario analysis 340–341
Secondary market
　meaning 446
Securities
　meaning 154
Securitisation 266–267
　advantages 242–243
　disadvantages 267
Security market line 281–282
Segment reporting 95–98
　disclosures for operating segments 97
　IFRS 8 thresholds and reporting segments 96–97
　International Financial Reporting Standard 8 95–96
　meaning 95
　operating segments 96
Sensitivity analysis 336–340
Share warrants 262
Shareholder value analysis 368–372
　calculation of shareholder value 371–372
　free cash flow 368–369
　strengths 372
　value creation 368
　value drivers 368
　weaknesses 372

Short-term finance 214–231
　external sources 215
　internal sources 224
　sources 214–231
Simulation modelling 341
Social accounting 22–25
Standard costing
　meaning 115
Statement of cash flows 74–84
　structure 75–84
Statement of changes in equity 72–74
　elements 73–74
Statement of financial position 61–67
　additional information 62
　components of equity 65–66
　current/non-current classification 64–65
　format 62–63
　line items 61–62
　share capital 65–66
Statement of profit or loss and other comprehensive income 67–72
　basic requirements 68–70
　discontinued operations 71–72
　other comprehensive income 70–71
　presentation 68–70
　profit or loss 70
Stocks
　meaning 240
Strategic report 88–91
　contents 89–91
　duty to prepare 88–89
　meaning 88
　purpose 89–91
Stock exchange
　meaning 243
　role of 244
Subsidiary company
　meaning 134
Systematic risk 279–281
　measuring 281

T
Temporary working capital 192
Test yourself answers 413–464
Tighter credit control 228–229
Traded company
　meaning 11
Treasury bills
　meaning 259
Trend analysis 165–171

U
UK company size limits 11
UK GAAP 15
　IFRS distinguished 18–19
Unit trusts 249
Unsystematic risk 279–280
US GAAP 15–16

V
Venture capital 248
Vertical analysis 165

W
Web resources 465
Weighted average cost 286
　meaning 116
Weighted average cost of capital 286–288
Window dressing
　meaning 182
Working capital 190–213
　controlling 224–225
　cycle 192–195
　　calculating 194
　　nature of industry, and 193
　efficiency ratios 197
　liquidity ratios 196
　management 190–213
　nature of 192
　profitability versus liquidity 195–196
　purpose 192
　ratios 196–200
Writing down allowances 330–331